Hard Press

The Fallen Leaves

by Wilkie Collins

THE PROLOGUE

I

The resistless influences which are one day to reign supreme over our poor hearts, and to shape the sad short course of our lives, are sometimes of mysteriously remote origin, and find their devious ways to us through the hearts and the lives of strangers.

While the young man whose troubled career it is here proposed to follow was wearing his first jacket, and bowling his first hoop, a domestic misfortune, falling on a household of strangers, was destined nevertheless to have its ultimate influence over his happiness, and to shape the whole aftercourse of his life.

For this reason, some First Words must precede the Story, and must present the brief narrative of what happened in the household of strangers. By what devious ways the event here related affected the chief personage of these pages, when he grew to manhood, it will be the business of the story to trace, over land and sea, among men and women, in bright days and dull days alike, until the end is reached, and the pen (God willing) is put back in the desk.

II

Old Benjamin Ronald (of the Stationers' Company) took a young wife at the ripe age of fifty, and carried with him into the holy estate of matrimony some of the habits of his bachelor life.

As a bachelor, he had never willingly left his shop (situated in that exclusively commercial region of London which is called "the City") from one year's end to another. As a married man, he persisted in following the same monotonous course; with this one difference, that he now had a woman to follow it with him. "Travelling by railway," he explained to his wife, "will make your head ache—it makes *my* head ache. Travelling by sea will make you sick—it makes *me* sick. If you want change of air, every sort of air is to be found in the City. If you admire the beauties of Nature, there is Finsbury Square with the beauties of Nature carefully selected and arranged. When we are in London, you (and I) are all right; and when we are out of London, you (and I) are all wrong." As surely as the autumn holiday season set in, so surely Old Ronald resisted his wife's petition for a change of scene in that form of words. A man habitually fortified behind his own inbred obstinacy and selfishness is for the most part an irresistible power within the limits of his domestic circle. As a rule, patient Mrs. Ronald yielded; and her husband stood revealed to his neighbours in the glorious character of a married man who had his own way.

But in the autumn of 1856, the retribution which sooner or later descends on all despotisms, great and small, overtook the iron rule of Old Ronald, and defeated the domestic tyrant on the battle-field of his own fireside.

The children born of the marriage, two in number, were both daughters. The elder had mortally offended her father by marrying imprudently—in a pecuniary sense. He had declared that she should never enter his house again; and he had mercilessly kept his word. The younger daughter (now eighteen years of age) proved to be also a source of parental inquietude, in another way. She was the passive cause of the revolt which set her father's authority at defiance. For some little time past she had been out of health. After many ineffectual trials of the mild influence of persuasion, her mother's patience at last gave way. Mrs. Ronald insisted—yes, actually insisted—on taking Miss Emma to the seaside.

"What's the matter with you?" Old Ronald asked; detecting something that perplexed him in his wife's look and manner, on the memorable occasion when she asserted a will of her own for the first time in her life.

A man of finer observation would have discovered the signs of no ordinary anxiety and alarm, struggling to show themselves openly in the poor woman's face. Her husband only saw a change that puzzled him. "Send for Emma," he said, his natural cunning inspiring him with the idea of confronting the mother and daughter, and of seeing what came of *that.* Emma appeared, plump and short, with large blue eyes, and full pouting lips, and splendid yellow hair: otherwise, miserably pale, languid in

4

her movements, careless in her dress, sullen in her manner. Out of health as her mother said, and as her father saw.

"You can see for yourself," said Mrs. Ronald, "that the girl is pining for fresh air. I have heard Ramsgate recommended."

Old Ronald looked at his daughter. She represented the one tender place in his nature. It was not a large place; but it did exist. And the proof of it is, that he began to yield—with the worst possible grace.

"Well, we will see about it," he said.

"There is no time to be lost," Mrs. Ronald persisted. "I mean to take her to Ramsgate tomorrow."

Mr. Ronald looked at his wife as a dog looks at the maddened sheep that turns on him. "You mean?" repeated the stationer. "Upon my soul—what next? You mean? Where is the money to come from? Answer me that."

Mrs. Ronald declined to be drawn into a conjugal dispute, in the presence of her daughter. She took Emma's arm, and led her to the door. There she stopped, and spoke. "I have already told you that the girl is ill," she said to her husband. "And I now tell you again that she must have the sea air. For God's sake, don't let us quarrel! I have enough to try me without that." She closed the door on herself and her daughter, and left her lord and master standing face to face with the wreck of his own outraged authority.

What further progress was made by the domestic revolt, when the bedroom candles were lit, and the hour of retirement had arrived with the night, is naturally involved in mystery. This alone is certain: On the next morning, the luggage was packed, and the cab was called to the door. Mrs. Ronald spoke her parting words to her husband in private.

"I hope I have not expressed myself too strongly about taking Emma to the seaside," she said, in gentle pleading tones. "I am anxious about our girl's health. If I have offended you—without meaning it, God knows!—say you forgive me before I go. I have tried honestly, dear, to be a good wife to you. And you have always trusted me, haven't you? And you trust me still?"

She took his lean cold hand, and pressed it fervently: her eyes rested on him with a strange mixture of timidity and anxiety. Still in the prime of her life, she preserved the personal attractions—the fair calm refined face, the natural grace of look and movement—which had made her marriage to a man old enough to be her father a cause of angry astonishment among all her friends. In the agitation that now possessed her, her colour rose, her eyes brightened; she looked for the moment almost young enough to be Emma's sister. Her husband opened his hard old eyes in surly bewilderment. "Why need you make this fuss?" he asked. "I don't understand you." Mrs. Ronald shrank at those words as if he had struck her. She kissed him in silence, and joined her daughter in the cab.

For the rest of that day, the persons in the stationer's employment had a hard time of it with their master in the shop. Something had upset Old Ronald. He ordered the shutters to be put up earlier that evening than usual. Instead of going to his club (at the tavern round the corner), he took a long walk in the lonely and lifeless streets of the City by night. There was no disguising it from himself; his wife's behaviour at parting had made him uneasy. He naturally swore at her for taking that liberty, while he lay awake alone in his bed. "Damn the woman! What does she mean?" The cry of the soul utters itself in various forms of expression. That was the cry of Old Ronald's soul, literally translated.

III

The next morning brought him a letter from Ramsgate.

"I write immediately to tell you of our safe arrival. We have found comfortable lodgings (as the address at the head of this letter will inform you) in Albion Place. I thank you, and Emma desires to thank you also, for your kindness in providing us with ample means for taking our little trip. It is beautiful weather today; the sea is calm, and the pleasure-boats are out. We do not of course expect to see you here. But if you do, by any chance, overcome your objection to moving out of London, I have a little request to make. Please let me hear of your visit beforehand—so that I may not omit all needful preparations. I know you dislike being troubled with letters (except on business), so I will not write too frequently. Be so good as to take no news for good news, in the intervals. When you have a few minutes to spare, you will write, I hope, and tell me how you and the shop are going on. Emma sends you her love, in which I beg to join." So the letter was expressed, and so it ended.

"They needn't be afraid of my troubling them. Calm seas and pleasure-boats! Stuff and nonsense!" Such was the first impression which his wife's report of herself produced on Old Ronald's mind. After a while, he looked at the letter again—and frowned, and reflected. "Please let me hear of your visit beforehand," he repeated to himself, as if the request had been, in some incomprehensible way, offensive to him. He opened the drawer of his desk, and threw the letter into it. When business was over for the day, he went to his club at the tavern, and made himself unusually disagreeable to everybody.

A week passed. In the interval he wrote briefly to his wife. "I'm all right, and the shop goes on as usual." He also forwarded one or two letters which came for Mrs. Ronald. No more news reached him from Ramsgate. "I suppose they're enjoying themselves," he reflected. "The house looks queer without them; I'll go to the club."

He stayed later than usual, and drank more than usual, that night. It was nearly one in the morning when he let himself in with his latch-key, and went upstairs to bed.

Approaching the toilette-table, he found a letter lying on it, addressed to "Mr. Ronald—private." It was not in his wife's handwriting; not in any handwriting known to him. The characters sloped the wrong way, and the envelope bore no postmark. He eyed it over and over suspiciously. At last he opened it, and read these lines:

"You are advised by a true friend to lose no time in looking after your wife. There are strange doings at the seaside. If you don't believe me, ask Mrs. Turner, Number 1, Slains Row, Ramsgate."

No address, no date, no signature—an anonymous letter, the first he had ever received in the long course of his life.

His hard brain was in no way affected by the liquor that he had drunk. He sat down on his bed, mechanically folding and refolding the letter. The reference to "Mrs. Turner" produced no impression on him of any sort: no person of that name, common as it was, happened to be numbered on the list of his friends or his customers. But for one circumstance, he would have thrown the letter aside, in contempt. His memory reverted to his wife's incomprehensible behaviour at parting. Addressing him through that remembrance, the anonymous warning assumed a certain importance to his mind. He went down to his desk, in the back office, and took his wife's letter out of the drawer, and read it through slowly. "Ha!" he said, pausing as he came across the sentence which requested him to write beforehand, in the unlikely event of his deciding to go to Ramsgate. He thought again of the strangely persistent way in which his wife had dwelt on his trusting her; he recalled her nervous anxious looks, her deepening colour, her agitation at one moment, and then her sudden silence and sudden retreat to the cab. Fed by these irritating influences, the inbred suspicion in his nature began to take fire slowly. She might be innocent enough in asking him to give her notice before he joined her at the seaside—she might naturally be anxious to omit no needful preparation for his comfort. Still, he didn't like it; no, he didn't like it. An appearance as of a slow collapse passed little by little over his rugged wrinkled face. He looked many years older than his age, as he sat at the desk, with the flaring candlelight close in front of him, thinking. The anonymous letter lay before him, side by side with his wife's letter. On a sudden, he lifted his gray head, and clenched his fist, and struck the venomous written warning as if it had been a living thing that could feel. "Whoever you are," he said, "I'll take your advice."

He never even made the attempt to go to bed that night. His pipe helped him through the comfortless and dreary hours. Once or twice he thought of his daughter. Why had her mother been so anxious about her? Why had her mother taken her to Ramsgate? Perhaps, as a blind—ah, yes, perhaps as a blind! More for the sake of something to do than for any other reason, he packed a handbag with a few necessaries. As soon as the servant was stirring, he ordered her to make him a cup of strong coffee. After that, it was time to show himself as usual, on the opening of the shop. To his astonishment, he found his clerk taking down the shutters, in place of the porter.

"What does this mean?" he asked. "Where is Farnaby?"

The clerk looked at his master, and paused aghast with a shutter in his hands.

"Good Lord! what has come to you?" he cried. "Are you ill?"

Old Ronald angrily repeated his question: "Where is Farnaby?"

"I don't know," was the answer.

"You don't know? Have you been up to his bedroom?"

8

"Yes."

"Well?"

"Well, he isn't in his bedroom. And, what's more, his bed hasn't been slept in last night. Farnaby's off, sir—nobody knows where."

Old Ronald dropped heavily into the nearest chair. This second mystery, following on the mystery of the anonymous letter, staggered him. But his business instincts were still in good working order. He held out his keys to the clerk. "Get the petty cash-book," he said, "and see if the money is all right."

The clerk received the keys under protest. *"That's* not the right reading of the riddle," he remarked.

"Do as I tell you!"

The clerk opened the money-drawer under the counter; counted the pounds, shillings and pence paid by chance customers up to the closing of the shop on the previous evening; compared the result with the petty cash-book, and answered, "Right to a halfpenny."

Satisfied so far, old Ronald condescended to approach the speculative side of the subject, with the assistance of his subordinate. "If what you said just now means anything," he resumed, "it means that you suspect the reason why Farnaby has left my service. Let's hear it."

"You know that I never liked John Farnaby," the clerk began. "An active young fellow and a clever young fellow, I grant you. But a bad servant for all that. False, Mr. Ronald—false to the marrow of his bones."

Mr. Ronald's patience began to give way. "Come to the facts," he growled. "Why has Farnaby gone off without a word to anybody? Do you know that?"

"I know no more than you do," the clerk answered coolly. "Don't fly into a passion. I have got some facts for you, if you will only give me time. Turn them over in your own mind, and see what they come to. Three days ago I was short of postage-stamps, and I went to the office. Farnaby was there, waiting at the desk where they pay the post-office orders. There must have been ten or a dozen people with letters, orders, and what not, between him and me. I got behind him quietly, and looked over his shoulder. I saw the clerk give him the money for his post-office order. Five pounds in gold, which I reckoned as they lay on the counter, and a bank-note besides, which he crumpled up in his hand. I can't tell you how much it was for; I only know it *was* a bank-note. Just ask yourself how a porter on twenty shillings a week (with a mother who takes in washing, and a father who takes in drink) comes to have a correspondent who sends him an order for five sovereigns—and a bank-note, value unknown. Say he's turned betting-man in secret. Very good. There's the post-office order, in that case, to show that he's got a run of luck. If he has got a run of luck, tell me this—why does he leave his place like a thief in the night? He's not a slave; he's not even an apprentice. When he thinks he can better himself, he has no earthly need to keep it a secret that he means to leave your service. He may have met with an accident, to be sure. But that's not *my* belief. I say he's up to some mischief And now comes the question: What are we to do?"

Mr. Ronald, listening with his head down, and without interposing a word on his own part, made an extraordinary answer. "Leave it," he said. "Leave it till tomorrow."

"Why?" the clerk answered, without ceremony.

Mr. Ronald made another extraordinary answer. "Because I am obliged to go out of town for the day. Look after the business. The ironmonger's man over the way will help you to put up the shutters at night. If anybody inquires for me, say I shall be back tomorrow." With those parting directions, heedless of the effect that he had produced on the clerk, he looked at his watch, and left the shop.

IV

The bell which gave five minutes' notice of the starting of the Ramsgate train had just rung.

While the other travellers were hastening to the platform, two persons stood passively apart as if they had not even yet decided on taking their places in the train. One of the two was a smart young man in a cheap travelling suit; mainly noticeable by his florid complexion, his restless dark eyes, and his profusely curling black hair. The other was a middle-aged woman in frowsy garments; tall and stout, sly and sullen. The smart young man stood behind the uncongenial-looking person with whom he had associated himself, using her as a screen to hide him while he watched the travellers on their way to the train. As the bell rang, the woman suddenly faced her companion, and pointed to the railway clock.

"Are you waiting to make up your mind till the train has gone?" she asked.

The young man frowned impatiently. "I am waiting for a person whom I expect to see," he answered. "If the person travels by this train, we shall travel by it. If not, we shall come back here, and look out for the next train, and so on till night-time, if it's necessary."

The woman fixed her small scowling gray eyes on the man as he replied in those terms. "Look here!" she broke out. "I like to see my way before me. You're a stranger, young Mister; and it's as likely as not you've given me a false name and address. That don't matter. False names are commoner than true ones, in my line of life. But mind this! I don't stir a step farther till I've got half the money in my hand, and my return-ticket there and back."

"Hold your tongue!" the man suddenly interposed in a whisper. "It's all right. I'll get the tickets."

He looked while he spoke at an elderly traveller, hastening by with his head down, deep in thought, noticing nobody. The traveller was Mr. Ronald. The young man, who had that moment recognized him, was his runaway porter, John Farnaby.

Returning with the tickets, the porter took his repellent travelling companion by the arm, and hurried her along the platform to the train. "The money!" she whispered, as they took their places. Farnaby handed it to her, ready wrapped up in a morsel of paper. She opened the paper, satisfied herself that no trick had been played her, and leaned back in her corner to go to sleep. The train started. Old Ronald travelled by the second class; his porter and his porter's companion accompanied him secretly by the third.

V

It was still early in the afternoon when Mr. Ronald descended the narrow street which leads from the high land of the South-Eastern railway station to the port of Ramsgate. Asking his way of the first policeman whom he met, he turned to the left, and reached the cliff on which the houses in Albion Place are situated. Farnaby followed him at a discreet distance; and the woman followed Farnaby.

Arrived in sight of the lodging-house, Mr. Ronald paused—partly to recover his breath, partly to compose himself. He was conscious of a change of feeling as he looked up at the windows: his errand suddenly assumed a contemptible aspect in his own eyes. He almost felt ashamed of himself. After twenty years of undisturbed married life, was it possible that he had doubted his wife—and that at the instigation of a stranger whose name even was unknown to him? "If she was to step out in the balcony, and see me down here," he thought, "what a fool I should look!" He felt half-inclined, at the moment when he lifted the knocker of the door, to put it back again quietly, and return to London. No! it was too late. The maid-servant was hanging up her birdcage in the area of the house; the maid-servant had seen him.

"Does Mrs. Ronald lodge here?" he asked.

The girl lifted her eyebrows and opened her mouth—stared at him in speechless confusion—and disappeared in the kitchen regions. This strange reception of his inquiry irritated him unreasonably. He knocked with the absurd violence of a man who vents his anger on the first convenient thing that he can find. The landlady opened the door, and looked at him in stern and silent surprise.

"Does Mrs. Ronald lodge here?" he repeated.

The landlady answered with some appearance of effort—the effort of a person who was carefully considering her words before she permitted them to pass her lips.

"Mrs. Ronald has taken rooms here. But she has not occupied them yet."

"Not occupied them yet?" The words bewildered him as if they had been spoken in an unknown tongue. He stood stupidly silent on the doorstep. His anger was gone; an all-mastering fear throbbed heavily at his heart. The landlady looked at him, and said to her secret self: "Just what I suspected; there *is* something wrong!"

"Perhaps I have not sufficiently explained myself, sir," she resumed with grave politeness. "Mrs. Ronald told me that she was staying at Ramsgate with friends. She would move into my house, she said, when her friends left—but they had not quite settled the day yet. She calls here for letters. Indeed, she was here early this morning, to pay the second week's rent. I asked when she thought of moving in. She didn't seem to know; her friends (as I understood) had not made up their minds. I must say I thought it a little odd. Would you like to leave any message?"

12

He recovered himself sufficiently to speak. "Can you tell me where her friends live?" he said.

The landlady shook her head. "No, indeed. I offered to save Mrs. Ronald the trouble of calling here, by sending letters or cards to her present residence. She declined the offer—and she has never mentioned the address. Would you like to come in and rest, sir? I will see that your card is taken care of, if you wish to leave it."

"Thank you, ma'am—it doesn't matter—good morning."

The landlady looked after him as he descended the house-steps. "It's the husband, Peggy," she said to the servant, waiting inquisitively behind her. "Poor old gentleman! And such a respectable-looking woman, too!"

Mr. Ronald walked mechanically to the end of the row of houses, and met the wide grand view of sea and sky. There were some seats behind the railing which fenced the edge of the cliff. He sat down, perfectly stupefied and helpless, on the nearest bench.

At the close of life, the loss of a man's customary nourishment extends its debilitating influence rapidly from his body to his mind. Mr. Ronald had tasted nothing but his cup of coffee since the previous night. His mind began to wander strangely; he was not angry or frightened or distressed. Instead of thinking of what had just happened, he was thinking of his young days when he had been a cricket-player. One special game revived in his memory, at which he had been struck on the head by the ball. "Just the same feeling," he reflected vacantly, with his hat off, and his hand on his forehead. "Dazed and giddy—just the same feeling!"

He leaned back on the bench, and fixed his eyes on the sea, and wondered languidly what had come to him. Farnaby and the woman, still following, waited round the corner where they could just keep him in view.

The blue lustre of the sky was without a cloud; the sunny sea leapt under the fresh westerly breeze. From the beach, the cries of children at play, the shouts of donkey-boys driving their poor beasts, the distant notes of brass instruments playing a waltz, and the mellow music of the small waves breaking on the sand, rose joyously together on the fragrant air. On the next bench, a dirty old boatman was prosing to a stupid old visitor. Mr. Ronald listened, with a sense of vacant content in the mere act of listening. The boatman's words found their way to his ears like the other sounds that were abroad in the air. "Yes; them's the Goodwin Sands, where you see the lightship. And that steamer there, towing a vessel into the harbour, that's the Ramsgate Tug. Do you know what I should like to see? I should like to see the Ramsgate Tug blow up. Why? I'll tell you why. I belong to Broadstairs; I don't belong to Ramsgate. Very well. I'm idling here, as you may see, without one copper piece in my pocket to rub against another. What trade do I belong to? I don't belong to no trade; I belong to a boat. The boat's rotting at Broadstairs, for want of work. And all along of what? All along of the Tug. The Tug has took the bread out of our mouths: me and my mates. Wait a bit; I'll show you how. What did a ship do, in the good old times, when she got on them sands—Goodwin Sands? Went to pieces, if it come on to blow; or got sucked down little by little when it was fair weather. Now I'm coming to it. What did We do (in the good old times, mind you) when we happened to see that ship in distress? Out with our boat; blow high or blow low, out with our boat. And saved the lives of the crew, did you say? Well, yes; saving the crew was part of the day's work, to be sure; the part we didn't get paid for. We saved *the cargo,* Master! and got salvage!! Hundreds of pounds, I tell you, divided amongst us by law!!! Ah, those times are gone. A parcel of sneaks get together, and subscribe to build a Steam-Tug. When a ship gets on the sands now, out goes the Tug, night and day alike, and brings her safe into harbour, and takes the bread out of our mouths. Shameful—that's what I call it—shameful."

The last words of the boatman's lament fell lower, lower, lower on Mr. Ronald's ears—he lost them altogether—he lost the view of the sea—he lost the sense of the wind blowing over him. Suddenly, he was roused as if from a deep sleep. On one side, the man from Broadstairs was shaking him by the collar. "I say, Master, cheer up; what's come to you?" On the other side, a compassionate lady was offering her smelling-bottle. "I am afraid, sir, you have fainted." He struggled to his feet, and vacantly thanked the lady. The man from Broadstairs—with an eye to salvage—took charge of the human wreck, and towed him to the nearest public-house. "A chop and a glass of brandy-and-water," said this good Samaritan of the nineteenth century. "That's what you want. I'm peckish myself, and I'll keep you company."

He was perfectly passive in the hands of any one who would take charge of him; he submitted as if he had been the boatman's dog, and had heard the whistle.

It could only be truly said that he had come to himself, when there had been time enough for him to feel the reanimating influence of the food and drink. Then he got to his feet, and looked with incredulous wonder at the companion of his meal. The man from Broadstairs opened his greasy lips, and was silenced by the sudden appearance of a gold coin between Mr. Ronald's finger and thumb. "Don't speak to me; pay the bill, and bring me the change outside." When the boatman joined him, he was reading a letter; walking to and fro, and speaking at intervals to himself. "God help me, have I lost my senses? I don't know what to do next." He referred to the letter again: "if you don't believe me, ask Mrs. Turner, Number 1, Slains Row, Ramsgate." He put the letter back in his pocket, and rallied suddenly. "Slains Row," he said, turning to the boatman. "Take me there directly, and keep the change for yourself."

The boatman's gratitude was (apparently) beyond expression in words. He slapped his pocket cheerfully, and that was all. Leading the way inland, he went downhill, and uphill again—then turned aside towards the eastern extremity of the town.

Farnaby, still following, with the woman behind him, stopped when the boatman diverged towards the east, and looked up at the name of the street. "I've got my

14

instructions," he said; "I know where he's going. Step out! We'll get there before him, by another way."

Mr. Ronald and his guide reached a row of poor little houses, with poor little gardens in front of them and behind them. The back windows looked out on downs and fields lying on either side of the road to Broadstairs. It was a lost and lonely spot. The guide stopped, and put a question with inquisitive respect. "What number, sir?" Mr. Ronald had sufficiently recovered himself to keep his own counsel. "That will do," he said. "You can leave me." The boatman waited a moment. Mr. Ronald looked at him. The boatman was slow to understand that his leadership had gone from him. "You're sure you don't want me any more?" he said. "Quite sure," Mr. Ronald answered. The man from Broadstairs retired—with his salvage to comfort him.

Number 1 was at the farther extremity of the row of houses. When Mr. Ronald rang the bell, the spies were already posted. The woman loitered on the road, within view of the door. Farnaby was out of sight, round the corner, watching the house over the low wooden palings of the back garden.

A lazy-looking man, in his shirt sleeves, opened the door. "Mrs. Turner at home?" he repeated. "Well, she's at home; but she's too busy to see anybody. What's your pleasure?" Mr. Ronald declined to accept excuses or to answer questions. "I must see Mrs. Turner directly," he said, "on important business." His tone and manner had their effect on the lazy man. "What name?" he asked. Mr. Ronald declined to mention his name. "Give my message," he said. "I won't detain Mrs. Turner more than a minute." The man hesitated—and opened the door of the front parlour. An old woman was fast asleep on a ragged little sofa. The man gave up the front parlour, and tried the back parlour next. It was empty. "Please to wait here," he said—and went away to deliver his message.

The parlour was a miserably furnished room. Through the open window, the patch of back garden was barely visible under fluttering rows of linen hanging out on lines to dry. A pack of dirty cards, and some plain needlework, littered the bare little table. A cheap American clock ticked with stern and steady activity on the mantelpiece. The smell of onions was in the air. A torn newspaper, with stains of beer on it, lay on the floor. There was some sinister influence in the place which affected Mr. Ronald painfully. He felt himself trembling, and sat down on one of the rickety chairs. The minutes followed one another wearily. He heard a trampling of feet in the room above—then a door opened and closed—then the rustle of a woman's dress on the stairs. In a moment more, the handle of the parlour door was turned. He rose, in anticipation of Mrs. Turner's appearance. The door opened. He found himself face to face with his wife.

VI

John Farnaby, posted at the garden paling, suddenly lifted his head and looked towards the open window of the back parlour. He reflected for a moment—and then joined his female companion on the road in front of the house.

"I want you at the back garden," he said. "Come along!"

"How much longer am I to be kept kicking my heels in this wretched hole?" the woman asked sulkily.

"As much longer as I please—if you want to go back to London with the other half of the money." He showed it to her as he spoke. She followed him without another word.

Arrived at the paling, Farnaby pointed to the window, and to the back garden door, which was left ajar. "Speak softly," he whispered. "Do you hear voices in the house?"

"I don't hear what they're talking about, if that's what you mean."

"I don't hear, either. Now mind what I tell you—I have reasons of my own for getting a little nearer to that window. Sit down under the paling, so that you can't be seen from the house. If you hear a row, you may take it for granted that I am found out. In that case, go back to London by the next train, and meet me at the terminus at two o'clock tomorrow afternoon. If nothing happens, wait where you are till you hear from me or see me again."

He laid his hand on the low paling, and vaulted over it. The linen hanging up in the garden to dry offered him a means of concealment (if any one happened to look out of the window) of which he skilfully availed himself. The dust-bin was at the side of the house, situated at a right angle to the parlour window. He was safe behind the bin, provided no one appeared on the path which connected the patch of garden at the back with the patch in front. Here, running the risk, he waited and listened.

The first voice that reached his ears was the voice of Mrs. Ronald. She was speaking with a firmness of tone that astonished him.

"Hear me to the end, Benjamin," she said. "I have a right to ask as much as that of my husband, and I do ask it. If I had been bent on nothing but saving the reputation of our miserable girl, you would have a right to blame me for keeping you ignorant of the calamity that has fallen on us—"

There the voice of her husband interposed sternly. "Calamity! Say disgrace, everlasting disgrace."

Mrs. Ronald did not notice the interruption. Sadly and patiently she went on.

"But I had a harder trial still to face," she said. "I had to save her, in spite of herself, from the wretch who has brought this infamy on us. He has acted throughout in cold blood; it is his interest to marry her, and from first to last he has plotted to force the marriage on us. For God's sake, don't speak loud! She is in the room above us; if she hears you it will be the death of her. Don't suppose I am talking at random; I have looked at his letters to her; I have got the confession of the servant-girl. Such a confession! Emma is his victim, body and soul. I know it! I know that she sent him money (*my* money) from this place. I know that the servant (at *her* instigation) informed him by telegraph of the birth of the child. Oh, Benjamin, don't curse the poor helpless infant—such a sweet little girl! don't think of it! I don't think of it! Show me the letter that brought you here; I want to see the letter. Ah, I can tell you who wrote it! *He* wrote it. In his own interests; always with his own interests in view. Don't you see it for yourself? If I succeed in keeping this shame and misery a secret from everybody—if I take Emma away, to some place abroad, on pretence of her health—there is an end of his hope of becoming your son-in-law; there is an end of his being taken into the business. Yes! he, the low-lived vagabond who puts up the shop-shutters, *he* looks forward to being taken into partnership, and succeeding you when you die! Isn't his object in writing that letter as plain to you now as the heaven above us? His one chance is to set your temper in a flame, to provoke the scandal of a discovery—and to force the marriage on us as the only remedy left. Am I wrong in making any sacrifice, rather than bind our girl for life, our own flesh and blood, to such a man as that? Surely you can feel for me, and forgive me, now. How could I own the truth to you, before I left London, knowing you as I do? How could I expect you to be patient, to go into hiding, to pass under a false name—to do all the degrading things that must be done, if we are to keep Emma out of this man's way? No! I know no more than you do where Farnaby is to be found. Hush! there is the door-bell. It's the doctor's time for his visit. I tell you again I don't know—on my sacred word of honour, I don't know where Farnaby is. Oh, be quiet! be quiet! there's the doctor going upstairs! don't let the doctor hear you!"

So far, she had succeeded in composing her husband. But the fury which she had innocently roused in him, in her eagerness to justify herself, now broke beyond all control. "You lie!" he cried furiously. "If you know everything else about it, you know where Farnaby is. I'll be the death of him, if I swing for it on the gallows! Where is he? Where is he?"

A shriek from the upper room silenced him before Mrs. Ronald could speak again. His daughter had heard him; his daughter had recognized his voice.

A cry of terror from her mother echoed the cry from above; the sound of the opening and closing of the door followed instantly. Then there was a momentary silence. Then Mrs. Ronald's voice was heard from the upper room calling to the nurse, asleep in the front parlour. The nurse's gruff tones were just audible, answering from the parlour door. There was another interval of silence; broken by another voice—a stranger's voice—speaking at the open window, close by.

"Follow me upstairs, sir, directly," the voice said in peremptory tones. "As your daughter's medical attendant, I tell you in the plainest terms that you have seriously frightened her. In her critical condition, I decline to answer for her life, unless you make the attempt at least to undo the mischief you have done. Whether you mean it or not, soothe her with kind words; say you have forgiven her. No! I have nothing to do with your domestic troubles; I have only my patient to think of. I don't care what she asks of you, you must give way to her now. If she falls into convulsions, she will die—and her death will be at your door."

So, with feebler and feebler interruptions from Mr. Ronald, the doctor spoke. It ended plainly in his being obeyed. The departing footsteps of the men were the next sounds to be heard. After that, there was a pause of silence—a long pause, broken by Mrs. Ronald, calling again from the upper regions. "Take the child into the back parlour, nurse, and wait till I come to you. It's cooler there, at this time of the day."

The wailing of an infant, and the gruff complaining of the nurse, were the next sounds that reached Farnaby in his hiding place. The nurse was grumbling to herself over the grievance of having been awakened from her sleep. "After being up all night, a person wants rest. There's no rest for anybody in this house. My head's as heavy as lead, and every bone in me has got an ache in it."

Before long, the renewed silence indicated that she had succeeded in hushing the child to sleep. Farnaby forgot the restraints of caution for the first time. His face flushed with excitement; he ventured nearer to the window, in his eagerness to find out what might happen next. After no long interval, the next sound came—a sound of heavy breathing, which told him that the drowsy nurse was falling asleep again. The window-sill was within reach of his hands. He waited until the heavy breathing deepened to snoring. Then he drew himself up by the window-sill, and looked into the room.

The nurse was fast asleep in an armchair; and the child was fast asleep on her lap.

He dropped softly to the ground again. Taking off his shoes, and putting them in his pockets, he ascended the two or three steps which led to the half-open back garden door. Arrived in the passage, he could just hear them talking upstairs. They were no doubt still absorbed in their troubles; he had only the servant to dread. The splashing of water in the kitchen informed him that she was safely occupied in washing. Slowly and softly he opened the back parlour door, and stole across the room to the nurse's chair.

One of her hands still rested on the child. The serious risk was the risk of waking her, if he lost his presence of mind and hurried it!

He glanced at the American clock on the mantelpiece. The result relieved him; it was not so late as he had feared. He knelt down, to steady himself, as nearly as possible on a level with the nurse's knees. By a hair's breadth at a time, he got both hands under the child. By a hair's breadth at a time, he drew the child away from

18

her; leaving her hand resting on her lap by degrees so gradual that the lightest sleeper could not have felt the change. That done (barring accidents), all was done. Keeping the child resting easily on his left arm, he had his right hand free to shut the door again. Arrived at the garden steps, a slight change passed over the sleeping infant's face—the delicate little creature shivered as it felt the full flow of the open air. He softly laid over its face a corner of the woollen shawl in which it was wrapped. The child reposed as quietly on his arm as if it had still been on the nurse's lap.

In a minute more he was at the paling. The woman rose to receive him, with the first smile that had crossed her face since they had left London.

"So you've got the baby," she said, "Well, you *are* a deep one!"

"Take it," he answered irritably. "We haven't a moment to lose."

Only stopping to put on his shoes, he led the way towards the more central part of the town. The first person he met directed him to the railway station. It was close by. In five minutes more the woman and the baby were safe in the train to London.

"There's the other half of the money," he said, handing it to her through the carriage window.

The woman eyed the child in her arms with a frowning expression of doubt. "All very well as long as it lasts," she said. "And what after that?"

"Of course, I shall call and see you," he answered.

She looked hard at him, and expressed the whole value she set on that assurance in four words. "Of course you will!"

The train started for London. Farnaby watched it, as it left the platform, with a look of unfeigned relief. "There!" he thought to himself. "Emma's reputation is safe enough now! When we are married, we mustn't have a love-child in the way of our prospects in life."

Leaving the station, he stopped at the refreshment room, and drank a glass of brandy-and-water. "Something to screw me up," he thought, "for what is to come." What was to come (after he had got rid of the child) had been carefully considered by him, on the journey to Ramsgate. "Emma's husband-that-is-to-be"—he had reasoned it out—"will naturally be the first person Emma wants to see, when the loss of the baby has upset the house. If Old Ronald has a grain of affection left in him, he must let her marry me after *that!*"

Acting on this view of his position, he took the way that led back to Slains Row, and rang the door-bell as became a visitor who had no reasons for concealment now.

The household was doubtless already disorganized by the discovery of the child's disappearance. Neither master nor servant was active in answering the bell. Farnaby submitted to be kept waiting with perfect composure. There are occasions on which a handsome man is bound to put his personal advantages to their best use. He took out his pocket-comb, and touched up the arrangement of his whiskers with a skilled and gentle hand. Approaching footsteps made themselves heard along the passage at last. Farnaby put back his comb, and buttoned his coat briskly. "Now for it!" he said, as the door was opened at last.

THE STORY

BOOK THE FIRST

AMELIUS AMONG THE SOCIALISTS

CHAPTER 1

Sixteen years after the date of Mr. Ronald's disastrous discovery at Ramsgate—that is to say, in the year 1872—the steamship *Aquila* left the port of New York, bound for Liverpool.

It was the month of September. The passenger-list of the *Aquila* had comparatively few names inscribed on it. In the autumn season, the voyage from America to England, but for the remunerative value of the cargo, would prove to be for the most part a profitless voyage to shipowners. The flow of passengers, at that time of year, sets steadily the other way. Americans are returning from Europe to their own country. Tourists have delayed the voyage until the fierce August heat of the United States has subsided, and the delicious Indian summer is ready to welcome them. At bed and board the passengers by the *Aquila* on her homeward voyage had plenty of room, and the choicest morsels for everybody alike on the well spread dinner-table.

The wind was favourable, the weather was lovely. Cheerfulness and good-humour pervaded the ship from stem to stern. The courteous captain did the honours of the cabin-table with the air of a gentleman who was receiving friends in his own house. The handsome doctor promenaded the deck arm-in-arm with ladies in course of rapid recovery from the first gastric consequences of travelling by sea. The excellent chief engineer, musical in his leisure moments to his fingers' ends, played the fiddle in his cabin, accompanied on the flute by that young Apollo of the Atlantic trade, the steward's mate. Only on the third morning of the voyage was the harmony on board the *Aquila* disturbed by a passing moment of discord—due to an unexpected addition to the ranks of the passengers, in the shape of a lost bird!

It was merely a weary little land-bird (blown out of its course, as the learned in such matters supposed); and it perched on one of the yards to rest and recover itself after its long flight.

The instant the creature was discovered, the insatiable Anglo-Saxon delight in killing birds, from the majestic eagle to the contemptible sparrow, displayed itself in its full frenzy. The crew ran about the decks, the passengers rushed into their cabins, eager to seize the first gun and to have the first shot. An old quarter-master of the *Aquila* was the enviable man, who first found the means of destruction ready to his hand. He lifted the gun to his shoulder, he had his finger on the trigger, when he was suddenly pounced upon by one of the passengers—a young, slim, sunburnt, active man—who snatched away the gun, discharged it over the side of the vessel, and turned furiously on the quarter-master. "You wretch! would you kill the poor weary bird that trusts our hospitality, and only asks us to give it a rest? That little harmless thing is as much one of God's creatures as you are. I'm ashamed of you—I'm horrified at you—you've got bird-murder in your face; I hate the sight of you!"

The quarter-master—a large grave fat man, slow alike in his bodily and his mental movements—listened to this extraordinary remonstrance with a fixed stare of amazement, and an open mouth from which the unspat tobacco-juice tricked in little brown streams. When the impetuous young gentleman paused (not for want of words, merely for want of breath), the quarter-master turned about, and addressed himself to the audience gathered round. "Gentlemen," he said, with a Roman brevity, "this young fellow is mad."

The captain's voice checked the general outbreak of laughter. "That will do, quarter-master. Let it be understood that nobody is to shoot the bird—and let me suggest to *you,* sir, that you might have expressed your sentiments quite as effectually in less violent language."

Addressed in those terms, the impetuous young man burst into another fit of excitement. "You're quite right, sir! I deserve every word you have said to me; I feel I have disgraced myself." He ran after the quartermaster, and seized him by both hands. "I beg your pardon; I beg your pardon with all my heart. You would have served me right if you had thrown me overboard after the language I used to you. Pray excuse my quick temper; pray forgive me. What do you say? 'Let bygones *be* bygones'? That's a capital way of putting it. You're a thorough good fellow. If I can ever be of the smallest use to you (there's my card and address in London), let me know it; I entreat you let me know it." He returned in a violent hurry to the captain. "I've made it up with the quarter-master, sir. He forgives me; he bears no malice. Allow me to congratulate you on having such a good Christian in your ship. I wish I was like him! Excuse me, ladies and gentlemen, for the disturbance I have made. It shan't happen again—I promise you that."

The male travellers in general looked at each other, and seemed to agree with the quarter-master's opinion of their fellow-passenger. The women, touched by his evident sincerity, and charmed with his handsome blushing eager face, agreed that he was quite right to save the poor bird, and that it would be all the better for the weaker part of creation generally if other men were more like him. While the various opinions were still in course of expression, the sound of the luncheon bell cleared the deck of the passengers, with two exceptions. One was the impetuous young man. The other was a middle-aged traveller, with a grizzled beard and a penetrating eye, who had silently observed the proceedings, and who now took the opportunity of introducing himself to the hero of the moment.

"Are you not going to take any luncheon?" he asked.

"No, sir. Among the people I have lived with we don't eat at intervals of three or four hours, all day long."

"Will you excuse me," pursued the other, "if I own I should like to know *what* people you have been living with? My name is Hethcote; I was associated, at one time of my life, with a college devoted to the training of young men. From what I have seen and heard this morning, I fancy you have not been educated on any of the recognized systems that are popular at the present day. Am I right?"

24

The excitable young man suddenly became the picture of resignation, and answered in a formula of words as if he was repeating a lesson.

"I am Claude-Amelius-Goldenheart. Aged twenty-one. Son, and only child, of the late Claude Goldenheart, of Shedfield Heath, Buckinghamshire, England. I have been brought up by the Primitive Christian Socialists, at Tadmor Community, State of Illinois. I have inherited an income of five hundred a year. And I am now, with the approval of the Community, going to London to see life."

Mr. Hethcote received this copious flow of information, in some doubt whether he had been made the victim of coarse raillery, or whether he had merely heard a quaint statement of facts.

Claude-Amelius-Goldenheart saw that he had produced an unfavourable impression, and hastened to set himself right.

"Excuse me, sir," he said, "I am not making game of you, as you seem to suppose. We are taught to be courteous to everybody, in our Community. The truth is, there seems to be something odd about me (I'm sure I don't know what), which makes people whom I meet on my travels curious to know who I am. If you'll please to remember, it's a long way from Illinois to New York, and curious strangers are not scarce on the journey. When one is obliged to keep on saying the same thing over and over again, a form saves a deal of trouble. I have made a form for myself—which is respectfully at the disposal of any person who does me the honour to wish for my acquaintance. Will that do, sir? Very well, then; shake hands, to show you're satisfied."

Mr. Hethcote shook hands, more than satisfied. He found it impossible to resist the bright honest brown eyes, the simple winning cordial manner of the young fellow with the quaint formula and the strange name. "Come, Mr. Goldenheart," he said, leading the way to a seat on deck, "let us sit down comfortably, and have a talk."

"Anything you like, sir—but don't call me Mr. Goldenheart."

"Why not?"

"Well, it sounds formal. And, besides, you're old enough to be my father; it's *my* duty to call *you* Mister—or Sir, as we say to our elders at Tadmor. I have left all my friends behind me at the Community—and I feel lonely out here on this big ocean, among strangers. Do me a kindness, sir. Call me by my Christian name; and give me a friendly slap on the back if you find we get along smoothly in the course of the day."

"Which of your names shall it be?" Mr. Hethcote asked, humouring this odd lad. "Claude?"

"No. Not Claude. The Primitive Christians said Claude was a finicking French name. Call me Amelius, and I shall begin to feel at home again. If you're in a hurry, cut it down to three letters (as they did at Tadmor), and call me Mel."

"Very good," said Mr. Hethcote. "Now, my friend Amelius (or Mel), I am going to speak out plainly, as you do. The Primitive Christian Socialists must have great confidence in their system of education, to turn you adrift in the world without a companion to look after you."

"You've hit it, sir," Amelius answered coolly. "They have unlimited confidence in their system of education. And I'm a proof of it."

"You have relations in London, I suppose?" Mr. Hethcote proceeded.

For the first time the face of Amelius showed a shadow of sadness on it.

"I have relations," he said. "But I have promised never to claim their hospitality. 'They are hard and worldly; and they will make you hard and worldly, too.' That's what my father said to me on his deathbed." He took off his hat when he mentioned his father's death, and came to a sudden pause—with his head bent down, like a man absorbed in thought. In less than a minute he put on his hat again, and looked up with his bright winning smile. "We say a little prayer for the loved ones who are gone, when we speak of them," he explained. "But we don't say it out loud, for fear of seeming to parade our religious convictions. We hate cant in our Community."

"I cordially agree with the Community, Amelius. But, my good fellow, have you really no friend to welcome you when you get to London?"

Amelius answered the question mysteriously. "Wait a little!" he said—and took a letter from the breast-pocket of his coat. Mr. Hethcote, watching him, observed that he looked at the address with unfeigned pride and pleasure.

"One of our brethren at the Community has given me this," he announced. "It's a letter of introduction, sir, to a remarkable man—a man who is an example to all the rest of us. He has risen, by dint of integrity and perseverance, from the position of a poor porter in a shop to be one of the most respected mercantile characters in the City of London."

With this explanation, Amelius handed his letter to Mr. Hethcote. It was addressed as follows:—

To John Farnaby, Esquire,
Messrs. Ronald & Farnaby,
Stationers,
Aldersgate Street, London.

26

CHAPTER 2

Mr. Hethcote looked at the address on the letter with an expression of surprise, which did not escape the notice of Amelius. "Do you know Mr. Farnaby?" he asked.

"I have some acquaintance with him," was the answer, given with a certain appearance of constraint.

Amelius went on eagerly with his questions. "What sort of man is he? Do you think he will be prejudiced against me, because I have been brought up in Tadmor?"

"I must be a little better acquainted, Amelius, with you and Tadmor before I can answer your question. Suppose you tell me how you became one of the Socialists, to begin with?"

"I was only a little boy, Mr. Hethcote, at that time."

"Very good. Even little boys have memories. Is there any objection to your telling me what you can remember?"

Amelius answered rather sadly, with his eyes bent on the deck. "I remember something happening which threw a gloom over us at home in England. I heard that my mother was concerned in it. When I grew older, I never presumed to ask my father what it was; and he never offered to tell me. I only know this: that he forgave her some wrong she had done him, and let her go on living at home—and that relations and friends all blamed him, and fell away from him, from that time. Not long afterwards, while I was at school, my mother died. I was sent for, to follow her funeral with my father. When we got back, and were alone together, he took me on his knee and kissed me. 'Which will you do, Amelius,' he said; 'stay in England with your uncle and aunt? or come with me all the way to America, and never go back to England again? Take time to think of it.' I wanted no time to think of it; I said, 'Go with you, papa.' He frightened me by bursting out crying; it was the first time I had ever seen him in tears. I can understand it now. He had been cut to the heart, and had borne it like a martyr; and his boy was his one friend left. Well, by the end of the week we were on board the ship; and there we met a benevolent gentleman, with a long gray beard, who bade my father welcome, and presented me with a cake. In my ignorance, I thought he was the captain. Nothing of the sort. He was the first Socialist I had ever seen; and it was he who had persuaded my father to leave England."

Mr. Hethcote's opinions of Socialists began to show themselves (a little sourly) in Mr. Hethcote's smile. "And how did you get on with this benevolent gentleman?" he asked. "After converting your father, did he convert you—with the cake?"

Amelius smiled. "Do him justice, sir; he didn't trust to the cake. He waited till we were in sight of the American land—and then he preached me a little sermon, on our arrival, entirely for my own use."

"A sermon?" Mr. Hethcote repeated. "Very little religion in it, I suspect."

"Very little indeed, sir," Amelius answered. "Only as much religion as there is in the New Testament. I was not quite old enough to understand him easily—so he wrote down his discourse on the fly-leaf of a story-book I had with me, and gave it to me to read when I was tired of the stories. Stories were scarce with me in those days; and, when I had exhausted my little stock, rather than read nothing I read my sermon— read it so often that I think I can remember every word of it now. 'My dear little boy, the Christian religion, as Christ taught it, has long ceased to be the religion of the Christian world. A selfish and cruel Pretence is set up in its place. Your own father is one example of the truth of this saying of mine. He has fulfilled the first and foremost duty of a true Christian—the duty of forgiving an injury. For this, he stands disgraced in the estimation of all his friends: they have renounced and abandoned him. He forgives them, and seeks peace and good company in the New World, among Christians like himself. You will not repent leaving home with him; you will be one of a loving family, and, when you are old enough, you will be free to decide for yourself what your future life shall be.' That was all I knew about the Socialists, when we reached Tadmor after our long journey."

Mr. Hethcote's prejudices made their appearance again. "A barren sort of place," he said, "judging by the name."

"Barren? What can you be thinking of? A prettier place I never saw, and never expect to see again. A clear winding river, running into a little blue lake. A broad hill-side, all laid out in flower-gardens, and shaded by splendid trees. On the top of the hill, the buildings of the Community, some of brick and some of wood, so covered with creepers and so encircled with verandahs that I can't tell you to this day what style of architecture they were built in. More trees behind the houses—and, on the other side of the hill, cornfields, nothing but cornfields rolling away and away in great yellow plains, till they reached the golden sky and the setting sun, and were seen no more. That was our first view of Tadmor, when the stage-coach dropped us at the town."

Mr. Hethcote still held out. "And what about the people who live in this earthly Paradise?" he asked. "Male and female saints—eh?"

"Oh dear no, sir! The very opposite of saints. They eat and drink like their neighbours. They never think of wearing dirty horsehair when they can get clean linen. And when they are tempted to misconduct themselves, they find a better way out of it than knotting a cord and thrashing their own backs. Saints! They all ran out together to bid us welcome like a lot of school-children; the first thing they did was to kiss us, and the next thing was to give us a mug of wine of their own making. Saints! Oh, Mr. Hethcote, what will you accuse us of being next? I declare your

28

suspicions of the poor Socialists keep cropping up again as fast as I cut them down. May I make a guess, sir, without offending you? From one or two things I have noticed, I strongly suspect you're a British clergyman."

Mr. Hethcote was conquered at last: he burst out laughing. "You have discovered me," he said, "travelling in a coloured cravat and a shooting jacket! I confess I should like to know how."

"It's easily explained, sir. Visitors of all sorts are welcome at Tadmor. We have a large experience of them in the travelling season. They all come with their own private suspicion of us lurking about the corners of their eyes. They see everything we have to show them, and eat and drink at our table, and join in our amusements, and get as pleasant and friendly with us as can be. The time comes to say goodbye— and then we find them out. If a guest who has been laughing and enjoying himself all day, suddenly becomes serious when he takes his leave, and shows that little lurking devil of suspicion again about the corners of his eyes—it's ten chances to one that he's a clergyman. No offence, Mr. Hethcote! I acknowledge with pleasure that the corners of *your* eyes are clear again. You're not a very clerical clergyman, sir, after all—I don't despair of converting you, yet!"

"Go on with your story, Amelius. You're the queerest fellow I have met with, for many a long day past."

"I'm a little doubtful about going on with my story, sir. I have told you how I got to Tadmor, and what it looks like, and what sort of people live in the place. If I am to get on beyond that, I must jump to the time when I was old enough to learn the Rules of the Community."

"Well—and what then?"

"Well, Mr. Hethcote, some of the Rules might offend you."

"Try!"

"All right, sir! don't blame me; *I'm* not ashamed of the Rules. And now, if I am to speak, I must speak seriously on a serious subject; I must begin with our religious principles. We find our Christianity in the spirit of the New Testament—not in the letter. We have three good reasons for objecting to pin our faith on the words alone, in that book. First, because we are not sure that the English translation is always to be depended on as accurate and honest. Secondly, because we know that (since the invention of printing) there is not a copy of the book in existence which is free from errors of the press, and that (before the invention of printing) those errors, in manuscript copies, must as a matter of course have been far more serious and far more numerous. Thirdly, because there is plain internal evidence (to say nothing of discoveries actually made in the present day) of interpolations and corruptions, introduced into the manuscript copies as they succeeded each other in ancient times.

These drawbacks are of no importance, however, in our estimation. We find, in the spirit of the book, the most simple and most perfect system of religion and morality that humanity has ever received—and with that we are content. To reverence God; and to love our neighbour as ourselves: if we had only those two commandments to guide us, we should have enough. The whole collection of Doctrines (as they are called) we reject at once, without even stopping to discuss them. We apply to them the test suggested by Christ himself: by their fruits ye shall know them. The fruits of Doctrines, in the past (to quote three instances only), have been the Spanish Inquisition, the Massacre of St. Bartholomew, and the Thirty Years' War—and the fruits, in the present, are dissension, bigotry, and opposition to useful reforms. Away with Doctrines! In the interests of Christianity, away with them! We are to love our enemies; we are to forgive injuries; we are to help the needy; we are to be pitiful and courteous, slow to judge others, and ashamed to exalt ourselves. That teaching doesn't lead to tortures, massacres, and wars; to envy, hatred, and malice—and for that reason it stands revealed to us as the teaching that we can trust. There is our religion, sir, as we find it in the Rules of the Community."

"Very well, Amelius. I notice, in passing, that the Community is in one respect like the Pope—the Community is infallible. We won't dwell on that. You have stated your principles. As to the application of them next? Nobody has a right to be rich among you, of course?"

"Put it the other way, Mr. Hethcote. All men have a right to be rich—provided they don't make other people poor, as a part of the process. We don't trouble ourselves much about money; that's the truth. We are farmers, carpenters, weavers, and printers; and what we earn (ask our neighbours if we don't earn it honestly) goes into the common fund. A man who comes to us with money puts it into the fund, and so makes things easy for the next man who comes with empty pockets. While they are with us, they all live in the same comfort, and have their equal share in the same profits—deducting the sum in reverse for sudden calls and bad times. If they leave us, the man who has brought money with him has his undisputed right to take it away again; and the man who has brought none bids us good-bye, all the richer for his equal share in the profits which he has personally earned. The only fuss at our place about money that I can remember was the fuss about my five hundred a year. I wanted to hand it over to the fund. It was my own, mind—inherited from my mother's property, on my coming of age. The Elders wouldn't hear of it: the Council wouldn't hear of it: the general vote of the Community wouldn't hear of it. 'We agreed with his father that he should decide for himself, when he grew to manhood'—that was how they put it. 'Let him go back to the Old World; and let him be free to choose, by the test of his own experience, what his future life shall be.' How do you think it will end, Mr. Hethcote? Shall I return to the Community? Or shall I stop in London?"

Mr. Hethcote answered, without a moment's hesitation. "You will stop in London."

"I'll bet you two to one, Sir, he goes back to the Community."

In those words, a third voice (speaking in a strong New England accent) insinuated itself into the conversation from behind. Amelius and Mr. Hethcote, looking round, discovered a long, lean, grave stranger—with his face overshadowed by a huge felt hat. "Have you been listening to our conversation?" Mr. Hethcote asked haughtily.

"I have been listening," answered the grave stranger, "with considerable interest. This young man, I find, opens a new chapter to me in the book of humanity. Do you accept my bet, Sir? My name is Rufus Dingwell; and my home is at Coolspring, Mass. You do *not* bet? I express my regret, and have the pleasure of taking a seat alongside of you. What is your name, Sir? Hethcote? We have one of that name at Coolspring. He is much respected. Mr. Claude A. Goldenheart, you are no stranger to me—no, Sir. I procured your name from the steward, when the little difficulty occurred just now about the bird. Your name considerably surprised me."

"Why?" Amelius asked.

"Well, sir—not to say that your surname (being Goldenheart) reminds one unexpectedly of *The Pilgrim's Progress*—I happen to be already acquainted with you. By reputation."

Amelius looked puzzled. "By reputation?" he said. "What does that mean?"

"It means, sir, that you occupy a prominent position in a recent number of our popular journal, entitled *The Coolspring Democrat*. The late romantic incident which caused the withdrawal of Miss Mellicent from your Community has produced a species of social commotion at Coolspring. Among our ladies, the tone of sentiment, Sir, is universally favourable to you. When I left, I do assure you, you were a popular character among us. The name of Claude A. Goldenheart was, so to speak, in everybody's mouth."

Amelius listened to this, with the colour suddenly deepening on his face, and with every appearance of heartfelt annoyance and regret. "There is no such thing as keeping a secret in America," he said, irritably. "Some spy must have got among us; none of *our* people would have exposed the poor lady to public comment. How would you like it, Mr. Dingwell, if the newspaper published the private sorrows of your wife or your daughter?"

Rufus Dingwell answered with the straightforward sincerity of feeling which is one of the indisputable virtues of his nation. "I had not thought of it in that light, sir," he said. "You have been good enough to credit me with a wife or a daughter. I do not possess either of those ladies; but your argument hits me, notwithstanding—hits me hard, I tell you." He looked at Mr. Hethcote, who sat silently and stiffly disapproving of all this familiarity, and applied himself in perfect innocence and good faith to making things pleasant in that quarter. "You are a stranger, Sir," said Rufus; "and you will doubtless wish to peruse the article which is the subject of conversation?" He took a newspaper slip from his pocket-book, and offered it to the astonished Englishman. "I shall be glad to hear your sentiments, sir, on the view propounded by our mutual friend, Claude A. Goldenheart."

Before Mr. Hethcote could reply, Amelius interposed in his own headlong way. "Give it to me! I want to read it first!"

He snatched at the newspaper slip. Rufus checked him with grave composure. "I am of a cool temperament myself, sir; but that don't prevent me from admiring heat in others. Short of boiling point—mind that!" With this hint, the wise New Englander permitted Amelius to take possession of the printed slip.

Mr. Hethcote, finding an opportunity of saying a word at last, asserted himself a little haughtily. "I beg you will both of you understand that I decline to read anything which relates to another person's private affairs."

Neither the one nor the other of his companions paid the slightest heed to this announcement. Amelius was reading the newspaper extract, and placid Rufus was watching him. In another moment, he crumpled up the slip, and threw it indignantly on the deck. "It's as full of lies as it can hold!" he burst out.

"It's all over the United States, by this time," Rufus remarked. "And I don't doubt we shall find the English papers have copied it, when we get to Liverpool. If you will take my advice, sir, you will cultivate a sagacious insensibility to the comments of the press."

"Do you think I care for myself?" Amelius asked indignantly. "It's the poor woman I am thinking of. What can I do to clear her character?"

"Well, sir," suggested Rufus, "in your place, I should have a notification circulated through the ship, announcing a lecture on the subject (weather permitting) in the course of the afternoon. That's the way we should do it at Coolspring."

Amelius listened without conviction. "It's certainly useless to make a secret of the matter now," he said; "but I don't see my way to making it more public still." He paused, and looked at Mr. Hethcote. "It so happens, sir," he resumed, "that this unfortunate affair is an example of some of the Rules of our Community, which I had not had time to speak of, when Mr. Dingwell here joined us. It will be a relief to me to contradict these abominable falsehoods to somebody; and I should like (if you don't mind) to hear what you think of my conduct, from your own point of view. It might prepare me," he added, smiling rather uneasily, "for what I may find in the English newspapers."

With these words of introduction he told his sad story—jocosely described in the newspaper heading as "Miss Mellicent and Goldenheart among the Socialists at Tadmor."

CHAPTER 3

"Nearly six months since," said Amelius, "we had notice by letter of the arrival of an unmarried English lady, who wished to become a member of our Community. You will understand my motive in keeping her family name a secret: even the newspaper has grace enough only to mention her by her Christian name. I don't want to cheat you out of your interest; so I will own at once that Miss Mellicent was not beautiful, and not young. When she came to us, she was thirty-eight years old, and time and trial had set their marks on her face plainly enough for anybody to see. Notwithstanding this, we all thought her an interesting woman. It might have been the sweetness of her voice; or perhaps it was something in her expression that took our fancy. There! I can't explain it; I can only say there were young women and pretty women at Tadmor who failed to win us as Miss Mellicent did. Contradictory enough, isn't it?"

Mr. Hethcote said he understood the contradiction. Rufus put an appropriate question: "Do you possess a photograph of this lady, sir?"

"No," said Amelius; "I wish I did. Well, we received her, on her arrival, in the Common Room—called so because we all assemble there every evening, when the work of the day is done. Sometimes we have the reading of a poem or a novel; sometimes debates on the social and political questions of the time in England and America; sometimes music, or dancing, or cards, or billiards, to amuse us. When a new member arrives, we have the ceremonies of introduction. I was close by the Elder Brother (that's the name we give to the chief of the Community) when two of the women led Miss Mellicent in. He's a hearty old fellow, who lived the first part of his life on his own clearing in one of the Western forests. To this day, he can't talk long, without showing, in one way or another, that his old familiarity with the trees still keeps its place in his memory. He looked hard at Miss Mellicent, under his shaggy old white eyebrows; and I heard him whisper to himself, 'Ah, dear me! Another of The Fallen Leaves!' I knew what he meant. The people who have drawn blanks in the lottery of life—the people who have toiled hard after happiness, and have gathered nothing but disappointment and sorrow; the friendless and the lonely, the wounded and the lost—these are the people whom our good Elder Brother calls The Fallen Leaves. I like the saying myself; it's a tender way of speaking of our poor fellow-creatures who are down in the world."

He paused for a moment, looking out thoughtfully over the vast void of sea and sky. A passing shadow of sadness clouded his bright young face. The two elder men looked at him in silence, feeling (in widely different ways) the same compassionate interest. What was the life that lay before him? And—God help him!—what would he do with it?

"Where did I leave off?" he asked, rousing himself suddenly.

"You left Miss Mellicent, sir, in the Common Room—the venerable citizen with the white eyebrows being suitably engaged in moralizing on her." In those terms the ever-ready Rufus set the story going again.

"Quite right," Amelius resumed. "There she was, poor thing, a little thin timid creature, in a white dress, with a black scarf over her shoulders, trembling and wondering in a room full of strangers. The Elder Brother took her by the hand, and kissed her on the forehead, and bade her heartily welcome in the name of the Community. Then the women followed his example, and the men all shook hands with her. And then our chief put the three questions, which he is bound to address to all new arrivals when they join us: 'Do you come here of your own free will? Do you bring with you a written recommendation from one of our brethren, which satisfies us that we do no wrong to ourselves or to others in receiving you? Do you understand that you are not bound to us by vows, and that you are free to leave us again if the life here is not agreeable to you?' Matters being settled so far, the reading of the Rules, and the Penalties imposed for breaking them, came next. Some of the Rules you know already; others of smaller importance I needn't trouble you with. As for the Penalties, if you incur the lighter ones, you are subject to public rebuke, or to isolation for a time from the social life of the Community. If you incur the heavier ones, you are either sent out into the world again for a given period, to return or not as you please; or you are struck off the list of members, and expelled for good and all. Suppose these preliminaries agreed to by Miss Mellicent with silent submission, and let us go on to the close of the ceremony—the reading of the Rules which settle the questions of Love and Marriage."

"Aha!" said Mr. Hethcote, "we are coming to the difficulties of the Community at last!"

"Are we also coming to Miss Mellicent, sir?" Rufus inquired. "As a citizen of a free country in which I can love in one State, marry in another, and be divorced in a third, I am not interested in your Rules—I am interested in your Lady."

"The two are inseparable in this case," Amelius answered gravely. "If I am to speak of Miss Mellicent, I must speak of the Rules; you will soon see why. Our Community becomes a despotism, gentlemen, in dealing with love and marriage. For example, it positively prohibits any member afflicted with hereditary disease from marrying at all; and it reserves to itself, in the case of every proposed marriage among us, the right of permitting or forbidding it, in council. We can't even fall in love with each other, without being bound, under penalties, to report it to the Elder Brother; who, in his turn, communicates it to the monthly council; who, in their turn, decide whether the courtship may go on or not. That's not the worst of it, even yet! In some cases—where we haven't the slightest intention of falling in love with each other—the governing body takes the initiative. 'You two will do well to marry; we see it, if you don't. Just think of it, will you?' You may laugh; some of our happiest marriages have been made in that way. Our governors in council act on an established principle: here it is in a nutshell. The results of experience in the matter of marriage, all over the world, show that a really wise choice of a husband or a wife is an exception to the rule; and that husbands and wives in general would be happier together if their marriages were managed for them by competent advisers on either side. Laws laid down on such lines as these, and others equally strict, which I have not mentioned yet, were not put in force, Mr. Hethcote, as you suppose, without serious difficulties— difficulties which threatened the very existence of the Community. But that was before my time. When I grew up, I found the husbands and wives about me content to acknowledge that the Rules fulfilled the purpose with which they had been made—the greatest happiness of the greatest number. It all looks very absurd, I dare say, from your point of view. But these queer regulations of ours answer the Christian test—by their fruits ye shall know them. Our married people don't live on separate sides of the house; our children are all healthy; wife-beating is unknown among us; and the practice in our divorce court wouldn't keep the most moderate lawyer on bread and cheese. Can you say as much for the success of the marriage laws in Europe? I leave you, gentlemen, to form your own opinions."

Mr. Hethcote declined to express an opinion. Rufus declined to resign his interest in the lady. "And what did Miss Mellicent say to it?" he inquired.

"She said something that startled us all," Amelius replied. "When the Elder Brother began to read the first words relating to love and marriage in the Book of Rules, she turned deadly pale; and rose up in her place with a sudden burst of courage or desperation—I don't know which. 'Must you read that to me?' she asked. 'I have nothing to do with love or marriage.' The Elder Brother laid aside his Book of Rules. 'If you are afflicted with an hereditary malady,' he said, 'the doctor from the town will examine you, and report to us.' She answered, 'I have no hereditary malady.' The Elder Brother took up his book again. 'In due course of time, my dear, the Council will decide for you whether you are to love and marry or not.' And he read the Rules. She sat down again, and hid her face in her hands, and never moved or spoke until he had done. The regular questions followed. Had she anything to say, in the way of objection? Nothing! In that case, would she sign the Rules? Yes! When the time came for supper, she excused herself, just like a child. 'I feel very tired; may I go to bed?' The unmarried women in the same dormitory with her anticipated some romantic confession when she grew used to her new friends. They proved to be wrong. 'My life has been one long disappointment,' was all she said. 'You will do me a kindness if you will take me as I am, and not ask me to talk about myself.' There was nothing sulky or ungracious in the expression of her wish to keep her own secret. A kinder and sweeter woman—never thinking of herself, always considerate of others—never lived. An accidental discovery made me her chief friend, among the men: it turned out that her childhood had been passed, where my childhood had been passed, at Shedfield Heath, in Buckinghamshire. She was never weary of consulting my boyish recollections, and comparing them with her own. 'I love the place,' she used to say; 'the only happy time of my life was the time passed there.' On my sacred word of honour, this was the sort of talk that passed between us, for week after week. What other talk could pass between a man whose one and twentieth birthday was then near at hand, and a woman who was close on forty? What could I do, when the poor, broken, disappointed creature met me on the hill or by the river, and said, 'You are going out for a walk; may I come with you?' I never attempted to intrude myself into her confidence; I never even asked her why she had joined the Community. You see what is coming, don't you? *I* never saw it. I didn't know what it meant, when some of the younger women, meeting us together, looked at me (not at her), and smiled maliciously. My stupid eyes were opened at last by the woman who slept in the next bed to her in the dormitory—a woman old enough to be my mother, who took care of me when I was a child at Tadmor. She stopped me one morning, on my way to fish in the river. 'Amelius,' she said, 'don't go to the fishing-house; Mellicent is waiting for you.' I stared at her in astonishment. She held up her finger at me: 'Take care, you foolish boy! You are drifting into a false position as fast as you can. Have you no suspicion of what is going on?' I looked all round me, in search of what was going on. Nothing out of the common was to be seen anywhere. 'What can you possibly mean?' I asked. 'You will only laugh at me, if I tell you,' she said. I promised not to laugh. She too looked all round her, as if she was afraid of somebody being near enough to hear us; and then she let out the secret. 'Amelius, ask for a holiday—and leave us for a while. Mellicent is in love with you.'"

CHAPTER 4

Amelius looked at his companions, in some doubt whether they would preserve their gravity at this critical point in his story. They both showed him that his apprehensions were well founded. He was a little hurt, and he instantly revealed it. "I own to my shame that I burst out laughing myself," he said. "But you two gentlemen are older and wiser than I am. I didn't expect to find you just as ready to laugh at poor Miss Mellicent as I was."

Mr. Hethcote declined to be reminded of his duties as a middle-aged gentleman in this backhanded manner. "Gently, Amelius! You can't expect to persuade us that a laughable thing is not a thing to be laughed at. A woman close on forty who falls in love with a young fellow of twenty-one—"

"Is a laughable circumstance," Rufus interposed. "Whereas a man of forty who fancies a young woman of twenty-one is all in the order of Nature. The men have settled it so. But why the women are to give up so much sooner than the men is a question, sir, on which I have long wished to hear the sentiments of the women themselves."

Mr. Hethcote dismissed the sentiments of the women with a wave of his hand. "Let us hear the rest of it, Amelius. Of course you went on to the fishing-house? And of course you found Miss Mellicent there?"

"She came to the door to meet me, much as usual," Amelius resumed, "and suddenly checked herself in the act of shaking hands with me. I can only suppose she saw something in my face that startled her. How it happened, I can't say; but I felt my good spirits forsake me the moment I found myself in her presence. I doubt if she had ever seen me so serious before. 'Have I offended you?' she asked. Of course, I denied it; but I failed to satisfy her. She began to tremble. 'Has somebody said something against me? Are you weary of my company?' Those were the next questions. It was useless to say No. Some perverse distrust of me, or some despair of herself, overpowered her on a sudden. She sank down on the floor of the fishing-house, and began to cry—not a good hearty burst of tears; a silent, miserable, resigned sort of crying, as if she had lost all claim to be pitied, and all right to feel wounded or hurt. I was so distressed, that I thought of nothing but consoling her. I meant well, and I acted like a fool. A sensible man would have lifted her up, I suppose, and left her to herself. I lifted her up, and put my arm round her waist. She looked at me as I did it. For just a moment, I declare she became twenty years younger! She blushed as I have never seen a woman blush before or since—the colour flowed all over her neck as well as her face. Before I could say a word, she caught hold of my hand, and (of all the confusing things in the world!) kissed it. 'No!' she cried, 'don't despise me! don't laugh at me! Wait, and hear what my life has been, and then you will understand why a little kindness overpowers me.' She looked round the corner of the fishing-house suspiciously. 'I don't want anybody else to hear us,' she said, 'all the pride isn't beaten out of me yet. Come to the lake, and row me about in the boat.' I took her out in the boat. Nobody could hear us

37

certainly; but she forgot, and I forgot, that anybody might see us, and that appearances on the lake might lead to false conclusions on shore."

Mr. Hethcote and Rufus exchanged significant looks. They had not forgotten the Rules of the Community, when two of its members showed a preference for each other's society.

Amelius proceeded. "Well, there we were on the lake. I paddled with the oars, and she opened her whole heart to me. Her troubles had begun, in a very common way, with her mother's death and her father's second marriage. She had a brother and a sister—the sister married a German merchant, settled in New York; the brother comfortably established as a sheep-farmer in Australia. So, you see, she was alone at home, at the mercy of the step-mother. I don't understand these cases myself, but people who do, tell me that there are generally faults on both sides. To make matters worse, they were a poor family; the one rich relative being a sister of the first wife, who disapproved of the widower marrying again, and never entered the house afterwards. Well, the step-mother had a sharp tongue, and Mellicent was the first person to feel the sting of it. She was reproached with being an encumbrance on her father, when she ought to be doing something for herself. There was no need to repeat those harsh words. The next day she answered an advertisement. Before the week was over, she was earning her bread as a daily governess."

Here Rufus stopped the narrative, having an interesting question to put. "Might I inquire, sir, what her salary was?"

"Thirty pounds a year," Amelius replied. "She was out teaching from nine o'clock to two—and then went home again."

"There seems to be nothing to complain of in that, as salaries go," Mr. Hethcote remarked.

"She made no complaint," Amelius rejoined. "She was satisfied with her salary; but she wasn't satisfied with her life. The meek little woman grew downright angry when she spoke of it. 'I had no reason to complain of my employers,' she said. 'I was civilly treated and punctually paid; but I never made friends of them. I tried to make friends of the children; and sometimes I thought I had succeeded—but, oh dear, when they were idle, and I was obliged to keep them to their lessons, I soon found how little hold I had on the love that I wanted them to give me. We see children in books who are perfect little angels; never envious or greedy or sulky or deceitful; always the same sweet, pious, tender, grateful, innocent creatures—and it has been my misfortune never to meet with them, go where I might! It is a hard world, Amelius, the world that I have lived in. I don't think there are such miserable lives anywhere as the lives led by the poor middle classes in England. From year's end to year's end, the one dreadful struggle to keep up appearances, and the heart-breaking monotony of an existence without change. We lived in the back street of a cheap suburb. I declare to you we had but one amusement in the whole long weary year—the annual concert the clergyman got up, in aid of his schools. The rest of the year it was all teaching for the first half of the day, and needlework for the young family for the other half. My father had religious scruples; he prohibited theatres, he prohibited dancing and light reading; he even prohibited looking in at the shop-windows, because we had no money to spare and they tempted us to buy. He went to business in the morning, and came back at night, and fell asleep after dinner, and woke up and read prayers—and next day to business and back, and sleeping and waking and reading prayers—and no break in it, week after week, month after month, except on Sunday, which was always the same Sunday; the same church, the same service, the same dinner, the same book of sermons in the evening. Even when we had a fortnight once a year at the seaside, we always went to the same place and lodged in the same cheap house. The few friends we had led just the same lives, and were beaten down flat by just the same monotony. All the women seemed to submit to it contentedly except my miserable self. I wanted so little! Only a change now and then; only a little sympathy when I was weary and sick at heart; only somebody whom I could love and serve, and be rewarded with a smile and a kind word in return. Mothers shook their heads, and daughters laughed at me. Have we time to be sentimental? Haven't we enough to do, darning and mending, and turning our dresses, and making the joint last as long as possible, and keeping the children clean, and doing the washing at home—and tea and sugar rising, and my husband grumbling every week when I have to ask him for the house-money. Oh, no more of it! no more of it! People meant for better things all ground down to the same sordid and selfish level—is that a pleasant sight to contemplate? I shudder when I think of the last twenty years of my life!' That's what she complained of, Mr. Hethcote, in the solitary middle of the lake, with nobody but me to hear her."

"In my country, sir," Rufus remarked, "the Lecture Bureau would have provided for her amusement, on economical terms. And I reckon, if a married life would fix her, she might have tried it among Us by way of a change."

"That's the saddest part of the story," said Amelius. "There came a time, only two years ago, when her prospects changed for the better. Her rich aunt (her mother's sister) died; and—what do you think?—left her a legacy of six thousand pounds. There was a gleam of sunshine in her life! The poor teacher was an heiress in a small way, with her fortune at her own disposal. They had something like a festival at home, for the first time; presents to everybody, and kissings and congratulations, and new dresses at last. And, more than that, another wonderful event happened before long. A gentleman made his appearance in the family circle, with an interesting object in view—a gentleman, who had called at the house in which she happened to be employed as teacher at the time, and had seen her occupied with her pupils. He had kept it to himself to be sure, but he had secretly admired her from that moment—and now it had come out! She had never had a lover before; mind that. And he was a remarkably handsome man: dressed beautifully, and sang and played, and was so humble and devoted with it all. Do you think it wonderful that she said Yes, when he proposed to marry her? I don't think it wonderful at all. For the first few weeks of the courtship, the sunshine was brighter than ever. Then the clouds began to rise. Anonymous letters came, describing the handsome gentleman (seen under his fair surface) as nothing less than a scoundrel. She tore up the letters indignantly—she was too delicate even to show them to him. Signed letters came

39

next, addressed to her father by an uncle and an aunt, both containing one and the same warning: 'If your daughter insists on having him, tell her to take care of her money.' A few days later, a visitor arrived—a brother, who spoke out more plainly still. As an honourable man, he could not hear of what was going on, without making the painful confession that his brother was forbidden to enter his house. That said, he washed his hands of all further responsibility. You two know the world, you will guess how it ended. Quarrels in the household; the poor middle-aged woman, living in her fool's paradise, blindly true to her lover; convinced that he was foully wronged; frantic when he declared that he would not connect himself with a family which suspected him. Ah, I have no patience when I think of it, and I almost wish I had never begun to tell the story! Do you know what he did? She was free of course, at her age, to decide for herself; there was no controlling her. The wedding day was fixed. Her father had declared he would not sanction it; and her step-mother kept him to his word. She went alone to the church, to meet her promised husband. He never appeared; he deserted her, mercilessly deserted her—after she had sacrificed her own relations to him—on her wedding-day. She was taken home insensible, and had a brain fever. The doctors declined to answer for her life. Her father thought it time to look to her banker's pass-book. Out of her six thousand pounds she had privately given no less than four thousand to the scoundrel who had deceived and forsaken her! Not a month afterwards he married a young girl—with a fortune of course. We read of such things in newspapers and books. But to have them brought home to one, after living one's own life among honest people—I tell you it stupefied me!"

He said no more. Below them in the cabin, voices were laughing and talking, to a cheerful accompaniment of clattering knives and forks. Around them spread the exultant glory of sea and sky. All that they heard, all that they saw, was cruelty out of harmony with the miserable story which had just reached its end. With one accord the three men rose and paced the deck, feeling physically the same need of some movement to lighten their spirits. With one accord they waited a little, before the narrative was resumed.

CHAPTER 5

Mr. Hethcote was the first to speak again.

"I can understand the poor creature's motive in joining your Community," he said. "To a person of any sensibility her position, among such relatives as you describe, must have been simply unendurable after what had happened. How did she hear of Tadmor and the Socialists?"

"She had read one of our books," Amelius answered; "and she had her married sister at New York to go to. There were moments, after her recovery (she confessed it to me frankly), when the thought of suicide was in her mind. Her religious scruples saved her. She was kindly received by her sister and her sister's husband. They proposed to keep her with them to teach their children. No! the new life offered to her was too like the old life—she was broken in body and mind; she had no courage to face it. We have a resident agent in New York; and he arranged for her journey to Tadmor. There is a gleam of brightness, at any rate, in this part of her story. She blessed the day, poor soul, when she joined us. Never before had she found herself among such kind-hearted, unselfish, simple people. Never before—" he abruptly checked himself, and looked a little confused.

Obliging Rufus finished the sentence for him. "Never before had she known a young man with such natural gifts of fascination as C.A.G. Don't you be too modest, sir; it doesn't pay, I assure you, in the nineteenth century."

Amelius was not as ready with his laugh as usual. "I wish I could drop it at the point we have reached now," he said. "But she has left Tadmor; and, in justice to her (after the scandals in the newspaper), I must tell you how she left it, and why. The mischief began when I was helping her out of the boat. Two of our young women met us on the bank of the lake, and asked me how I got on with my fishing. They didn't mean any harm—they were only in their customary good spirits. Still, there was no mistaking their looks and tones when they put the question. Miss Mellicent, in her confusion, made matters worse. She coloured up, and snatched her hand out of mine, and ran back to the house by herself. The girls, enjoying their own foolish joke, congratulated me on my prospects. I must have been out of sorts in some way—upset, perhaps, by what I had heard in the boat. Anyhow, I lost my temper, and *I* made matters worse, next. I said some angry words, and left them. The same evening I found a letter in my room. 'For your sake, I must not be seen alone with you again. It is hard to lose the comfort of your sympathy, but I must submit. Think of me as kindly as I think of you. It has done me good to open my heart to you.' Only those lines, signed by Mellicent's initials. I was rash enough to keep the letter, instead of destroying it. All might have ended well, nevertheless, if she had only held to her resolution. But, unluckily, my twenty-first birthday was close at hand; and there was talk of keeping it as a festival in the Community. I was up with sunrise when the day came; having some farming work to look after, and wanting to get it over in good time. My shortest way back to breakfast was through a wood. In the wood I met her."

41

"Alone?" Mr. Hethcote asked.

Rufus expressed his opinion of the wisdom of putting this question with his customary plainness of language. "When there's a rash thing to be done by a man and a woman together, sir, philosophers have remarked that it's always the woman who leads the way. Of course she was alone."

"She had a little present for me on my birthday," Amelius explained—"a purse of her own making. And she was afraid of the ridicule of the young women, if she gave it to me openly. 'You have my heart's dearest wishes for your happiness; think of me sometimes, Amelius, when you open your purse.' If you had been in my place, could you have told her to go away, when she said that, and put her gift into your hand? Not if she had been looking at you at the moment—I'll swear you couldn't have done it!"

The lean yellow face of Rufus Dingwell relaxed for the first time into a broad grin. "There are further particulars, sir, stated in the newspaper," he said slily.

"Damn the newspaper!" Amelius answered.

Rufus bowed, serenely courteous, with the air of a man who accepted a British oath as an unwilling compliment paid by the old country to the American press. "The newspaper report states, sir, that she kissed you."

"It's a lie!" Amelius shouted.

"Perhaps it's an error of the press," Rufus persisted. "Perhaps, *you* kissed *her?"*

"Never mind what I did," said Amelius savagely.

Mr. Hethcote felt it necessary to interfere. He addressed Rufus in his most magnificent manner. "In England, Mr. Dingwell, a gentleman is not in the habit of disclosing these—er—these—er, er—"

"These kissings in a wood?" suggested Rufus. "In my country, sir, we do not regard kissing, in or out of a wood, in the light of a shameful proceeding. Quite the contrary, I do assure you."

Amelius recovered his temper. The discussion was becoming too ridiculous to be endured by the unfortunate person who was the object of it.

"Don't let us make mountains out of molehills," he said. "I did kiss her—there! A woman pressing the prettiest little purse you ever saw into your hand, and wishing you many happy returns of the day with the tears in her eyes; I should like to know what else was to be done but to kiss her. Ah, yes, smooth out your newspaper report,

42

and have another look at it! She *did* rest her head on my shoulder, poor soul, and she *did* say, 'Oh, Amelius, I thought my heart was turned to stone; feel how you have made it beat!' When I remembered what she had told me in the boat, I declare to God I almost burst out crying myself—it was so innocent and so pitiful."

Rufus held out his hand with true American cordiality. "I do assure you, sir, I meant no harm," he said. "The right grit is in you, and no mistake—and there goes the newspaper!" He rolled up the slip, and flung it overboard.

Mr. Hethcote nodded his entire approval of this proceeding. Amelius went on with his story.

"I'm near the end now," he said. "If I had known it would have taken so long to tell—never mind! We got out of the wood at last, Mr. Rufus; and left it without a suspicion that we had been watched. I was prudent enough (when it was too late, you will say) to suggest to her that we had better be careful for the future. Instead of taking it seriously, she laughed. 'Have you altered your mind, since you wrote to me?' I asked. 'To be sure I have,' she said. 'When I wrote to you I forgot the difference between your age and mine. Nothing that *we* do will be taken seriously. I am afraid of their laughing at me, Amelius; but I am afraid of nothing else.' I did my best to undeceive her. I told her plainly that people unequally matched in years—women older than men, as well as men older than women—were not uncommonly married among us. The council only looked to their being well suited in other ways, and declined to trouble itself about the question of age. I don't think I produced much effect; she seemed, for once in her life, poor thing, to be too happy to look beyond the passing moment. Besides, there was the birthday festival to keep her mind from dwelling on doubts and fears that were not agreeable to her. And the next day there was another event to occupy our attention—the arrival of the lawyer's letter from London, with the announcement of my inheritance on coming of age. It was settled, as you know, that I was to go out into the world, and to judge for myself; but the date of my departure was not fixed. Two days later, the storm that had been gathering for weeks past burst on us—we were cited to appear before the council to answer for an infraction of the Rules. Everything that I have confessed to you, and some things besides that I have kept to myself, lay formally inscribed on a sheet of paper placed on the council table—and pinned to the sheet of paper was Mellicent's letter to me, found in my room. I took the whole blame on myself, and insisted on being confronted with the unknown person who had informed against us. The council met this by a question:—'Is the information, in any particular, false?' Neither of us could deny that it was, in every particular, true. Hearing this, the council decided that there was no need, on our own showing, to confront us with the informer. From that day to this, I have never known who the spy was. Neither Mellicent nor I had an enemy in the Community. The girls who had seen us on the lake, and some other members who had met us together, only gave their evidence on compulsion—and even then they prevaricated, they were so fond of us and so sorry for us. After waiting a day, the governing body pronounced their judgment. Their duty was prescribed to them by the Rules. We were sentenced to six months' absence from the Community; to return or not as we pleased. A hard sentence,

43

gentlemen—whatever *we* may think of it—to homeless and friendless people, to the Fallen Leaves that had drifted to Tadmor. In my case it had been already arranged that I was to leave. After what had happened, my departure was made compulsory in four-and-twenty hours; and I was forbidden to return, until the date of my sentence had expired. In Mellicent's case they were still more strict. They would not trust her to travel by herself. A female member of the Community was appointed to accompany her to the house of her married sister at New York: she was ordered to be ready for the journey by sunrise the next morning. We both understood, of course, that the object of this was to prevent our travelling together. They might have saved themselves the trouble of putting obstacles in our way."

"So far as You were concerned, I suppose?" said Mr. Hethcote.

"So far as She was concerned also," Amelius answered.

"How did she take it, sir?" Rufus inquired.

"With a composure that astonished us all," said Amelius. "We had anticipated tears and entreaties for mercy. She stood up perfectly calm, far calmer than I was, with her head turned towards me, and her eyes resting quietly on my face. If you can imagine a woman whose whole being was absorbed in looking into the future; seeing what no mortal creature about her saw; sustained by hopes that no mortal creature about her could share—you may see her as I did, when she heard her sentence pronounced. The members of the Community, accustomed to take leave of an erring brother or sister with loving and merciful words, were all more or less distressed as they bade her farewell. Most of the women were in tears as they kissed her. They said the same kind words to her over and over again. 'We are heartily sorry for you, dear; we shall all be glad to welcome you back.' They sang our customary hymn at parting—and broke down before they got to the end. It was *she* who consoled *them!* Not once, through all that melancholy ceremony, did she lose her strange composure, her rapt mysterious look. I was the last to say farewell; and I own I couldn't trust myself to speak. She held my hand in hers. For a moment, her face lighted up softly with a radiant smile—then the strange preoccupied expression flowed over her again, like shadow over a light. Her eyes, still looking into mine, seemed to look beyond me. She spoke low, in sad steady tones. 'Be comforted, Amelius; the end is not yet.' She put her hands on my head, and drew it down to her. 'You will come back to me,' she whispered—and kissed me on the forehead, before them all. When I looked up again, she was gone. I have neither seen her nor heard from her since. It's all told, gentlemen—and some of it has distressed me in the telling. Let me go away for a minute by myself, and look at the sea."

BOOK THE SECOND

AMELIUS IN LONDON

CHAPTER 1

Oh, Rufus Dingwell, it is such a rainy day! And the London street which I look out on from my hotel window presents such a dirty and such a miserable view! Do you know, I hardly feel like the same Amelius who promised to write to you when you left the steamer at Queenstown. My spirits are sinking; I begin to feel old. Am I in the right state of mind to tell you what are my first impressions of London? Perhaps I may alter my opinion. At present (this is between ourselves), I don't like London or London people—excepting two ladies, who, in very different ways, have interested and charmed me.

Who are the ladies? I must tell you what I heard about them from Mr. Hethcote, before I present them to you on my own responsibility.

After you left us, I found the last day of the voyage to Liverpool dull enough. Mr. Hethcote did not seem to feel it in the same way: on the contrary, he grew more familiar and confidential in his talk with me. He has some of the English stiffness, you see, and your American pace was a little too fast for him. On our last night on board, we had some more conversation about the Farnabys. You were not interested enough in the subject to attend to what he said about them while you were with us; but if you are to be introduced to the ladies, you must be interested now. Let me first inform you that Mr. and Mrs. Farnaby have no children; and let me add that they have adopted the daughter and orphan child of Mrs. Farnaby's sister. This sister, it seems, died many years ago, surviving her husband for a few months only. To complete the story of the past, death has also taken old Mr. Ronald, the founder of the stationer's business, and his wife, Mrs. Farnaby's mother. Dry facts these—I don't deny it; but there is something more interesting to follow. I have next to tell you how Mr. Hethcote first became acquainted with Mrs. Farnaby. Now, Rufus, we are coming to something romantic at last!

It is some time since Mr. Hethcote ceased to perform his clerical duties, owing to a malady in the throat, which made it painful for him to take his place in the reading-desk or the pulpit. His last curacy attached him to a church at the West-end of London; and here, one Sunday evening, after he had preached the sermon, a lady in trouble came to him in the vestry for spiritual advice and consolation. She was a regular attendant at the church, and something which he had said in that evening's sermon had deeply affected her. Mr. Hethcote spoke with her afterwards on many occasions at home. He felt a sincere interest in her, but he disliked her husband; and, when he gave up his curacy, he ceased to pay visits to the house. As to what Mrs. Farnaby's troubles were, I can tell you nothing. Mr. Hethcote spoke very gravely and sadly when he told me that the subject of his conversations with her must be kept a secret. "I doubt whether you and Mr. Farnaby will get on well together," he said to me; "but I shall be astonished if you are not favourably impressed by his wife and her niece."

This was all I knew when I presented my letter of introduction to Mr. Farnaby at his place of business.

46

It was a grand stone building, with great plate-glass windows—all renewed and improved, they told me, since old Mr. Ronald's time. My letter and my card went into an office at the back, and I followed them after a while. A lean, hard, middle-aged man, buttoned up tight in a black frock-coat, received me, holding my written introduction open in his hand. He had a ruddy complexion not commonly seen in Londoners, so far as my experience goes. His iron-gray hair and whiskers (especially the whiskers) were in wonderfully fine order—as carefully oiled and combed as if he had just come out of a barber's shop. I had been in the morning to the Zoological Gardens; his eyes, when he lifted them from the letter to me, reminded me of the eyes of the eagles—glassy and cruel. I have a fault that I can't cure myself of. I like people, or dislike them, at first sight, without knowing, in either case, whether they deserve it or not. In the one moment when our eyes met, I felt the devil in me. In plain English, I hated Mr. Farnaby!

"Good morning, sir," he began, in a loud, harsh, rasping voice. "The letter you bring me takes me by surprise."

"I thought the writer was an old friend of yours," I said.

"An old friend of mine," Mr. Farnaby answered, "whose errors I deplore. When he joined your Community, I looked upon him as a lost man. I am surprised at his writing to me."

It is quite likely I was wrong, knowing nothing of the usages of society in England. I thought this reception of me downright rude. I had laid my hat on a chair; I took it up in my hand again, and delivered a parting shot at the brute with the oily whiskers.

"If I had known what you now tell me," I said, "I should not have troubled you by presenting that letter. Good morning."

This didn't in the least offend him. A curious smile broke out on his face; it widened his eyes, and it twitched up his mouth at one corner. He held out his hand to stop me. I waited, in case he felt bound to make an apology. He did nothing of the sort— he only made a remark.

"You are young and hasty," he said. "I may lament my friend's extravagances, without failing on that account in what is due to an old friendship. You are probably not aware that we have no sympathy in England with Socialists."

I hit him back again. "In that case, sir, a little Socialism in England would do you no harm. We consider it a part of our duty as Christians to feel sympathy with all men who are honest in their convictions—no matter how mistaken (in our opinion) the convictions may be." I rather thought I had him there; and I took up my hat again, to get off with the honours of victory while I had the chance.

I am sincerely ashamed of myself, Rufus, in telling you all this. I ought to have given him back "the soft answer that turneth away wrath"—my conduct was a disgrace to my Community. What evil influence was at work in me? Was it the air of London? or was it a possession of the devil?

He stopped me for the second time—not in the least disconcerted by what I had said to him. His inbred conviction of his own superiority to a young adventurer like me was really something magnificent to witness. He did me justice—the Philistine-Pharisee did me justice! Will you believe it? He made his remarks next on my good points, as if I had been a young bull at a prize cattle show.

"Excuse me for noticing it," he said. "Your manners are perfectly gentlemanlike, and you speak English without any accent. And yet you have been brought up in America. What does it mean?"

I grew worse and worse—I got downright sulky now.

"I suppose it means," I answered, "that some of us, in America, cultivate ourselves as well as our land. We have our books and music, though you seem to think we only have our axes and spades. Englishmen don't claim a monopoly of good manners at Tadmor. We see no difference between an American gentleman and an English gentleman. And as for speaking English with an accent, the Americans accuse *us* of doing that."

He smiled again. "How very absurd!" he said, with a superb compassion for the benighted Americans. By this time, I suspect he began to feel that he had had enough of me. He got rid of me with an invitation.

"I shall be glad to receive you at my private residence, and introduce you to my wife and her niece—our adopted daughter. There is the address. We have a few friends to dinner on Saturday next, at seven. Will you give us the pleasure of your company?"

We are all aware that there is a distinction between civility and cordiality; but I myself never knew how wide that distinction might be, until Mr. Farnaby invited me to dinner. If I had not been curious (after what Mr. Hethcote had told me) to see Mrs. Farnaby and her niece, I should certainly have slipped out of the engagement. As it was, I promised to dine with Oily-Whiskers.

He put his hand into mine at parting. It felt as moistly cold as a dead fish. After getting out again into the street, I turned into the first tavern I passed, and ordered a drink. Shall I tell you what else I did? I went into the lavatory, and washed Mr. Farnaby off my hand. (N.B.—If I had behaved in this way at Tadmor, I should have been punished with the lighter penalty—taking my meals by myself, and being forbidden to enter the Common Room for eight and forty hours.) I feel I am getting wickeder and wickeder in London—I have half a mind to join you in Ireland. What does Tom Moore say of his countrymen—he ought to know, I suppose? "For though they love women and golden store: Sir Knight, they love honour and virtue more!" They must have been all Socialists in Tom Moore's time. Just the place for me.

I have been obliged to wait a little. A dense fog has descended on us by way of variety. With a stinking coal fire, with the gas lit and the curtains drawn at half-past eleven in the forenoon, I feel that I am in my own country again at last. Patience, my friend—patience! I am coming to the ladies.

Entering Mr. Farnaby's private residence on the appointed day, I became acquainted with one more of the innumerable insincerities of modern English life. When a man asks you to dine with him at seven o'clock, in other countries, he means what he says. In England, he means half-past seven, and sometimes a quarter to eight. At seven o'clock I was the only person in Mr. Farnaby's drawing-room. At ten minutes past seven, Mr. Farnaby made his appearance. I had a good mind to take his place in the middle of the hearth-rug, and say, "Farnaby, I am glad to see you." But I looked at his whiskers; and *they* said to me, as plainly as words could speak, "Better not!"

In five minutes more, Mrs. Farnaby joined us.

I wish I was a practised author—or, no, I would rather, for the moment, be a competent portrait-painter, and send you Mrs. Farnaby's likeness enclosed. How I am to describe her in words, I really don't know. My dear fellow, she almost frightened me. I never before saw such a woman; I never expect to see such a woman again. There was nothing in her figure, or in her way of moving, that produced this impression on me—she is little and fat, and walks with a firm, heavy step, like the step of a man. Her face is what I want to make you see as plainly as I saw it myself: it was her face that startled me.

So far as I can pretend to judge, she must have been pretty, in a healthy way, when she was young. I declare I hardly know whether she is not pretty now. She certainly has no marks or wrinkles; her hair either has no gray in it, or is too light to show the gray. She has preserved her fair complexion; perhaps with art to assist it—I can't say. As for her lips—I am not speaking disrespectfully, I am only describing them truly, when I say that they invite kisses in spite of her. In two words, though she has been married (as I know from what one of the guests told me after dinner) for sixteen years, she would be still an irresistible little woman, but for the one startling drawback of her eyes. Don't mistake me. In themselves, they are large, well-opened blue eyes, and may at one time have been the chief attraction in her face. But now there is an expression of suffering in them—long, unsolaced suffering, as I believe— so despairing and so dreadful, that she really made my heart ache when I looked at her. I will swear to it, that woman lives in some secret hell of her own making, and longs for the release of death; and is so inveterately full of bodily life and strength, that she may carry her burden with her to the utmost verge of life. I am digging the pen into the paper, I feel this so strongly, and I am so wretchedly incompetent to express my feeling. Can you imagine a diseased mind, imprisoned in a healthy body? I don't care what doctors or books may say—it is that, and nothing else.

Nothing else will solve the mystery of the smooth face, the fleshy figure, the firm step, the muscular grip of her hand when she gives it to you—and the soul in torment that looks at you all the while out of her eyes. It is useless to tell me that such a contradiction as this cannot exist. I have seen the woman; and she does exist.

Oh yes! I can fancy you grinning over my letter—I can hear you saying to yourself, "Where did he pick up his experience, I wonder?" I have no experience—I only have something that serves me instead of it, and I don't know what. The Elder Brother, at Tadmor, used to say it was sympathy. But *he* is a sentimentalist.

Well, Mr. Farnaby presented me to his wife—and then walked away as if he was sick of us both, and looked out of the window.

For some reason or other, Mrs. Farnaby seemed to be surprised, for the moment, by my personal appearance. Her husband had, very likely, not told her how young I was. She got over her momentary astonishment, and, signing to me to sit by her on the sofa, said the necessary words of welcome—evidently thinking something else all the time. The strange miserable eyes looked over my shoulder, instead of looking at me.

"Mr. Farnaby tells me you have been living in America."

The tone in which she spoke was curiously quiet and monotonous. I have heard such tones, in the Far West, from lonely settlers without a neighbouring soul to speak to. Has Mrs. Farnaby no neighbouring soul to speak to, except at dinner parties?

"You are an Englishman, are you not?" she went on.

I said Yes, and cast about in my mind for something to say to her. She saved me the trouble by making me the victim of a complete series of questions. This, as I afterwards discovered, was *her* way of finding conversation for strangers. Have you ever met with absent-minded people to whom it is a relief to ask questions mechanically, without feeling the slightest interest in the answers?

She began. "Where did you live in America?"

"At Tadmor, in the State of Illinois."

"What sort of place is Tadmor?"

I described the place as well as I could, under the circumstances.

"What made you go to Tadmor?"

50

It was impossible to reply to this, without speaking of the Community. Feeling that the subject was not in the least likely to interest her, I spoke as briefly as I could. To my astonishment, I evidently began to interest her from that moment. The series of questions went on—but now she not only listened, she was eager for the answers.

"Are there any women among you?"

"Nearly as many women as men."

Another change! Over the weary misery of her eyes there flashed a bright look of interest which completely transformed them. Her articulation even quickened when she put her next question.

"Are any of the women friendless creatures, who came to you from England?"

"Yes, some of them."

I thought of Mellicent as I spoke. Was this new interest that I had so innocently aroused, an interest in Mellicent? Her next question only added to my perplexity. Her next question proved that my guess had completely failed to hit the mark.

"Are there any *young* women among them?"

Mr. Farnaby, standing with his back to us thus far, suddenly turned and looked at her, when she inquired if there were "young" women among us.

"Oh yes," I said. "Mere girls."

She pressed so near to me that her knees touched mine. "How old?" she asked eagerly.

Mr. Farnaby left the window, walked close up to the sofa, and deliberately interrupted us.

"Nasty muggy weather, isn't it?" he said. "I suppose the climate of America—"

Mrs. Farnaby deliberately interrupted her husband. "How old?" she repeated, in a louder tone.

I was bound, of course, to answer the lady of the house. "Some girls from eighteen to twenty. And some younger."

"How much younger?"

"Oh, from sixteen to seventeen."

She grew more and more excited; she positively laid her hand on my arm in her eagerness to secure my attention all to herself. "American girls or English?" she resumed, her fat, firm fingers closing on me with a tremulous grasp.

"Shall you be in town in November?" said Mr. Farnaby, purposely interrupting us again. "If you would like to see the Lord Mayor's Show—"

Mrs. Farnaby impatiently shook me by the arm. "American girls or English?" she reiterated, more obstinately than ever.

Mr. Farnaby gave her one look. If he could have put her on the blazing fire and have burnt her up in an instant by an effort of will, I believe he would have made the effort. He saw that I was observing him, and turned quickly from his wife to me. His ruddy face was pale with suppressed rage. My early arrival had given Mrs. Farnaby an opportunity of speaking to me, which he had not anticipated in inviting me to dinner. "Come and see my pictures," he said.

His wife still held me fast. Whether he liked it or not, I had again no choice but to answer her. "Some American girls, and some English," I said.

Her eyes opened wider and wider in unutterable expectation. She suddenly advanced her face so close to mine, that I felt her hot breath on my cheeks as the next words burst their way through her lips.

"Born in England?"

"No. Born at Tadmor."

She dropped my arm. The light died out of her eyes in an instant. In some inconceivable way, I had utterly destroyed some secret expectation that she had fixed on me. She actually left me on the sofa, and took a chair on the opposite side of the fireplace. Mr. Farnaby, turning paler and paler, stepped up to her as she changed her place. I rose to look at the pictures on the wall nearest to me. You remarked the extraordinary keenness of my sense of hearing, while we were fellow passengers on the steamship. When he stooped over her, and whispered in her ear, I heard him—though nearly the whole breadth of the room was between us. "You hell-cat!"—that was what Mr. Farnaby said to his wife.

The clock on the mantelpiece struck the half-hour after seven. In quick succession, the guests at the dinner now entered the room.

I was so staggered by the extraordinary scene of married life which I had just witnessed, that the guests produced only a very faint impression upon me. My mind was absorbed in trying to find the true meaning of what I had seen and heard. Was Mrs. Farnaby a little mad? I dismissed that idea as soon as it occurred to me; nothing that I had observed in her justified it. The truer conclusion appeared to be, that she was deeply interested in some absent (and possibly lost) young creature; whose age, judging by actions and tones which had sufficiently revealed that part of the secret to me, could not be more than sixteen or seventeen years. How long had she cherished the hope of seeing the girl, or hearing of her? It must have been, anyhow, a hope very deeply rooted, for she had been perfectly incapable of controlling herself when I had accidentally roused it. As for her husband, there could be no doubt that the subject was not merely distasteful to him, but so absolutely infuriating that he could not even keep his temper, in the presence of a third person invited to his house. Had he injured the girl in any way? Was he responsible for her disappearance? Did his wife know it, or only suspect it? Who *was* the girl? What was the secret of Mrs. Farnaby's extraordinary interest in her—-Mrs. Farnaby, whose marriage was childless; whose interest one would have thought should be naturally concentrated on her adopted daughter, her sister's orphan child? In conjectures such as these, I completely lost myself. Let me hear what your ingenuity can make of the puzzle; and let me return to Mr. Farnaby's dinner, waiting on Mr. Farnaby's table.

The servant threw open the drawing-room door, and the most honoured guest present led Mrs. Farnaby to the dining-room. I roused myself to some observation of what was going on about me. No ladies had been invited; and the men were all of a certain age. I looked in vain for the charming niece. Was she not well enough to appear at the dinner-party? I ventured on putting the question to Mr. Farnaby.

"You will find her at the tea-table, when we return to the drawing-room. Girls are out of place at dinner-parties." So he answered me—not very graciously.

As I stepped out on the landing, I looked up; I don't know why, unless I was the unconscious object of magnetic attraction. Anyhow, I had my reward. A bright young face peeped over the balusters of the upper staircase, and modestly withdrew itself again in a violent hurry. Everybody but Mr. Farnaby and myself had disappeared in the dining-room. Was she having a peep at the young Socialist?

Another interruption to my letter, caused by another change in the weather. The fog has vanished; the waiter is turning off the gas, and letting in the drab-coloured daylight. I ask him if it is still raining. He smiles, and rubs his hands, and says, "It looks like clearing up soon, sir." This man's head is gray; he has been all his life a waiter in London—and he can still see the cheerful side of things. What native strength of mind cast away on a vocation that is unworthy of it!

Well—and now about the Farnaby dinner. I feel a tightness in the lower part of my waistcoat, Rufus, when I think of the dinner; there was such a quantity of it, and Mr. Farnaby was so tyrannically resolute in forcing his luxuries down the throats of his guests. His eye was on me, if I let my plate go away before it was empty—his eye said "I have paid for this magnificent dinner, and I mean to see you eat it." Our printed list of the dishes, as they succeeded each other, also informed us of the varieties of wine which it was imperatively necessary to drink with each dish. I got into difficulties early in the proceedings. The taste of sherry, for instance, is absolutely nauseous to me; and Rhine wine turns into vinegar ten minutes after it has passed my lips. I asked for the wine that I could drink, out of its turn. You should have seen Mr. Farnaby's face, when I violated the rules of his dinner-table! It was the one amusing incident of the feast—the one thing that alleviated the dreary and mysterious spectacle of Mrs. Farnaby. There she sat, with her mind hundreds of miles away from everything that was going on about her, entangling the two guests, on her right hand and on her left, in a network of vacant questions, just as she had entangled me. I discovered that one of these gentlemen was a barrister and the other a ship-owner, by the answers which Mrs. Farnaby absently extracted from them on the subject of their respective vocations in life. And while she questioned incessantly, she ate incessantly. Her vigorous body insisted on being fed. She would have emptied her wineglass (I suspect) as readily as she plied her knife and fork— but I discovered that a certain system of restraint was established in the matter of wine. At intervals, Mr. Farnaby just looked at the butler—and the butler and his bottle, on those occasions, deliberately passed her by. Not the slightest visible change was produced in her by the eating and drinking; she was equal to any demands that any dinner could make on her. There was no flush in her face, no change in her spirits, when she rose, in obedience to English custom, and retired to the drawing-room.

Left together over their wine, the men began to talk politics.

I listened at the outset, expecting to get some information. Our readings in modern history at Tadmor had informed us of the dominant political position of the middle classes in England, since the time of the first Reform Bill. Mr. Farnaby's guests represented the respectable mediocrity of social position, the professional and commercial average of the nation. They all talked glibly enough—I and an old gentleman who sat next to me being the only listeners. I had spent the morning lazily in the smoking-room of the hotel, reading the day's newspapers. And what did I hear now, when the politicians set in for their discussion? I heard the leading articles of the day's newspapers translated into bald chat, and coolly addressed by one man to another, as if they were his own individual views on public affairs! This absurd imposture positively went the round of the table, received and respected by everybody with a stolid solemnity of make-believe which it was downright shameful to see. Not a man present said, "I saw that today in the *Times* or the *Telegraph.*" Not a man present had an opinion of his own; or, if he had an opinion, ventured to express it; or, if he knew nothing of the subject, was honest enough to say so. One enormous Sham, and everybody in a conspiracy to take it for the real thing: that is an accurate description of the state of political feeling among the representative men at Mr. Farnaby's dinner. I am not judging rashly by one example only; I have been taken to clubs and public festivals, only to hear over and over again what I heard in Mr. Farnaby's dining-room. Does it need any great foresight to see that such a state of things as this cannot last much longer, in a country which has not done with reforming itself yet? The time is coming, in England, when the people who *have* opinions of their own will be heard, and when Parliament will be forced to open the door to them.

This is a nice outbreak of republican freedom! What does my long-suffering friend think of it—waiting all the time to be presented to Mr. Farnaby's niece? Everything in its place, Rufus. The niece followed the politics, at the time; and she shall follow them now.

You shall hear first what my next neighbour said of her—a quaint old fellow, a retired doctor, if I remember correctly. He seemed to be as weary of the second-hand newspaper talk as I was; he quite sparkled and cheered up when I introduced the subject of Miss Regina. Have I mentioned her name yet? If not, here it is for you in full:—Miss Regina Mildmay.

"I call her the brown girl," said the old gentleman. "Brown hair, brown eyes, and a brown skin. No, not a brunette; not dark enough for that—a warm, delicate brown; wait till you see it! Takes after her father, I should tell you. He was a fine-looking man in his time; foreign blood in his veins, by his mother's side. Miss Regina gets her queer name by being christened after his mother. Never mind her name; she's a charming person. Let's drink her health."

We drank her health. Remembering that he had called her "the brown girl," I said I supposed she was still quite young.

"Better than young," the doctor answered; "in the prime of life. I call her a girl, by habit. Wait till you see her!"

"Has she a good figure, sir?"

"Ha! you're like the Turks, are you? A nice-looking woman doesn't content you—you must have her well-made too. We can accommodate you, sir; we are slim and tall, with a swing of our hips, and we walk like a goddess. Wait and see how her head is put on her shoulders—I say no more. Proud? Not she! A simple, unaffected, kind-hearted creature. Always the same; I never saw her out of temper in my life; I never heard her speak ill of anybody. The man who gets her will be a man to be envied, I can tell you!"

"Is she engaged to be married?"

"No. She has had plenty of offers; but she doesn't seem to care for anything of that sort—so far. Devotes herself to Mrs. Farnaby, and keeps up her school-friendships. A splendid creature, with the vital thermometer at temperate heart—a calm, meditative, equable person. Pass me the olives. Only think! the man who discovered olives is unknown; no statue of him erected in any part of the civilized earth. I know few more remarkable instances of human ingratitude."

I risked a bold question—but not on the subject of olives. "Isn't Miss Regina's life rather a dull one in this house?"

The doctor cautiously lowered his voice. "It would be dull enough to some women. Regina's early life has been a hard one. Her mother was Mr. Ronald's eldest daughter. The old brute never forgave her for marrying against his wishes. Mrs. Ronald did all she could, secretly, to help the young wife in disgrace. But old Ronald had sole command of the money, and kept it to himself. From Regina's earliest childhood there was always distress at home. Her father harassed by creditors, trying one scheme after another, and failing in all; her mother and herself, half starved—with their very bedclothes sometimes at the pawnbrokers. I attended them in their illnesses, and though they hid their wretchedness from everybody else (proud as Lucifer, both of them!), they couldn't hide it from me. Fancy the change to this house! I don't say that living here in clover is enough for such a person as Regina; I only say it has its influence. She is one of those young women, sir, who delight in sacrificing themselves to others—she is devoted, for instance, to Mrs. Farnaby. I only hope Mrs. Farnaby is worthy of it! Not that it matters to Regina. What she does, she does out of her own sweetness of disposition. She brightens this household, I can tell you! Farnaby did a wise thing, in his own domestic interests, when he adopted her as his daughter. She thinks she can never be grateful enough to him—the good creature!—though she has repaid him a hundredfold. He'll find that out, one of these days, when a husband takes her away. Don't suppose that I want to disparage our host—he's an old friend of mine; but he's a little too apt to take the good things that fall to his lot as if they were nothing but a just recognition of his own merits. I have told him that to his face, often enough to have a right to say it of him when he doesn't hear me. Do you smoke? I wish they would drop their politics, and take to tobacco. I say Farnaby! I want a cigar."

This broad hint produced an adjournment to the smoking-room, the doctor leading the way. I began to wonder how much longer my introduction to Miss Regina was to be delayed. It was not to come until I had seen a new side of my host's character, and had found myself promoted to a place of my own in Mr. Farnaby's estimation.

As we rose from table one of the guests spoke to me of a visit that he had recently paid to the part of Buckinghamshire which I come from. "I was shown a remarkably picturesque old house on the heath," he said. "They told me it had been inhabited for centuries by the family of the Goldenhearts. Are you in any way related to them?" I answered that I was very nearly related, having been born in the house—and there, as I suppose, the matter ended. Being the youngest man of the party, I waited, of course, until the rest of the gentlemen had passed out to the smoking-room. Mr. Farnaby and I were left together. To my astonishment, he put his arm cordially into mine, and led me out of the dining-room with the genial familiarity of an old friend!

"I'll give you such a cigar," he said, "as you can't buy for money in all London. You have enjoyed yourself, I hope? Now we know what wine you like, you won't have to ask the butler for it next time. Drop in any day, and take pot-luck with us." He came to a standstill in the hall; his brassy rasping voice assumed a new tone—a sort of parody of respect. "Have you been to your family place," he asked, "since your return to England?"

He had evidently heard the few words exchanged between his friend and myself. It seemed odd that he should take any interest in a place belonging to people who were strangers to him. However, his question was easily answered. I had only to inform him that my father had sold the house when he left England.

"Oh dear, I'm sorry to hear that!" he said. "Those old family places ought to be kept up. The greatness of England, sir, strikes its roots in the old families of England. They may be rich, or they may be poor—that don't matter. An old family *is* an old family; it's sad to see their hearths and homes sold to wealthy manufacturers who don't know who their own grandfathers were. Would you allow me to ask what is the family motto of the Goldenhearts?"

Shall I own the truth? The bottles circulated freely at Mr. Farnaby's table—I began to wonder whether he was quite sober. I said I was sorry to disappoint him, but I really did not know what my family motto was.

He was unaffectedly shocked. "I think I saw a ring on your finger," he said, as soon as he recovered himself. He lifted my left hand in his own cold-fishy paw. The one ring I wear is of plain gold; it belonged to my father and it has his initials inscribed on the signet.

"Good gracious, you haven't got your coat-of-arms on your seal!" cried Mr. Farnaby. "My dear sir, I am old enough to be your father, and I must take the freedom of remonstrating with you. Your coat-of-arms and your motto are no doubt at the Heralds' Office—why don't you apply for them? Shall I go there for you? I will do it with pleasure. You shouldn't be careless about these things—you shouldn't indeed."

I listened in speechless astonishment. Was he ironically expressing his contempt for old families? We got into the smoking-room at last; and my friend the doctor enlightened me privately in a corner. Every word Mr. Farnaby had said had been spoken in earnest. This man, who owes his rise from the lowest social position entirely to himself—who, judging by his own experience, has every reason to despise the poor pride of ancestry—actually feels a sincerely servile admiration for the accident of birth! "Oh, poor human nature!" as Somebody says. How cordially I agree with Somebody!

We went up to the drawing-room; and I was introduced to "the brown girl" at last. What impression did she produce on me?

Do you know, Rufus, there is some perverse reluctance in me to go on with this inordinately long letter just when I have arrived at the most interesting part of it. I can't account for my own state of mind; I only know that it is so. The difficulty of describing the young lady doesn't perplex me like the difficulty of describing Mrs. Farnaby. I can see her now, as vividly as if she was present in the room. I even remember (and this is astonishing in a man) the dress that she wore. And yet I shrink from writing about her, as if there was something wrong in it. Do me a kindness, good friend, and let me send off all these sheets of paper, the idle work of an idle morning, just as they are. When I write next, I promise to be ashamed of my own capricious state of mind, and to paint the portrait of Miss Regina at full length.

In the mean while, don't run away with the idea that she has made a disagreeable impression upon me. Good heavens! it is far from that. You have had the old doctor's opinion of her. Very well. Multiply this opinion by ten—and you have mine.

[NOTE:—A strange indorsement appears on this letter, dated several months after the period at which it was received:—*"Ah, poor Amelius! He had better have gone back to Miss Mellicent, and put up with the little drawback of her age. What a bright, lovable fellow he was! Goodbye to Goldenheart!"*

These lines are not signed. They are known, however, to be in the handwriting of Rufus Dingwell.]

CHAPTER 2

I particularly want you to come and lunch with us, dearest Cecilia, the day after tomorrow. Don't say to yourself, "The Farnaby's house is dull, and Regina is too slow for me," and don't think about the long drive for the horses, from your place to London. This letter has an interest of its own, my dear—I have got something new for you. What do you think of a young man, who is clever and handsome and agreeable—and, wonder of wonders, quite unlike any other young Englishman you ever saw in your life? You are to meet him at luncheon; and you are to get used to his strange name beforehand. For which purpose I enclose his card.

He made his first appearance at our house, at dinner yesterday evening.

When he was presented to me at the tea-table, he was not to be put off with a bow—he insisted on shaking hands. "Where I have been," he explained, "we help a first introduction with a little cordiality." He looked into his tea-cup, after he said that, with the air of a man who could say something more, if he had a little encouragement. Of course, I encouraged him. "I suppose shaking hands is much the same form in America that bowing is in England?" I said, as suggestively as I could.

He looked up directly, and shook his head. "We have too many forms in this country," he said. "The virtue of hospitality, for instance, seems to have become a form in England. In America, when a new acquaintance says, 'Come and see me,' he means it. When he says it here, in nine cases out of ten he looks unaffectedly astonished if you are fool enough to take him at his word. I hate insincerity, Miss Regina—and now I have returned to my own country, I find insincerity one of the established institutions of English Society. 'Can we do anything for you?' Ask them to do something for you—and you will see what it means. 'Thank you for such a pleasant evening!' Get into the carriage with them when they go home—and you will find that it means, 'What a bore!' 'Ah, Mr. So-and-so, allow me to congratulate you on your new appointment.' Mr. So-and-so passes out of hearing—and you discover what the congratulations mean. 'Corrupt old brute! he has got the price of his vote at the last division.' 'Oh, Mr. Blank, what a charming book you have written!' Mr. Blank passes out of hearing—and you ask what his book is about. 'To tell you the truth, I haven't read it. Hush! he's received at Court; one must say these things.' The other day a friend took me to a grand dinner at the Lord Mayor's. I accompanied him first to his club; many distinguished guests met there before going to the dinner. Heavens, how they spoke of the Lord Mayor! One of them didn't know his name, and didn't want to know it; another wasn't certain whether he was a tallow-chandler or a button-maker; a third, who had met with him somewhere, described him as a damned ass; a fourth said, 'Oh, don't be hard on him; he's only a vulgar old Cockney, without an *h* in his whole composition.' A chorus of general agreement followed, as the dinner-hour approached: 'What a bore!' I whispered to my friend, 'Why do they go?' He answered, 'You see, one must do this sort of thing.' And when we got to the Mansion House, they did that sort of thing with a vengeance! When the speech-making set in, these very men who had been all expressing their profound contempt for the Lord Mayor behind his back, now flattered him to his face in such a shamelessly servile way, with such a meanly complete insensibility to their own baseness, that I did really and literally turn sick. I slipped out into the fresh air, and fumigated myself, after the company I had kept, with a cigar. No, no! it's useless to excuse these things (I could quote dozens of other instances that have come under my own observation) by saying that they are trifles. When trifles make themselves habits of yours or of mine, they become a part of your character or mine. We have an inveterately false and vicious system of society in England. If you want to trace one of the causes, look back to the little organized insincerities of English life."

Of course you understand, Cecilia, that this was not all said at one burst, as I have written it here. Some of it came out in the way of answers to my inquiries, and some of it was spoken in the intervals of laughing, talking, and tea-drinking. But I want to show you how very different this young man is from the young men whom we are in the habit of meeting, and so I huddle his talk together in one sample, as Papa Farnaby would call it.

My dear, he is decidedly handsome (I mean our delightful Amelius); his face has a bright, eager look, indescribably refreshing as a contrast to the stolid composure of the ordinary young Englishman. His smile is charming; he moves as gracefully— with as little self-consciousness—as my Italian greyhound. He has been brought up among the strangest people in America; and (would you believe it?) he is actually a Socialist. Don't be alarmed. He shocked us all dreadfully by declaring that his Socialism was entirely learnt out of the New Testament. I have looked at the New Testament, since he mentioned some of his principles to me; and, do you know, I declare it is true!

Oh, I forgot—the young Socialist plays and sings! When we asked him to go to the piano, he got up and began directly. "I don't do it well enough," he said, "to want a great deal of pressing." He sang old English songs, with great taste and sweetness. One of the gentlemen of our party, evidently disliking him, spoke rather rudely, I thought. "A Socialist who sings and plays," he said, "is a harmless Socialist indeed. I begin to feel that my balance is safe at my banker's, and that London won't be set on fire with petroleum this time." He got his answer, I can tell you. "Why should we set London on fire? London takes a regular percentage of your income from you, sir, whether you like it or not, on sound Socialist principles. You are the man who has got the money, and Socialism says:—You must and shall help the man who has got none. That is exactly what your own Poor Law says to you, every time the collector leaves the paper at your house." Wasn't it clever?—and it was doubly severe, because it was good-humouredly said.

Between ourselves, Cecilia, I think he is struck with me. When I walked about the room, his bright eyes followed me everywhere. And, when I took a chair by somebody else, not feeling it quite right to keep him all to myself, he invariably contrived to find a seat on the other side of me. His voice, too, had a certain tone, addressed to me, and to no other person in the room. Judge for yourself when you come here; but don't jump to conclusions, if you please. Oh no—I am not going to

60

fall in love with him! It isn't in me to fall in love with anybody. Do you remember what the last man whom I refused said of me? "She has a machine on the left side of her that pumps blood through her body, but she has no heart." I pity the woman who marries *that* man!

One thing more, my dear. This curious Amelius seems to notice trifles which escape men in general, just as *we* do. Towards the close of the evening, poor Mamma Farnaby fell into one of her vacant states; half asleep and half awake on the sofa in the back drawing-room. "Your aunt interests me," he whispered. "She must have suffered some terrible sorrow, at some past time in her life." Fancy a man seeing that! He dropped some hints, which showed that he was puzzling his brains to discover how I got on with her, and whether I was in her confidence or not: he even went the length of asking what sort of life I led with the uncle and aunt who have adopted me. My dear, it was done so delicately, with such irresistible sympathy and such a charming air of respect, that I was quite startled when I remembered, in the wakeful hours of the night, how freely I had spoken to him. Not that I have betrayed any secrets; for, as you know, I am as ignorant as everybody else of what the early troubles of my poor dear aunt may have been. But I did tell him how I came into the house a helpless little orphan girl; and how generously these two good relatives adopted me; and how happy it made me to find that I could really do something to cheer their sad childless lives. "I wish I was half as good as you are," he said. "I can't understand how you became fond of Mrs. Farnaby. Perhaps it began in sympathy and compassion?" Just think of that, from a young Englishman! He went on confessing his perplexities, as if we had known one another from childhood. "I am a little surprised to see Mrs. Farnaby present at parties of this sort; I should have thought she would have stayed in her own room." "That's just what she objects to do," I answered; "She says people will report that her husband is ashamed of her, or that she is not fit to be seen in society, if she doesn't appear at the parties—and she is determined not to be misrepresented in that way." Can you understand my talking to him with so little reserve? It is a specimen, Cecilia, of the odd manner in which my impulses carry me away, in this man's company. He is so nice and gentle—and yet so manly. I shall be curious to see if you can resist him, with your superior firmness and knowledge of the world.

But the strangest incident of all I have not told you yet—feeling some hesitation about the best way of describing it, so as to interest you in what has deeply interested me. I must tell it as plainly as I can, and leave it to speak for itself.

Who do you think has invited Amelius Goldenheart to luncheon? Not Papa Farnaby, who only invites him to dinner. Not I, it is needless to say. Who is it, then? Mamma Farnaby herself. He has actually so interested her that she has been thinking of him, and dreaming of him, in his absence!

I heard her last night, poor thing, talking and grinding her teeth in her sleep; and I went into her room to try if I could quiet her, in the usual way, by putting my cool hand on her forehead, and pressing it gently. (The old doctor says it's magnetism, which is ridiculous.) Well, it didn't succeed this time; she went on muttering, and making that dreadful sound with her teeth. Occasionally a word was spoken clearly enough to be intelligible. I could make no connected sense of what I heard; but I could positively discover this—that she was dreaming of our guest from America!

I said nothing about it, of course, when I went upstairs with her cup of tea this morning. What do you think was the first thing she asked for? Pen, ink, and paper. Her next request was that I would write Mr. Goldenheart's address on an envelope. "Are you going to write to him?" I asked. "Yes," she said, "I want to speak to him, while John is out of the way at business," "Secrets?" I said, turning it off with a laugh. She answered, speaking gravely and earnestly. "Yes; secrets." The letter was written, and sent to his hotel, inviting him to lunch with us on the first day when he was disengaged. He has replied, appointing the day after tomorrow. By way of trying to penetrate the mystery, I inquired if she wished me to appear at the luncheon. She considered with herself, before she answered that. "I want him to be amused, and put in a good humour," she said, "before I speak to him. You must lunch with us—and ask Cecilia." She stopped, and considered once more. "Mind one thing," she went on. "Your uncle is to know nothing about it. If you tell him, I will never speak to you again."

Is this not extraordinary? Whatever her dream may have been, it has evidently produced a strong impression on her. I firmly believe she means to take him away with her to her own room, when the luncheon is over. Dearest Cecilia, you must help me to stop this! I have never been trusted with her secrets; they may, for all I know, be innocent secrets enough, poor soul! But it is surely in the highest degree undesirable that she should take into her confidence a young man who is only an acquaintance of ours: she will either make herself ridiculous, or do something worse. If Mr. Farnaby finds it out, I really tremble for what may happen.

For the sake of old friendship, don't leave me to face this difficulty by myself. A line, only one line, dearest, to say that you will not fail me.

62

BOOK THE THIRD

MRS. FARNABY'S FOOT

CHAPTER 1

It is an afternoon concert; and modern German music was largely represented on the programme. The patient English people sat in closely-packed rows, listening to the pretentious instrumental noises which were impudently offered to them as a substitute for melody. While these docile victims of the worst of all quackeries (musical quackery) were still toiling through their first hour of endurance, a passing ripple of interest stirred the stagnant surface of the audience caused by the sudden rising of a lady overcome by the heat. She was quickly led out of the concert-room (after whispering a word of explanation to two young ladies seated at her side) by a gentleman who made a fourth member of the party. Left by themselves, the young ladies looked at each other, whispered to each other, half rose from their places, became confusedly conscious that the wandering attention of the audience was fixed on them, and decided at last on following their companions out of the hall.

But the lady who had preceded them had some reason of her own for not waiting to recover herself in the vestibule. When the gentleman in charge of her asked if he should get a glass of water, she answered sharply, "Get a cab—and be quick about it."

The cab was found in a moment; the gentleman got in after her, by the lady's invitation. "Are you better now?" he asked.

"I have never had anything the matter with me," she replied, quietly; "tell the man to drive faster."

Having obeyed his instructions, the gentleman (otherwise Amelius) began to look a little puzzled. The lady (Mrs. Farnaby herself) perceived his condition of mind, and favoured him with an explanation.

"I had my own motive for asking you to luncheon today," she began, in that steady downright way of speaking that was peculiar to her. "I wanted to have a word with you privately. My niece Regina—don't be surprised at my calling her my niece, when you have heard Mr. Farnaby call her his daughter. She *is* my niece. Adopting her is a mere phrase. It doesn't alter facts; it doesn't make her Mr. Farnaby's child or mine, does it?"

She had ended with a question, but she seemed to want no answer to it. Her face was turned towards the cab-window, instead of towards Amelius. He was one of those rare people who are capable of remaining silent when they have nothing to say. Mrs. Farnaby went on.

"My niece Regina is a good creature in her way; but she suspects people. She has some reason of her own for trying to prevent me from taking you into my confidence; and her friend Cecilia is helping her. Yes, yes; the concert was the obstacle which they had arranged to put in my way. You were obliged to go, after

64

telling them you wanted to hear the music; and I couldn't complain, because they had got a fourth ticket for me. I made up my mind what to do; and I have done it. Nothing wonderful in my being taken ill with the heat; nothing wonderful in your doing your duty as a gentleman and looking after me—and what is the consequence? Here we are together, on our way to my room, in spite of them. Not so bad for a poor helpless creature like me, is it?"

Inwardly wondering what it all meant, and what she could possibly want with him, Amelius suggested that the young ladies might leave the concert-room, and, not finding them in the vestibule, might follow them back to the house.

Mrs. Farnaby turned her head from the window, and looked him in the face for the first time. "I have been a match for them so far," she said; "leave it to me, and you will find I can be a match for them still."

After saying this, she watched the puzzled face of Amelius with a moment's steady scrutiny. Her full lips relaxed into a faint smile; her head sank slowly on her bosom. "I wonder whether he thinks I am a little crazy?" she said quietly to herself. "Some women in my place would have gone mad years ago. Perhaps it might have been better for *me.*" She looked up again at Amelius. "I believe you are a good-tempered fellow," she went on. "Are you in your usual temper now? Did you enjoy your lunch? Has the lively company of the young ladies put you in a good humour with women generally? I want you to be in a particularly good humour with me."

She spoke quite gravely. Amelius, a little to his own astonishment, found himself answering gravely on his side; assuring her, in the most conventional terms, that he was entirely at her service. Something in her manner affected him disagreeably. If he had followed his impulse, he would have jumped out of the cab, and have recovered his liberty and his light-heartedness at one and the same moment, by running away at the top of his speed.

The driver turned into the street in which Mr. Farnaby's house was situated. Mrs. Farnaby stopped him, and got out at some little distance from the door. "You think the young ones will follow us back," she said to Amelius. "It doesn't matter, the servants will have nothing to tell them if they do." She checked him in the act of knocking, when they reached the house door. "It's tea-time downstairs," she whispered, looking at her watch. "You and I are going into the house, without letting the servants know anything about it. *Now* do you understand?"

She produced from her pocket a steel ring, with several keys attached to it. "A duplicate of Mr. Farnaby's key," she explained, as she chose one, and opened the street door. "Sometimes, when I find myself waking in the small hours of the morning, I can't endure my bed; I must go out and walk. My key lets me in again, just as it lets us in now, without disturbing anybody. You had better say nothing about it to Mr. Farnaby. Not that it matters much; for I should refuse to give up my key if he asked me. But you're a good-natured fellow—and you don't want to make bad blood between man and wife, do you? Step softly, and follow me."

Amelius hesitated. There was something repellent to him in entering another man's house under these clandestine conditions. "All right!" whispered Mrs. Farnaby, perfectly understanding him. "Consult your dignity; go out again, and knock at the door, and ask if I am at home. I only wanted to prevent a fuss and an interruption when Regina comes back. If the servants don't know we are here, they will tell her we haven't returned—don't you see?"

It would have been absurd to contest the matter, after this. Amelius followed her submissively to the farther end of the hall. There, she opened the door of a long narrow room, built out at the back of the house.

"This is my den," she said, signing to Amelius to pass in. "While we are here, nobody will disturb us." She laid aside her bonnet and shawl, and pointed to a box of cigars on the table. "Take one," she resumed. "I smoke too, when nobody sees me. That's one of the reasons, I dare say, why Regina wished to keep you out of my room. I find smoking composes me. What do *you* say?"

She lit a cigar, and handed the matches to Amelius. Finding that he stood fairly committed to the adventure, he resigned himself to circumstances with his customary facility. He too lit a cigar, and took a chair by the fire, and looked about him with an impenetrable composure worthy of Rufus Dingwell himself.

The room bore no sort of resemblance to a boudoir. A faded old turkey carpet was spread on the floor. The common mahogany table had no covering; the chintz on the chairs was of a truly venerable age. Some of the furniture made the place look like a room occupied by a man. Dumb-bells and clubs of the sort used in athletic exercises hung over the bare mantelpiece; a large ugly oaken structure with closed doors, something between a cabinet and a wardrobe, rose on one side to the ceiling; a turning lathe stood against the opposite wall. Above the lathe were hung in a row four prints, in dingy old frames of black wood, which especially attracted the attention of Amelius. Mostly foreign prints, they were all discoloured by time, and they all strangely represented different aspects of the same subject—infants parted from their parents by desertion or robbery. The young Moses was there, in his ark of bulrushes, on the river bank. Good St. Francis appeared next, roaming the streets, and rescuing forsaken children in the wintry night. A third print showed the foundling hospital of old Paris, with the turning cage in the wall, and the bell to ring when the infant was placed in it. The next and last subject was the stealing of a child from the lap of its slumbering nurse by a gipsy woman. These sadly suggestive subjects were the only ornaments on the walls. No traces of books or music were visible; no needlework of any sort was to be seen; no elegant trifles; no china or flowers or delicate lacework or sparkling jewelry—nothing, absolutely nothing, suggestive of a woman's presence appeared in any part of Mrs. Farnaby's room.

"I have got several things to say to you," she began; "but one thing must be settled first. Give me your sacred word of honour that you will not repeat to any mortal creature what I am going to tell you now." She reclined in her chair, and drew in a mouthful of smoke and puffed it out again, and waited for his reply.

66

Young and unsuspicious as he was, this unscrupulous method of taking his confidence by storm startled Amelius. His natural tact and good sense told him plainly that Mrs. Farnaby was asking too much.

"Don't be angry with me, ma'am," he said; "I must remind you that you are going to tell me your secrets, without any wish to intrude on them on my part—"

She interrupted him there. "What does that matter?" she asked coolly.

Amelius was obstinate; he went on with what he had to say. "I should like to know," he proceeded, "that I am doing no wrong to anybody, before I give you my promise?"

"You will be doing a kindness to a miserable creature," she answered, as quietly as ever; "and you will be doing no wrong to yourself or to anybody else, if you promise. That is all I can say. Your cigar is out. Take a light."

Amelius took a light, with the dog-like docility of a man in a state of blank amazement. She waited, watching him composedly until his cigar was in working order again.

"Well?" she asked. "Will you promise now?"

Amelius gave her his promise.

"On your sacred word of honour?" she persisted.

Amelius repeated the formula. She reclined in her chair once more. "I want to speak to you as if I was speaking to an old friend," she explained. "I suppose I may call you Amelius?"

"Certainly."

"Well, Amelius, I must tell you first that I committed a sin, many long years ago. I have suffered the punishment; I am suffering it still. Ever since I was a young woman, I have had a heavy burden of misery on my heart. I am not reconciled to it, I cannot submit to it, yet. I never shall be reconciled to it, I never shall submit to it, if I live to be a hundred. Do you wish me to enter into particulars? or will you have mercy on me, and be satisfied with what I have told you so far?"

It was not said entreatingly, or tenderly, or humbly: she spoke with a savage self-contained resignation in her manner and in her voice. Amelius forgot his cigar again—and again she reminded him of it. He answered her as his own generous impulsive temperament urged him; he said, "Tell me nothing that causes you a moment's pain; tell me only how I can help you." She handed him the box of matches; she said, "Your cigar is out again."

He laid down his cigar. In his brief span of life he had seen no human misery that expressed itself in this way. "Excuse me," he answered; "I won't smoke just now."

She laid her cigar aside like Amelius, and crossed her arms over her bosom, and looked at him, with the first softening gleam of tenderness that he had seen in her face. "My friend," she said, "yours will be a sad life—I pity you. The world will wound that sensitive heart of yours; the world will trample on that generous nature. One of these days, perhaps, you will be a wretch like me. No more of that. Get up; I have something to show you."

Rising herself, she led the way to the large oaken press, and took her bunch of keys out of her pocket again.

"About this old sorrow of mine," she resumed. "Do me justice, Amelius, at the outset. I haven't treated it as some women treat their sorrows—I haven't nursed it and petted it and made the most of it to myself and to others. No! I have tried every means of relief, every possible pursuit that could occupy my mind. One example of what I say will do as well as a hundred. See it for yourself."

She put the key in the lock. It resisted her first efforts to open it. With a contemptuous burst of impatience and a sudden exertion of her rare strength, she tore open the two doors of the press. Behind the door on the left appeared a row of open shelves. The opposite compartment, behind the door on the right, was filled by drawers with brass handles. She shut the left door; angrily banging it to, as if the opening of it had disclosed something which she did not wish to be seen. By the merest chance, Amelius had looked that way first. In the one instant in which it was possible to see anything, he had noticed, carefully laid out on one of the shelves, a baby's long linen frock and cap, turned yellow by the lapse of time.

The half-told story of the past was more than half told now. The treasured relics of the infant threw their little glimmer of light on the motive which had chosen the subjects of the prints on the wall. A child deserted and lost! A child who, by bare possibility, might be living still!

She turned towards Amelius suddenly, "There is nothing to interest you on *that* side," she said. "Look at the drawers here; open them for yourself." She drew back as she spoke, and pointed to the uppermost of the row of drawers. A narrow slip of paper was pasted on it, bearing this inscription:—*"Dead Consolations."*

Amelius opened the drawer; it was full of books. "Look at them," she said. Amelius, obeying her, discovered dictionaries, grammars, exercises, poems, novels, and histories—all in the German language.

"A foreign language tried as a relief," said Mrs. Farnaby, speaking quietly behind him. "Month after month of hard study—all forgotten now. The old sorrow came back in spite of it. A dead consolation! Open the next drawer."

The next drawer revealed water-colours and drawing materials huddled together in a corner, and a heap of poor little conventional landscapes filling up the rest of the space. As works of art, they were wretched in the last degree; monuments of industry and application miserably and completely thrown away.

"I had no talent for that pursuit, as you see," said Mrs. Farnaby. "But I persevered with it, week after week, month after month. I thought to myself, 'I hate it so, it costs me such dreadful trouble, it so worries and persecutes and humiliates me, that *this* surely must keep my mind occupied and my thoughts away from myself!' No; the old sorrow stared me in the face again on the paper that I was spoiling, through the colours that I couldn't learn to use. Another dead consolation! Shut it up."

She herself opened a third and a fourth drawer. In one there appeared a copy of Euclid, and a slate with the problems still traced on it; the other contained a microscope, and the treatises relating to its use. "Always the same effort," she said, shutting the door of the press as she spoke; "and always the same result. You have had enough of it, and so have I." She turned, and pointed to the lathe in the corner, and to the clubs and dumb-bells over the mantelpiece. "I can look at *them* patiently," she went on; "they give me bodily relief. I work at the lathe till my back aches; I swing the clubs till I'm ready to drop with fatigue. And then I lie down on the rug there, and sleep it off, and forget myself for an hour or two. Come back to the fire again. You have seen my dead consolations; you must hear about my living consolation next. In justice to Mr. Farnaby—ah, how I hate him!"

She spoke those last vehement words to herself, but with such intense bitterness of contempt that the tones were quite loud enough to be heard. Amelius looked furtively towards the door. Was there no hope that Regina and her friend might return and interrupt them? After what he had seen and heard, could *he* hope to console Mrs. Farnaby? He could only wonder what object she could possibly have in view in taking him into her confidence. "Am I always to be in a mess with women?" he thought to himself. "First poor Mellicent, and now this one. What next?" He lit his cigar again. The brotherhood of smokers, and they alone, will understand what a refuge it was to him at that moment.

"Give me a light," said Mrs. Farnaby, recalled to the remembrance of her own cigar. "I want to know one thing before I go on. Amelius, I watched those bright eyes of yours at luncheon-time. Did they tell me the truth? You're not in love with my niece, are you?"

Amelius took his cigar out of his mouth, and looked at her.

"Out with it boldly!" she said.

Amelius let it out, to a certain extent. "I admire her very much," he answered.

"Ah," Mrs. Farnaby remarked, "you don't know her as well as I do."

The disdainful indifference of her tone irritated Amelius. He was still young enough to believe in the existence of gratitude; and Mrs. Farnaby had spoken ungratefully. Besides, he was fond enough of Regina already to feel offended when she was referred to slightingly.

"I am surprised to hear what you say of her," he burst out. "She is quite devoted to you."

"Oh yes," said Mrs. Farnaby, carelessly. "She is devoted to me, of course—she is the living consolation I told you of just now. That was Mr. Farnaby's notion in adopting her. Mr. Farnaby thought to himself, 'Here's a ready-made daughter for my wife—that's all this tiresome woman wants to comfort her: now we shall do.' Do you know what I call that? I call it reasoning like an idiot. A man may be very clever at his business—and may be a contemptible fool in other respects. Another woman's child a consolation to *me!* Pah! it makes me sick to think of it. I have one merit, Amelius, I don't cant. It's my duty to take care of my sister's child; and I do my duty willingly. Regina's a good sort of creature—I don't dispute it. But she's like all those tall darkish women: there's no backbone in her, no dash; a kind, feeble, goody-goody, sugarish disposition; and a deal of quiet obstinacy at the bottom of it, I can tell you. Oh yes, I do her justice; I don't deny that she's devoted to me, as you say. But I am making a clean breast of it now. And you ought to know, and you shall know, that Mr. Farnaby's living consolation is no more a consolation to me than the things you have seen in the drawers. There! now we've done with Regina. No: there's one thing more to be cleared up. When you say you admire her, what do you mean? Do you mean to marry her?"

For once in his life Amelius stood on his dignity. "I have too much respect for the young lady to answer your question," he said loftily.

"Because, if you do," Mrs. Farnaby proceeded, "I mean to put every possible obstacle in your way. In short, I mean to prevent it."

This plain declaration staggered Amelius. He confessed the truth by implication in one word.

"Why?" he asked sharply.

"Wait a little, and recover your temper," she answered.

There was a pause. They sat, on either side of the fireplace, and eyed each other attentively.

70

"Now are you ready?" Mrs. Farnaby resumed. "Here is my reason. If you marry Regina, or marry anybody, you will settle down somewhere, and lead a dull life."

"Well," said Amelius; "and why not, if I like it?"

"Because I want you to remain a roving bachelor; here today and gone tomorrow—travelling all over the world, and seeing everything and everybody."

"What good will that do to *you,* Mrs. Farnaby?"

She rose from her own side of the fireplace, crossed to the side on which Amelius was sitting, and, standing before him, placed her hands heavily on his shoulders. Her eyes grew radiant with a sudden interest and animation as they looked down on him, riveted on his face.

"I am still waiting, my friend, for the living consolation that may yet come to me," she said. "And, hear this, Amelius! After all the years that have passed, you may be the man who brings it to me."

In the momentary silence that followed, they heard a double knock at the house-door.

"Regina!" said Mrs. Farnaby.

As the name passed her lips, she sprang to the door of the room, and turned the key in the lock.

CHAPTER 2

Amelius rose impulsively from his chair.

Mrs. Farnaby turned at the same moment, and signed to him to resume his seat. "You have given me your promise," she whispered. "All I ask of you is to be silent." She softly drew the key out of the door, and showed it to him. "You can't get out," she said, "unless you take the key from me by force!"

Whatever Amelius might think of the situation in which he now found himself, the one thing that he could honourably do was to say nothing, and submit to it. He remained quietly by the fire. No imaginable consideration (he mentally resolved) should induce him to consent to a second confidential interview in Mrs. Farnaby's room.

The servant opened the house-door. Regina's voice was heard in the hall.

"Has my aunt come in?"

"No, miss."

"Have you heard nothing of her?"

"Nothing, miss."

"Has Mr. Goldenheart been here?"

"No, miss."

"Very extraordinary! What can have become of them, Cecilia?"

The voice of the other lady was heard in answer. "We have probably missed them, on leaving the concert room. Don't alarm yourself, Regina. I must go back, under any circumstances; the carriage will be waiting for me. If I see anything of your aunt, I will say that you are expecting her at home."

"One moment, Cecilia! (Thomas, you needn't wait.) Is it really true that you don't like Mr. Goldenheart?"

"What! has it come to that, already? I'll try to like him, Regina. Goodbye again."

The closing of the street door told that the ladies had separated. The sound was followed, in another moment, by the opening and closing of the dining-room door. Mrs. Farnaby returned to her chair at the fireplace.

"Regina has gone into the dining-room to wait for us," she said. "I see you don't like your position here; and I won't keep you more than a few minutes longer. You are of course at a loss to understand what I was saying to you, when the knock at the door interrupted us. Sit down again for five minutes; it fidgets me to see you standing there, looking at your boots. I told you I had one consolation still possibly left. Judge for yourself what the hope of it is to me, when I own to you that I should long since have put an end to my life, without it. Don't think I am talking nonsense; I mean what I say. It is one of my misfortunes that I have no religious scruples to restrain me. There was a time when I believed that religion might comfort me. I once opened my heart to a clergyman—a worthy person, who did his best to help me. All useless! My heart was too hard, I suppose. It doesn't matter—except to give you one more proof that I am thoroughly in earnest. Patience! patience! I am coming to the point. I asked you some odd questions, on the day when you first dined here? You have forgotten all about them, of course?"

"I remember them perfectly well," Amelius answered.

"You remember them? That looks as if you had thought about them afterwards. Come! tell me plainly what you did think?"

Amelius told her plainly. She became more and more interested, more and more excited, as he went on.

"Quite right!" she exclaimed, starting to her feet and walking swiftly backwards and forwards in the room. "There *is* a lost girl whom I want to find; and she is between sixteen and seventeen years old, as you thought. Mind! I have no reason—not the shadow of a reason—for believing that she is still a living creature. I have only my own stupid obstinate conviction; rooted here," she pressed both hands fiercely on her heart, "so that nothing can tear it out of me! I have lived in that belief—Oh, don't ask me how long! it is so far, so miserably far, to look back!" She stopped in the middle of the room. Her breath came and went in quick heavy gasps; the first tears that had softened the hard wretchedness in her eyes rose in them now, and transfigured them with the divine beauty of maternal love. "I won't distress you," she said, stamping on the floor, as she struggled with the hysterical passion that was raging in her. "Give me a minute, and I'll force it down again."

She dropped into a chair, threw her arms heavily on the table, and laid her head on them. Amelius thought of the child's frock and cap hidden in the cabinet. All that was manly and noble in his nature felt for the unhappy woman, whose secret was dimly revealed to him now. The little selfish sense of annoyance at the awkward situation in which she had placed him, vanished to return no more. He approached her, and put his hand gently on her shoulder. "I am truly sorry for you," he said. "Tell me how I can help you, and I will do it with all my heart."

"Do you really mean that?" She roughly dashed the tears from her eyes, and rose as she put the question. Holding him with one hand, she parted the hair back from his forehead with the other. "I must see your whole face," she said—"your face will tell me. Yes: you do mean it. The world hasn't spoilt you, yet. Do you believe in dreams?"

Amelius looked at her, startled by the sudden transition. She deliberately repeated her question.

"I ask you seriously," she said; "do you believe in dreams?"

Amelius answered seriously, on his side, "I can't honestly say that I do."

"Ah!" she exclaimed, "like me. I don't believe in dreams, either—I wish I did! But it's not in me to believe in superstitions; I'm too hard—and I'm sorry for it. I have seen people who were comforted by their superstitions; happy people, possessed of faith. Don't you even believe that dreams are sometimes fulfilled by chance?"

"Nobody can deny that," Amelius replied; "the instances of it are too many. But for one dream fulfilled by a coincidence, there are—"

"A hundred at least that are *not* fulfilled," Mrs. Farnaby interposed. "Very well. I calculate on that. See how little hope can live on! There is just the barest possibility that what I dreamed of you the other night may come to pass. It's a poor chance; but it has encouraged me to take you into my confidence, and ask you to help me."

This strange confession—this sad revelation of despair still unconsciously deceiving itself under the disguise of hope—only strengthened the compassionate sympathy which Amelius already felt for her. "What did you dream about me?" he asked gently.

"It's nothing to tell," she replied. "I was in a room that was quite strange to me; and the door opened, and you came in leading a young girl by the hand. You said, 'Be happy at last; here she is.' My heart knew her instantly, though my eyes had never seen her since the first days of her life. And I woke myself, crying for joy. Wait! it's not all told yet. I went to sleep again, and dreamed it again, and woke, and lay awake for awhile, and slept once more, and dreamed it for the third time. Ah, if I could only feel some people's confidence in three times! No; it produced an impression on me—and that was all. I got as far as thinking to myself, there is just a chance; I haven't a creature in the world to help me; I may as well speak to him. O, you needn't remind me that there is a rational explanation of my dream. I have read it all up, in the Encyclopædia in the library. One of the ideas of wise men is that we think of something, consciously or unconsciously, in the daytime, and then reproduce it in a dream. That's my case, I daresay. When you were first introduced to me, and when I heard where you had been brought up, I thought directly that *she* might have been one among the many forlorn creatures who had drifted to your Community, and that I might find her through you. Say that thought went to my bed with me—and we have the explanation of my dream. Never mind! There is my one poor chance in a hundred still left. You will remember me, Amelius, if you *should* meet with her, won't you?"

The implied confession of her own intractable character, without religious faith to ennoble it, without even imagination to refine it—the unconscious disclosure of the one tender and loving instinct in her nature still piteously struggling for existence, with no sympathy to sustain it, with no light to guide it—would have touched the heart of any man not incurably depraved. Amelius spoke with the fervour of his young enthusiasm. "I would go to the uttermost ends of the earth, if I thought I could do you any good. But, oh, it sounds so hopeless!"

She shook her head, and smiled faintly.

"Don't say that! You are free, you have money, you will travel about in the world and amuse yourself. In a week you will see more than stay-at-home people see in a year. How do we know what the future has in store for us? I have my own idea. She may be lost in the labyrinth of London, or she may be hundreds of thousands of miles away. Amuse yourself, Amelius—amuse yourself. Tomorrow or ten years hence, you might meet with her!"

In sheer mercy to the poor creature, Amelius refused to encourage her delusion. "Even supposing such a thing could happen," he objected, "how am I to know the lost girl? You can't describe her to me; you have not seen her since she was a child. Do you know anything of what happened at the time—I mean at the time when she was lost?"

"I know nothing."

"Absolutely nothing?"

"Absolutely nothing."

"Have you never felt a suspicion of how it happened?"

Her face changed: she frowned as she looked at him. "Not till weeks and months had passed," she said, "not till it was too late. I was ill at the time. When my mind got clear again, I began to suspect one particular person—little by little, you know; noticing trifles, and thinking about them afterwards." She stopped, evidently restraining herself on the point of saying more.

Amelius tried to lead her on. "Did you suspect the person—?" he began.

"I suspected him of casting the child helpless on the world!" Mrs. Farnaby interposed, with a sudden burst of fury. "Don't ask me any more about it, or I shall break out and shock you!" She clenched her fists as she said the words. "It's well for that man," she muttered between her teeth, "that I have never got beyond suspecting, and never found out the truth! Why did you turn my mind that way? You shouldn't have done it. Help me back again to what we were saying a minute ago. You made some objection; you said—?"

"I said," Amelius reminded her, "that, even if I did meet with the missing girl, I couldn't possibly know it. And I must say more than that—I don't see how you yourself could be sure of recognizing her, if she stood before you at this moment."

He spoke very gently, fearing to irritate her. She showed no sign of irritation—she looked at him, and listened to him, attentively.

"Are you setting a trap for me?" she asked. "No!" she cried, before Amelius could answer, "I am not mean enough to distrust you—I forgot myself. You have innocently said something that rankles in my mind. I can't leave it where you have left it; I don't like to be told that I shouldn't recognize her. Give me time to think. I must clear this up."

She consulted her own thoughts, keeping her eyes fixed on Amelius.

"I am going to speak plainly," she announced, with a sudden appearance of resolution. "Listen to this. When I banged to the door of that big cupboard of mine, it was because I didn't want you to see something on the shelves. Did you see anything in spite of me?"

The question was not an easy one to answer. Amelius hesitated. Mrs. Farnaby insisted on a reply.

"Did you see anything?" she reiterated

Amelius owned that he had seen something.

She turned away from him, and looked into the fire. Her firm full tones sank so low, when she spoke next, that he could barely hear them.

"Was it something belonging to a child?"

"Yes."

"Was it a baby's frock and cap? Answer me. We have gone too far to go back. I don't want apologies or explanations—I want, Yes or No."

"Yes."

There was an interval of silence. She never moved; she still looked into fire—looked, as if all her past life was pictured there in the burning coals.

76

"Do you despise me?" she asked at last, very quietly.

"As God hears me, I am only sorry for you!" Amelius answered.

Another woman would have melted into tears. This woman still looked into the fire—and that was all. "What a good fellow!" she said to herself, "what a good fellow he is!"

There was another pause. She turned towards him again as abruptly as she had turned away.

"I had hoped to spare you, and to spare myself," she said. "If the miserable truth has come out, it is through no curiosity of yours, and (God knows!) against every wish of mine. I don't know if you really felt like a friend towards me before—you must be my friend now. Don't speak! I know I can trust you. One last word, Amelius, about my lost child. You doubt whether I should recognize her, if she stood before me now. That might be quite true, if I had only my own poor hopes and anxieties to guide me. But I have something else to guide me—and, after what has passed between us, you may as well know what it is: it might even, by accident, guide you. Don't alarm yourself; it's nothing distressing this time. How can I explain it?" she went on; pausing, and speaking in some perplexity to herself. "It would be easier to show it—and why not?" She addressed herself to Amelius once more. "I'm a strange creature," she resumed. "First, I worry you about my own affairs—then I puzzle you—then I make you sorry for me—and now (would you think it?) I am going to amuse you! Amelius, are you an admirer of pretty feet?"

Amelius had heard of men (in books) who had found reason to doubt whether their own ears were not deceiving them. For the first time, he began to understand those men, and to sympathize with them. He admitted, in a certain bewildered way, that he was an admirer of pretty feet—and waited for what was to come next.

"When a woman has a pretty hand," Mrs. Farnaby proceeded; "she is ready enough to show it. When she goes out to a ball, she favours you with a view of her bosom, and a part of her back. Now tell me! If there is no impropriety in a naked bosom—where is the impropriety in a naked foot?"

Amelius agreed, like a man in a dream.

"Where, indeed!" he remarked—and waited again for what was to come next.

"Look out of the window," said Mrs. Farnaby.

Amelius obeyed. The window had been opened for a few inches at the top, no doubt to ventilate the room. The dull view of the courtyard was varied by the stables at the farther end, and by the kitchen skylight rising in the middle of the open space. As Amelius looked out, he observed that some person at that moment in the kitchen required apparently a large supply of fresh air. The swinging window, on the side of the skylight which was nearest to him, was invisibly and noiselessly pulled open from below; the similar window, on the other side, being already wide open also. Judging by appearance, the inhabitants of the kitchen possessed a merit which is exceedingly rare among domestic servants—they understood the laws of ventilation, and appreciated the blessing of fresh air.

"That will do," said Mrs. Farnaby. "You can turn round now."

Amelius turned. Mrs. Farnaby's boots and stockings were on the hearthrug, and one of Mrs. Farnaby's feet was placed, ready for inspection, on the chair which he had just left. "Look at my right foot first," she said, speaking gravely and composedly in her ordinary tone.

It was well worth looking at—a foot equally beautiful in form and in colour: the instep arched and high, the ankle at once delicate and strong, the toes tinged with rose-colour at the tips. In brief, it was a foot to be photographed, to be cast in plaster, to be fondled and kissed. Amelius attempted to express his admiration, but was not allowed to get beyond the first two or three words. "No," Mrs. Farnaby explained, "this is not vanity—simply information. You have seen my right foot; and you have noticed that there is nothing the matter with it. Very well. Now look at my left foot."

She put her left foot up on the chair. "Look between the third toe and the fourth," she said.

Following his instructions, Amelius discovered that the beauty of the foot was spoilt, in this case, by a singular defect. The two toes were bound together by a flexible web, or membrane, which held them to each other as high as the insertion of the nail on either side.

"Do you wonder," Mrs. Farnaby asked, "why I show you the fault in my foot? Amelius! my poor darling was born with my deformity—and I want you to know exactly what it is, because neither you nor I can say what reason for remembering it there may not be in the future." She stopped, as if to give him an opportunity of speaking. A man shallow and flippant by nature might have seen the disclosure in a grotesque aspect. Amelius was sad and silent. "I like you better and better," she went on. "You are not like the common run of men. Nine out of ten of them would have turned what I have just told you into a joke—nine out of ten would have said, 'Am I to ask every girl I meet to show me her left foot?' You are above that; you understand me. Have I no means of recognizing my own child, now?"

She smiled, and took her foot off the chair—then, after a moment's thought, she pointed to it again.

"Keep this as strictly secret as you keep everything else," she said. "In the past days, when I used to employ people privately to help me to find her, it was my only defence against being imposed upon. Rogues and vagabonds thought of other marks and signs—but not one of them could guess at such a mark as that. Have you got your pocket-book, Amelius? In case we are separated at some later time, I want to write the name and address in it of a person whom we can trust. I persist, you see, in providing for the future. There's the one chance in a hundred that my dream may come true—and you have so many years before you, and so many girls to meet with in that time!"

She handed back the pocket-book, which Amelius had given to her, after having inscribed a man's name and address on one of the blank leaves.

"He was my father's lawyer," she explained; "and he and his son are both men to be trusted. Suppose I am ill, for instance—no, that's absurd; I never had a day's illness in my life. Suppose I am dead (killed perhaps by some accident, or perhaps by my own hand), the lawyers have my written instructions, in the case of my child being found. Then again—I am such an unaccountable woman—I may go away somewhere, all by myself. Never mind! The lawyers shall have my address, and my positive orders (though they keep it a secret from all the world besides) to tell it to you. I don't ask your pardon, Amelius, for troubling you. The chances are so terribly against me; it is all but impossible that I shall ever see you—as I saw you in my dream—coming into the room, leading my girl by the hand. Odd, isn't it? This is how I veer about between hope and despair. Well, it may amuse you to remember it, one of these days. Years hence, when I am at rest in mother earth, and when you are a middle aged married man, you may tell your wife how strangely you once became the forlorn hope of the most wretched woman that ever lived—and you may say to each other, as you sit by your snug fireside, 'Perhaps that poor lost daughter is still living somewhere, and wondering who her mother was.' No! I won't let you see the tears in my eyes again—I'll let you go at last."

She led the way to the door—a creature to be pitied, if ever there was a pitiable creature yet: a woman whose whole nature was maternal, who was nothing if not a mother; and who had lived through sixteen years of barren life, in the hopeless anticipation of recovering her lost child!

"Goodbye, and thank you," she said. "I want to be left by myself, my dear, with that little frock and cap which you found out in spite of me. Go, and tell my niece it's all right—and don't be stupid enough to fall in love with a girl who has no love to give you in return." She pushed Amelius into the hall. "Here he is, Regina!" she called out; "I have done with him."

Before Amelius could speak, she had shut herself into her room. He advanced along the hall, and met Regina at the door of the dining-room.

CHAPTER 3

The young lady spoke first.

"Mr. Goldenheart," she said, with the coldest possible politeness, "perhaps you will be good enough to explain what this means?"

She turned back into the dining-room. Amelius followed her in silence. "Here I am, in another scrape with a woman!" he thought to himself. "Are men in general as unlucky as I am, I wonder?"

"You needn't close the door," said Regina maliciously. "Everybody in the house is welcome to hear what *I* have to say to you."

Amelius made a mistake at the outset—he tried what a little humility would do to help him. There is probably no instance on record in which humility on the part of a man has ever really found its way to the indulgence of an irritated woman. The best and the worst of them alike have at least one virtue in common—they secretly despise a man who is not bold enough to defend himself when they are angry with him.

"I hope I have not offended you?" Amelius ventured to say.

She tossed her head contemptuously. "Oh dear, no! I am not offended. Only a little surprised at your being so very ready to oblige my aunt."

In the short experience of her which had fallen to the lot of Amelius, she had never looked so charmingly as she looked now. The nervous irritability under which she was suffering brightened her face with the animation which was wanting in it at ordinary times. Her soft brown eyes sparkled; her smooth dusky cheeks glowed with a warm red flush; her tall supple figure asserted its full dignity, robed in a superb dress of silken purple and black lace, which set off her personal attractions to the utmost advantage. She not only roused the admiration of Amelius—she unconsciously gave him back the self-possession which he had, for the moment, completely lost. He was man enough to feel the humiliation of being despised by the one woman in the world whose love he longed to win; and he answered with a sudden firmness of tone and look that startled her.

"You had better speak more plainly still, Miss Regina," he said. "You may as well blame me at once for the misfortune of being a man."

She drew back a step. "I don't understand you," she answered.

"Do I owe no forbearance to a woman who asks a favour of me?" Amelius went on. "If a man had asked me to steal into the house on tiptoe, I should have said—well! I should have said something I had better not repeat. If a man had stood between me and the door when you came back, I should have taken him by the collar and pulled him out of my way. Could I do that, if you please, with Mrs. Farnaby?"

Regina saw the weak point of this defence with a woman's quickness of perception. "I can't offer any opinion," she said; "especially when you lay all the blame on my aunt."

Amelius opened his lips to protest—and thought better of it. He wisely went straight on with what he had still to say.

"If you will let me finish," he resumed, "you will understand me a little better than that. Whatever blame there may be, Miss Regina, I am quite ready to take on myself. I merely wanted to remind you that I was put in an awkward position, and that I couldn't civilly find a way out of it. As for your aunt, I will only say this: I know of hardly any sacrifice that I would not submit to, if I could be of the smallest service to her. After what I heard, while I was in her room—"

Regina interrupted him at that point. "I suppose it's a secret between you?" she said.

"Yes; it's a secret," Amelius proceeded, "as you say. But one thing I may tell you, without breaking my promise. Mrs. Farnaby has—well! has filled me with kindly feeling towards her. She has a claim, poor soul, to my truest sympathy. And I shall remember her claim. And I shall be faithful to what I feel towards her as long as I live!"

It was not very elegantly expressed; but the tone was the tone of true feeling in his voice trembled, his colour rose. He stood before her, speaking with perfect simplicity straight from his heart—and the woman's heart felt it instantly. This was the man whose ridicule she had dreaded, if her aunt's rash confidence struck him in an absurd light! She sat down in silence, with a grave sad face, reproaching herself for the wrong which her too ready distrust had inflicted on him; longing to ask his pardon, and yet hesitating to say the simple words.

He approached her chair, and, placing his hand on the back of it, said gently, "do you think a little better of me now?"

She had taken off her gloves: she silently folded and refolded them in her lap.

"Your good opinion is very precious to me," Amelius pleaded, bending a little nearer to her. "I can't tell you how sorry I should be—" He stopped, and put it more strongly. "I shall never have courage enough to enter the house again, if I have made you think meanly of me."

A woman who cared nothing for him would have easily answered this. The calm heart of Regina began to flutter: something warned her not to trust herself to speak.

Little as he suspected it, Amelius had troubled the tranquil temperament of this woman. He had found his way to those secret reserves of tenderness—placid and deep—of which she was hardly conscious herself, until his influence had enlightened her. She was afraid to look up at him; her eyes would have told him the truth. She lifted her long, finely shaped, dusky hand, and offered it to him as the best answer that she could make.

Amelius took it, looked at it, and ventured on his first familiarity with her—he kissed it. She only said, "Don't!" very faintly.

"The Queen would let me kiss her hand if I went to Court," Amelius reminded her, with a pleasant inner conviction of his wonderful readiness at finding an excuse.

She smiled in spite of herself. "Would the Queen let you hold it?" she asked, gently releasing her hand, and looking at him as she drew it away. The peace was made without another word of explanation. Amelius took a chair at her side. "I'm quite happy now you have forgiven me," he said. "You don't know how I admire you— and how anxious I am to please you, if I only knew how!"

He drew his chair a little nearer; his eyes told her plainly that his language would soon become warmer still, if she gave him the smallest encouragement. This was one reason for changing the subject. But there was another reason, more cogent still. Her first painful sense of having treated him unjustly had ceased to make itself keenly felt; the lower emotions had their opportunity of asserting themselves. Curiosity, irresistible curiosity, took possession of her mind, and urged her to penetrate the mystery of the interview between Amelius and her aunt.

"Will you think me very indiscreet," she began slyly, "if I made a little confession to you?"

Amelius was only too eager to hear the confession: it would pave the way for something of the same sort on his part.

"I understand my aunt making the heat in the concert-room a pretence for taking you away with her," Regina proceeded; "but what astonishes me is that she should have admitted you to her confidence after so short an acquaintance. You are still—what shall I say?—you are still a new friend of ours."

"How long will it be before I become an old friend?" Amelius asked. "I mean," he added, with artful emphasis, "an old friend of *yours?"*

Confused by the question, Regina passed it over without notice. "I am Mrs. Farnaby's adopted daughter," she resumed. "I have been with her since I was a little girl—and yet she has never told me any of her secrets. Pray don't suppose that I am tempting you to break faith with my aunt! I am quite incapable of such conduct as that."

Amelius saw his way to a thoroughly commonplace compliment which possessed the charm of complete novelty so far as his experience was concerned. He would actually have told her that she was incapable of doing anything which was not perfectly becoming to a charming person, if she had only given him time! She was too eager in the pursuit of her own object to give him time. "I *should* like to know," she went on, "whether my aunt has been influenced in any way by a dream that she had about you."

Amelius started. "Has she told you of her dream?" he asked, with some appearance of alarm.

Regina blushed and hesitated, "My room is next to my aunt's," she explained. "We keep the door between us open. I am often in and out when she is disturbed in her sleep. She was talking in her sleep, and I heard your name—nothing more. Perhaps I ought not to have mentioned it? Perhaps I ought not to expect you to answer me?"

"There is no harm in my answering you," said Amelius. "The dream really had something to do with her trusting me. You may not think quite so unfavourably of her conduct now you know that."

"It doesn't matter what I think," Regina replied constrainedly. "If my aunt's secrets have interested you—what right have I to object? I am sure I shall say nothing. Though I am not in my aunt's confidence, nor in your confidence, you will find I can keep a secret."

She folded up her gloves for the twentieth time at least, and gave Amelius his opportunity of retiring by rising from her chair. He made a last effort to recover the ground that he had lost, without betraying Mrs. Farnaby's trust in him.

"I am sure you can keep a secret," he said. "I should like to give you one of my secrets to keep—only I mustn't take the liberty, I suppose, just yet?"

She new perfectly well what he wanted to say. Her heart began to quicken its beat; she was at a loss how to answer. After an awkward silence, she made an attempt to dismiss him. "Don't let me detain you," she said, "if you have any engagement."

Amelius silently looked round him for his hat. On a table behind him a monthly magazine lay open, exhibiting one of those melancholy modern "illustrations" which present the English art of our day in its laziest and lowest state of degradation. A vacuous young giant, in flowing trousers, stood in a garden, and stared at a plump young giantess with enormous eyes and rotund hips, vacantly boring holes in the grass with the point of her parasol. Perfectly incapable of explaining itself, this imbecile production put its trust in the printer, whose charitable types helped it, at the bottom of the page, with the title of "Love at First Sight." On those remarkable words Amelius seized, with the desperation of the drowning man, catching at the proverbial straw. They offered him a chance of pleading his cause, this time, with a happy indirectness of allusion at which not even a young lady's susceptibility could take offence.

"Do you believe in that?" he said, pointing to the illustration.

Regina declined to understand him. "In what?" she asked.

"In love at first sight."

It would be speaking with inexcusable rudeness to say plainly that she told him a lie. Let the milder form of expression be, that she modestly concealed the truth. "I don't know anything about it," she said.

"*I* do," Amelius remarked smartly.

She persisted in looking at the illustration. Was there an infection of imbecility in that fatal work? She was too simple to understand him, even yet! "You do—what?" she inquired innocently.

"I know what love at first sight is," Amelius burst out.

Regina turned over the leaves of the magazine. "Ah," she said, "you have read the story."

"I haven't read the story," Amelius answered. "I know what I felt myself—on being introduced to a young lady."

She looked up at him with a sly smile. "A young lady in America?" she asked.

"In England, Miss Regina." He tried to take her hand—but she kept it out of his reach. "In London," he went on, drifting back into his customary plainness of speech. "In this very street," he resumed, seizing her hand before she was aware of him. Too much bewildered to know what else to do, Regina took refuge desperately in shaking hands with him. "Goodbye, Mr. Goldenheart," she said—and gave him his dismissal for the second time.

Amelius submitted to his fate; there was something in her eyes which warned him that he had ventured far enough for that day.

"May I call again, soon?" he asked piteously.

"No!" answered a voice at the door which they both recognized—the voice of Mrs. Farnaby.

"Yes!" Regina whispered to him, as her aunt entered the room. Mrs. Farnaby's interference, following on the earlier events of the day, had touched the young lady's usually placable temper in a tender place—and Amelius reaped the benefit of it.

Mrs. Farnaby walked straight up to him, put her hand in his arm, and led him out into the hall.

"I had my suspicions," she said; "and I find they have not misled me. Twice already, I have warned you to let my niece alone. For the third, and last time, I tell you that she is as cold as ice. She will trifle with you as long as it flatters her vanity; and she will throw you over, as she has thrown other men over. Have your fling, you foolish fellow, before you marry anybody. Pay no more visits to this house, unless they are visits to me. I shall expect to hear from you." She paused, and pointed to a statue which was one of the ornaments in the hall. "Look at that bronze woman with the clock in her hand. That's Regina. Be off with you—goodbye!"

Amelius found himself in the street. Regina was looking out at the dining-room window. He kissed his hand to her: she smiled and bowed. "Damn the other men!" Amelius said to himself. "I'll call on her tomorrow."

CHAPTER 4

Returning to his hotel, he found three letters waiting for him on the sitting-room table.

The first letter that he opened was from his landlord, and contained his bill for the past week. As he looked at the sum total, Amelius presented to perfection the aspect of a serious young man. He took pen, ink, and paper, and made some elaborate calculations. Money that he had too generously lent, or too freely given away, appeared in his statement of expenses, as well as money that he had spent on himself. The result may be plainly stated in his own words: "Goodbye to the hotel; I must go into lodgings."

Having arrived at this wise decision, he opened the second letter. It proved to be written by the lawyers who had already communicated with him at Tadmor, on the subject of his inheritance.

"DEAR SIR,

"The enclosed, insufficiently addressed as you will perceive, only reached us this day. We beg to remain, *etc*."

Amelius opened the letter enclosed, and turned to the signature for information. The name instantly took him back to the Community: the writer was Mellicent.

Her letter began abruptly, in these terms:

"Do you remember what I said to you when we parted at Tadmor? I said, 'Be comforted, Amelius, the end is not yet.' And I said again, 'You will come back to me.'

"I remind you of this, my friend—directing to your lawyers, whose names I remember when their letter to you was publicly read in the Common Room. Once or twice a year I shall continue to remind you of those parting words of mine: there will be a time perhaps when you will thank me for doing so.

"In the mean while, light your pipe with my letters; my letters don't matter. If I can comfort you, and reconcile you to your life—years hence, when you, too, my Amelius, may be one of the Fallen Leaves like me—then I shall not have lived and suffered in vain; my last days on earth will be the happiest days that I have ever seen.

"Be pleased not to answer these lines, or any other written words of mine that may follow, so long as you are prosperous and happy. With *that* part of your life I have nothing to do. You will find friends wherever you go—among the women especially. Your generous nature shows itself frankly in your face; your manly gentleness and sweetness speak in every tone of your voice; we poor women feel drawn towards you by an attraction which we are not able to resist. Have you fallen in love already with some beautiful English girl? Oh, be careful and prudent! Be sure, before you set your heart on her, that she is worthy of you! So many women are cruel and deceitful. Some of them will make you believe you have won their love, when you have only flattered their vanity; and some are poor weak creatures whose minds are set on their own interests, and who may let bad advisers guide them, when you are not by. For your own sake, take care!

"I am living with my sister, at New York. The days and weeks glide by me quietly; you are in my thoughts and my prayers; I have nothing to complain of; I wait and hope. When the time of my banishment from the Community has expired, I shall go back to Tadmor; and there you will find me, Amelius, the first to welcome you when your spirits are sinking under the burden of life, and your heart turns again to the friends of your early days.

"Goodbye, my dear—goodbye!"

Amelius laid the letter aside, touched and saddened by the artless devotion to him which it expressed. He was conscious also of a feeling of uneasy surprise, when he read the lines which referred to his possible entanglement with some beautiful English girl. Here, with widely different motives, was Mrs. Farnaby's warning repeated, by a stranger writing from another quarter of the globe! It was an odd coincidence, to say the least of it. After thinking for a while, he turned abruptly to the third letter that was waiting for him. He was not at ease; his mind felt the need of relief.

The third letter was from Rufus Dingwell; announcing the close of his tour in Ireland, and his intention of shortly joining Amelius in London. The excellent American expressed, with his customary absence of reserve, his fervent admiration of Irish hospitality, Irish beauty, and Irish whisky. "Green Erin wants but one thing more," Rufus predicted, "to be a Paradise on earth—it wants the day to come when we shall send an American minister to the Irish Republic." Laughing over this quaint outbreak, Amelius turned from the first page to the second. As his eyes fell on the next paragraph, a sudden change passed over him; he let the letter drop on the floor.

"One last word," the American wrote, "about that nice long bright letter of yours. I have read it with strict attention, and thought over it considerably afterwards. Don't be riled, friend Amelius, if I tell you in plain words, that your account of the Farnabys doesn't make me happy—quite the contrary, I do assure you. My back is set up, sir, against that family. You will do well to drop them; and, above all things, mind what you are about with the brown miss, who has found her way to your favourable opinion in such an almighty hurry. Do me a favour, my good boy. Just wait till I have seen her, will you?"

Mrs. Farnaby, Mellicent, Rufus—all three strangers to each other; and all three agreed nevertheless in trying to part him from the beautiful young Englishwoman! "I don't care," Amelius thought to himself "They may say what they please—I'll marry Regina, if she will have me!"

BOOK THE FOURTH

LOVE AND MONEY

CHAPTER 1

In an interval of no more than three weeks what events may not present themselves? what changes may not take place? Behold Amelius, on the first drizzling day of November, established in respectable lodgings, at a moderate weekly rent. He stands before his small fireside, and warms his back with an Englishman's severe sense of enjoyment. The cheap looking-glass on the mantelpiece reflects the head and shoulders of a new Amelius. His habits are changed; his social position is in course of development. Already, he is a strict economist. Before long, he expects to become a married man.

It is good to be economical: it is, perhaps, better still to be the accepted husband of a handsome young woman. But, for all that, a man in a state of moral improvement, with prospects which his less favoured fellow creatures may reasonably envy, is still a man subject to the mischievous mercy of circumstances, and capable of feeling it keenly. The face of the new Amelius wore an expression of anxiety, and, more remarkable yet, the temper of the new Amelius was out of order.

For the first time in his life he found himself considering trivial questions of sixpences, and small favours of discount for cash payments—an irritating state of things in itself. There were more serious anxieties, however, to trouble him than these. He had no reason to complain of the beloved object herself. Not twelve hours since he had said to Regina, with a voice that faltered, and a heart that beat wildly, "Are you fond enough of me to let me marry you?" And she had answered placidly, with a heart that would have satisfied the most exacting stethoscope in the medical profession, "Yes, if you like." There was a moment of rapture, when she submitted for the first time to be kissed, and when she consented, on being gently reminded that it was expected of her, to return the kiss—once, and no more. But there was also an attendant train of serious considerations which followed on the heels of Amelius when the kissing was over, and when he had said goodbye for the day.

He had two women for enemies, both resolutely against him in the matter of his marriage.

Regina's correspondent and bosom friend, Cecilia, who had begun by disliking him, without knowing why, persisted in maintaining her unfavourable opinion of the new friend of the Farnabys. She was a young married woman; and she had an influence over Regina which promised, when the fit opportunity came, to make itself felt. The second, and by far the more powerful hostile influence, was the influence of Mrs. Farnaby. Nothing could exceed the half sisterly, half motherly, goodwill with which she received Amelius on those rare occasions when they happened to meet, unembarrassed by the presence of a third person in the room. Without actually reverting to what had passed between them during their memorable interview, Mrs. Farnaby asked questions, plainly showing that the forlorn hope which she associated with Amelius was a hope still firmly rooted in her mind. "Have you been much about London lately?" "Have you met with any girls who have taken your fancy?" "Are you getting tired of staying in the same place, and are you going to travel soon?" Inquiries such as these she was, sooner or later, sure to make when they were alone. But if Regina happened to enter the room, or if Amelius contrived to find his way to her in some other part of the house, Mrs. Farnaby deliberately shortened the interview and silenced the lovers—still as resolute as ever to keep Amelius exposed to the adventurous freedom of a bachelor's life. For the last week, his only opportunities of speaking to Regina had been obtained for him secretly by the well-rewarded devotion of her maid. And he had now the prospect before him of asking Mr. Farnaby for the hand of his adopted daughter, with the certainty of the influence of two women being used against him—even if he succeeded in obtaining a favourable reception for his proposal from the master of the house.

Under such circumstances as these—alone, on a rainy November day, in a lodging on the dreary eastward side of the Tottenham Court Road—even Amelius bore the aspect of a melancholy man. He was angry with his cigar because it refused to light freely. He was angry with the poor deaf servant-of-all-work, who entered the room, after one thumping knock at the door, and made, in muffled tones, the barbarous announcement, "Here's somebody a-wantin' to see yer."

"Who the devil is Somebody?" Amelius shouted.

"Somebody is a citizen of the United States," answered Rufus, quietly entering the room. "And he's sorry to find Claude A. Goldenheart's temperature at boiling-point already!"

He had not altered in the slightest degree since he had left the steamship at Queenstown. Irish hospitality had not fattened him; the change from sea to land had not suggested to him the slightest alteration in his dress. He still wore the huge felt hat in which he had first presented himself to notice on the deck of the vessel. The maid-of-all-work raised her eyes to the face of the long lean stranger, overshadowed by the broadbrimmed hat, in reverent amazement. "My love to you, miss," said Rufus, with his customary grave cordiality; "*I'll* shut the door." Having dismissed the maid with that gentle hint, he shook hands heartily with Amelius. "Well, I call this a juicy morning," he said, just as if they had met at the cabin breakfast-table as usual.

For the moment, at least, Amelius brightened at the sight of his fellow-traveller. "I am really glad to see you," he said. "It's lonely in these new quarters, before one gets used to them."

Rufus relieved himself of his hat and great coat, and silently looked about the room. "I'm big in the bones," he remarked, surveying the rickety lodging-house furniture with some suspicion; "and I'm a trifle heavier than I look. I shan't break one of these chairs if I sit down on it, shall I?" Passing round the table (littered with books and letters) in search of the nearest chair, he accidentally brushed against a sheet of paper with writing on it. "Memorandum of friends in London, to be informed of my change of address," he read, looking at the paper, as he picked it up, with the friendly freedom that characterized him. "You have made pretty good use of your time, my son, since I took my leave of you in Queenstown harbour. I call this a reasonable long list of acquaintances made by a young stranger in London."

"I met with an old friend of my family at the hotel," Amelius explained. "He was a great loss to my poor father, when he got an appointment in India; and, now he has returned, he has been equally kind to me. I am indebted to his introduction for most of the names on that list."

"Yes?" said Rufus, in the interrogative tone of a man who was waiting to hear more. "I'm listening, though I may not look like it. Git along."

Amelius looked at his visitor, wondering in what precise direction he was to "git along."

"I'm no friend to partial information," Rufus proceeded; "I like to round it off complete, as it were, in my own mind. There are names on this list that you haven't accounted for yet. Who provided you, sir, with the balance of your new friends?"

Amelius answered, not very willingly, "I met them at Mr. Farnaby's house."

Rufus looked up from the list with the air of a man surprised by disagreeable information, and unwilling to receive it too readily. "How?" he exclaimed, using the old English equivalent (often heard in America) for the modern "What?"

"I met them at Mr. Farnaby's," Amelius repeated.

"Did you happen to receive a letter of my writing, dated Dublin?" Rufus asked.

"Yes."

"Do you set any particular value on my advice?"

"Certainly!"

"And you cultivate social relations with Farnaby and family, notwithstanding?"

"I have motives for being friendly with them, which—which I haven't had time to explain to you yet."

Rufus stretched out his long legs on the floor, and fixed his shrewd grave eyes steadily on Amelius.

"My friend," he said, quietly, "in respect of personal appearance and pleasing elasticity of spirits, I find you altered for the worse, I do. It may be Liver, or it may be Love. I reckon, now I think of it, you're too young yet for Liver. It's the brown miss—that's what 'tis. I hate that girl, sir, by instinct."

"A nice way of talking of a young lady you never saw!" Amelius broke out.

Rufus smiled grimly. "Go ahead!" he said. "If you can get vent in quarrelling with me, go ahead, my son."

He looked round the room again, with his hands in his pockets, whistling. Descending to the table in due course of time, his quick eye detected a photograph placed on the open writing desk which Amelius had been using earlier in the day. Before it was possible to stop him, the photograph was in his hand. "I believe I've got her likeness," he announced. "I do assure you I take pleasure in making her acquaintance in this sort of way. Well, now, I declare she's a columnar creature! Yes, sir; I do justice to your native produce—your fine fleshy beef-fed English girl. But I tell you this: after a child or two, that sort runs to fat, and you find you have married more of her than you bargained for. To what lengths may you have proceeded, Amelius, with this splendid and spanking person?"

Amelius was just on the verge of taking offence. "Speak of her respectfully," he said, "if you expect me to answer you."

Rufus stared in astonishment. "I'm paying her all manner of compliments," he protested, "and you're not satisfied yet. My friend, I still find something about you, on this occasion, which reminds me of meat cut against the grain. You're almost nasty—you are! The air of London, I reckon, isn't at all the thing for you. Well, it don't matter to me; I like you. Afloat or ashore, I like you. Do you want to know what I should do, in your place, if I found myself steering a little too nigh to the brown miss? I should—well, to put it in one word, I should scatter. Where's the harm, I'll ask you, if you try another girl or two, before you make your mind up. I shall be proud to introduce you to our slim and snaky sort at Coolspring. Yes. I mean what I say; and I'll go back with you across the pond." Referring in this disrespectful manner to the Atlantic Ocean, Rufus offered his hand in token of unalterable devotion and goodwill.

Who could resist such a man as this? Amelius, always in extremes, wrung his hand, with an impetuous sense of shame. "I've been sulky," he said, "I've been rude, I ought to be ashamed of myself—and I am. There's only one excuse for me, Rufus. I love her with all my heart and soul; and I'm engaged to be married to her. And yet, if you understand my way of putting it, I'm—in short, I'm in a mess."

With this characteristic preface, he described his position as exactly as he could; having due regard to the necessary reserve on the subject of Mrs. Farnaby. Rufus listened, with the closest attention, from beginning to end; making no attempt to disguise the unfavourable impression which the announcement of the marriage-engagement had made on him. When he spoke next, instead of looking at Amelius as usual, he held his head down, and looked gloomily at his boots.

"Well," he said, "you've gone ahead this time, and that's a fact. She didn't raise any difficulties that a man could ride off on—did she?"

"She was all that was sweet and kind!" Amelius answered, with enthusiasm.

"She was all that was sweet and kind," Rufus absently repeated, still intent on the solid spectacle of his own boots. "And how about uncle Farnaby? Perhaps he's sweet and kind likewise, or perhaps he cuts up rough? Possible—is it not, sir?"

"I don't know; I haven't spoken to him yet."

Rufus suddenly looked up. A faint gleam of hope irradiated his long lank face. "Mercy be praised! there's a last chance for you," he remarked. "Uncle Farnaby may say No."

"It doesn't matter what he says," Amelius rejoined. "She's old enough to choose for herself, he can't stop the marriage."

Rufus lifted one wiry yellow forefinger, in a state of perpendicular protest. "He cannot stop the marriage," the sagacious New Englander admitted; "but he can stop the money, my son. Find out how you stand with him before another day is over your head."

"I can't go to him this evening." said Amelius; "he dines out."

"Where is he now?"

"At his place of business."

"Fix him at his place of business. Right away!" cried Rufus, springing with sudden energy to his feet.

"I don't think he would like it," Amelius objected. "He's not a very pleasant fellow, anywhere; but he's particularly disagreeable at his place of business."

Rufus walked to the window, and looked out. The objections to Mr. Farnaby appeared to fail, so far, in interesting him.

"To put it plainly," Amelius went on, "there's something about him that I can't endure. And—though he's very civil to me, in his way—I don't think he has ever got over the discovery that I am a Christian Socialist."

Rufus abruptly turned round from the window, and became attentive again. "So you told him that—did you?" he said.

94

"Of course!" Amelius rejoined, sharply. "Do you suppose I am ashamed of the principles in which I have been brought up?"

"You don't care, I reckon, if all the world knows your principles, persisted Rufus, deliberately leading him on.

"Care?" Amelius reiterated. "I only wish I had all the world to listen to me. They should hear of my principles, with no bated breath, I promise you!"

There was a pause. Rufus turned back again to the window. "When Farnaby's at home, where does he live?" he asked suddenly—still keeping his face towards the street.

Amelius mentioned the address. "You don't mean that you are going to call there?" he inquired, with some anxiety.

"Well, I reckoned I might catch him before dinner-time. You seem to be sort of feared to speak to him yourself. I'm your friend, Amelius—and I'll speak for you."

The bare idea of the interview struck Amelius with terror. "No, no!" he said. "I'm much obliged to you, Rufus. But in a matter of this sort, I shouldn't like to transfer the responsibility to my friend. I'll speak to Mr. Farnaby in a day or two."

Rufus was evidently not satisfied with this. "I do suppose, now," he suggested, "you're not the only man moving in this metropolis who fancies Miss Regina. Query, my son: if you put off Farnaby much longer—" He paused and looked at Amelius. "Ah," he said, "I reckon I needn't enlarge further: there *is* another man. Well, it's the same in my country; I don't know what he does, with You: he always turns up, with Us, just at the time when you least want to see him."

There *was* another man—an older and a richer man than Amelius; equally assiduous in his attentions to the aunt and to the niece; submissively polite to his favoured young rival. He was the sort of person, in age and in temperament, who would be perfectly capable of advancing his own interests by means of the hostile influence of Mrs. Farnaby. Who could say what the result might be if, by some unlucky accident, he made the attempt before Amelius had secured for himself the support of the master of the house? In his present condition of nervous irritability, he was ready to believe in any coincidence of the disastrous sort. The wealthy rival was a man of business, a near city neighbour of Mr. Farnaby. They might be together at that moment; and Regina's fidelity to her lover might be put to a harder test than she was prepared to endure. Amelius remembered the gentle conciliatory smile (too gentle by half) with which his placid mistress had received his first kisses—and, without stopping to weigh conclusions, snatched up his hat. "Wait here for me, Rufus, like a good fellow. I'm off to the stationer's shop." With those parting words, he hurried out of the room.

Left by himself, Rufus began to rummage the pockets of his frockcoat—a long, loose, and dingy garment which had become friendly and comfortable to him by dint of ancient use. Producing a handful of correspondence, he selected the largest envelope of all; shook out on the table several smaller letters enclosed; picked one out of the number; and read the concluding paragraph only, with the closest attention.

"I enclose letters of introduction to the secretaries of literary institutions in London, and in some of the principal cities of England. If you feel disposed to lecture yourself, or if you can persuade friends and citizens known to you to do so, I believe it may be in your power to advance in this way the interests of our Bureau. Please take notice that the more advanced institutions, which are ready to countenance and welcome free thought in religion, politics, and morals, are marked on the envelopes with a cross in red ink. The envelopes without a mark are addressed to platforms on which the customary British prejudices remain rampant, and in which the charge for places reaches a higher figure than can be as yet obtained in the sanctuaries of free thought."

Rufus laid down the letter, and, choosing one among the envelopes marked in red ink, looked at the introduction enclosed. "If the right sort of invitation reached Amelius from this institution," he thought, "the boy would lecture on Christian Socialism with all his heart and soul. I wonder what the brown miss and her uncle would say to that?"

He smiled to himself, and put the letter back in the envelope, and considered the subject for a while. Below the odd rough surface, he was a man in ten thousand; no more single-hearted and more affectionate creature ever breathed the breath of life. He had not been understood in his own little circle; there had been a want of sympathy with him, and even a want of knowledge of him, at home. Amelius, popular with everybody, had touched the great heart of this man. He perceived the peril that lay hidden under the strange and lonely position of his fellow-voyager—so innocent in the ways of the world, so young and so easily impressed His fondness for Amelius, it is hardly too much to say, was the fondness of a father for a son. With a sigh, he shook his head, and gathered up his letters, and put them back in his pockets. "No, not yet," he decided. "The poor boy really loves her; and the girl may be good enough to make the happiness of his life." He got up and walked about the room. Suddenly he stopped, struck by a new idea. "Why shouldn't I judge for myself?" he thought. "I've got the address—I reckon I'll look in on the Farnabys, in a friendly way."

He sat down at the desk, and wrote a line, in the event of Amelius being the first to return to the lodgings:

DEAR BOY,

"I don't find her photograph tells me quite so much as I want to know. I have a mind to see the living original. Being your friend, you know, it's only civil to pay my respects to the family. Expect my unbiased opinion when I come back.

"Yours,

"RUFUS."

Having enclosed and addressed these lines, he took up his greatcoat—and checked himself in the act of putting it on. The brown miss was a British miss. A strange New Englander had better be careful of his personal appearance, before he ventured into her presence. Urged by this cautious motive, he approached the looking-glass, and surveyed himself critically.

"I doubt I might be the better," it occurred to him, "if I brushed my hair, and smelt a little of perfume. Yes. I'll make a toilet. Where's the boy's bedroom, I wonder?"

He observed a second door in the sitting-room, and opened it at hazard. Fortune had befriended him, so far: he found himself in his young friend's bedchamber.

The toilet of Amelius, simple as it was, had its mysteries for Rufus. He was at a loss among the perfumes. They were all contained in a modest little dressing case, without labels of any sort to describe the contents of the pots and bottles. He examined them one after another, and stopped at some recently invented French shaving-cream. "It smells lovely," he said, assuming it to be some rare pomatum. "Just what I want, it seems, for my head." He rubbed the shaving cream into his bristly iron-gray hair, until his arms ached. When he had next sprinkled his handkerchief and himself profusely, first with rose water, and then (to make quite sure) with eau-de-cologne used as a climax, he felt that he was in a position to appeal agreeably to the senses of the softer sex. In five minutes more, he was on his way to Mr. Farnaby's private residence.

CHAPTER 2

The rain that had begun with the morning still poured on steadily in the afternoon. After one look out of the window, Regina decided on passing the rest of the day luxuriously, in the company of a novel, by her own fireside. With her feet on the tender, and her head on the soft cushion of her favourite easy-chair, she opened the book. Having read the first chapter and part of the second, she was just lazily turning over the leaves in search of a love scene, when her languid interest in the novel was suddenly diverted to an incident in real life. The sitting-room door was gently opened, and her maid appeared in a state of modest confusion.

"If you please, miss, here's a strange gentleman who comes from Mr. Goldenheart. He wishes particularly to say—"

She paused, and looked behind her. A faint and curious smell of mingled soap and scent entered the room, followed closely by a tall, calm, shabbily-dressed man, who laid a wiry yellow hand on the maid's shoulder, and stopped her effectually before she could say a word more.

"Don't you think of troubling yourself to git through with it, my dear; I'm here, and I'll finish for you." Addressing the maid in these encouraging terms, the stranger advanced to Regina, and actually attempted to shake hands with her! Regina rose—and looked at him. It was a look that ought to have daunted the boldest man living; it produced no sort of effect on *this* man. He still held out his hand; his lean face broadened with a pleasant smile. "My name is Rufus Dingwell," he said. "I come from Coolspring, Mass.; and Amelius is my introduction to yourself and family."

Regina silently acknowledged this information by a frigid bow, and addressed herself to the maid, waiting at the door: "Don't leave the room, Phoebe."

Rufus, inwardly wondering what Phoebe was wanted for, proceeded to express the cordial sentiments proper to the occasion. "I have heard about you, miss; and I take pleasure in making your acquaintance."

The unwritten laws of politeness obliged Regina to say something. "I have not heard Mr. Goldenheart mention your name," she remarked. "Are you an old friend of his?"

Rufus explained with genial alacrity. "We crossed the Pond together, miss. I like the boy; he's bright and spry; he refreshes me—he does. We go ahead with most things in my country; and friendship's one of them. How *do* you find yourself? Won't you shake hands?" He took her hand, without waiting to be repelled this time, and shook it with the heartiest good-will.

Regina shuddered faintly: she summoned assistance in case of further familiarity. "Phoebe, tell my aunt."

Rufus added a message on his own account. "And say this, my dear. I sincerely desire to make the acquaintance of Miss Regina's aunt, and any other members of the family circle."

Phoebe left the room, smiling. Such an amusing visitor as this was a rare person in Mr. Farnaby's house. Rufus looked after her, with unconcealed approval. The maid appeared to be more to his taste than the mistress. "Well, that's a pretty creature, I do declare," he said to Regina. "Reminds me of our American girls—slim in the waist, and carries her head nicely. How old may she be, now?"

Regina expressed her opinion of this familiar question by pointing, with silent dignity, to a chair.

"Thank you, miss; not that one," said Rufus. "You see, I'm long in the legs, and if I once got down as low as that, I reckon I should have to restore the balance by putting my feet up on the grate; and that's not manners in Great Britain—and quite right too."

He picked out the highest chair he could find, and admired the workmanship as he drew it up to the fireplace. "Most sumptuous and elegant," he said. "The style of the Re_nay_sance, as they call it." Regina observed with dismay that he had not got his hat in his hand like other visitors. He had left it no doubt in the hall; he looked as if he had dropped in to spend the day, and stay to dinner.

"Well, miss, I've seen your photograph," he resumed; "and I don't much approve of it, now I see You. My sentiments are not altogether favourable to that art. I delivered a lecture on photographic portraiture at Coolspring; and I described it briefly as justice without mercy. The audience took the idea; they larfed, they did. Larfin' reminds me of Amelius. Do you object to his being a Christian Socialist, miss?"

The young lady's look, when she answered the question, was not lost on Rufus. He registered it, mentally, in case of need. "Amelius will soon get over all that nonsense," she said, "when he has been a little longer in London."

"Possible," Rufus admitted. "The boy is fond of you. Yes: he loves you. I have noticed him, and I can certify to that. I may also remark that he wants a deal of love in return. No doubt, miss, you have observed that circumstance yourself?"

Regina resented this last inquiry as an outrage on propriety. "What next will he say?" she thought to herself. "I must put this presuming man in his proper place." She darted another annihilating look at him, as she spoke in her turn. "May I ask, Mr.—Mr.——?"

"Dingwell," said Rufus, prompting her.

"May I ask, Mr. Dingwell, if you have favoured me by calling here at the request of Mr. Goldenheart?"

Genial and simple-minded as he was, eagerly as he desired to appreciate at her full value the young lady who was one day to be the wife of Amelius, Rufus felt the tone in which those words were spoken. It was not easy to stimulate his modest sense of what was fairly due to him into asserting itself, but the cold distrust, the deliberate distance of Regina's manner, exhausted the long-suffering indulgence of this singularly patient man. "The Lord, in his mercy, preserve Amelius from marrying You," he thought, as he rose from his chair, and advanced with a certain simple dignity to take leave of her.

"It did not occur to me, miss, to pay my respects to you, till Amelius and I had parted company," he said. "Please to excuse me. I should have been welcome, in my country, with no better introduction than being (as I may say) his friend and well-wisher. If I have made a mistake—"

He stopped. Regina had suddenly changed colour. Instead of looking at him, she was looking over his shoulder, apparently at something behind him. He turned to see what it was. A lady, short and stout, with strange wild sorrowful eyes, had noiselessly entered the room while he was speaking: she was waiting, as it seemed, until he had finished what he had to say. When they confronted each other, she moved to meet him, with a firm heavy step, and with her hand held out in token of welcome.

"You may feel equally sure, sir, of a friendly reception here," she said, in her steady self-possessed way. "I am this young lady's aunt; and I am glad to see the friend of Amelius in my house." Before Rufus could answer, she turned to Regina. "I waited," she went on, "to give you an opportunity of explaining yourself to this gentleman. I am afraid he has mistaken your coldness of manner for intentional rudeness."

The colour rushed back into Regina's face—she vibrated for a moment between anger and tears. But the better nature in her broke its way through the constitutional shyness and restraint which habitually kept it down. "I meant no harm, sir," she said, raising her large beautiful eyes submissively to Rufus; "I am not used to receiving strangers. And you did ask me some very strange questions," she added, with a sudden burst of self-assertion. "Strangers are not in the habit of saying such things in England." She looked at Mrs. Farnaby, listening with impenetrable composure, and stopped in confusion. Her aunt would not scruple to speak to the stranger about Amelius in her presence—there was no knowing what she might not have to endure. She turned again to Rufus. "Excuse me," she said, "if I leave you with my aunt—I have an engagement." With that trivial apology, she made her escape from the room.

"She has no engagement," Mrs. Farnaby briefly remarked as the door closed. "Sit down, sir."

For once, even Rufus was not as his ease. "I can hit it off, ma'am, with most people," he said. "I wonder what I've done to offend your niece?"

"My niece (with many good qualities) is a narrow-minded young woman," Mrs. Farnaby explained. "You are not like the men she is accustomed to see. She doesn't understand you—you are not a commonplace gentleman. For instance," Mrs. Farnaby continued, with the matter-of-fact gravity of a woman innately inaccessible to a sense of humour, "you have got something strange on your hair. It seems to be melting, and it smells like soap. No: it's no use taking out your handkerchief—your handkerchief won't mop it up. I'll get a towel." She opened an inner door, which disclosed a little passage, and a bath-room beyond it. "I'm the strongest person in the house," she resumed, returning with a towel in her hand, as gravely as ever. "Sit still, and don't make apologies. If any of us can rub you dry, I'm the woman." She set to work with the towel, as if she had been Rufus's mother, making him presentable in the days of his boyhood. Giddy under the violence of the rubbing, staggered by the contrast between the cold reception accorded to him by the niece, and the more than friendly welcome offered by the aunt, Rufus submitted to circumstances in docile and silent bewilderment. "There; you'll do till you get home—nobody can laugh at you now," Mrs. Farnaby announced. "You're an absent-minded man, I suppose? You wanted to wash your head, and you forgot the warm water and the towel. Was that how it happened, sir?"

"I thank you with all my heart, ma'am; I took it for pomatum," Rufus answered. "Would you object to shaking hands again? This cordial welcome of yours reminds me, I do assure you, of home. Since I left New England, I've never met with the like of you. I do suppose now it was my hair that set Miss Regina's back up? I'm not quite easy in my mind, ma'am, about your niece. I'm sort of feared of what she may say of me to Amelius. I meant no harm, Lord knows."

The secret of Mrs. Farnaby's extraordinary alacrity in the use of the towel began slowly to show itself now. The tone of her American guest had already become the friendly and familiar tone which it had been her object to establish. With a little management, he might be made an invaluable ally in the great work of hindering the marriage of Amelius.

"You are very fond of your young friend?" she began quietly.

"That is so, ma'am."

"And he has told you that he has taken a liking to my niece?"

"And shown me her likeness," Rufus added.

"And shown you her likeness. And you thought you would come here, and see for yourself what sort of girl she was?"

"Naturally," Rufus admitted.

Mrs. Farnaby revealed, without further hesitation, the object that she had in view. "Amelius is little more than a lad, still," she said. "He has got all his life before him. It would be a sad thing, if he married a girl who didn't make him happy." She turned in her chair, and pointed to the door by which Regina had left them. "Between ourselves," she resumed, dropping her voice to a whisper, "do you believe my niece will make him happy?"

Rufus hesitated.

"I'm above family prejudices," Mrs. Farnaby proceeded. "You needn't be afraid of offending me. Speak out."

Rufus would have spoken out to any other woman in the universe. *This* woman had preserved him from ridicule—*this* woman had rubbed his head dry. He prevaricated.

"I don't suppose I understand the ladies in this country," he said.

But Mrs. Farnaby was not to be trifled with. "If Amelius was your son, and if he asked you to consent to his marriage with my niece," she rejoined, "would you say Yes?"

This was too much for Rufus. "Not if he went down on both his knees to ask me," he answered.

Mrs. Farnaby was satisfied at last, and owned it without reserve. "My own opinion," she said, "exactly expressed! don't be surprised. Didn't I tell you I had no family prejudices? Do you know if he has spoken to my husband, yet?"

Rufus looked at his watch. "I reckon he's just about done it by this time."

Mrs. Farnaby paused, and reflected for a moment. She had already attempted to prejudice her husband against Amelius, and had received an answer which Mr. Farnaby considered to be final. "Mr. Goldenheart honours us if he seeks our alliance; he is the representative of an old English family." Under these circumstances, it was quite possible that the proposals of Amelius had been accepted. Mrs. Farnaby was not the less determined that the marriage should never take place, and not the less eager to secure the assistance of her new ally. "When will Amelius tell you about it?" she asked.

"When I go back to his lodgings, ma'am."

"Go back at once—and bear this in mind as you go. If you can find out any likely way of parting these two young people (in their own best interests), depend on one thing—if I can help you, I will. I'm as fond of Amelius as you are. Ask him if I haven't done my best to keep him away from my niece. Ask him if I haven't expressed my opinion, that she's not the right wife for him. Come and see me again as soon as you like. I'm fond of Americans. Good morning."

Rufus attempted to express his sense of gratitude, in his own briefly eloquent way. He was not allowed a hearing. With one and the same action, Mrs. Farnaby patted him on the shoulder, and pushed him out of the room.

"If that woman was an American citizen," Rufus reflected, on his way through the streets, "she'd be the first female President of the United States!" His admiration of Mrs. Farnaby's energy and resolution, expressed in these strong terms, acknowledged but one limit. Highly as he approved of her, there was nevertheless an unfathomable something in the woman's eyes that disturbed and daunted him.

CHAPTER 3

Rufus found his friend at the lodgings, prostrate on the sofa, smoking furiously. Before a word had passed between them, it was plain to the New Englander that something had gone wrong.

"Well," he asked; "and what does Farnaby say?"

"Damn Farnaby!"

Rufus was secretly conscious of an immense sense of relief. "I call that a stiff way of putting it," he quietly remarked; "but the meaning's clear. Farnaby has said No."

Amelius jumped off the sofa, and planted himself defiantly on the hearthrug.

"You're wrong for once," he said, with a bitter laugh. "The exasperating part of it is that Farnaby has said neither Yes nor No. The oily-whiskered brute—you haven't seen him yet, have you?—began by saying Yes. 'A man like me, the heir of a fine old English family, honoured him by making proposals; he could wish no more brilliant prospect for his dear adopted child. She would fill the high position that was offered to her, and fill it worthily.' That was the fawning way in which he talked to me at first! He squeezed my hand in his horrid cold shiny paw till, I give you my word of honour, I felt as if I was going to be sick. Wait a little; you haven't heard the worst of it yet. He soon altered his tone—it began with his asking me, if I had 'considered the question of settlements'. I didn't know what he meant. He had to put it in plain English; he wanted to hear what my property was. 'Oh, that's soon settled,' I said. 'I've got five hundred a year; and Regina is welcome to every farthing of it.' He fell back in his chair as if I had shot him; he turned—it was worse than pale, he positively turned green. At first he wouldn't believe me; he declared I must be joking. I set him right about that immediately. His next change was a proud impudence. 'Have you not observed, sir, in what style Regina is accustomed to live in my house? Five hundred a year? Good heavens! With strict economy, five hundred a year might pay her milliner's bill and the keep of her horse and carriage. Who is to pay for everything else—the establishment, the dinner-parties and balls, the tour abroad, the children, the nurses, the doctor? I tell you this, Mr. Goldenheart, I'm willing to make a sacrifice to you, as a born gentleman, which I would certainly not consent to in the case of any self-made man. Enlarge your income, sir, to no more than four times five hundred pounds, and I guarantee a yearly allowance to Regina of half as much again, besides the fortune which she will inherit at my death. That will make your income three thousand a year to start with. I know something of domestic expenses, and I tell you positively, you can't do it on a farthing less.' That was his language, Rufus. The insolence of his tone I can't attempt to describe. If I hadn't thought of Regina, I should have behaved in a manner unworthy of a Christian—I believe I should have taken my walking-cane, and given him a sound thrashing."

Rufus neither expressed surprise nor offered advice. He was lost in meditation on the wealth of Mr. Farnaby. "A stationer's business seems to eventuate in a lively profit, in this country," he said.

"A stationer's business?" Amelius repeated disdainfully. "Farnaby has half a dozen irons in the fire besides that. He's got a newspaper, and a patent medicine, and a new bank, and I don't know what else. One of his own friends said to me, 'Nobody knows whether Farnaby is rich or poor; he is going to do one of two things—he is going to die worth millions, or to die bankrupt.' Oh, if I can only live to see the day when Socialism will put that sort of man in his right place!"

"Try a republic, on our model, first," said Rufus. "When Farnaby talks of the style his young woman is accustomed to live in, what does he mean?"

"He means," Amelius answered smartly, "a carriage to drive out in, champagne on the table, and a footman to answer the door."

"Farnaby's ideas, sir, have crossed the water and landed in New York," Rufus remarked. "Well, and what did you say to him, on your side?"

"I gave it to him, I can tell you! 'That's all ostentation,' I said. 'Why can't Regina and I begin life modestly? What do we want with a carriage to drive out in, and champagne on the table, and a footman to answer the door? We want to love each other and be happy. There are thousands of as good gentlemen as I am, in England, with wives and families, who would ask for nothing better than an income of five hundred a year. The fact is, Mr. Farnaby, you're positively saturated with the love of money. Get your New Testament and read what Christ says of rich people.' What do you think he did, when I put it in that unanswerable way? He held up his hand, and looked horrified. 'I can't allow profanity in my office,' says he. 'I have my New Testament read to me in church, sir, every Sunday.' That's the sort of Christian, Rufus, who is the average product of modern times! He was as obstinate as a mule; he wouldn't give way a single inch. His adopted daughter, he said, was accustomed to live in a certain style. In that same style she should live when she was married, so long as he had a voice in the matter. Of course, if she chose to set his wishes and feelings at defiance, in return for all that he had done for her, she was old enough to take her own way. In that case, he would tell me as plainly as he meant to tell her, that she must not look to a single farthing of his money to help her, and not expect to find her name down in his will. He felt the honour of a family alliance with me as sincerely as ever. But he must abide by the conditions that he had stated. On those terms, he would be proud to give me the hand of Regina at the altar, and proud to feel that he had done his duty by his adopted child. I let him go on till he had run himself out—and then I asked quietly, if he could tell me the way to increase my income to two thousand a year. How do you think he answered me?"

"Perhaps he offered to utilise your capital in his business," Rufus guessed.

"Not he! He considered business quite beneath me; my duty to myself, as a gentleman, was to adopt a profession. On reflection, it turned out that there was but one likely profession to try, in my case—the Law. I might be called to the Bar, and (with luck) I might get remunerative work to do, in eight or ten years' time. That, I declare to you, was the prospect he set before me, if I chose to take his advice. I asked if he was joking. Certainly not! I was only one-and-twenty years old (he reminded me); I had plenty of time to spare—I should still marry young if I married at thirty. I took up my hat, and gave him a bit of my mind at parting. 'If you really mean anything,' I said, 'you mean that Regina is to pine and fade and be a middle-aged woman, and that I am to resist the temptations that beset a young man in London, and lead the life of a monk for the next ten years—and all for what? For a carriage to ride out in, champagne on the table, and a footman to answer the door! Keep your money, Mr. Farnaby; Regina and I will do without it.'—What are you laughing at? I don't think you could have put it more strongly yourself."

Rufus suddenly recovered his gravity. "I tell you this, Amelius," he replied; "you afford (as we say in my country) meaty fruit for reflection—you do."

"What do you mean by that?"

"Well, I reckon you remember when we were aboard the boat. You gave us a narrative of what happened in that Community of yours, which I can truly cha_rac_terise as a combination of native eloquence and chastening good sense. I put the question to myself, sir, what has become of that well-informed and discreet young Christian, now he has changed the sphere to England and mixed with the Farnabys? It's not to be denied that I see him before me in the flesh when I look across the table here; but it's equally true that I miss him altogether, in the spirit."

Amelius sat down again on the sofa. "In plain words," he said, "you think I have behaved like a fool in this matter?"

Rufus crossed his long legs, and nodded his head in silent approval. Instead of taking offence, Amelius considered a little.

"It didn't strike me before," he said. "But, now you mention it, I can understand that I appear to be a simple sort of fellow in what is called Society here; and the reason, I suspect, is that it's not the society in which I have been accustomed to mix. The Farnabys are new to me, Rufus. When it comes to a question of my life at Tadmor, of what I saw and learnt and felt in the Community—then, I can think and speak like a reasonable being, because I am thinking and speaking of what I know thoroughly well. Hang it, make some allowance for the difference of circumstances! Besides, I'm in love, and that alters a man—and, I have heard some people say, not always for the better. Anyhow, I've done it with Farnaby, and it can't be undone. There will be no peace for me now, till I have spoken to Regina. I have read the note you left for me. Did you see her, when you called at the house?"

106

The quiet tone in which the question was put surprised Rufus. He had fully expected, after Regina's reception of him, to be called to account for the liberty that he had taken. Amelius was too completely absorbed by his present anxieties to consider trivial questions of etiquette. Hearing that Rufus had seen Regina, he never even asked for his friend's opinion of her. His mind was full of the obstacles that might be interposed to his seeing her again.

"Farnaby is sure, after what has passed between us, to keep her out of my way if he can," Amelius said. "And Mrs. Farnaby, to my certain knowledge, will help him. They don't suspect *you*. Couldn't you call again—you're old enough to be her father—and make some excuse to take her out with you for a walk?"

The answer of Rufus to this was Roman in its brevity. He pointed to the window, and said, "Look at the rain."

"Then I must try her maid once more," said Amelius, resignedly. He took his hat and umbrella. "Don't leave me, old fellow," he resumed as he opened the door. "This is the turning-point of my life. I'm sorely in need of a friend."

"Do you think she will marry you against the will of her uncle and aunt?" Rufus asked.

"I am certain of it," Amelius answered. With that he left the room.

Rufus looked after him sadly. Sympathy and sorrow were expressed in every line of his rugged face. "My poor boy! how will he bear it, if she says No? What will become of him, if she says Yes?" He rubbed his hand irritably across his forehead, like a man whose own thoughts were repellent to him. In a moment more, he plunged into his pockets, and drew out again the letters introducing him to the secretaries of public institutions. "If there's salvation for Amelius," he said, "I reckon I shall find it here."

CHAPTER 4

The medium of correspondence between Amelius and Regina's maid was an old woman who kept a shop for the sale of newspapers and periodicals, in a by-street not far from Mr. Farnaby's house. From this place his letters were delivered to the maid, under cover of the morning newspapers—and here he found the answers waiting for him later in the day. "If Rufus could only have taken her out for a walk, I might have seen Regina this afternoon," thought Amelius. "As it is, I may have to wait till to-morrow, or later still. And then, there's the sovereign to Phoebe." He sighed as he thought of the fee. Sovereigns were becoming scarce in our young Socialist's purse.

Arriving in sight of the newsvendor's shop, Amelius noticed a man leaving it, who walked away towards the farther end of the street. When he entered the shop himself a minute afterwards, the woman took up a letter from the counter. "A young man has just left this for you," she said.

Amelius recognised the maid's handwriting on the address. The man whom he had seen leaving the shop was Phoebe's messenger.

He opened the letter. Her mistress, Phoebe explained, was too much flurried to be able to write. The master had astonished the whole household by appearing among them at least three hours before the time at which he was accustomed to leave his place of business. He had found "Mrs. Ormond" (otherwise Regina's friend and correspondent, Cecilia) paying a visit to his niece, and had asked to speak with her in private, before she took leave. The result was an invitation to Regina, from Mrs. Ormond, to stay for a little while at her house in the neighbourhood of Harrow. The ladies were to leave London together, in Mrs. Ormond's carriage, that afternoon. Under stress of strong persuasion, on the part of her uncle and aunt as well as her friend, Regina had ended in giving way. But she had not forgotten the interests of Amelius. She was willing to see him privately on the next day, provided he left London by the train which reached Harrow soon after eleven in the forenoon. If it happened to rain, then he must put off his journey until the first fine day, arriving in any case at the same hour. The place at which he was to wait was described to him; and with these instructions the letter ended.

The rapidity with which Mr. Farnaby had carried out his resolution to separate the lovers placed the weakness of Regina's character before Amelius in a new and startling light. Why had she not stood on her privileges, as a woman who had arrived at years of discretion, and refused to leave London until she had first heard what her lover had to say? Amelius had left his American friend, feeling sure that Regina's decision would be in his favour, when she was called upon to choose between the man who was ready to marry her, and the man who was nothing but her uncle by courtesy. For the first time, he now felt that his own confident anticipations might, by bare possibility, deceive him. He returned to his lodgings, in such a state of depression, that compassionate Rufus insisted on taking him out to dinner, and hurried him off afterwards to the play. Thoroughly prostrated, Amelius submitted to the genial influence of his friend. He had not even energy enough to feel surprised when Rufus stopped, on their way to the tavern, at a dingy building adorned with a Grecian portico, and left a letter and a card in charge of a servant at the side-door.

The next day, by a happy interposition of Fortune, proved to be a day without rain. Amelius followed his instructions to the letter. A little watery sunshine showed itself as he left the station at Harrow. His mind was still in such a state of doubt and disturbance that it drew from superstition a faint encouragement to hope. He hailed the feeble November sunlight as a good omen.

Mr. and Mrs. Ormond's place of residence stood alone, surrounded by its own grounds. A wooden fence separated the property, on one side, from a muddy little by-road, leading to a neighbouring farm. At a wicket-gate in this fence, giving admission to a shrubbery situated at some distance from the house, Amelius now waited for the appearance of the maid.

After a delay of a few minutes only, the faithful Phoebe approached the gate with a key in her hand. "Where is she?" Amelius asked, as the girl opened the gate for him.

"Waiting for you in the shrubbery. Stop, sir; I have something to say to you first."

Amelius took out his purse, and produced the fee. Even he had observed that Phoebe was perhaps a little too eager to get her money!

"Thank you, sir. Please to look at your watch. You mustn't be with Miss Regina a moment longer than a quarter of an hour."

"Why not?"

"This is the time, sir, when Mrs. Ormond is engaged every day with her cook and housekeeper. In a quarter of an hour the orders will be given—and Mrs. Ormond will join Miss Regina for a walk in the grounds. You will be the ruin of me, sir, if she finds you here." With that warning, the maid led the way along the winding paths of the shrubbery.

"I must thank you for your letter, Phoebe," said Amelius, as he followed her. "By-the-by, who was your messenger?"

Phoebe's answer was no answer at all. "Only a young man, sir," she said.

"In plain words, your sweetheart, I suppose?"

Phoebe's expressive silence was her only reply. She turned a corner, and pointed to her mistress standing alone before the entrance of a damp and deserted summer-house.

Regina put her handkerchief to her eyes, when the maid had discreetly retired. "Oh," she said softly, "I am afraid this is very wrong."

Amelius removed the handkerchief by the exercise of a little gentle force, and administered comfort under the form of a kiss. Having opened the proceedings in this way, he put his first question, "Why did you leave London?"

"How could I help it!" said Regina, feebly. "They were all against me. What else could I do?"

It occurred to Amelius that she might, at her age, have asserted a will of her own. He kept his idea, however, to himself, and, giving her his arm, led her slowly along the path of the shrubbery. "You have heard, I suppose, what Mr. Farnaby expects of me?" he said.

"Yes, dear."

"*I* call it worse than mercenary—I call it downright brutal."

"Oh, Amelius, don't talk so!"

Amelius came suddenly to a standstill. "Does that mean you agree with him?" he asked.

"Don't be angry with me, dear. I only meant there was some excuse for him."

"What excuse?"

"Well, you see, he has a high idea of your family, and he thought you were rich people. And—I know you didn't mean it, Amelius—but, still, you did disappoint him."

Amelius dropped her arm. This mildly-persistent defence of Mr. Farnaby exasperated him.

"Perhaps I have disappointed *you?*" he said.

"Oh, no, no! Oh, how cruel you are!" The ready tears showed themselves again in her magnificent eyes—gentle considerate tears that raised no storm in her bosom, and produced no unbecoming results in her face. "Don't be hard on me!" she said, appealing to him helplessly, like a charming overgrown child.

Some men might have still resisted her; but Amelius was not one of them. He took her hand, and pressed it tenderly.

110

"Regina," he said, "do you love me?"

"You know I do!"

He put his arm round her waist, he concentrated the passion that was in him into a look, and poured the look into her eyes. "Do you love me as dearly as I love you?" he whispered.

She felt it with all the little passion that was in her. After a moment of hesitation, she put one arm timidly round his neck, and, bending her grand head, laid it on his bosom. Her finely-rounded, supple, muscular figure trembled, as if she had been the most fragile woman living. "Dear Amelius!" she murmured inaudibly. He tried to speak to her—his voice failed him. She had, in perfect innocence, fired his young blood. He drew her closer and closer to him: he lifted her head, with a masterful resolution which she was not able to resist, and pressed his kisses in hot and breathless succession on her lips. His vehemence frightened her. She tore herself out of his arms with a sudden exertion of strength that took him completely by surprise. "I didn't think you would have been rude to me!" With that mild reproach, she turned away, and took the path which led from the shrubbery to the house. Amelius followed her, entreating that she would accept his excuses and grant him a few minutes more. He modestly laid all the blame on her beauty—lamented that he had not resolution enough to resist the charm of it. When did that commonplace compliment ever fail to produce its effect? Regina smiled with the weakly complacent good-nature, which was only saved from being contemptible by its association with her personal attractions. "Will you promise to behave?" she stipulated. And Amelius, not very eagerly, promised.

"Shall we go into the summer-house?" he suggested.

"It's very damp at this time of year," Regina answered, with placid good sense. "Perhaps we might catch cold—we had better walk about."

They walked accordingly. "I wanted to speak to you about our marriage," Amelius resumed.

She sighed softly. "We have some time to wait," she said, "before we can think of that."

He passed this reply over without notice. "You know," he went on, "that I have an income of five hundred a year?"

"Yes, dear."

"There are hundreds of thousands of respectable artisans, Regina, (with large families), who live comfortably on less than half my income."

"Do they, dear?"

"And many gentlemen are not better off. Curates, for instance. Do you see what I am coming to, my darling?"

"No, dear."

"Could you live with me in a cottage in the country, with a nice garden, and one little maid to wait on us, and two or three new dresses in a year?"

Regina lifted her fine eyes in sober ecstasy to the sky. "It sounds very tempting," she remarked, in the sweetest tones of her voice.

"And it could all be done," Amelius proceeded, "on five hundred a year."

"Could it, dear?"

"I have calculated it—allowing the necessary margin—and I am sure of what I say. And I have done something else; I have asked about the Marriage License. I can easily find lodgings in the neighbourhood. We might be married at Harrow in a fortnight."

Regina started: her eyes opened widely, and rested on Amelius with an expression of incredulous wonder. "Married in a fortnight?" she repeated. "What would my uncle and aunt say?"

"My angel, our happiness doesn't depend on your uncle and aunt—our happiness depends on ourselves. Nobody has any power to control us. I am a man, and you are a woman; and we have a right to be married whenever we like." Amelius pronounced this last oracular sentence with his head held high, and a pleasant inner persuasion of the convincing manner in which he had stated his case.

"Without my uncle to give me away!" Regina exclaimed. "Without my aunt! With no bridesmaids, and no friends, and no wedding-breakfast! Oh, Amelius, what *can* you be thinking of?" She drew back a step, and looked at him in helpless consternation.

For the moment, and the moment only, Amelius lost all patience with her. "If you really loved me," he said bitterly, "you wouldn't think of the bridesmaids and the breakfast!" Regina had her answer ready in her pocket—she took out her handkerchief. Before she could lift it to her eyes, Amelius recovered himself. "No, no," he said, "I didn't mean that—I am sure you love me—take my arm again. Do you know, Regina, I doubt whether your uncle has told you everything that passed between us. Are you really aware of the hard terms that he insists on? He expects me to increase my five hundred a year to two thousand, before he will sanction our marriage."

112

"Yes, dear, he told me that."

"I have as much chance of earning fifteen hundred a year, Regina, as I have of being made King of England. Did he tell you *that?*"

"He doesn't agree with you, dear—he thinks you might earn it (with your abilities) in ten years."

This time it was the turn of Amelius to look at Regina in helpless consternation. "Ten years?" he repeated. "Do you coolly contemplate waiting ten years before we are married? Good heavens! is it possible that you are thinking of the money? that *you* can't live without carriages and footmen, and ostentation and grandeur—?"

He stopped. For once, even Regina showed that she had spirit enough to be angry. "You ought to be ashamed of yourself to speak to me in that way!" she broke out indignantly. "If you have no better opinion of me than that, I won't marry you at all—no, not if you had fifty thousand a year, sir, to-morrow! Am I to have no sense of duty to my uncle—to the good man who has been a second father to me? Do you think I am ungrateful enough to set his wishes at defiance? Oh yes, I know you don't like him! I know that a great many people don't like him. That doesn't make any difference to Me! But for dear uncle Farnaby, I might have gone to the workhouse, I might have been a starving needlewoman, a poor persecuted maid-of-all-work. Am I to forget that, because you have no patience, and only think of yourself? Oh, I wish I had never met with you! I wish I had never been fool enough to be as fond of you as I am!" With that confession, she turned her back on him, and took refuge in her handkerchief once more.

Amelius stood looking at her in silent despair. After the tone in which she had spoken of her obligations to her uncle, it was useless to anticipate any satisfactory result from the exertion of his influence over Regina. Recalling what he had seen and heard, in Mrs. Farnaby's room, Amelius could not doubt that the motive of pacifying his wife was the motive which had first led Farnaby to receive Regina into his house. Was it unreasonable or unjust to infer, that the orphan child must have been mainly indebted to Mrs. Farnaby's sense of duty to the memory of her sister for the parental protection afforded to her, from that time forth? It would have been useless, and worse than useless, to place before Regina such considerations as these. Her exaggerated idea of the gratitude that she owed to her uncle was beyond the limited reach of reason. Nothing was to be gained by opposition; and no sensible course was left but to say some peace-making words and submit.

"I beg your pardon, Regina, if I have offended you. You have sadly disappointed me. I haven't deliberately misjudged you; I can say no more."

She turned round quickly, and looked at him. There was an ominous change to resignation in his voice, there was a dogged submission in his manner, that alarmed her. She had never yet seen him under the perilously-patient aspect in which he now presented himself, after his apology had been made.

113

"I forgive you, Amelius, with all my heart," she said—and timidly held out her hand.

He took it, raised it silently to his lips, and dropped it again.

She suddenly turned pale. All the love that she had in her to give to a man, she had given to Amelius. Her heart sank; she asked herself, in blank terror, if she had lost him.

"I am afraid it is *I* who have offended *you,"* she said. "Don't be angry with me, Amelius! don't make me more unhappy than I am!"

"I am not in the least angry," he answered, still in the quiet subdued way that terrified her. "You can't expect me, Regina, to contemplate a ten years' engagement cheerfully."

She took his hand, and held it in both her own hands—held it, as if his love for her was there and she was determined not to let it go.

"If you will only leave it to me," she pleaded, "the engagement shan't be so long as that. Try my uncle with a little kindness and respect, Amelius, instead of saying hard words to him. Or let *me* try him, if you are too proud to give way. May I say that you had no intention of offending him, and that you are willing to leave the future to me?"

"Certainly," said Amelius, "if you think it will be of the slightest use." His tone added plainly, "I don't believe in your uncle, mind, as you do."

She still persisted. "It will be of the greatest use," she went on. "He will let me go home again, and he will not object to your coming to see me. He doesn't like to be despised and set at defiance—who does? Be patient, Amelius; and I will persuade him to expect less money from you—only what you may earn, dear, with your talents, long before ten years have passed." She waited for a word of reply which might show that she had encouraged him a little. He only smiled. "You talk of loving me," she said, drawing back from him with a look of reproach; "and you don't even believe what I say to you." She stopped, and looked behind her with a faint cry of alarm. Hurried footsteps were audible on the other side of the evergreens that screened them. Amelius stepped back to a turn in the path, and discovered Phoebe.

"Don't stay a moment longer, sir!" cried the girl. "I've been to the house—and Mrs. Ormond isn't there—and nobody knows where she is. Get out by the gate, sir, while you have the chance."

Amelius returned to Regina. "I mustn't get the girl into a scrape," he said. "You know where to write to me. Good-bye."

Regina made a sign to the maid to retire. Amelius had never taken leave of her as he was taking leave of her now. She forgot the fervent embrace and the daring kisses— she was desperate at the bare idea of losing him. "Oh, Amelius, don't doubt that I love you! Say you believe I love you! Kiss me before you go!"

He kissed her—but, ah, not as he had kissed her before. He said the words she wanted him to say—but only to please her, not with all his heart. She let him go; reproaches would be wasted at that moment.

Phoebe found her pale and immovable, rooted to the spot on which they had parted. "Dear, dear me, miss, what's gone wrong?"

And her mistress answered wildly, in words that had never before passed her placid lips, "O Phoebe, I wish I was dead!"

Such was the impression left on the mind of Regina by the interview in the shrubbery.

The impression left on the mind of Amelius was stated in equally strong language, later in the day. His American friend asked innocently for news, and was answered in these terms:

"Find something to occupy my mind, Rufus, or I shall throw the whole thing over and go to the devil."

The wise man from New England was too wise to trouble Amelius with questions, under these circumstances. "Is that so?" was all he said. Then he put his hand in his pocket, and, producing a letter, laid it quietly on the table.

"For me?" Amelius asked.

"You wanted something to occupy your mind," the wily Rufus answered. "There 'tis."

Amelius read the letter. It was dated, "Hampden Institution." The secretary invited Amelius, in highly complimentary terms, to lecture, in the hall of the Institution, on Christian Socialism as taught and practised in the Community at Tadmor. He was offered two-thirds of the profits derived from the sale of places, and was left free to appoint his own evening (at a week's notice) and to issue his own advertisements. Minor details were reserved to be discussed with the secretary, when the lecturer had consented to the arrangement proposed to him.

Having finished the letter, Amelius looked at his friend. "This is your doing," he said.

Rufus admitted it, with his customary candour. He had a letter of introduction to the secretary, and he had called by appointment that morning. The Institution wanted something new to attract the members and the public. Having no present intention of lecturing himself, he had thought of Amelius, and had spoken his thought. "I mentioned," Rufus added slyly, "that I didn't reckon you would mount the platform. But he's a sanguine creature, that secretary—and he said he'd try."

"Why should I say No?" Amelius asked, a little irritably. "The secretary pays me a compliment, and offers me an opportunity of spreading our principles. Perhaps," he added, more quietly, after a moment's reflection, "you thought I might not be equal to the occasion—and, in that case, I don't say you were wrong."

Rufus shook his head. "If you had passed your life in this decrepit little island," he replied, "I might have doubted you, likely enough. But Tadmor's situated in the United States. If they don't practise the boys in the art of orating, don't you tell me there's an American citizen with a voice in *that* society. Guess again, my son. You won't? Well, then, 'twas uncle Farnaby I had in my mind. I said to myself—not to the secretary—Amelius is bound to consider uncle Farnaby. Oh, my! what would uncle Farnaby say?"

The hot temper of Amelius took fire instantly. "What the devil do I care for Farnaby's opinions?" he burst out. "If there's a man in England who wants the principles of Christian Socialism beaten into his thick head, it's Farnaby. Are you going to see the secretary again?"

"I might look in," Rufus answered, "in the course of the evening."

"Tell him I'll give the lecture—with my compliments and thanks. If I can only succeed," pursued Amelius, hearing himself with the new idea, "I may make a name as a lecturer, and a name means money, and money means beating Farnaby with his own weapons. It's an opening for me, Rufus, at the crisis of my life."

"That is so," Rufus admitted. "I may as well look up the secretary."

"Why shouldn't I go with you?" Amelius suggested.

"Why not?" Rufus agreed.

They left the house together.

116

BOOK THE FIFTH

THE FATAL LECTURE

CHAPTER 1

Late that night Amelius sat alone in his room, making notes for the lecture which he had now formally engaged himself to deliver in a week's time.

Thanks to his American education (as Rufus had supposed), he had not been without practice in the art of public speaking. He had learnt to face his fellow-creatures in the act of oratory, and to hear the sound of his own voice in a silent assembly, without trembling from head to foot. English newspapers were regularly sent to Tadmor, and English politics were frequently discussed in the little parliament of the Community. The prospect of addressing a new audience, with their sympathies probably against him at the outset, had its terrors undoubtedly. But the more formidable consideration, to the mind of Amelius, was presented by the limits imposed on him in the matter of time. The lecture was to be succeeded (at the request of a clerical member of the Institution) by a public discussion; and the secretary's experience suggested that the lecturer would do well to reduce his address within the compass of an hour. "Socialism is a large subject to be squeezed into that small space," Amelius had objected. And the secretary sighed, and answered, "They won't listen any longer."

Making notes, from time to time, of the points on which it was most desirable to insist, and on the relative positions which they should occupy in his lecture, the memory of Amelius became more and more absorbed in recalling the scenes in which his early life had been passed. /

He laid down his pen, as the clock of the nearest church struck the first dark hour of the morning, and let his thoughts take him back again, without interruption or restraint, to the hills and vales of Tadmor. Once more the kind old Elder Brother taught him the noble lessons of Christianity as they came from the inspired Teacher's own lips; once more he took his turn of healthy work in the garden and the field; once more the voices of his companions joined with him in the evening songs, and the timid little figure of Mellicent stood at his side, content to hold the music-book and listen. How poor, how corrupt, did the life look that he was leading now, by comparison with the life that he had led in those earlier and happier days! How shamefully he had forgotten the simple precepts of Christian humility, Christian sympathy, and Christian self-restraint, in which his teachers had trusted as the safeguards that were to preserve him from the foul contact of the world! Within the last two days only, he had refused to make merciful allowance for the errors of a man, whose life had been wasted in the sordid struggle upward from poverty to wealth. And, worse yet, he had cruelly distressed the poor girl who loved him, at the prompting of those selfish passions which it was his first and foremost duty to restrain. The bare remembrance of it was unendurable to him, in his present frame of mind. With his customary impetuosity, he snatched up the pen, to make atonement before he went to rest that night. He wrote in few words to Mr. Farnaby, declaring that he regretted having spoken impatiently and contemptuously at the interview between them, and expressing the hope that their experience of each other, in the time to come, might perhaps lead to acceptable concessions on either side. His letter to Regina was written, it is needless to say, in warmer terms and at much greater length: it was the honest outpouring of his love and his penitence. When the letters were safe in their envelopes he was not satisfied, even yet. No matter what the hour might be, there was no ease of mind for Amelius, until he had actually posted his letters. He stole downstairs, and softly unbolted the door, and hurried away to the nearest letter-box. When he had let himself in again with his latch-key, his mind was relieved at last. "Now," he thought, as he lit his bed-room candle, "I can go to sleep!"

A visit from Rufus was the first event of the day.

The two set to work together to draw out the necessary advertisement of the lecture. It was well calculated to attract attention in certain quarters. The announcement addressed itself, in capital letters, to all honest people who were poor and discontented. "Come, and hear the remedy which Christian Socialism provides for your troubles, explained to you by a friend and a brother; and pay no more than sixpence for the place that you occupy." The necessary information as to time and place followed this appeal; including the offer of reserved seats at higher prices. By advice of the secretary, the advertisement was not sent to any journal having its circulation among the wealthier classes of society. It appeared prominently in one daily paper and in two weekly papers; the three possessing an aggregate sale of four hundred thousand copies. "Assume only five readers to each copy," cried sanguine Amelius, "and we appeal to an audience of two millions. What a magnificent publicity!"

There was one inevitable result of magnificent publicity which Amelius failed to consider. His advertisements were certain to bring people together, who might otherwise never have met in the great world of London, under one roof. All over England, Scotland, and Ireland, he invited unknown guests to pass the evening with him. In such circumstances, recognitions may take place between persons who have lost sight of each other for years; conversations may be held, which might otherwise never have been exchanged; and results may follow, for which the hero of the evening may be innocently responsible, because two or three among his audience happen to be sitting to hear him on the same bench. A man who opens his doors, and invites the public indiscriminately to come in, runs the risk of playing with inflammable materials, and can never be sure at what time or in what direction they may explode.

Rufus himself took the fair copies of the advertisement to the nearest agent. Amelius stayed at home to think over his lecture.

He was interrupted by the arrival of Mr. Farnaby's answer to his letter. The man of the oily whiskers wrote courteously and guardedly. He was evidently flattered and pleased by the advance that had been made to him; and he was quite willing "under the circumstances" to give the lovers opportunities of meeting at his house. At the same time, he limited the number of the opportunities. "Once a week, for the present, my dear sir. Regina will doubtless write to you, when she returns to London."

Regina wrote, by return of post. The next morning Amelius received a letter from her which enchanted him. She had never loved him as she loved him now; she longed to see him again; she had prevailed on Mrs. Ormond to let her shorten her visit, and to intercede for her with the authorities at home. They were to return together to London on the afternoon of the next day. Amelius would be sure to find her, if he arranged to call in time for five-o'clock tea.

Towards four o'clock on the next day, while Amelius was putting the finishing touches to his dress, he was informed that "a young person wished to see him." The visitor proved to be Phoebe, with her handkerchief to her eyes; indulging in grief, in humble imitation of her young mistress's gentle method of proceeding on similar occasions.

"Good God!" cried Amelius, "has anything happened to Regina?"

"No, sir," Phoebe murmured behind the handkerchief. "Miss Regina is at home, and well."

"Then what are you crying about?"

Phoebe forgot her mistress's gentle method. She answered, with an explosion of sobs, "I'm ruined, sir!"

"What do you mean by being ruined? Who's done it?"

"You've done it, sir!"

Amelius started. His relations with Phoebe had been purely and entirely of the pecuniary sort. She was a showy, pretty girl, with a smart little figure—but with some undeniably bad lines, which only observant physiognomists remarked, about her eyebrows and her mouth. Amelius was not a physiognomist; but he was in love with Regina, which at his age implied faithful love. It is only men over forty who can court the mistress, with reserves of admiration to spare for the maid.

"Sit down," said Amelius; "and tell me in two words what you mean."

Phoebe sat down, and dried her eyes. "I have been infamously treated, sir, by Mrs. Farnaby," she began—and stopped, overpowered by the bare remembrance of her wrongs. She was angry enough, at that moment, to be off her guard. The vindictive nature that was in the girl found its way outward, and showed itself in her face. Amelius perceived the change, and began to doubt whether Phoebe was quite worthy of the place which she had hitherto held in his estimation.

"Surely there must be some mistake," he said. "What opportunity has Mrs. Farnaby had of ill-treating you? You have only just got back to London."

"I beg your pardon, sir, we got back sooner than we expected. Mrs. Ormond had business in town: and she left Miss Regina at her own door, nearly two hours since."

"Well?"

"Well, sir, I had hardly taken off my bonnet and shawl, when I was sent for by Mrs. Farnaby. 'Have you unpacked your box yet?' says she. I told her I hadn't had time to do so. 'You needn't trouble yourself to unpack,' says she. 'You are no longer in Miss Regina's service. There are your wages—with a month's wages besides, in place of the customary warning.' I'm only a poor girl, sir, but I up and spoke to her as plain as she spoke to me. 'I want to know,' I says, 'why I am sent away in this uncivil manner?' I couldn't possibly repeat what she said. My blood boils when I think of it," Phoebe declared, with melodramatic vehemence. "Somebody has found us out, sir. Somebody has told Mrs. Farnaby of your private meeting with Miss Regina in the shrubbery, and the money you kindly gave me. I believe Mrs. Ormond is at the bottom of it; you remember nobody knew where she was, when I thought she was in the house speaking to the cook. That's guess-work, I allow, so far. What is certain is, that I have been spoken to as if I was the lowest creature that walks the streets. Mrs. Farnaby refuses to give me a character, sir. She actually said she would call in the police, if I didn't leave the house in half an hour. How am I to get another place, without a character? I'm a ruined girl, that's what I am—and all through You!"

Threatened at this point with an illustrative outburst of sobbing Amelius was simple enough to try the consoling influence of a sovereign. "Why don't you speak to Miss Regina?" he asked. "You know she will help you."

"She has done all she can, sir. I have nothing to say against Miss Regina—she's a good creature. She came into the room, and begged, and prayed, and took all the blame on herself. Mrs. Farnaby wouldn't hear a word. 'I'm mistress here,' she says; 'you had better go back to your room.' Ah, Mr. Amelius, I can tell you Mrs. Farnaby is your enemy as well as mine! you'll never marry her niece if *she* can stop it. Mark my words, sir, that's the secret of the vile manner in which she has used me. My conscience is clear, thank God. I've tried to serve the cause of true love—and I'm not ashamed of it. Never mind! my turn is to come. I'm only a poor servant, sent adrift in the world without a character. Wait a little! you see if I am not even (and better than even) with Mrs. Farnaby, before long! *I know what I know.* I am not going to say any more than that. She shall rue the day," cried Phoebe, relapsing into melodrama again, "when she turned me out of the house like a thief!"

"Come! come!" said Amelius, sharply, "you mustn't speak in that way."

Phoebe had got her money: she could afford to be independent. She rose from her chair. The insolence which is the almost invariable accompaniment of a sense of injury among Englishwomen of her class expressed itself in her answer to Amelius. "I speak as I think, sir. I have some spirit in me; I am not a woman to be trodden underfoot—and so Mrs. Farnaby shall find, before she is many days older."

"Phoebe! Phoebe! you are talking like a heathen. If Mrs. Farnaby has behaved to you with unjust severity, set her an example of moderation on your side. It's your duty as a Christian to forgive injuries."

Phoebe burst out laughing. "Hee-hee-hee! Thank you, sir, for a sermon as well as a sovereign. You have been most kind, indeed!" She changed suddenly from irony to anger. "I never was called a heathen before! Considering what I have done for you, I think you might at least have been civil. Good afternoon, sir." She lifted her saucy little snub-nose, and walked with dignity out of the room.

For the moment, Amelius was amused. As he heard the house-door closed, he turned laughing to the window, for a last look at Phoebe in the character of an injured Christian. In an instant the smile left his lips—he drew back from the window with a start.

A man had been waiting for Phoebe, in the street. At the moment when Amelius looked out, she had just taken his arm. He glanced back at the house, as they walked away together. Amelius immediately recognised, in Phoebe's companion (and sweetheart), a vagabond Irishman, nicknamed Jervy, whose face he had last seen at Tadmor. Employed as one of the agents of the Community in transacting their business with the neighbouring town, he had been dismissed for misconduct, and had been unwisely taken back again, at the intercession of a respectable person who believed in his promises of amendment. Amelius had suspected this man of being the spy who officiously informed against Mellicent and himself, but having discovered no evidence to justify his suspicions, he had remained silent on the subject. It was now quite plain to him that Jervy's appearance in London could only be attributed to a second dismissal from the service of the Community, for some offence sufficiently serious to oblige him to take refuge in England. A more disreputable person it was hardly possible for Phoebe to have become acquainted with. In her present vindictive mood, he would be emphatically a dangerous companion and counsellor. Amelius felt this so strongly, that he determined to follow them, on the chance of finding out where Jervy lived. Unhappily, he had only arrived at this resolution after a lapse of a minute or two. He ran into the street but it was too late; not a trace of them was to be discovered. Pursuing his way to Mr. Farnaby's house, he decided on mentioning what had happened to Regina. Her aunt had not acted wisely in refusing to let the maid refer to her for a character. She would do well to set herself right with Phoebe, in this particular, before it was too late.

CHAPTER 2

Mrs. Farnaby stood at the door of her own room, and looked at her niece with an air of contemptuous curiosity.

"Well? You and your lover have had a fine time of it together, I suppose? What do you want here?"

"Amelius wishes particularly to speak to you, aunt."

"Tell him to save himself the trouble. He may reconcile your uncle to his marriage—he won't reconcile Me."

"It's not about that, aunt; it's about Phoebe."

"Does he want me to take Phoebe back again?"

At that moment Amelius appeared in the hall, and answered the question himself. "I want to give you a word of warning," he said.

Mrs. Farnaby smiled grimly. "That excites my curiosity," she replied. "Come in. I don't want *you,"* she added, dismissing her niece at the door. "So you're willing to wait ten years for Regina?" she continued, when Amelius was alone with her. "I'm disappointed in you; you're a poor weak creature, after all. What about that young hussy, Phoebe?"

Amelius told her unreservedly all that had passed between the discarded maid and himself, not forgetting, before he concluded, to caution her on the subject of the maid's companion. "I don't know what that man may not do to mislead Phoebe," he said. "If I were you, I wouldn't drive her into a corner."

Mrs. Farnaby eyed him scornfully from head to foot. "You used to have the spirit of a man in you," she answered. "Keeping company with Regina has made you a milksop already. If you want to know what I think of Phoebe and her sweetheart—" she stopped, and snapped her fingers. "There!" she said, "that's what I think! Now go back to Regina. I can tell you one thing—she will never be your wife."

Amelius looked at her in quiet surprise. "It seems odd," he remarked, "that you should treat me as you do, after what you said to me, the last time I was in this room. You expect me to help you in the dearest wish of your life—and you do everything you can to thwart the dearest wish of *my* life. A man can't keep his temper under continual provocation. Suppose I refuse to help you?"

Mrs. Farnaby looked at him with the most exasperating composure. "I defy you to do it," she answered.

"You defy me to do it!" Amelius exclaimed.

"Do you take me for a fool?" Mrs. Farnaby went on. "Do you think I don't know you better than you know yourself?" She stepped up close to him; her voice sank suddenly to low and tender tones. "If that last unlikely chance should turn out in my favour," she went on; "if you really did meet with my poor girl, one of these days, and knew that you had met with her—do you mean to say you could be cruel enough, no matter how badly I behaved to you, to tell me nothing about it? Is *that* the heart I can feel beating under my hand? Is *that* the Christianity you learnt at Tadmor? Pooh, pooh, you foolish boy! Go back to Regina; and tell her you have tried to frighten me, and you find it won't do."

The next day was Saturday. The advertisement of the lecture appeared in the newspapers. Rufus confessed that he had been extravagant enough, in the case of the two weekly journals, to occupy half a page. "The public," he explained, "have got a nasty way of overlooking advertisements of a modest and retiring character. Hit 'em in the eyes when they open the paper, or you don't hit 'em at all."

Among the members of the public attracted by the new announcement, Mrs. Farnaby was one. She honoured Amelius with a visit at his lodgings. "I called you a poor weak creature yesterday" (these were her first words on entering the room); "I talked like a fool. You're a splendid fellow; I respect your courage, and I shall attend your lecture. Never mind what Mr. Farnaby and Regina say. Regina's poor little conventional soul is shaken, I dare say; you needn't expect to have my niece among your audience. But Farnaby is a humbug, as usual. He affects to be horrified; he talks big about breaking off the match. In his own self, he's bursting with curiosity to know how you will get through with it. I tell you this—he will sneak into the hall and stand at the back where nobody can see him. I shall go with him; and, when you're on the platform, I'll hold up my handkerchief like this. Then you'll know he's there. Hit him hard, Amelius—hit him hard! Where is your friend Rufus? just gone away? I like that American. Give him my love, and tell him to come and see me." She left the room as abruptly as she had entered it. Amelius looked after her in amazement. Mrs. Farnaby was not like herself; Mrs. Farnaby was in good spirits!

Regina's opinion of the lecture arrived by post.

Every other word in her letter was underlined; half the sentences began with "Oh!"; Regina was shocked, astonished, ashamed, alarmed. What would Amelius do next? Why had he deceived her, and left her to find it out in the papers? He had undone all the good effect of those charming letters to her father and herself. He had no idea of the disgust and abhorrence which respectable people would feel at his odious Socialism. Was she never to know another happy moment? and was Amelius to be the cause of it? and so on, and so on.

Mr. Farnaby's protest followed, delivered by Mr. Farnaby himself. He kept his gloves on when he called; he was solemn and pathetic; he remonstrated, in the character of one of the ancestors of Amelius; he pitied the ancient family "mouldering in the silent grave," he would abstain from deciding in a hurry, but his daughter's feelings were outraged, and he feared it might be his duty to break off the match. Amelius, with perfect good temper, offered him a free admission, and asked him to hear the lecture and decide for himself whether there was any harm in it. Mr. Farnaby turned his head away from the ticket as if it was something indecent. "Sad! sad!" That was his only farewell to the gentleman-Socialist.

On the Sunday (being the only day in London on which a man can use his brains without being interrupted by street music), Amelius rehearsed his lecture. On the Monday, he paid his weekly visit to Regina.

She was reported—whether truly or not it was impossible for him to discover—to have gone out in the carriage with Mrs. Ormond. Amelius wrote to her in soothing and affectionate terms, suggesting, as he had suggested to her father, that she should wait to hear the lecture before she condemned it. In the mean time, he entreated her to remember that they had promised to be true to one another, in time and eternity— Socialism notwithstanding.

The answer came back by private messenger. The tone was serious. Regina's principles forbade her to attend a Socialist lecture. She hoped Amelius was in earnest in writing as he did about time and eternity. The subject was very awful to a rightly-constituted mind. On the next page, some mitigation of this severity followed in a postscript. Regina would wait at home to see Amelius, the day after his "regrettable appearance in public."

The evening of Tuesday was the evening of the lecture.

Rufus posted himself at the ticket-taker's office, in the interests of Amelius. "Even sixpences do sometimes stick to a man's fingers, on their way from the public to the money-box," he remarked. The sixpences did indeed flow in rapidly; the advertisements had, so far, produced their effect. But the reserved seats sold very slowly. The members of the Institution, who were admitted for nothing, arrived in large numbers, and secured the best places. Towards eight o'clock (the hour at which the lecture was to begin), the sixpenny audience was still pouring in. Rufus recognised Phoebe among the late arrivals, escorted by a person in the dress of a gentleman, who was palpably a blackguard nevertheless. A short stout lady followed, who warily shook hands with Rufus, and said, "Let me introduce you to Mr. Farnaby." Mr. Farnaby's mouth and chin were shrouded in a wrapper; his hat was over his eyebrows. Rufus observed that he looked as if he was ashamed of himself. A gaunt, dirty, savage old woman, miserably dressed, offered her sixpence to the moneytaker, while the two gentlemen were shaking hands; the example, it is needless to say, being set by Rufus. The old woman looked attentively at all that was visible of Mr. Farnaby—that is to say, at his eyes and his whiskers—by the gas-lamp hanging in the corridor. She instantly drew back, though she had got her ticket; waited until Mr. Farnaby had paid for his wife and himself, and then followed close behind them, into the hall.

And why not? The advertisements addressed this wretched old creature as one of the poor and discontented public. Sixteen years ago, John Farnaby had put his own child into that woman's hands at Ramsgate, and had never seen either of them since.

CHAPTER 3

Entering the hall, Mr. Farnaby discovered without difficulty the position of modest retirement of which he was in search.

The cheap seats were situated, as usual, on that part of the floor of the building which was farthest from the platform. A gallery at this end of the hall threw its shadow over the hindermost benches and the gangway by which they were approached. In the sheltering obscurity thus produced, Mr. Farnaby took his place; standing in the corner formed by the angle it which the two walls of the building met, with his dutiful wife at his side.

Still following them, unnoticed in the crowd, the old woman stopped at the extremity of the hindermost bench, looked close at a smartly-dressed young man who occupied the last seat at the end, and who paid marked attention to a pretty girl sitting by him, and whispered in his ear, "Now then, Jervy! can't you make room for Mother Sowler?"

The man started and looked round. "You here?" he exclaimed, with an oath.

Before he could say more, Phoebe whispered to him on the other side, "What a horrid old creature! How did you ever come to know her?"

At the same moment, Mrs. Sowler reiterated her request in more peremptory language. "Do you hear, Jervy—do you hear? Sit a little closer."

Jervy apparently had his reasons for treating the expression of Mrs. Sowler's wishes with deference, shabby as she was. Making abundant apologies, he asked his neighbours to favour him by sitting a little nearer to each other, and so contrive to leave a morsel of vacant space at the edge of the bench.

Phoebe, making room under protest, began to whisper again. "What does she mean by calling you Jervy? She looks like a beggar. Tell her your name is Jervis."

The reply she received did not encourage her to say more. "Hold your tongue; I have reasons for being civil to her—you be civil too."

He turned to Mrs. Sowler, with the readiest submission to circumstances. Under the surface of his showy looks and his vulgar facility of manner, there lay hidden a substance of callous villainy and impenetrable cunning. He had in him the materials out of which the clever murderers are made, who baffle the police. If he could have done it with impunity, he would have destroyed without remorse the squalid old creature who sat by him, and who knew enough of his past career in England to send him to penal servitude for life. As it was, he spoke to her with a spurious condescension and good humour. "Why, it must be ten years, Mrs. Sowler, since I last saw you! What have you been doing?"

The woman frowned at him as she answered. "Can't you look at me, and see? Starving!" She eyed his gaudy watch and chain greedily. "Money don't seem to be scarce with you. Have you made your fortune in America?"

He laid his hand on her arm, and pressed it warningly. "Hush!" he said, under his breath. "We'll talk about that, after the lecture." His bright shifty black eyes turned furtively towards Phoebe—and Mrs. Sowler noticed it. The girl's savings in service had paid for his jewelry and his fine clothes. She silently resented his rudeness in telling her to "hold her tongue"; sitting, sullen, with her impudent little nose in the air. Jervy tried to include her indirectly in his conversation with his shabby old friend. "This young lady," he said, "knows Mr. Goldenheart. She feels sure he'll break down; and we've come here to see the fun. I don't hold with Socialism myself—I am for, what my favourite newspaper calls, the Altar and the Throne. In short, my politics are Conservative."

"Your politics are in your girl's pocket," muttered Mrs. Sowler. "How long will her money last?"

Jervy turned a deaf ear to the interruption. "And what has brought you here?" he went on, in his most ingratiating way. "Did you see the advertisement in the papers?"

Mrs. Sowler answered loud enough to be heard above the hum of talking in the sixpenny places. "I was having a drop of gin, and I saw the paper at the public-house. I'm one of the discontented poor. I hate rich people; and I'm ready to pay my sixpence to hear them abused."

"Hear, hear!" said a man near, who looked like a shoemaker.

"I hope he'll give it to the aristocracy," added one of the shoemaker's neighbours, apparently a groom out of place.

"I'm sick of the aristocracy," cried a woman with a fiery face and a crushed bonnet. "It's them as swallows up the money. What business have they with their palaces and their parks, when my husband's out of work, and my children hungry at home?"

The acquiescent shoemaker listened with admiration. "Very well put," he said; "very well put."

These expressions of popular feeling reached the respectable ears of Mr. Farnaby. "Do you hear those wretches?" he said to his wife.

Mrs. Farnaby seized the welcome opportunity of irritating him. "Poor things!" she answered. "In their place, we should talk as they do."

128

"You had better go into the reserved seats," rejoined her husband, turning from her with a look of disgust. "There's plenty of room. Why do you stop here?"

"I couldn't think of leaving you, my dear! How did you like my American friend?"

"I am astonished at your taking the liberty of introducing him to me. You knew perfectly well that I was here incognito. What do I care about a wandering American?"

Mrs. Farnaby persisted as maliciously as ever. "Ah, but you see, I like him. The wandering American is my ally."

"Your ally! What do you mean?"

"Good heavens, how dull you are! don't you know that I object to my niece's marriage engagement? I was quite delighted when I heard of this lecture, because it's an obstacle in the way. It disgusts Regina, and it disgusts You—and my dear American is the man who first brought it about. Hush! here's Amelius. How well he looks! So graceful and so gentlemanlike," cried Mrs. Farnaby, signalling with her handkerchief to show Amelius their position in the hall. "I declare I'm ready to become a Socialist before he opens his lips!"

The personal appearance of Amelius took the audience completely by surprise. A man who is young and handsome is not the order of man who is habitually associated in the popular mind with the idea of a lecture. After a moment of silence, there was a spontaneous burst of applause. It was renewed when Amelius, first placing on his table a little book, announced his intention of delivering the lecture extempore. The absence of the inevitable manuscript was in itself an act of mercy that cheered the public at starting.

The orator of the evening began.

"Ladies and gentlemen, thoughtful people accustomed to watch the signs of the times in this country, and among the other nations of Europe, are (so far as I know) agreed in the conclusion, that serious changes are likely to take place in present forms of government, and in existing systems of society, before the century in which we live has reached its end. In plain words, the next revolution is not so unlikely, and not so far off, as it pleases the higher and wealthier classes among European populations to suppose. I am one of those who believe that the coming convulsion will take the form, this time, of a social revolution, and that the man at the head of it will not be a military or a political man—but a Great Citizen, sprung from the people, and devoted heart and soul to the people's cause. Within the limits assigned to me to-night, it is impossible that I should speak to you of government and society among other nations, even if I possessed the necessary knowledge and experience to venture on so vast a subject. All that I can now attempt to do is (first) to point out some of the causes which are paving the way for a coming change in the social and political condition of this country; and (secondly) to satisfy you that the only trustworthy remedy for existing abuses is to be found in the system which Christian Socialism extracts from this little book on my table—the book which you all know under the name of The New Testament. Before, however, I enter on my task, I feel it a duty to say one preliminary word on the subject of my claim to address you, such as it is. I am most unwilling to speak of myself—but my position here forces me to do so. I am a stranger to all of you; and I am a very young man. Let me tell you, then, briefly, what my life has been, and where I have been brought up—and then decide for yourselves whether it is worth your while to favour me with your attention, or not."

"A very good opening," remarked the shoemaker.

"A nice-looking fellow," said the fiery-faced woman, "I should like to kiss him."

"He's too civil by half," grumbled Mrs. Sowler; "I wish I had my sixpence back in my pocket."

"Give him time." whispered Jervy, "and he'll warm up. I say, Phoebe, he doesn't begin like a man who is going to break down. I don't expect there will be much to laugh at to-night."

"What an admirable speaker!" said Mrs. Farnaby to her husband. "Fancy such a man as that, being married to such an idiot as Regina!"

"There's always a chance for him," returned Mr. Farnaby, savagely, "as long as he's not married to such a woman as You!"

In the mean time, Amelius had claimed national kindred with his audience as an Englishman, and had rapidly sketched his life at Tadmor, in its most noteworthy points. This done, he put the question whether they would hear him. His frankness and freshness had already won the public: they answered by a general shout of applause.

"Very well," Amelius proceeded, "now let us get on. Suppose we take a glance (we have no time to do more) at the present state of our religious system, first. What is the public aspect of the thing called Christianity, in the England of our day? A hundred different sects all at variance with each other. An established church, rent in every direction by incessant wrangling—disputes about black gowns or white; about having candlesticks on tables, or off tables; about bowing to the east or bowing to the west; about which doctrine collects the most respectable support and possesses the largest sum of money, the doctrine in my church, or the doctrine in your church, or the doctrine in the church over the way. Look up, if you like, from this multitudinous and incessant squabbling among the rank and file, to the high regions in which the right reverend representatives of state religion sit apart. Are they Christians? If they are, show me the Bishop who dare assert his Christianity in the

House of Lords, when the ministry of the day happens to see its advantage in engaging in a war! Where is that Bishop, and how many supporters does he count among his own order? Do you blame me for using intemperate language—language which I cannot justify? Take a fair test, and try me by that. The result of the Christianity of the New Testament is to make men true, humane, gentle, modest, strictly scrupulous and strictly considerate in their dealings with their neighbours. Does the Christianity of the churches and the sects produce these results among us? Look at the staple of the country, at the occupation which employs the largest number of Englishmen of all degrees—Look at our Commerce. What is its social aspect, judged by the morality which is in this book in my hand? Let those organised systems of imposture, masquerading under the disguise of banks and companies, answer the question—there is no need for me to answer it. You know what respectable names are associated, year after year, with the shameless falsification of accounts, and the merciless ruin of thousands on thousands of victims. You know how our poor Indian customer finds his cotton-print dress a sham that falls to pieces; how the savage who deals honestly with us for his weapon finds his gun a delusion that bursts; how the half-starved needlewoman who buys her reel of thread finds printed on the label a false statement of the number of yards that she buys; you know that, in the markets of Europe, foreign goods are fast taking the place of English goods, because the foreigner is the most honest manufacturer of the two—and, lastly, you know, what is worse than all, that these cruel and wicked deceptions, and many more like them, are regarded, on the highest commercial authority, as 'forms of competition' and justifiable proceedings in trade. Do you believe in the honourable accumulation of wealth by men who hold such opinions and perpetrate such impostures as these? I don't! Do you find any brighter and purer prospect when you look down from the man who deceives you and me on the great scale, to the man who deceives us on the small? I don't! Everything we eat, drink, and wear is a more or less adulterated commodity; and that very adulteration is sold to us by the tradesmen at such outrageous prices, that we are obliged to protect ourselves on the Socialist principle, by setting up cooperative shops of our own. Wait! and hear me out, before you applaud. Don't mistake the plain purpose of what I am saying to you; and don't suppose that I am blind to the brighter side of the dark picture that I have drawn. Look within the limits of private life, and you will find true Christians, thank God, among clergymen and laymen alike; you will find men and women who deserve to be called, in the highest sense of the word, disciples of Christ. But my business is not with private life—my business is with the present public aspect of the religion, morals, and politics of this country; and again I say it, that aspect presents one wide field of corruption and abuse, and reveals a callous and shocking insensibility on the part of the nation at large to the spectacle of its own demoralisation and disgrace."

There Amelius paused, and took his first drink of water.

Reserved seats at public performances seem, by some curious affinity, to be occupied by reserved persons. The select public, seated nearest to the orator, preserved discreet silence. But the hearty applause from the sixpenny places made ample amends. There was enough of the lecturer's own vehemence and impetuosity in this opening attack—sustained as it undeniably was by a sound foundation of truth—to appeal strongly to the majority of his audience. Mrs. Sowler began to think that her sixpence had been well laid out, after all; and Mrs. Farnaby pointed the direct application to her husband of all the hardest hits at commerce, by nodding her head at him as they were delivered.

Amelius went on.

"The next thing we have to discover is this: Will our present system of government supply us with peaceable means for the reform of the abuses which I have already noticed? not forgetting that other enormous abuse, represented by our intolerable national expenditure, increasing with every year. Unless you insist on it, I do not propose to waste our precious time by saying anything about the House of Lords, for three good reasons. In the first place, that assembly is not elected by the people, and it has therefore no right of existence in a really free country. In the second place, out of its four hundred and eighty-five members, no less than one hundred and eighty-four directly profit by the expenditure of the public money; being in the annual receipt, under one pretence or another, of more than half a million sterling. In the third place, if the assembly of the Commons has in it the will, as well as the capacity, to lead the way in the needful reforms, the assembly of the Lords has no alternative but to follow, or to raise the revolution which it only escaped, by a hair's-breadth, some forty years since. What do you say? Shall we waste our time in speaking of the House of Lords?"

Loud cries from the sixpenny benches answered No; the ostler and the fiery-faced woman being the most vociferous of all. Here and there, certain dissentient individuals raised a little hiss—led by Jervy, in the interests of "the Altar and the Throne."

Amelius resumed.

"Well, will the House of Commons help us to get purer Christianity, and cheaper government, by lawful and sufficient process of reform? Let me again remind you that this assembly has the power—if it has the will. Is it so constituted at present as to have the will? There is the question! The number of members is a little over six hundred and fifty. Out of this muster, one fifth only represent (or pretend to represent) the trading interests of the country. As for the members charged with the interests of the working class, they are more easily counted still—they are two in number! Then, in heaven's name (you will ask), what interest does the majority of members in this assembly represent? There is but one answer—the military and aristocratic interest. In these days of the decay of representative institutions, the House of Commons has become a complete misnomer. The Commons are not represented; modern members belong to classes of the community which have really no interest in providing for popular needs and lightening popular burdens. In one word, there is no sort of hope for us in the House of Commons. And whose fault is this? I own it with shame and sorrow—it is emphatically the fault of the people. Yes, I say to you plainly, it is the disgrace and the peril of England that the people themselves have elected the representative assembly which ignores the people's wants! You voters, in town and county alike, have had every conceivable freedom and encouragement secured to you in the exercise of your sacred trust—and there is the modern House of Commons to prove that you are thoroughly unworthy of it!"

These bold words produced an outbreak of disapprobation from the audience, which, for the moment, completely overpowered the speaker's voice. They were prepared to listen with inexhaustible patience to the enumeration of their virtues and their wrongs—but they had not paid sixpence each to be informed of the vicious and contemptible part which they play in modern politics. They yelled and groaned and hissed—and felt that their handsome young lecturer had insulted them!

Amelius waited quietly until the disturbance had worn itself out.

"I am sorry I have made you angry with me," he said, smiling. "The blame for this little disturbance really rests with the public speakers who are afraid of you and who flatter you—especially if you belong to the working classes. You are not accustomed to have the truth told you to your faces. Why, my good friends, the people in this country, who are unworthy of the great trust which the wise and generous English constitution places in their hands, are so numerous that they can be divided into distinct classes! There is the highly-educated class which despairs, and holds aloof. There is the class beneath—without self-respect, and therefore without public spirit—which can be bribed indirectly, by the gift of a place, by the concession of a lease, even by an invitation to a party at a great house which includes the wives and the daughters. And there is the lower class still—mercenary, corrupt, shameless to the marrow of its bones—which sells itself and its liberties for money and drink. When I began this discourse, and adverted to great changes that are to come, I spoke of them as revolutionary changes. Am I an alarmist? Do I unjustly ignore the capacity for peaceable reformation which has preserved modern England from revolutions, thus far? God forbid that I should deny the truth, or that I should alarm you without need! But history tells me, if I look no farther back than to the first French Revolution, that there are social and political corruptions, which strike their roots in a nation so widely and so deeply, that no force short of the force of a revolutionary convulsion can tear them up and cast them away. And I do personally fear (and older and wiser men than I agree with me), that the corruptions at which I have only been able to hint, in this brief address, are fast extending themselves—in England, as well as in Europe generally—beyond the reach of that lawful and bloodless reform which has served us so well in past years. Whether I am mistaken in this view (and I hope with all my heart it may be so), or whether events yet in the future will prove that I am right, the remedy in either case, the one sure foundation on which a permanent, complete, and worthy reformation can be built—whether it prevents a convulsion or whether it follows a convulsion—is only to be found within the covers of this book. Do not, I entreat you, suffer yourselves to be persuaded by those purblind philosophers who assert that the divine virtue of Christianity is a virtue which is wearing out with the lapse of time. It is the abuse and corruption of Christianity that is wearing out—as all falsities and all impostures must and do wear out. Never, since Christ and his apostles first showed men the way to be better and happier, have the nations stood in sorer need of a return to that teaching, in its pristine purity and simplicity, than now! Never, more certainly than at this critical time, was it the interest as well as the duty of mankind to turn a deaf ear to the turmoil of false teachers, and to trust in that all-wise and all-merciful Voice which only ceased to exalt, console, and purify humanity, when it expired in darkness under the torture of the cross! Are these the wild words of an enthusiast? Is this the dream of an earthly Paradise in which it is sheer folly to believe? I can tell you of one existing community (one among others) which numbers some hundreds of persons; and which has found prosperity and happiness, by reducing the whole art and mystery of government to the simple solution set forth in the New Testament—fear God, and love thy neighbour as thyself."

By these gradations Amelius arrived at the second of the two parts into which he had divided his address.

He now repeated, at greater length and with a more careful choice of language, the statement of the religious and social principles of the Community at Tadmor, which he had already addressed to his two fellow-travellers on the voyage to England. While he confined himself to plain narrative, describing a mode of life which was entirely new to his hearers, he held the attention of the audience. But when he began to argue the question of applying Christian Socialism to the government of large populations as well as small—when he inquired logically whether what he had proved to be good for some hundreds of persons was not also good for some thousands, and, conceding that, for some hundreds of thousands, and so on until he had arrived, by dint of sheer argument, at the conclusion that what had succeeded at Tadmor must necessarily succeed on a fair trial in London—then the public interest began to flag. People remembered their coughs and colds, and talked in whispers, and looked about them with a vague feeling of relief in staring at each other. Mrs. Sowler, hitherto content with furtively glancing at Mr. Farnaby from time to time, now began to look at him more boldly, as he stood in his corner with his eyes fixed sternly on the platform at the other end of the hall. He too began to feel that the lecture was changing its tone. It was no longer the daring outbreak which he had come to hear, as his sufficient justification (if necessary) for forbidding Amelius to enter his house. "I have had enough of it," he said, suddenly turning to his wife, "let us go."

If Mrs. Farnaby could have been forewarned that she was standing in that assembly of strangers, not as one of themselves, but as a woman with a formidable danger hanging over her head—or if she had only happened to look towards Phoebe, and had felt a passing reluctance to submit herself to the possibly insolent notice of a discharged servant—she might have gone out with her husband, and might have so escaped the peril that had been lying in wait for her, from the fatal moment when she first entered the hall. As it was she refused to move. "You forget the public discussion," she said. "Wait and see what sort of fight Amelius makes of it when the lecture is over."

She spoke loud enough to be heard by some of the people seated nearest to her. Phoebe, critically examining the dresses of the few ladies in the reserved seats, twisted round on the bench, and noticed for the first time the presence of Mr. and Mrs. Farnaby in their dim corner. "Look!" she whispered to Jervy, "there's the wretch who turned me out of her house without a character, and her husband with her."

Jervy looked round, in his turn, a little doubtful of the accuracy of his sweetheart's information. "Surely they wouldn't come to the sixpenny places," he said. "Are you certain it's Mr. and Mrs. Farnaby?"

He spoke in cautiously-lowered tones; but Mrs. Sowler had seen him look back at the lady and gentleman in the corner, and was listening attentively to catch the first words that fell from his lips.

"Which is Mr. Farnaby?" she asked.

"The man in the corner there, with the white silk wrapper over his mouth, and his hat down to his eyebrows."

Mrs. Sowler looked round for a moment—to make sure that Jervy's man and her man were one and the same.

"Farnaby?" she muttered to herself, in the tone of a person who heard the name for the first time. She considered a little, and leaning across Jervy, addressed herself to his companion. "My dear," she whispered, "did that gentleman ever go by the name of Morgan, and have his letters addressed to the George and Dragon, in Tooley-street?"

Phoebe lifted her eyebrows with a look of contemptuous surprise, which was an answer in itself. "Fancy the great Mr. Farnaby going by an assumed name, and having his letters addressed to a public-house!" she said to Jervy.

Mrs. Sowler asked no more questions. She relapsed into muttering to herself, under her breath. "His whiskers have turned gray, to be sure—but I know his eyes again; I'll take my oath to it, there's no mistaking *his* eyes!" She suddenly appealed to Jervy. "Is Mr. Farnaby rich?" she asked.

"Rolling in riches!" was the answer.

"Where does he live?"

Jervy was cautious how he replied to that; he consulted Phoebe. "Shall I tell her?"

Phoebe answered petulantly, "I'm turned out of the house; I don't care what you tell her!"

Jervy again addressed the old woman, still keeping his information in reserve. "Why do you want to know where he lives?"

"He owes me money," said Mrs. Sowler.

Jervy looked hard at her, and emitted a long low whistle, expressive of blank amazement. The persons near, annoyed by the incessant whispering, looked round irritably, and insisted on silence. Jervy ventured nevertheless on a last interruption. "You seem to be tired of this," he remarked to Phoebe; "let's go and get some oysters." She rose directly. Jervy tapped Mrs. Sowler on the shoulder, as they passed her. "Come and have some supper," he said; "I'll stand treat."

The three were necessarily noticed by their neighbours as they passed out. Mrs. Farnaby discovered Phoebe—when it was too late. Mr. Farnaby happened to look first at the old woman. Sixteen years of squalid poverty effectually disguised her, in that dim light. He only looked away again, and said to his wife impatiently, "Let us go too!"

Mrs. Farnaby was still obstinate. "You can go if you like," she said; "I shall stay here."

CHAPTER 4

"Three dozen oysters, bread-and-butter, and bottled stout; a private room and a good fire." Issuing these instructions, on his arrival at the tavern, Jervy was surprised by a sudden act of interference on the part of his venerable guest. Mrs. Sowler actually took it on herself to order her own supper!

"Nothing cold to eat or drink for me," she said. "Morning and night, waking and sleeping, I can't keep myself warm. See for yourself, Jervy, how I've lost flesh since you first knew me! A steak, broiling hot from the gridiron, and gin-and-water, hotter still—that's the supper for me."

"Take the order, waiter," said Jervy, resignedly; "and let us see the private room."

The tavern was of the old-fashioned English sort, which scorns to learn a lesson of brightness and elegance from France. The private room can only be described as a museum for the exhibition of dirt in all its varieties. Behind the bars of the rusty little grate a dying fire was drawing its last breath. Mrs. Sowler clamoured for wood and coals; revived the fire with her own hands; and seated herself shivering as close to the fender as the chair would go. After a while, the composing effect of the heat began to make its influence felt: the head of the half-starved wretch sank: a species of stupor overcame her—half faintness, and half sleep.

Phoebe and her sweetheart sat together, waiting the appearance of the supper, on a little sofa at the other end of the room. Having certain objects to gain, Jervy put his arm round her waist, and looked and spoke in his most insinuating manner.

"Try and put up with Mother Sowler for an hour or two," he said. "My sweet girl, I know she isn't fit company for you! But how can I turn my back on an old friend?"

"That's just what surprises me," Phoebe answered. "I don't understand such a person being a friend of yours."

Always ready with the necessary lie, whenever the occasion called for it, Jervy invented a pathetic little story, in two short parts. First part: Mrs. Sowler, rich and respected; a widow inhabiting a villa-residence, and riding in her carriage. Second part: a villainous lawyer; misplaced confidence; reckless investments; death of the villain; ruin of Mrs. Sowler. "Don't talk about her misfortunes when she wakes," Jervy concluded, "or she'll burst out crying, to a dead certainty. Only tell me, dear Phoebe, would *you* turn your back on a forlorn old creature because she has outlived all her other friends, and hasn't a farthing left in the world? Poor as I am, I can help her to a supper, at any rate."

Phoebe expressed her admiration of these noble sentiments by an inexpensive ebullition of tenderness, which failed to fulfill Jervy's private anticipations. He had aimed straight at her purse—and he had only hit her heart! He tried a broad hint next. "I wonder whether I shall have a shilling or two left to give Mrs. Sowler, when I have paid for the supper?" He sighed, and pulled out some small change, and looked at it in eloquent silence. Phoebe was hit in the right place at last. She handed him her purse. "What is mine will be yours, when we are married," she said; "why not now?" Jervy expressed his sense of obligation with the promptitude of a grateful man; he repeated those precious words, "My sweet girl!" Phoebe laid her head on his shoulder—and let him kiss her, and enjoyed it in silent ecstasy with half-closed eyes. The scoundrel waited and watched her, until she was completely under his influence. Then, and not till then, he risked the gradual revelation of the purpose which had induced him to withdraw from the hall, before the proceedings of the evening had reached their end.

"Did you hear what Mrs. Sowler said to me, just before we left the lecture?" he asked.

"No, dear."

"You remember that she asked me to tell her Farnaby's address?"

"Oh yes! And she wanted to know if he had ever gone by the name of Morgan. Ridiculous—wasn't it?"

"I'm not so sure of that, my dear. She told me, in so many words, that Farnaby owed her money. He didn't make his fortune all at once, I suppose. How do we know what he might have done in his young days, or how he might have humbugged a feeble woman. Wait till our friend there at the fire has warmed her old bones with some hot grog—and I'll find out something more about Farnaby's debt."

"Why, dear? What is it to you?"

Jervy reflected for a moment, and decided that the time had come to speak more plainly.

"In the first place," he said, "it would only be an act of common humanity, on my part, to help Mrs. Sowler to get her money. You see that, don't you? Very well. Now, I am no Socialist, as you are aware; quite the contrary. At the same time, I am a remarkably just man; and I own I was struck by what Mr. Goldenheart said about the uses to which wealthy people are put, by the Rules at Tadmor. 'The man who has got the money is bound, by the express law of Christian morality, to use it in assisting the man who has got none.' Those were his words, as nearly as I can remember them. He put it still more strongly afterwards; he said, 'A man who hoards up a large fortune, from a purely selfish motive—either because he is a miser, or because he looks only to the aggrandisement of his own family after his death—is, in either case, an essentially unchristian person, who stands in manifest need of enlightenment and control by Christian law.' And then, if you remember, some of the people murmured; and Mr. Goldenheart stopped them by reading a line from the

138

New Testament, which said exactly what he had been saying—only in fewer words. Now, my dear girl, Farnaby seems to me to be one of the many people pointed at in this young gentleman's lecture. Judging by looks, I should say he was a hard man."

"That's just what he is—hard as iron! Looks at his servants as if they were dirt under his feet; and never speaks a kind word to them from one year's end to another."

"Suppose I guess again? He's not particularly free-handed with his money—is he?"

"He! He will spend anything on himself and his grandeur; but he never gave away a halfpenny in his life."

Jervy pointed to the fireplace, with a burst of virtuous indignation. "And there's that poor old soul starving for want of the money he owes her! Damn it, I agree with the Socialists; it's a virtue to make that sort of man bleed. Look at you and me! We are the very people he ought to help—we might be married at once, if we only knew where to find a little money. I've seen a deal of the world, Phoebe; and my experience tells me there's something about that debt of Farnaby's which he doesn't want to have known. Why shouldn't we screw a few five-pound notes for ourselves out of the rich miser's fears?"

Phoebe was cautious. "It's against the law—ain't it?" she said.

"Trust me to keep clear of the law," Jervy answered. "I won't stir in the matter till I know for certain that he daren't take the police into his confidence. It will be all easy enough when we are once sure of that. You have been long enough in the family to find out Farnaby's weak side. Would it do, if we got at him, to begin with, through his wife?"

Phoebe suddenly reddened to the roots of her hair. "Don't talk to me about his wife!" she broke out fiercely; "I've got a day of reckoning to come with that lady—" She looked at Jervy and checked herself. He was watching her with an eager curiosity, which not even his ready cunning was quick enough to conceal.

"I wouldn't intrude on your little secrets, darling, for the world!" he said, in his most persuasive tones. "But, if you want advice, you know that I am heart and soul at your service."

Phoebe looked across the room at Mrs. Sowler, still nodding over the fire.

"Never mind now," she said; "I don't think it's a matter for a man to advise about—it's between Mrs. Farnaby and me. Do what you like with her husband; I don't care; he's a brute, and I hate him. But there's one thing I insist on—I won't have Miss Regina frightened or annoyed; mind that! She's a good creature. There, read the letter she wrote to me yesterday, and judge for yourself."

Jervy looked at the letter. It was not very long. He resignedly took upon himself the burden of reading it.

"DEAR PHOEBE,

"Don't be downhearted. I am your friend always, and I will help you to get another place. I am sorry to say that it was indeed Mrs. Ormond who found us out that day. She had her suspicions, and she watched us, and told my aunt. This she owned to me with her own lips. She said, 'I would do anything, my dear, to save you from an ill-assorted marriage.' I am very wretched about it, because I can never look on her as my friend again. My aunt, as you know, is of Mrs. Ormond's way of thinking. You must make allowances for her hot temper. Remember, out of your kindness towards me, you had been secretly helping forward the very thing which she was most anxious to prevent. That made her very angry; but, never fear, she will come round in time. If you don't want to spend your little savings, while you are waiting for another situation, let me know. A share of my pocket-money is always at your service.

"Your friend,

"REGINA."

"Very nice indeed," said Jervy, handing the letter back, and yawning as he did it. "And convenient, too, if we run short of money. Ah, here's the waiter with the supper, at last! Now, Mrs. Sowler, there's a time for everything—it's time to wake up."

He lifted the old woman off her chair, and settled her before the table, like a child. The sight of the hot food and drink roused her to a tigerish activity. She devoured the meat with her eyes as well as her teeth; she drank the hot gin-and-water in fierce gulps, and set down the glass with audible gasps of relief. "Another one," she cried, "and I shall begin to feel warm again!"

Jervy, watching her from the opposite side of the table, with Phoebe close by him as usual, had his own motives for encouraging her to talk, by the easy means of encouraging her to drink. He sent for another glass of the hot grog. Phoebe, daintily picking up her oysters with her fork, affected to be shocked at Mrs. Sowler's coarse method of eating and drinking. She kept her eyes on her plate, and only consented to taste malt liquor under modest protest. When Jervy lit a cigar, after finishing his supper, she reminded him, in an impressively genteel manner, of the consideration which he owed to the presence of an elderly lady. "I like it myself, dear," she said mincingly; "but perhaps Mrs. Sowler objects to the smell?"

Mrs. Sowler burst into a hoarse laugh. "Do I look as if I was likely to be squeamish about smells?" she asked, with the savage contempt for her own poverty, which was one of the dangerous elements in her character. "See the place I live in, young woman, and then talk about smells if you like!"

This was indelicate. Phoebe picked a last oyster out of its shell, and kept her eyes modestly fixed on her plate. Observing that the second glass of gin-and-water was fast becoming empty, Jervy risked the first advances, on his way to Mrs. Sowler's confidence.

"About that debt of Farnaby's?" he began. "Is it a debt of long standing?"

Mrs. Sowler was on her guard. In other words, Mrs. Sowler's head was only assailable by hot grog, when hot grog was administered in large quantities. She said it was a debt of long standing, and she said no more.

"Has it been standing seven years?"

Mrs. Sowler emptied her glass, and looked hard at Jervy across the table. "My memory isn't good for much, at my time of life." She gave him that answer, and she gave him no more.

Jervy yielded with his best grace. "Try a third glass," he said; "there's luck, you know, in odd numbers."

Mrs. Sowler met this advance in the spirit in which it was made. She was obliging enough to consult her memory, even before the third glass made its appearance. "Seven years, did you say?" she repeated. "More than twice seven years, Jervy! What do you think of that?"

Jervy wasted no time in thinking. He went on with his questions.

"Are you quite sure that the man I pointed out to you, at the lecture, is the same man who went by the name of Morgan, and had his letters addressed to the public-house?"

"Quite sure. I'd swear to him anywhere—only by his eyes."

"And have you never yet asked him to pay the debt?"

"How could I ask him, when I never knew what his name was till you told me to-night?"

"What amount of money does he owe you?"

Whether Mrs. Sowler had her mind prophetically fixed on a fourth glass of grog, or whether she thought it time to begin asking questions on her own account, is not easy to say. Whatever her motive might be, she slyly shook her head, and winked at Jervy. "The money's my business," she remarked. "You tell me where he lives— and I'll make him pay me."

Jervy was equal to the occasion. "You won't do anything of the sort," he said.

Mrs. Sowler laughed defiantly. "So you think, my fine fellow!"

"I don't think at all, old lady—I'm certain. In the first place, Farnaby don't owe you the debt by law, after seven years. In the second place, just look at yourself in the glass there. Do you think the servants will let you in, when you knock at Farnaby's door? You want a clever fellow to help you—or you'll never recover that debt."

Mrs. Sowler was accessible to reason (even half-way through her third glass of grog), when reason was presented to her in convincing terms. She came to the point at once. "How much do you want?" she asked.

"Nothing," Jervy answered; "I don't look to *you* to pay my commission."

Mrs. Sowler reflected a little—and understood him. "Say that again," she insisted, "in the presence of your young woman as witness."

Jervy touched his young woman's hand under the table, warning her to make no objection, and to leave it to him. Having declared for the second time that he would not take a farthing from Mrs. Sowler, he went on with his inquiries.

"I'm acting in your interests, Mother Sowler," he said; "and you'll be the loser, if you don't answer my questions patiently, and tell me the truth. I want to go back to the debt. What is it for?"

"For six weeks' keep of a child, at ten shillings a week."

Phoebe looked up from her plate.

"Whose child?" Jervy asked, noticing the sudden movement.

"Morgan's child—the same man you said was Farnaby."

"Do you know who the mother was?"

"I wish I did! I should have got the money out of her long ago."

Jervy stole a look at Phoebe. She had turned pale; she was listening, with her eyes riveted on Mrs. Sowler's ugly face.

142

"How long ago was it?" Jervy went on.

"Better than sixteen years."

"Did Farnaby himself give you the child?"

"With his own hands, over the garden-paling of a house at Ramsgate. He saw me and the child into the train for London. I had ten pounds from him, and no more. He promised to see me, and settle everything, in a month's time. I have never set eyes on him from that day, till I saw him paying his money this evening at the door of the hall."

Jervy stole another look at Phoebe. She was still perfectly unconscious that he was observing her. Her attention was completely absorbed by Mrs. Sowler's replies. Speculating on the possible result, Jervy abandoned the question of the debt, and devoted his next inquiries to the subject of the child.

"I promise you every farthing of your money, Mother Sowler," he said, "with interest added to it. How old was the child when Farnaby gave it to you?"

"Old? Not a week old, I should say!"

"Not a week old?" Jervy repeated, with his eye on Phoebe. "Dear, dear me, a newborn baby, one may say!"

The girl's excitement was fast getting beyond control. She leaned across the table, in her eagerness to hear more.

"And how long was this poor child under your care?" Jervy went on.

"How can I tell you, at this distance of time? For some months, I should say. This I'm certain of—I kept it for six good weeks after the ten pounds he gave me were spent. And then—" she stopped, and looked at Phoebe.

"And then you got rid of it?"

Mrs. Sowler felt for Jervy's foot under the table, and gave it a significant kick. "I have done nothing to be ashamed of, miss," she said, addressing her answer defiantly to Phoebe. "Being too poor to keep the little dear myself, I placed it under the care of a good lady, who adopted it."

Phoebe could restrain herself no longer. She burst out with the next question, before Jervy could open his lips.

"Do you know where the lady is now?"

"No," said Mrs. Sowler shortly; "I don't."

"Do you know where to find the child?"

Mrs. Sowler slowly stirred up the remains of her grog. "I know no more than you do. Any more questions, miss?"

Phoebe's excitement completely blinded her to the evident signs of a change in Mrs. Sowler's temper for the worse. She went on headlong.

"Have you never seen the child since you gave her to the lady?"

Mrs. Sowler set down her glass, just as she was raising it to her lips. Jervy paused, thunderstruck, in the act of lighting a second cigar.

"Her?" Mrs. Sowler repeated slowly, her eyes fixed on Phoebe with a lowering expression of suspicion and surprise. "Her?" She turned to Jervy. "Did you ask me if the child was a girl or a boy?"

"I never even thought of it," Jervy replied.

"Did I happen to say it myself, without being asked?"

Jervy deliberately abandoned Phoebe to the implacable old wretch, before whom she had betrayed herself. It was the only likely way of forcing the girl to confess everything. "No," he answered; "you never said it without being asked."

Mrs. Sowler turned once more to Phoebe. "How do you know the child was a girl?" she inquired.

Phoebe trembled, and said nothing. She sat with her head down, and her hands, fast clasped together, resting on her lap.

"Might I ask, if you please," Mrs. Sowler proceeded, with a ferocious assumption of courtesy, "how old you are, miss? You're young enough and pretty enough not to mind answering to your age, I'm sure."

Even Jervy's villainous experience of the world failed to forewarn him of what was coming. Phoebe, it is needless to say, instantly fell into the trap.

"Twenty-four," she replied, "next birthday."

"And the child was put into my hands, sixteen years ago," said Mrs. Sowler. "Take sixteen from twenty-four, and eight remains. I'm more surprised than ever, miss, at your knowing it to be a girl. It couldn't have been your child—could it?"

144

Phoebe started to her feet, in a state of fury. "Do you hear that?" she cried, appealing to Jervy. "How dare you bring me here to be insulted by that drunken wretch?"

Mrs. Sowler rose, on her side. The old savage snatched up her empty glass—intending to throw it at Phoebe. At the same moment, the ready Jervy caught her by the arm, dragged her out of the room, and shut the door behind them.

There was a bench on the landing outside. He pushed Mrs. Sowler down on the bench with one hand, and took Phoebe's purse out of his pocket with the other. "Here's a pound," he said, "towards the recovery of that debt of yours. Go home quietly, and meet me at the door of this house tomorrow evening, at six."

Mrs. Sowler, opening her lips to protest, suddenly closed them again, fascinated by the sight of the gold. She clutched the coin, and became friendly and familiar in a moment. "Help me downstairs, deary," she said, "and put me into a cab. I'm afraid of the night air."

"One word more, before I put you into a cab," said Jervy. "What did you really do with the child?"

Mrs. Sowler grinned hideously, and whispered her reply, in the strictest confidence.

"Sold her to Moll Davies, for five-and-sixpence."

"Who was Moll Davis?"

"A cadger."

"And you really know nothing now of Moll Davis or the child?"

"Should I want you to help me if I did?" Mrs. Sowler asked contemptuously. "They may be both dead and buried, for all I know to the contrary."

Jervy put her into the cab, without further delay. "Now for the other one!" he said to himself, as he hurried back to the private room.

CHAPTER 5

Some men would have found it no easy task to console Phoebe, under the circumstances. Jervy had the immense advantage of not feeling the slightest sympathy for her: he was in full command of his large resources of fluent assurance and ready flattery. In less than five minutes, Phoebe's tears were dried, and her lover had his arm round her waist again, in the character of a cherished and forgiven man.

"Now, my angel!" he said (Phoebe sighed tenderly; he had never called her his angel before), "tell me all about it in confidence. Only let me know the facts, and I shall see my way to protecting you against any annoyance from Mrs. Sowler in the future. You have made a very extraordinary discovery. Come closer to me, my dear girl. Did it happen in Farnaby's house?"

"I heard it in the kitchen," said Phoebe.

Jervy started. "Did any one else hear it?" he asked.

"No. They were all in the housekeeper's room, looking at the Indian curiosities which her son in Canada had sent to her. I had left my bird on the dresser—and I ran into the kitchen to put the cage in a safe place, being afraid of the cat. One of the swinging windows in the skylight was open; and I heard voices in the back room above, which is Mrs. Farnaby's room."

"Whose voices did you hear?"

"Mrs. Farnaby's voice, and Mr. Goldenheart's."

"Mrs. Farnaby?" Jervy repeated, in surprise. "Are you sure it was *Mrs.?*"

"Of course I am! Do you think I don't know that horrid woman's voice? She was saying a most extraordinary thing when I first heard her—she was asking if there was anything wrong in showing her naked foot. And a man answered, and the voice was Mr. Goldenheart's. You would have felt curious to hear more, if you had been in my place, wouldn't you? I opened the second window in the kitchen, so as to make sure of not missing anything. And what do you think I heard her say?"

"You mean Mrs. Farnaby?"

"Yes. I heard her say, 'Look at my right foot—you see there's nothing the matter with it.' And then, after a while, she said, 'Look at my left foot—look between the third toe and the fourth.' Did you ever hear of such a audacious thing for a married woman to say to a young man?"

"Go on! go on! What did *he* say?"

"Nothing; I suppose he was looking at her foot."

"Her left foot?"

"Yes. Her left foot was nothing to be proud of, I can tell you! By her own account, she has some horrid deformity in it, between the third toe and the fourth. No; I didn't hear her say what the deformity was. I only heard her call it so—and she said her 'poor darling' was born with the same fault, and that was her defence against being imposed upon by rogues—I remember the very words—'in the past days when I employed people to find her.' Yes! she said *her.* I heard it plainly. And she talked afterwards of her 'poor lost daughter', who might be still living somewhere, and wondering who her mother was. Naturally enough, when I heard that hateful old drunkard talking about a child given to her by Mr. Farnaby, I put two and two together. Dear me, how strangely you look! What's wrong with you?"

"I'm only very much interested—that's all. But there's one thing I don't understand. What had Mr. Goldenheart to do with all this?"

"Didn't I tell you?"

"No."

"Well, then, I tell you now. Mrs. Farnaby is not only a heartless wretch, who turns a poor girl out of her situation, and refuses to give her a character—she's a fool besides. That precious exhibition of her nasty foot was to inform Mr. Goldenheart of something she wanted him to know. If he happened to meet with a girl, in his walks or his travels, and if he found that she had the same deformity in the same foot, then he might know for certain—"

"All right! I understand. But why Mr. Goldenheart?"

"Because she had a dream that Mr. Goldenheart had found the lost girl, and because she thought there was one chance in a hundred that her dream might come true! Did you ever hear of such a fool before? From what I could make out, I believe she actually cried about it. And that same woman turns me into the street to be ruined, for all she knows or cares. Mind this! I would have kept her secret—it was no business of mine, after all—if she had behaved decently to me. As it is, I mean to be even with her; and what I heard down in the kitchen is more than enough to help me to it. I'll expose her somehow—I don't quite know how; but that will come with time. You will keep the secret, dear, I'm sure. We are soon to have all our secrets in common, when we are man and wife, ain't we? Why, you're not listening to me! What *is* the matter with you?"

Jervy suddenly looked up. His soft insinuating manner had vanished; he spoke roughly and impatiently.

"I want to know something. Has Farnaby's wife got money of her own?"

Phoebe's mind was still disturbed by the change in her lover. "You speak as if you were angry with me," she said.

Jervy recovered his insinuating tones, with some difficulty. "My dear girl, I love you! How can I be angry with you? You've set me thinking—and it bothers me a little, that's all. Do you happen to know if Mrs. Farnaby has got money of her own?"

Phoebe answered this time. "I've heard Miss Regina say that Mrs. Farnaby's father was a rich man," she said.

"What was his name?"

"Ronald."

"Do you know when he died?"

"No."

Jervy fell into thought again, biting his nails in great perplexity. After a moment or two, an idea came to him. "The tombstone will tell me!" he exclaimed, speaking to himself. He turned to Phoebe, before she could express her surprise, and asked if she knew where Mr. Ronald was buried.

"Yes," said Phoebe, "I've heard that. In Highgate cemetery. But why do you want to know?"

Jervy looked at his watch. "It's getting late," he said; "I'll see you safe home."

"But I want to know—"

"Put on your bonnet, and wait till we are out in the street."

Jervy paid the bill, with all needful remembrance of the waiter. He was generous, he was polite; but he was apparently in no hurry to favour Phoebe with the explanation that he had promised. They had left the tavern for some minutes—and he was still rude enough to remain absorbed in his own reflections. Phoebe's patience gave way.

"I have told you everything," she said reproachfully; "I don't call it fair dealing to keep me in the dark after that."

He roused himself directly. "My dear girl, you entirely mistake me!"

148

The reply was as ready as usual; but it was spoken rather absently. Only that moment, he had decided on informing Phoebe (to some extent, at least) of the purpose which he was then meditating. He would infinitely have preferred using Mrs. Sowler as his sole accomplice. But he knew the girl too well to run that risk. If he refused to satisfy her curiosity, she would be deterred by no scruples of delicacy from privately watching him; and she might say something (either by word of month or by writing) to the kind young mistress who was in correspondence with her, which might lead to disastrous results. It was of the last importance to him, so far to associate Phoebe with his projected enterprise, as to give her an interest of her own in keeping his secrets.

"I have not the least wish," he resumed, "to conceal any thing from you. So far as I can see my way at present, you shall see it too." Reserving in this dexterous manner the freedom of lying, whenever he found it necessary to depart from the truth, he smiled encouragingly, and waited to be questioned.

Phoebe repeated the inquiry she had made at the tavern. "Why do you want to know where Mr. Ronald is buried?" she asked bluntly.

"Mr. Ronald's tombstone, my dear, will tell me the date of Mr. Ronald's death," Jervy rejoined. "When I have got the date, I shall go to a place near St. Paul's, called Doctors' Commons; I shall pay a shilling fee, and I shall have the privilege of looking at Mr. Ronald's will."

"And what good will that do you?"

"Very properly put, Phoebe! Even shillings are not to be wasted, in our position. But my shilling will buy two sixpennyworths of information. I shall find out what sum of money Mr. Ronald has left to his daughter; and I shall know for certain whether Mrs. Farnaby's husband has any power over it, or not."

"Well?" said Phoebe, not much interested so far—"and what then?"

Jervy looked about him. They were in a crowded thoroughfare at the time. He preserved a discreet silence, until they had arrived at the first turning which led down a quiet street.

"What I have to tell you," he said, "must not be accidentally heard by anybody. Here, my dear, we are all but out of the world—and here I can speak to you safely. I promise you two good things. You shall bring Mrs. Farnaby to that day of reckoning; and we will find money enough to marry on comfortably as soon as you like."

Phoebe's languid interest in the subject began to revive: she insisted on having a clearer explanation than this. "Do you mean to get the money out of Mr. Farnaby?" she inquired.

"I will have nothing to do with Mr. Farnaby—unless I find that his wife's money is not at her own disposal. What you heard in the kitchen has altered all my plans. Wait a minute—and you will see what I am driving at. How much do you think Mrs. Farnaby would give me, if I found that lost daughter of hers?"

Phoebe suddenly stood still, and looked at the sordid scoundrel who was tempting her in blank amazement.

"But nobody knows where the daughter is," she objected.

"You and I know that the daughter has a deformity in her left foot," Jervy replied; "and you and I know exactly in what part of the foot it is. There's not only money to be made out of that knowledge—but money made easily, without the slightest risk. Suppose I managed the matter by correspondence, without appearing in it personally? Don't you think Mrs. Farnaby would open her purse beforehand, if I mentioned the exact position of that little deformity, as a proof that I was to be depended on?"

Phoebe was unable, or unwilling, to draw the obvious conclusion, even now.

"But, what would you do," she said, "when Mrs. Farnaby insisted on seeing her daughter?"

There was something in the girl's tone—half fearful, half suspicious—which warned Jervy that he was treading on dangerous ground. He knew perfectly well what he proposed to do, in the case that had been so plainly put him. It was the simplest thing in the world. He had only to make an appointment with Mrs. Farnaby for a meeting on a future day, and to take to flight in the interval; leaving a polite note behind him to say that it was all a mistake, and that he regretted being too poor to return the money. Having thus far acknowledged the design he had in view, could he still venture on answering his companion without reserve? Phoebe was vain, Phoebe was vindictive; and, more promising still, Phoebe was a fool. But she was not yet capable of consenting to an act of the vilest infamy, in cold blood. Jervy looked at her—and saw that the foreseen necessity for lying had come at last.

"That's just the difficulty," he said; "that's just where I don't see my way plainly yet. Can you advise me?"

Phoebe started, and drew back from him. "*I* advise you!" she exclaimed. "It frightens me to think of it. If you make her believe she is going to see her daughter, and if she finds out that you have robbed and deceived her, I can tell you this—with her furious temper—you would drive her mad."

Jervy's reply was a model of well-acted indignation. "Don't talk of anything so horrible," he exclaimed. "If you believe me capable of such cruelty as that, go to Mrs. Farnaby, and warn her at once!"

150

"It's too bad to speak to me in that way!" Phoebe rejoined, with the frank impetuosity of an offended woman. "You know I would die, rather than get you into trouble. Beg my pardon directly—or I won't walk another step with you!"

Jervy made the necessary apologies, with all possible humility. He had gained his end—he could now postpone any further discussion of the subject, without arousing Phoebe's distrust. "Let us say no more about it, for the present," he suggested; "we will think it over, and talk of pleasanter things in the mean time. Kiss me, my dear girl; there's nobody looking."

So he made peace with his sweetheart, and secured to himself, at the same time, the full liberty of future action of which he stood in need. If Phoebe asked any more questions, the necessary answer was obvious to the meanest capacity. He had merely to say, "The matter is beset with difficulties which I didn't see at first—I have given it up."

Their nearest way back to Phoebe's lodgings took them through the street which led to the Hampden Institution. Passing along the opposite side of the road, they saw the private door opened. Two men stepped out. A third man, inside, called after one of them. "Mr. Goldenheart! you have left the statement of receipts in the waiting-room." "Never mind," Amelius answered; "the night's receipts are so small that I would rather not be reminded of them again." "In my country," a third voice remarked, "if he had lectured as he has lectured to-night, I reckon I'd have given him three hundred dollars, gold (sixty pounds, English currency), and have made my own profit by the transaction. The British nation has lost its taste, sir, for intellectual recreation. I wish you good evening."

Jervy hurried Phoebe out of the way, just as the two gentlemen were crossing the street. He had not forgotten events at Tadmor—and he was by no means eager to renew his former acquaintance with Amelius.

CHAPTER 6

Rufus and his young friend walked together silently as far as a large square. Here they stopped, having reached the point at which it was necessary to take different directions on their way home.

"I've a word of advice, my son, for your private ear," said the New Englander. "The barometer behind your waistcoat points to a downhearted state of the moral atmosphere. Come along to home with me—you want a whisky cocktail badly."

"No, thank you, my dear fellow," Amelius answered a little sadly. "I own I'm downhearted, as you say. You see, I expected this lecture to be a new opening for me. Personally, as you know, I don't care two straws about money. But my marriage depends on my adding to my income; and the first attempt I've made to do it has ended in a total failure. I'm all abroad again, when I look to the future—and I'm afraid I'm fool enough to let it weigh on my spirits. No, the cocktail isn't the right remedy for me. I don't get the exercise and fresh air, here, that I used to get at Tadmor. My head burns after all that talking to-night. A good long walk will put me right, and nothing else will."

Rufus at once offered to accompany him. Amelius shook his head. "Did you ever walk a mile in your life, when you could ride?" he asked good-humouredly. "I mean to be on my legs for four or five hours; I should only have to send you home in a cab. Thank you, old fellow, for the brotherly interest you take in me. I'll breakfast with you to-morrow, at your hotel. Good night."

Some curious prevision of evil seemed to trouble the mind of the good New Englander. He held Amelius fast by the hand: he said, very earnestly, "It goes against the grit with me to see you wandering off by yourself at this time of night—it does, I tell you! Do me a favour for once, my bright boy—go right away to bed."

Amelius laughed, and released his hand. "I shouldn't sleep, if I did go to bed. Breakfast to-morrow, at ten o'clock. Goodnight, again!"

He started on his walk, at a pace which set pursuit on the part of Rufus at defiance. The American stood watching him, until he was lost to sight in the darkness. "What a grip that young fellow has got on me, in no more than a few months!" Rufus thought, as he slowly turned away in the direction of his hotel. "Lord send the poor boy may keep clear of mischief this night!"

Meanwhile, Amelius walked on swiftly, straight before him, careless in what direction he turned his steps, so long as he felt the cool air and kept moving.

His thoughts were not at first occupied with the doubtful question of his marriage; the lecture was still the uppermost subject in his mind. He had reserved for the conclusion of his address the justification of his view of the future, afforded by the widespread and frightful poverty among the millions of the population of London alone. On this melancholy theme he had spoken with the eloquence of true feeling, and had produced a strong impression, even on those members of the audience who were most resolutely opposed to the opinions which he advocated. Without any undue exercise of self-esteem, he could look back on the close of his lecture with the conviction that he had really done justice to himself and to his cause. The retrospect of the public discussion that had followed failed to give him the same pleasure. His warm temper, his vehemently sincere belief in the truth of his own convictions, placed him at a serious disadvantage towards the more self-restrained speakers (all older than himself) who rose, one after another, to combat his views. More than once he had lost his temper, and had been obliged to make his apologies. More than once he had been indebted to the ready help of Rufus, who had taken part in the battle of words, with the generous purpose of covering his retreat. "No!" he thought to himself, with bitter humility, "I'm not fit for public discussions. If they put me into Parliament tomorrow, I should only get called to order and do nothing."

He reached the bank of the Thames, at the eastward end of the Strand.

Walking straight on, as absently as ever, he crossed Waterloo Bridge, and followed the broad street that lay before him on the other side. He was thinking of the future again: Regina was in his mind now. The one prospect that he could see of a tranquil and happy life—with duties as well as pleasures; duties that might rouse him to find the vocation for which he was fit—was the prospect of his marriage. What was the obstacle that stood in his way? The vile obstacle of money; the contemptible spirit of ostentation which forbade him to live humbly on his own sufficient little income, and insisted that he should purchase domestic happiness at the price of the tawdry splendour of a rich tradesman and his friends. And Regina, who was free to follow her own better impulses—Regina, whose heart acknowledged him as its master— bowed before the golden image which was the tutelary deity of her uncle's household, and said resignedly, Love must wait!

Still walking blindly on, he was roused on a sudden to a sense of passing events. Crossing a side-street at the moment, a man caught him roughly by the arm, and saved him from being run over. The man had a broom in his hand; he was a crossing-sweeper. "I think I've earned my penny, sir!" he said.

Amelius gave him half-a-crown. The man shouldered his broom, and tossed up the money, in a transport of delight. "Here's something to go home with!" he cried, as he caught the half-crown again.

"Have you got a family at home?" Amelius asked.

"Only one, sir," said the man. "The others are all dead. She's as good a girl and as pretty a girl as ever put on a petticoat—though I say it that shouldn't. Thank you kindly, sir. Good night!"

Amelius looked after the poor fellow, happy at least for that night! "If I had only been lucky enough to fall in love with the crossing-sweeper's daughter," he thought bitterly, "*she* would have married me when I asked her."

He looked along the street. It curved away in the distance, with no visible limit to it. Arrived at the next side-street on his left, Amelius turned down it, weary of walking longer in the same direction. Whither it might lead him he neither knew nor cared. In his present humour it was a pleasurable sensation to feel himself lost in London.

The short street suddenly widened; a blaze of flaring gaslight dazzled his eyes; he heard all round him the shouting of innumerable voices. For the first time since he had been in London, he found himself in one of the street-markets of the poor.

On either side of the road, the barrows of the costermongers—the wandering tradesmen of the highway—were drawn up in rows; and every man was advertising his wares, by means of the cheap publicity of his own voice. Fish and vegetables; pottery and writing-paper; looking-glasses, saucepans, and coloured prints—all appealed together to the scantily filled purses of the crowds who thronged the pavement. One lusty vagabond stood up in a rickety donkey-cart, knee-deep in apples, selling a great wooden measure full for a penny, and yelling louder than all the rest. "Never was such apples sold in the public streets before! Sweet as flowers, and sound as a bell. Who says the poor ain't looked after," cried the fellow, with ferocious irony, "when they can have such apple-sauce as this to their loin of pork? Here's nobby apples; here's a penn'orth for your money. Sold again! Hullo, you! you look hungry. Catch! there's an apple for nothing, just to taste. Be in time, be in time before they're all sold!" Amelius moved forward a few steps, and was half deafened by rival butchers, shouting, "Buy, buy, buy!" to audiences of ragged women, who fingered the meat doubtfully, with longing eyes. A little farther—and there was a blind man selling staylaces, and singing a Psalm; and, beyond him again, a broken-down soldier playing "God save the Queen" on a tin flageolet. The one silent person in this sordid carnival was a Lascar beggar, with a printed placard round his neck, addressed to "The Charitable Public." He held a tallow candle to illuminate the copious narrative of his misfortunes; and the one reader he obtained was a fat man, who scratched his head, and remarked to Amelius that he didn't like foreigners. Starving boys and girls lurked among the costermongers' barrows, and begged piteously on pretence of selling cigar-lights and comic songs. Furious women stood at the doors of public-houses, and railed on their drunken husbands for spending the house-money in gin. A thicker crowd, towards the middle of the street, poured in and out at the door of a cookshop. Here the people presented a less terrible spectacle—they were even touching to see. These were the patient poor, who bought hot morsels of sheep's heart and liver at a penny an ounce, with lamentable little mouthfuls of peas-pudding, greens, and potatoes at a halfpenny each. Pale children in corners supped on penny basins of soup, and looked with hungry admiration at their enviable neighbours who could afford to buy stewed eels for twopence. Everywhere there was the same noble resignation to their hard fate, in old and young alike. No impatience, no complaints. In this wretched place, the language of true gratitude was still to be heard, thanking the good-natured cook for a little spoonful of gravy thrown in for nothing—and here, humble mercy that had its one superfluous halfpenny to spare gave that halfpenny to utter destitution, and gave it with right good-will. Amelius spent all his shillings and sixpences, in doubling and trebling the poor little pennyworths of food—and left the place with tears in his eyes.

He was near the end of the street by this time. The sight of the misery about him, and the sense of his own utter inability to remedy it, weighed heavily on his spirits. He thought of the peaceful and prosperous life at Tadmor. Were his happy brethren of the Community and these miserable people about him creatures of the same all-merciful God? The terrible doubts which come to all thinking men—the doubts which are not to be stifled by crying "Oh, fie!" in a pulpit—rose darkly in his mind. He quickened his pace. "Let me let out of it," he said to himself, "let me get out of it!"

BOOK THE SIXTH

FILIA DOLOROSA

CHAPTER 1

Amelius found it no easy matter to pass quickly through the people loitering and gossiping about him. There was greater freedom for a rapid walker in the road. He was on the point of stepping off the pavement, when a voice behind him—a sweet soft voice, though it spoke very faintly—said, "Are you good-natured, sir?"

He turned, and found himself face to face with one of the saddest sisterhood on earth—the sisterhood of the streets.

His heart ached as he looked at her, she was so poor and so young. The lost creature had, to all appearance, barely passed the boundary between childhood and girlhood—she could hardly be more than fifteen or sixteen years old. Her eyes, of the purest and loveliest blue, rested on Amelius with a vacantly patient look, like the eyes of a suffering child. The soft oval outline of her face would have been perfect if the cheeks had been filled out; they were wasted and hollow, and sadly pale. Her delicate lips had none of the rosy colour of youth; and her finely modelled chin was disfigured by a piece of plaster covering some injury. She was little and thin; her worn and scanty clothing showed her frail youthful figure still waiting for its perfection of growth. Her pretty little bare hands were reddened by the raw night air. She trembled as Amelius looked at her in silence, with compassionate wonder. But for the words in which she had accosted him, it would have been impossible to associate her with the lamentable life that she led. The appearance of the girl was artlessly virginal and innocent; she looked as if she had passed through the contamination of the streets without being touched by it, without fearing it, or feeling it, or understanding it. Robed in pure white, with her gentle blue eyes raised to heaven, a painter might have shown her on his canvas as a saint or an angel; and the critical world would have said, Here is the true ideal—Raphael himself might have painted this!

"You look very pale," said Amelius. "Are you ill?"

"No, sir—only hungry."

Her eyes half closed; she reeled from sheer weakness as she said the words. Amelius held her up, and looked round him. They were close to a stall at which coffee and slices of bread-and-butter were sold. He ordered some coffee to be poured out, and offered her the food. She thanked him and tried to eat. "I can't help it, sir," she said faintly. The bread dropped from her hand; her weary head sank on his shoulder.

Two young women—older members of the sad sisterhood—were passing at the moment. "She's too far gone, sir, to eat," said one of them. "I know what would do her good, if you don't mind going into a public-house."

"Where is it?" said Amelius. "Be quick!"

157

One of the women led the way. The other helped Amelius to support the girl. They entered the crowded public-house. In less than a minute, the first woman had forced her way through the drunken customers at the bar, and had returned with a glass of port-wine and cloves. The girl revived as the stimulant passed her lips. She opened her innocent blue eyes again, in vague surprise. "I shan't die this time," she said quietly.

A corner of the place was not occupied; a small empty cask stood there. Amelius made the poor creature sit down and rest a little. He had only gold in his purse; and, when the woman had paid for the wine, he offered her some of the change. She declined to take it. "I've got a shilling or two, sir," she said; "and I can take care of myself. Give it to Simple Sally."

"You'll save her a beating, sir, for one night at least," said the other woman. "We call her Simple Sally, because she's a little soft, poor soul—hasn't grown up, you know, in her mind, since she was a child. Give her some of your change, sir, and you'll be doing a kind thing."

All that is most unselfish, all that is most divinely compassionate and self-sacrificing in a woman's nature, was as beautiful and as undefiled as ever in these women—the outcasts of the hard highway!

Amelius turned to the girl. Her head had sunk on her bosom; she was half asleep. She looked up as he approached her.

"Would you have been beaten to-night," he asked, "if you had not met with me?"

"Father always beats me, sir," said Simple Sally, "if I don't bring money home. He threw a knife at me last night. It didn't hurt much—it only cut me here," said the girl, pointing to the plaster on her chin.

One of the women touched Amelius on the shoulder, and whispered to him. "He's no more her father, sir, than I am. She's a helpless creature—and he takes advantage of her. If I only had a place to take her to, he should never set eyes on her again. Show the gentleman your bosom, Sally."

She opened her poor threadbare little shawl. Over the lovely girlish breast, still only growing to the rounded beauty of womanhood, there was a hideous blue-black bruise. Simple Sally smiled, and said, "That *did* hurt me, sir. I'd rather have the knife."

Some of the nearest drinkers at the bar looked round and laughed. Amelius tenderly drew the shawl over the girl's cold bosom. "For God's sake, let us get away from this place!" he said.

The influence of the cool night air completed Simple Sally's recovery. She was able to eat now. Amelius proposed retracing his steps to the provision-shop, and giving her the best food that the place afforded. She preferred the bread-and-butter at the coffee-stall. Those thick slices, piled up on the plate, tempted her as a luxury. On trying the luxury, one slice satisfied her. "I thought I was hungry enough to eat the whole plateful," said the girl, turning away from the stall, in the vacantly submissive manner which it saddened Amelius to see. He bought more of the bread-and-butter, on the chance that her appetite might revive. While he was wrapping it in a morsel of paper, one of her elder companions touched him and whispered, "There he is, sir!" Amelius looked at her. "The brute who calls himself her father," the woman explained impatiently.

Amelius turned, and saw Simple Sally with her arm in the grasp of a half-drunken ruffian; one of the swarming wild beasts of Low London, dirtied down from head to foot to the colour of the street mud—the living danger and disgrace of English civilization. As Amelius eyed him, he drew the girl away a step or two. "You've got a gentleman this time," he said to her; "I shall expect gold to-night, or else—!" He finished the sentence by lifting his monstrous fist, and shaking it in her face. Cautiously as he had lowered his tones in speaking, the words had reached the keenly sensitive ears of Amelius. Urged by his hot temper, he sprang forward. In another moment, he would have knocked the brute down—but for the timely interference of the arm of the law, clad in a policeman's great-coat. "Don't get yourself into trouble, sir," said the man good-humouredly. "Now, you Hell-fire (that's the nice name they know him by, sir, in these parts), be off with you!" The wild beast on two legs cowered at the voice of authority, like the wild beast on four: he was lost to sight, at the dark end of the street, in a moment.

"I saw him threaten her with his fist," said Amelius, his eyes still aflame with indignation. "He has bruised her frightfully on the breast. Is there no protection for the poor creature?"

"Well, sir," the policeman answered, "you can summon him if you like. I dare say he'd get a month's hard labour. But, don't you see, it would be all the worse for her when he came out of prison."

The policeman's view of the girl's position was beyond dispute. Amelius turned to her gently; she was shivering with cold or terror, perhaps with both. "Tell me," he said, "is that man really your father?"

"Lord bless you, sir!" interposed the policeman, astonished at the gentleman's simplicity, "Simple Sally hasn't got father or mother—have you, my girl?"

She paid no heed to the policeman. The sorrow and sympathy, plainly visible in Amelius, filled her with a childish interest and surprise. She dimly understood that it was sorrow and sympathy for *her*. The bare idea of distressing this new friend, so unimaginably kind and considerate, seemed to frighten her. "Don't fret about *me,* sir," she said timidly; "I don't mind having no father nor mother; I don't mind being beaten." She appealed to the nearest of her two women-friends. "We get used to everything, don't we, Jenny?"

Amelius could bear no more. "It's enough to break one's heart to hear you, and see you!" he burst out—and suddenly turned his head aside. His generous nature was touched to the quick; he could only control himself by an effort of resolution that shook him, body and soul. "I can't and won't let that unfortunate creature go back to be beaten and starved!" he said, passionately addressing himself to the policeman. "Oh, look at her! How helpless, and how young!"

The policeman stared. These were strange words to him. But all true emotion carries with it, among all true people, its own title to respect. He spoke to Amelius with marked respect.

"It's a hard case, sir, no doubt," he said. "The girl's a quiet, well-disposed creature—and the other two there are the same. They're of the sort that keep to themselves, and don't drink. They all of them do well enough, as long as they don't let the liquor overcome them. Half the time it's the men's fault when they do drink. Perhaps the workhouse might take her in for the night. What's this you've got girl, in your hand? Money?"

Amelius hastened to say that he had given her the money. "The workhouse!" he repeated. "The very sound of it is horrible."

"Make your mind easy, sir," said the policeman; "they won't take her in at the workhouse, with money in her hand."

In sheer despair, Amelius asked helplessly if there was no hotel near. The policeman pointed to Simple Sally's threadbare and scanty clothes, and left them to answer the question for themselves. "There's a place they call a coffee-house," he said, with the air of a man who thought he had better provoke as little further inquiry on that subject as possible.

Too completely pre-occupied, or too innocent in the ways of London, to understand the man, Amelius decided on trying the coffee-house. A suspicious old woman met them at the door, and spied the policeman in the background. Without waiting for any inquiries, she said, "All full for to-night,"—and shut the door in their faces.

"Is there no other place?" said Amelius.

"There's a lodging-house," the policeman answered, more doubtfully than ever. "It's getting late, sir; and I'm afraid you'll find 'em packed like herrings in a barrel. Come, and see for yourself."

160

He led the way into a wretchedly lighted by-street, and knocked with his foot on a trap-door in the pavement. The door was pushed open from below, by a sturdy boy with a dirty night-cap on his head.

"Any of 'em wanted to-night, sir?" asked the sturdy boy, the moment he saw the policeman.

"What does he mean?" said Amelius.

"There's a sprinkling of thieves among them, sir," the policeman explained. "Stand out of the way, Jacob, and let the gentleman look in."

He produced his lantern, and directed the light downwards, as he spoke. Amelius looked in. The policeman's figure of speech, likening the lodgers to "herrings in a barrel," accurately described the scene. On the floor of a kitchen, men, women, and children lay all huddled together in closely packed rows. Ghastly faces rose terrified out of the seething obscurity, when the light of the lantern fell on them. The stench drove Amelius back, sickened and shuddering.

"How's the sore place on your head, Jacob?" the policeman inquired. "This is a civil boy," he explained to Amelius, "and I like to encourage him."

"I'm getting better, sir, as fast as I can," said the boy.

"Good night, Jacob."

"Good night, sir." The trap-door fell—and the lodging-house disappeared like the vision of a frightful dream.

There was a moment of silence among the little group on the pavement. It was not easy to solve the question of what to do next. "There seems to be some difficulty," the policeman remarked, "about housing this girl for the night."

"Why shouldn't we take her along with us?" one of the women suggested. "She won't mind sleeping three in a bed, I know."

"What are you thinking of?" the other woman remonstrated. "When he finds she don't come home, our place will be the first place he looks for her in."

Amelius settled the difficulty, in his own headlong way, "I'll take care of her for the night," he said. "Sally, will you trust yourself with me?"

She put her hand in his, with the air of a child who was ready to go home. Her wan face brightened for the first time. "Thank you, sir," she said; "I'll go anywhere along with you."

The policeman smiled. The two women looked thunderstruck. Before they had recovered themselves, Amelius forced them to take some money from him, and cordially shook hands with them. "You're good creatures," he said, in his eager, hearty way; "I'm sincerely sorry for you. Now, Mr. Policeman, show me where to find a cab—and take that for the trouble I am giving you. You're a humane man, and a credit to the force."

In five minutes more, Amelius was on the way to his lodgings, with Simple Sally by his side. The act of reckless imprudence which he was committing was nothing but an act of Christian duty, to his mind. Not the slightest misgiving troubled him. "I shall provide for her in some way!" he thought to himself cheerfully. He looked at her. The weary outcast was asleep already in her corner of the cab. From time to time she still shivered, even in her sleep. Amelius took off his great-coat, and covered her with it. How some of his friends at the club would have laughed, if they had seen him at that moment!

He was obliged to wake her when the cab stopped. His key admitted them to the house. He lit his candle in the hall, and led her up the stairs. "You'll soon be asleep again, Sally," he whispered.

She looked round the little sitting-room with drowsy admiration. "What a pretty place to live in!" she said.

"Are you hungry again?" Amelius asked.

She shook her head, and took off her shabby bonnet; her pretty light-brown hair fell about her face and her shoulders. "I think I'm too tired, sir, to be hungry. Might I take the sofa-pillow, and lay down on the hearth-rug?"

Amelius opened the door of his bedroom. "You are to pass the night more comfortably than that," he answered. "There is a bed for you here."

She followed him in, and looked round the bedroom, with renewed admiration of everything that she saw. At the sight of the hairbrushes and the comb, she clapped her hands in ecstasy. "Oh, how different from mine!" she exclaimed. "Is the comb tortoise-shell, sir, like one sees in the shop-windows?" The bath and the towels attracted her next; she stood, looking at them with longing eyes, completely forgetful of the wonderful comb. "I've often peeped into the ironmongers' shops," she said, "and thought I should be the happiest girl in the world, if I had such a bath as that. A little pitcher is all I have got of my own, and they swear at me when I want it filled more than once. In all my life, I have never had as much water as I should like." She paused, and thought for a moment. The forlorn, vacant look appeared again, and dimmed the beauty of her blue eyes. "It will be hard to go back, after seeing all these pretty things," she said to herself—and sighed, with that inborn submission to her fate so melancholy to see in a creature so young.

162

"You shall never go back again to that dreadful life," Amelius interposed. "Never speak of it, never think of it any more. Oh, don't look at me like that!"

She was listening with an expression of pain, and with both her hands lifted to her head. There was something so wonderful in the idea which he had suggested to her, that her mind was not able to take it all in at once. "You make my head giddy," she said. "I'm such a poor stupid girl—I feel out of myself, like, when a gentleman like you sets me thinking of new things. Would you mind saying it again, sir?"

"I'll say it to-morrow morning," Amelius rejoined kindly. "You are tired, Sally—go to rest."

She roused herself, and looked at the bed. "Is that your bed, sir?"

"It's your bed to-night," said Amelius. "I shall sleep on the sofa, in the next room."

Her eyes rested on him, for a moment, in speechless surprise; she looked back again at the bed. "Are you going to leave me by myself?" she asked wonderingly. Not the faintest suggestion of immodesty— nothing that the most profligate man living could have interpreted impurely—showed itself in her look or manner, as she said those words.

Amelius thought of what one of her women-friends had told him. "She hasn't grown up, you know, in her mind, since she was a child." There were other senses in the poor victim that were still undeveloped, besides the mental sense. He was at a loss how to answer her, with the respect which was due to that all-atoning ignorance. His silence amazed and frightened her.

"Have I said anything to make you angry with me?" she asked.

Amelius hesitated no longer. "My poor girl," he said, "I pity you from the bottom of my heart! Sleep well, Simple Sally—sleep well." He left her hurriedly, and shut the door between them.

She followed him as far as the closed door; and stood there alone, trying to understand him, and trying all in vain! After a while, she found courage enough to whisper through the door. "If you please, sir—" She stopped, startled by her own boldness. He never heard her; he was standing at the window, looking out thoughtfully at the night; feeling less confident of the future already. She still stood at the door, wretched in the firm persuasion that she had offended him. Once she lifted her hand to knock at the door, and let it drop again at her side. A second time she made the effort, and desperately summoned the resolution to knock. He opened the door directly.

"I'm very sorry if I said anything wrong," she began faintly, her breath coming and going in quick hysteric gasps. "Please forgive me, and wish me good night."

Amelius took her hand; he said good night with the utmost gentleness, but he said it sorrowfully. She was not quite comforted yet. "Would you mind, sir—?" She paused awkwardly, afraid to go on. There was something so completely childlike in the artless perplexity of her eyes, that Amelius smiled. The change in his expression gave her back her courage in an instant; her pale delicate lips reflected his smile prettily. "Would you mind giving me a kiss, sir?" she said. Amelius kissed her. Let the man who can honestly say he would have done otherwise, blame him. He shut the door between them once more. She was quite happy now. He heard her singing to herself as she got ready for bed.

Once, in the wakeful watches of the night, she startled him. He heard a cry of pain or terror in the bedroom. "What is it?" he asked through the door; "what has frightened you?" There was no answer. After a minute or two, the cry was repeated. He opened the door, and looked in. She was sleeping, and dreaming as she slept. One little thin white arm was lifted in the air, and waved restlessly to and fro over her head. "Don't kill me!" she murmured, in low moaning tones—"oh, don't kill me!" Amelius took her arm gently, and laid it back on the coverlet of the bed. His touch seemed to exercise some calming influence over her: she sighed, and turned her head on the pillow; a faint flush rose on her wasted cheeks, and passed away again—she sank quietly into dreamless sleep.

Amelius returned to his sofa, and fell into a broken slumber. The hours of the night passed. The sad light of the November morning dawned mistily through the uncurtained window, and woke him.

He started up, and looked at the bedroom door. "Now what is to be done?" That was his first thought, on waking: he was beginning to feel his responsibilities at last.

CHAPTER 2

The landlady of the lodgings decided what was to be done.

"You will be so good, sir, as to leave my apartments immediately," she said to Amelius. "I make no claim to the week's rent, in consideration of the short notice. This is a respectable house, and it shall be kept respectable at any sacrifice."

Amelius explained and protested; he appealed to the landlady's sense of justice and sense of duty, as a Christian woman.

The reasoning which would have been irresistible at Tadmor was reasoning completely thrown away in London. The landlady remained as impenetrable as the Egyptian Sphinx. "If that creature in the bedroom is not out of my house in an hour's time, I shall send for the police." Having answered her lodger's arguments in those terms, she left the room, and banged the door after her.

"Thank you, sir, for being so kind to me. I'll go away directly—and then, perhaps, the lady will forgive you."

Amelius looked round. Simple Sally had heard it all. She was dressed in her wretched clothes, and was standing at the open bedroom door, crying,

"Wait a little," said Amelius, wiping her eyes with his own handkerchief; "and we will go away together. I want to get you some better clothes; and I don't exactly know how to set about it. Don't cry, my dear—don't cry."

The deaf maid-of-all-work came in, as he spoke. She too was in tears. Amelius had been good to her, in many little ways—and she was the guilty person who had led to the discovery in the bedroom. "If you had only told me, sir," she said penitently, "I'd have kep' it secret. But, there, I went in with your 'ot water, as usual, and, O Lor', I was that startled I dropped the jug, and run downstairs again—!"

Amelius stopped the further progress of the apology. "I don't blame you, Maria," he said; "I'm in a difficulty. Help me out of it; and you will do me a kindness."

Maria partially heard him, and no more. Afraid of reaching the landlady's ears, as well as the maid's ears, if he raised his voice, he asked if she could read writing. Yes, she could read writing, if it was plain. Amelius immediately reduced the expression of his necessities to writing, in large text. Maria was delighted. She knew the nearest shop at which ready-made outer clothing for women could be obtained, and nothing was wanted, as a certain guide to an ignorant man, but two pieces of string. With one piece, she measured Simple Sally's height, and with the other she took the slender girth of the girl's waist—while Amelius opened his writing-desk, and supplied himself with the last sum of spare money that he possessed. He had just closed the desk again, when the voice of the merciless landlady was heard, calling imperatively for Maria.

The maid-of-all-work handed the two indicative strings to Amelius. "They'll 'elp you at the shop," she said—and shuffled out of the room.

Amelius turned to Simple Sally. "I am going to get you some new clothes," he began.

The girl stopped him there: she was incapable of listening to a word more. Every trace of sorrow vanished from her face in an instant. She clapped her hands. "Oh!" she cried, "new clothes! clean clothes! Let me go with you."

Even Amelius saw that it was impossible to take her out in the streets with him in broad daylight, dressed as she was then. "No, no," he said, "wait here till you get your new things. I won't be half an hour gone. Lock yourself in if you're afraid, and open the door to nobody till I come back!"

Sally hesitated; she began to look frightened.

"Think of the new dress, and the pretty bonnet," suggested Amelius, speaking unconsciously in the tone in which he might have promised a toy to a child.

He had taken the right way with her. Her face brightened again. "I'll do anything you tell me," she said.

He put the key in her hand, and was out in the street directly.

Amelius possessed one valuable moral quality which is exceedingly rare among Englishmen. He was not in the least ashamed of putting himself in a ridiculous position, when he was conscious that his own motives justified him. The smiling and tittering of the shop-women, when he stated the nature of his errand, and produced his two pieces of string, failed to annoy him in the smallest degree. He laughed too. "Funny, isn't it," he said, "a man like me buying gowns and the rest of it? She can't come herself—and you'll advise me, like good creatures, won't you?" They advised their handsome young customer to such good purpose, that he was in possession of a gray walking costume, a black cloth jacket, a plain lavender-coloured bonnet, a pair of black gloves, and a paper of pins, in little more than ten minutes' time. The nearest trunk-maker supplied a travelling-box to hold all these treasures; and a passing cab took Amelius back to his lodgings, just as the half-hour was out. But one event had happened during his absence. The landlady had knocked at the door, had called through it in a terrible voice, "Half an hour more!" and had retired again without waiting for an answer.

Amelius carried the box into the bedroom. "Be as quick as you can, Sally," he said—and left her alone, to enjoy the full rapture of discovering the new clothes.

166

When she opened the door and showed herself, the change was so wonderful that Amelius was literally unable to speak to her. Joy flushed her pale cheeks, and diffused its tender radiance over her pure blue eyes. A more charming little creature, in that momentary transfiguration of pride and delight, no man's eyes ever looked on. She ran across the room to Amelius, and threw her arms round his neck. "Let me be your servant!" she cried; "I want to live with you all my life. Jump me up! I'm wild—I want to fly through the window." She caught sight of herself in the looking-glass, and suddenly became composed and serious. "Oh," she said, with the quaintest mixture of awe and astonishment, "was there ever such another bonnet as this? Do look at it—do please look at it!"

Amelius good-naturedly approached to look at it. At the same moment the sitting-room door was opened, without any preliminary ceremony of knocking—and Rufus walked into the room. "It's half after ten," he said, "and the breakfast is spoiling as fast as it can."

Before Amelius could make his excuses for having completely forgotten his engagement, Rufus discovered Sally. No woman, young or old, high in rank or low in rank, ever found the New Englander unprepared with his own characteristic acknowledgment of the debt of courtesy which he owed to the sex. With his customary vast strides, he marched up to Sally and insisted on shaking hands with her. "How do you find yourself, miss? I take pleasure in making your acquaintance." The girl turned to Amelius with wide-eyed wonder and doubt. "Go into the next room, Sally, for a minute or two," he said. "This gentleman is a friend of mine, and I have something to say to him."

"That's an *active* little girl," said Rufus, looking after her as she ran to the friendly shelter of the bedroom. "Reminds me of one of our girls at Coolspring—she does. Well, now, and who may Sally be?"

Amelius answered the question, as usual, without the slightest reserve. Rufus waited in impenetrable silence until he had completed his narrative—then took him gently by the arm, and led him to the window. With his hands in his pockets and his long legs planted wide apart on his big feet, the American carefully studied the face of his young friend under the strongest light that could fall on it.

"No," said Rufus, speaking quietly to himself, "the boy is not raving mad, so far as I can see. He has every appearance on him of meaning what he says. And this is what comes of the Community of Tadmor, is it? Well, civil and religious liberty is dearly purchased sometimes in the United States—and that's a fact."

Amelius turned away to pack his portmanteau. "I don't understand you," he said.

"I don't suppose you do," Rufus remarked. "I am at a similar loss myself to understand *you*. My store of sensible remarks is copious on most occasions—but I'm darned if I ain't dried up in the face of this! Might I venture to ask what that venerable Chief Christian at Tadmor would say to the predicament in which I find my young Socialist this morning?"

"What would he say?" Amelius repeated. "Just what he said when Mellicent first came among us. 'Ah, dear me! Another of the Fallen Leaves!' I wish I had the dear old man here to help me. *He* would know how to restore that poor starved, outraged, beaten creature to the happy place on God's earth which God intended her to fill!"

Rufus abruptly took him by the hand. "You mean that?" he said.

"What else could I mean?" Amelius rejoined sharply.

"Bring her right away to breakfast at the hotel!" cried Rufus, with every appearance of feeling infinitely relieved. "I don't say I can supply you with the venerable Chief Christian—but I can find a woman to fix you, who is as nigh to being an angel, barring the wings, as any she-creature since the time of mother Eve." He knocked at the bedroom door, turning a deaf ear to every appeal for further information which Amelius could address to him. "Breakfast is waiting, miss!" he called out; "and I'm bound to tell you that the temper of the cook at our hotel is a long way on the wrong side of uncertain. Well, Amelius, this is the age of exhibition. If there's ever an exhibition of ignorance in the business of packing a portmanteau, you run for the Gold Medal—and a unanimous jury will vote it, I reckon, to a young man from Tadmor. Clear out, will you, and leave it to me."

He pulled off his coat, and conquered the difficulties of packing in a hurry, as if he had done nothing else all his life. The landlady herself, appearing with pitiless punctuality exactly at the expiration of the hour, "smoothed her horrid front" in the polite and placable presence of Rufus. He insisted on shaking hands with her; he took pleasure in making her acquaintance; she reminded him, he did assure her, of the lady of the captain-general of the Coolspring Branch of the St. Vitus Commandery; and he would take the liberty to inquire whether they were related or not. Under cover of this fashionable conversation, Simple Sally was taken out of the room by Amelius without attracting notice. She insisted on carrying her threadbare old clothes away with her in the box which had contained the new dress. "I want to look at them sometimes," she said, "and think how much better off I am now." Rufus was the last to take his departure; he persisted in talking to the landlady all the way down the stairs and out to the street door.

While Amelius was waiting for his friend on the house-steps, a young man driving by in a cab leaned out and looked at him. The young man was Jervy, on his way from Mr. Ronald's tombstone to Doctors' Commons.

168

CHAPTER 3

With a rapid succession of events the morning had begun. With a rapid succession of events the day went on.

The breakfast being over, rooms at the hotel were engaged by Rufus for his "two young friends." After this, the next thing to be done was to provide Simple Sally with certain necessary, but invisible, articles of clothing, which Amelius had never thought of. A note to the nearest shop produced the speedy arrival of a smart lady, accompanied by a boy and a large basket. There was some difficulty in persuading Sally to trust herself alone in her room with the stranger. She was afraid, poor soul, of everybody but Amelius. Even the good American failed to win her confidence. The distrust implanted in her feeble mind by the terrible life that she had led, was the instinctive distrust of a wild animal. "Why must I go among other people?" she whispered piteously to Amelius. "I only want to be with You!" It was as completely useless to reason with her as it would have been to explain the advantages of a comfortable cage to a newly caught bird. There was but one way of inducing her to submit to the most gently exerted interference. Amelius had only to say, "Do it, Sally, to please me." And Sally sighed, and did it.

In her absence Amelius reiterated his inquiries, in relation to that unknown friend whom Rufus had not scrupled to describe as "an angel—barring the wings."

The lady in question, the American briefly explained, was an Englishwoman—the wife of one of his countrymen, established in London as a merchant. He had known them both intimately before their departure from the United States; and the old friendship had been cordially renewed on his arrival in England. Associated with many other charitable institutions, Mrs. Payson was one of the managing committee of a "Home for Friendless Women," especially adapted to receive poor girls in Sally's melancholy position. Rufus offered to write a note to Mrs. Payson; inquiring at what hour she could receive his friend and himself, and obtain permission for them to see the "Home." Amelius, after some hesitation, accepted the proposal. The messenger had not been long despatched with the note before the smart person from the shop made her appearance once more, reporting that "the young lady's outfit had been perfectly arranged," and presenting the inevitable result in the shape of a bill. The last farthing of ready money in the possession of Amelius proved to be insufficient to discharge the debt. He accepted a loan from Rufus, until he could give his bankers the necessary order to sell out some of his money invested in the Funds. His answer, when Rufus protested against this course, was characteristic of the teaching which he owed to the Community. "My dear fellow, I am bound to return the money you have lent to me—in the interests of our poor brethren. The next friend who borrows of you may not have the means of paying you back."

After waiting for the return of Simple Sally, and waiting in vain, Amelius sent a chambermaid to her room, with a message to her. Rufus disapproved of this hasty proceeding. "Why disturb the girl at her looking-glass?" asked the old bachelor, with his quaintly humorous smile.

Sally came in with no bright pleasure in her eyes this time; the girl looked worn and haggard. She drew Amelius away into a corner, and whispered to him. "I get a pain sometimes where the bruise is," she said; "and I've got it bad, now." She glanced, with an odd furtive jealousy, at Rufus. "I kept away from you," she explained, "because I didn't want *him* to know." She stopped, and put her hand on her bosom, and clenched her teeth fast. "Never mind," she said cheerfully, as the pang passed away again; "I can bear it."

Amelius, acting on impulse, as usual, instantly ordered the most comfortable carriage that the hotel possessed. He had heard terrible stories of the possible result of an injury to a woman's bosom. "I shall take her to the best doctor in London," he announced. Sally whispered to him again—still with her eye on Rufus. "Is *he* going with us?" she asked. "No," said Amelius; "one of us must stay here to receive a message." Rufus looked after them very gravely, as the two left the room together.

Applying for information to the mistress of the hotel, Amelius obtained the address of a consulting surgeon of great celebrity, while Sally was getting ready to go out.

"Why don't you like my good friend upstairs?" he said to the girl as they drove away from the house. The answer came swift and straight from the heart of the daughter of Eve. "Because *you* like him!" Amelius changed the subject: he asked if she was still in pain. She shook her head impatiently. Pain or no pain, the uppermost idea in her mind was still that idea of being his servant, which had already found expression in words before they left the lodgings. "Will you let me keep my beautiful new dress for going out on Sundays?" she asked. "The shabby old things will do when I am your servant. I can black your boots, and brush your clothes, and keep your room tidy—and I will try hard to learn, if you will have me taught to cook." Amelius attempted to change the subject again. He might as well have talked to her in an unknown tongue. The glorious prospect of being his servant absorbed the whole of her attention. "I'm little and I'm stupid," she went on; "but I do think I could learn to cook, if I knew I was doing it for *You."* She paused, and looked at him anxiously. "Do let me try!" she pleaded; "I haven't had much pleasure in my life—and I should like it so!" It was impossible to resist this. "You shall be as happy as I can make you, Sally," Amelius answered; "God knows it isn't much you ask for!"

Something in those compassionate words set her thinking in another direction. It was sad to see how slowly and painfully she realized the idea that had been suggested to her.

"I wonder whether you *can* make me happy?" she said. "I suppose I have been happy before this—but I don't know when. I don't remember a time when I was not hungry or cold. Wait a bit. I do think I *was* happy once. It was a long while ago, and it took me a weary time to do it—but I did learn at last to play a tune on the fiddle. The old man and his wife took it in turns to teach me. Somebody gave me to the old man and his wife; I don't know who it was, and I don't remember their names. They were musicians. In the fine streets they sang hymns, and in the poor streets they sang comic songs. It was cold, to be sure, standing barefoot on the

170

pavement—but I got plenty of halfpence. The people said I was so little it was a shame to send me out, and so I got halfpence. I had bread and apples for supper, and a nice little corner under the staircase, to sleep in. Do you know, I do think I did enjoy myself at that time," she concluded, still a little doubtful whether those faint and far-off remembrances were really to be relied on.

Amelius tried to lead her to other recollections. He asked her how old she was when she played the fiddle.

"I don't know," she answered; "I don't know how old I am now. I don't remember anything before the fiddle. I can't call to mind how long it was first—but there came a time when the old man and his wife got into trouble. They went to prison, and I never saw them afterwards. I ran away with the fiddle; to get the halfpence, you know, all to myself. I think I should have got a deal of money, if it hadn't been for the boys. They're so cruel, the boys are. They broke my fiddle. I tried selling pencils after that; but people didn't seem to want pencils. They found me out begging. I got took up, and brought before the what-do-you-call-him—the gentleman who sits in a high place, you know, behind a desk. Oh, but I was frightened, when they took me before the gentleman! He looked very much puzzled. He says, 'Bring her up here; she's so small I can hardly see her.' He says, 'Good God! what am I to do with this unfortunate child?' There was plenty of people about. One of them says, 'The workhouse ought to take her.' And a lady came in, and she says, 'I'll take her, sir, if you'll let me.' And he knew her, and he let her. She took me to a place they called a Refuge—for wandering children, you know. It was very strict at the Refuge. They did give us plenty to eat, to be sure, and they taught us lessons. They told us about Our Father up in Heaven. I said a wrong thing—I said, 'I don't want him up in Heaven; I want him down here.' They were very much ashamed of me when I said that. I was a bad girl; I turned ungrateful. After a time, I ran away. You see, it was so strict, and I was so used to the streets. I met with a Scotchman in the streets. He wore a kilt, and played the pipes; he taught me to dance, and dressed me up like a Scotch girl. He had a curious wife, a sort of half-black woman. She used to dance too—on a bit of carpet, you know, so as not to spoil her fine shoes. They taught me songs; he taught me a Scotch song. And one day his wife said *she* was English (I don't know how that was, being a half-black woman), and I should learn an English song. And they quarrelled about it. And she had her way. She taught me 'Sally in our Alley'. That's how I come to be called Sally. I hadn't any name of my own—I always had nicknames. Sally was the last of them, and Sally has stuck to me. I hope it isn't too common a name to please you? Oh, what a fine house! Are we really going in? Will they let *me* in? How stupid I am! I forgot my beautiful clothes. You won't tell them, will you, if they take me for a lady?"

The carriage had stopped at the great surgeon's house: the waiting-room was full of patients. Some of them were trying to read the books and newspapers on the table; and some of them were looking at each other, not only without the slightest sympathy, but occasionally even with downright distrust and dislike. Amelius took up a newspaper, and gave Sally an illustrated book to amuse her, while they waited to see the Surgeon in their turn.

Two long hours passed, before the servant summoned Amelius to the consulting-room. Sally was wearily asleep in her chair. He left her undisturbed, having questions to put relating to the imperfectly developed state of her mind, which could not be asked in her presence. The surgeon listened, with no ordinary interest, to the young stranger's simple and straightforward narrative of what had happened on the previous night. "You are very unlike other young men," he said; "may I ask how you have been brought up?" The reply surprised him. "This opens quite a new view of Socialism," he said. "I thought your conduct highly imprudent at first—it seems to be the natural result of your teaching now. Let me see what I can do to help you."

He was very grave and very gentle, when Sally was presented to him. His opinion of the injury to her bosom relieved the anxiety of Amelius: there might be pain for some little time to come, but there were no serious consequences to fear. Having written his prescription, and having put several questions to Sally, the surgeon sent her back, with marked kindness of manner, to wait for Amelius in the patients' room.

"I have young daughters of my own," he said, when the door was closed; "and I cannot but feel for that unhappy creature, when I contrast her life with theirs. So far as I can see it, the natural growth of her senses—her higher and her lower senses alike—has been stunted, like the natural growth of her body, by starvation, terror, exposure to cold, and other influences inherent in the life that she has led. With nourishing food, pure air, and above all kind and careful treatment, I see no reason, at her age, why she should not develop into an intelligent and healthy young woman. Pardon me if I venture on giving you a word of advice. At your time of life, you will do well to place her at once under competent and proper care. You may live to regret it, if you are too confident in your own good motives in such a case as this. Come to me again, if I can be of any use to you. No," he continued, refusing to take his fee; "my help to that poor lost girl is help given freely." He shook hands with Amelius—a worthy member of the noble order to which he belonged.

The surgeon's parting advice, following on the quaint protest of Rufus, had its effect on Amelius. He was silent and thoughtful when he got into the carriage again.

Simple Sally looked at him with a vague sense of alarm. Her heart beat fast, under the perpetually recurring fear that she had done something or said something to offend him. "Was it bad behaviour in me," she asked, "to fall asleep in the chair?" Reassured, so far, she was still as anxious as ever to get at the truth. After long hesitation, and long previous thought, she ventured to try another question. "The gentleman sent me out of the room—did he say anything to set you against me?"

"The gentleman said everything that was kind of you," Amelius replied, "and everything to make me hope that you will live to be a happy girl."

172

She said nothing to that; vague assurances were no assurances to her—she only looked at him with the dumb fidelity of a dog. Suddenly, she dropped on her knees in the carriage, hid her face in her hands, and cried silently. Surprised and distressed, he attempted to raise her and console her. "No!" she said obstinately. "Something has happened to vex you, and you won't tell me what it is. Do, do, do tell me what it is!"

"My dear child," said Amelius, "I was only thinking anxiously about you, in the time to come."

She looked up at him quickly. "What! have you forgotten already?" she exclaimed. "I'm to be your servant in the time to come." She dried her eyes, and took her place again joyously by his side. "You did frighten me," she said, "and all for nothing. But you didn't mean it, did you?"

An older man might have had the courage to undeceive her: Amelius shrank from it. He tried to lead her back to the melancholy story—so common and so terrible; so pitiable in its utter absence of sentiment or romance—the story of her past life.

"No," she answered, with that quick insight where her feelings were concerned, which was the only quick insight that she possessed. "I don't like making you sorry; and you did look sorry—you did—when I talked about it before. The streets, the streets, the streets; little girl, or big girl, it's only the streets; and always being hungry or cold; and cruel men when it isn't cruel boys. I want to be happy! I want to enjoy my new clothes! You tell me about your own self. What makes you so kind? I can't make it out; try as I may, I can't make it out."

Some time elapsed before they got back to the hotel. Amelius drove as far as the City, to give the necessary instructions to his bankers.

On returning to the sitting-room at last, he discovered that his American friend was not alone. A gray-haired lady with a bright benevolent face was talking earnestly to Rufus. The instant Sally discovered the stranger, she started back, fled to the shelter of her bedchamber, and locked herself in. Amelius, entering the room after a little hesitation, was presented to Mrs. Payson.

"There was something in my old friend's note," said the lady, smiling and turning to Rufus, "which suggested to me that I should do well to answer it personally. I am not too old yet to follow the impulse of the moment, sometimes; and I am very glad that I did so. I have heard what is, to me, a very interesting story. Mr. Goldenheart, I respect you! And I will prove it by helping you, with all my heart and soul, to save that poor little girl who has just run away from me. Pray don't make excuses for her; I should have run away too, at her age. We have arranged," she continued, looking again at Rufus, "that I shall take you both to the Home, this afternoon. If we can prevail on Sally to go with us, one serious obstacle in our way will be overcome. Tell me the number of her room. I want to try if I can't make friends with her. I have had some experience; and I don't despair of bringing her back here, hand in hand with the terrible person who has frightened her."

The two men were left together. Amelius attempted to speak.

"Keep it down," said Rufus; "no premature outbreak of opinion, if you please, yet awhile. Wait till she has fixed Sally, and shown us the Paradise of the poor girls. It's within the London postal district, and that's all I know about it. Well, now, and did you go to the doctor? Thunder! what's come to the boy? Seems as though he had left his complexion in the carriage! He looks, I do declare, as if he wanted medical tinkering himself."

Amelius explained that his past night had been a wakeful one, and that the events of the day had not allowed him any opportunities of repose. "Since the morning," he said, "things have hurried so, one on the top of the other, that I am beginning to feel a little dazed and weary." Without a word of remark, Rufus produced the remedy. The materials were ready on the sideboard—he made a cocktail.

"Another?" asked the New Englander, after a reasonable lapse of time.

Amelius declined taking another. He stretched himself on the sofa; his good friend considerately took up a newspaper. For the first time that day, he had now the prospect of a quiet interval for rest and thought. In less than a minute the delusive prospect vanished. He started to his feet again, disturbed by a new anxiety. Having leisure to think, he had thought of Regina. "Good heavens!" he exclaimed; "she's waiting to see me—and I never remembered it till this moment!" He looked at his watch: it was five o'clock. "What am I to do?" he said helplessly.

Rufus laid down the newspaper, and considered the new difficulty in its various aspects.

"We are bound to go with Mrs. Payson to the Home," he said; "and, I tell you this, Amelius, the matter of Sally is not a matter to be played with; it's a thing that's got to be done. In your place I should write politely to Miss Regina, and put it off till to-morrow."

In ninety-nine cases out of a hundred, a man who took Rufus for his counsellor was a man who acted wisely in every sense of the word. Events, however, of which Amelius and his friend were both ignorant alike, had so ordered it, that the American's well-meant advice, in this one exceptional case, was the very worst advice that could have been given. In an hour more, Jervy and Mrs. Sowler were to meet at the tavern door. The one last hope of protecting Mrs. Farnaby from the abominable conspiracy of which she was the destined victim, rested solely on the fulfilment by Amelius of his engagement with Regina for that day. Always ready to interfere with the progress of the courtship, Mrs. Farnaby would be especially eager to seize the first opportunity of speaking to her young Socialist friend on the subject

174

of his lecture. In the course of the talk between them, the idea which, in the present disturbed state of his mind, had not struck him yet—the idea that the outcast of the streets might, by the barest conceivable possibility, be identified with the lost daughter—would, in one way or another, be almost infallibly suggested to Amelius; and, at the eleventh hour, the conspiracy would be foiled. If, on the other hand, the American's fatal advice was followed, the next morning's post might bring a letter from Jervy to Mrs. Farnaby—with this disastrous result. At the first words spoken by Amelius, she would put an end to all further interest in the subject on his part, by telling him that the lost girl had been found, and found by another person.

Rufus pointed to the writing-materials on a side table, which he had himself used earlier in the day. The needful excuse was, unhappily, quite easy to find. A misunderstanding with his landlady had obliged Amelius to leave his lodgings at an hour's notice, and had occupied him in trying to find a new residence for the rest of the day. The note was written. Rufus, who was nearest to the bell, stretched out his hand to ring for the messenger. Amelius suddenly stopped him.

"She doesn't like me to disappoint her," he said. "I needn't stay long—I might get there and back in half an hour, in a fast cab."

His conscience was not quite easy. The sense of having forgotten Regina—no matter how naturally and excusably—oppressed him with a feeling of self-reproach. Rufus raised no objection; the hesitation of Amelius was unquestionably creditable to him. "If you must do it, my son," he said, "do it right away—and we'll wait for you."

Amelius took up his hat. The door opened as he approached it, and Mrs. Payson entered the room, leading Simple Sally by the hand.

"We are all going together," said the genial old lady, "to see my large family of daughters at the Home. We can have our talk in the carriage. It's an hour's drive from this place—and I must be back again to dinner at half-past seven."

Amelius and Rufus looked at each other. Amelius thought of pleading an engagement, and asking to be excused. Under the circumstances, it was assuredly not a very gracious thing to do. Before he could make up his mind, one way or the other, Sally stole to his side, and put her hand on his arm. Mrs. Payson had done wonders in conquering the girl's inveterate distrust of strangers, and, to a certain extent at least, winning her confidence. But no early influence could shake Sally's dog-like devotion to Amelius. Her jealous instinct discovered something suspicious in his sudden silence. "You must go with us," she said, "I won't go without you."

"Certainly not," Mrs. Payson added; "I promised her that, of course, beforehand."

Rufus rang the bell, and despatched the messenger to Regina. "That's the one way out of it, my son," he whispered to Amelius, as they followed Mrs. Payson and Sally down the stairs of the hotel.

They had just driven up to the gates of the Home, when Jervy and his accomplice met at the tavern, and entered on their consultation in a private room.

In spite of her poverty-stricken appearance, Mrs. Sowler was not absolutely destitute. In various underhand and wicked ways, she contrived to put a few shillings in her pocket from week to week. If she was half starved, it was for the very ordinary reason, among persons of her vicious class, that she preferred spending her money on drink. Stating his business with her, as reservedly and as cunningly as usual, Jervy found, to his astonishment, that even this squalid old creature presumed to bargain with him. The two wretches were on the point of a quarrel which might have delayed the execution of the plot against Mrs. Farnaby, but for the vile self-control which made Jervy one of the most formidable criminals living. He gave way on the question of money—and, from that moment, he had Mrs. Sowler absolutely at his disposal.

"Meet me to-morrow morning, to receive your instructions," he said. "The time is ten sharp; and the place is the powder-magazine in Hyde Park. And mind this! You must be decently dressed—you know where to hire the things. If I smell you of spirits to-morrow morning, I shall employ somebody else. No; not a farthing now. You will have your money—first instalment only, mind!—to-morrow at ten."

Left by himself, Jervy sent for pen, ink, and paper. Using his left hand, which was just as serviceable to him as his right, he traced these lines:—

"You are informed, by an unknown friend, that a certain lost young lady is now living in a foreign country, and may be restored to her afflicted mother on receipt of a sufficient sum to pay expenses, and to reward the writer of this letter, who is undeservedly, in distressed circumstances.

"Are you, madam, the mother? I ask the question in the strictest confidence, knowing nothing certainly but that your husband was the person who put the young lady out to nurse in her infancy.

"I don't address your husband, because his inhuman desertion of the poor baby does not incline me to trust him. I run the risk of trusting you—to a certain extent—at starting. Shall I drop a hint which may help you to identify the child, in your own mind? It would be inexcusably foolish on my part to speak too plainly, just yet. The hint must be a vague one. Suppose I use a poetical expression, and say that the young lady is enveloped in mystery from head to foot—especially the foot?

"In the event of my addressing the right person, I beg to offer a suggestion for a preliminary interview.

176

"If you will take a walk on the bridge over the Serpentine River, on Kensington Gardens side, at half-past ten o'clock to-morrow morning, holding a white handkerchief in your left hand, you will meet the much-injured woman, who was deceived into taking charge of the infant child at Ramsgate, and will be satisfied so far that you are giving your confidence to persons who really deserve it."

Jervy addressed this infamous letter to Mrs. Farnaby, in an ordinary envelope, marked "Private." He posted it, that night, with his own hand.

CHAPTER 4

"Rufus! I don't quite like the way you look at me. You seem to think—"

"Give it tongue, my son. What do I seem to think?"

"You think I'm forgetting Regina. You don't believe I'm just as fond of her as ever. The fact is, you're an old bachelor."

"That is so. Where's the harm, Amelius?"

"I don't understand—"

"You're out there, my bright boy. I reckon I understand more than you think for. The wisest thing you ever did in your life is what you did this evening, when you committed Sally to the care of those ladies at the Home."

"Good night, Rufus. We shall quarrel if I stay here any longer."

"Good night, Amelius. We shan't quarrel, stay here as long as you like."

The good deed had been done; the sacrifice—already a painful sacrifice—had been made. Mrs. Payson was old enough to speak plainly, as well as seriously, to Amelius of the absolute necessity of separating himself from Simple Sally, without any needless delay. "You have seen for yourself," she said, "that the plan on which this little household is ruled is the unvarying plan of patience and kindness. So far as Sally is concerned, you can be quite sure that she will never hear a harsh word, never meet with a hard look, while she is under our care. The lamentable neglect under which the poor creature has suffered, will be tenderly remembered and atoned for, here. If we can't make her happy among us, I promise that she shall leave the Home, if she wishes it, in six weeks' time. As to yourself, consider your position if you persist in taking her back with you. Our good friend Rufus has told me that you are engaged to be married. Think of the misinterpretations, to say the least of it, to which you would subject yourself—think of the reports which would sooner or later find their way to the young lady's ears, and of the deplorable consequences that would follow. I believe implicitly in the purity of your motives. But remember Who taught us to pray that we may not be led into temptation—and complete the good work that you have begun, by leaving Sally among friends and sisters in this house."

To any honourable man, these were unanswerable words. Coming after what Rufus and the surgeon had already said to him, they left Amelius no alternative but to yield. He pleaded for leave to write to Sally, and to see her, at a later interval, when she might be reconciled to her new life. Mrs. Payson had just consented to both requests, Rufus had just heartily congratulated him on his decision—when the door was thrown violently open. Simple Sally ran into the room, followed by one of the women-attendants in a state of breathless surprise.

178

"She showed me a bedroom," cried Sally, pointing indignantly to the woman; "and she asked if I should like to sleep there." She turned to Amelius, and caught him by the hand to lead him away. The ineradicable instinct of distrust had been once more roused in her by the too zealous attendant. "I'm not going to stay here," she said; "I'm going away with You!"

Amelius glanced at Mrs. Payson. Sally tried to drag him to the door. He did his best to reassure her by a smile; he spoke confusedly some composing words. But his honest face, always accustomed to tell the truth, told the truth now. The poor lost creature, whose feeble intelligence was so slow to discern, so inapt to reflect, looked at him with the heart's instantaneous perception, and saw her doom. She let go of his hand. Her head sank. Without word or cry, she dropped on the floor at his feet.

The attendant instantly raised her, and placed her on a sofa. Mrs. Payson saw how resolutely Amelius struggled to control himself, and felt for him with all her heart. Turning aside for a moment, she hastily wrote a few lines, and returned to him. "Go, before we revive her," she whispered; "and give what I have written to the coachman. You shall suffer no anxiety that I can spare you," said the excellent woman; "I will stay here myself to-night, and reconcile her to the new life."

She held out her hand; Amelius kissed it in silence. Rufus led him out. Not a word dropped from his lips on the long drive back to London.

His mind was disturbed by other subjects besides the subject of Sally. He thought of his future, darkened by the doubtful marriage-engagement that was before him. Alone with Rufus, for the rest of the evening, he petulantly misunderstood the sympathy with which the kindly American regarded him. Their bedrooms were next to each other. Rufus heard him walking restlessly to and fro, and now and then talking to himself. After a while, these sounds ceased. He was evidently worn out, and was getting the rest that he needed, at last.

The next morning he received a few lines from Mrs. Payson, giving a favourable account of Sally, and promising further particulars in a day or two.

Encouraged by this good news, revived by a long night's sleep, he went towards noon to pay his postponed visit to Regina. At that early hour, he could feel sure that his interview with her would not be interrupted by visitors. She received him quietly and seriously, pressing his hand with a warmer fondness than usual. He had anticipated some complaint of his absence on the previous day, and some severe allusion to his appearance in the capacity of a Socialist lecturer. Regina's indulgence, or Regina's interest in circumstances of more pressing importance, preserved a merciful silence on both subjects.

"It is a comfort to me to see you, Amelius," she said; "I am in trouble about my uncle, and I am weary of my own anxious thoughts. Something unpleasant has happened in Mr. Farnaby's business. He goes to the City earlier, and he returns much later, than usual. When he does come back, he doesn't speak to me—he locks himself into his room; and he looks worn and haggard when I make his breakfast for him in the morning. You know that he is one of the directors of the new bank? There was something about the bank in the newspaper yesterday which upset him dreadfully; he put down his cup of coffee—and went away to the City, without eating his breakfast. I don't like to worry you about it, Amelius. But my aunt seems to take no interest in her husband's affairs—and it is really a relief to me to talk of my troubles to you. I have kept the newspaper; do look at what it says about the bank, and tell me if you understand it!"

Amelius read the passage pointed out to him. He knew as little of banking business as Regina. "So far as I can make it out," he said, "they're paying away money to their shareholders which they haven't earned. How do they do that, I wonder?"

Regina changed the subject in despair. She asked Amelius if he had found new lodgings. Hearing that he had not yet succeeded in the search for a residence, she opened a drawer of her work-table, and took out a card.

"The brother of one of my schoolfellows is going to be married," she said. "He has a pretty bachelor cottage in the neighbourhood of the Regent's Park—and he wants to sell it, with the furniture, just as it is. I don't know whether you care to encumber yourself with a little house of your own. His sister has asked me to distribute some of his cards, with the address and the particulars. It might be worth your while, perhaps, to look at the cottage when you pass that way."

Amelius took the card. The small feminine restraints and gentlenesses of Regina, her quiet even voice, her serene grace of movement, had a pleasantly soothing effect on his mind after the anxieties of the last four and twenty hours. He looked at her bending over her embroidery, deftly and gracefully industrious—and drew his chair closer to her. She smiled softly over her work, conscious that he was admiring her, and placidly pleased to receive the tribute.

"I would buy the cottage at once," said Amelius, "if I thought you would come and live in it with me."

She looked up gravely, with her needle suspended in her hand.

"Don't let us return to that," she answered, and went on again with her embroidery.

"Why not?" Amelius asked.

She persisted in working, as industriously as if she had been a poor needlewoman, with serious reasons for being eager to get her money. "It is useless," she replied, "to speak of what cannot be for some time to come."

Amelius stopped the progress of the embroidery by taking her hand. Her devotion to her work irritated him.

180

"Look at me, Regina," he said, steadily controlling himself. "I want to propose that we shall give way a little on both sides. I won't hurry you; I will wait a reasonable time. If I promise that, surely you may yield a little in return. Money seems to be a hard taskmaster, my darling, after what you have told me about your uncle. See how he suffers because he is bent on being rich; and ask yourself if it isn't a warning to us not to follow his example! Would you like to see *me* too wretched to speak to you, or to eat my breakfast—and all for the sake of a little outward show? Come, come! let us think of ourselves. Why should we waste the best days of our life apart, when we are both free to be happy together? I have another good friend besides Rufus—the good friend of my father before me. He knows all sorts of great people, and he will help me to some employment. In six months' time I might have a little salary to add to my income. Say the sweetest words, my darling, that ever fell from your lips—say you will marry me in six months!"

It was not in a woman's nature to be insensible to such pleading as this. She all but yielded. "I should like to say it, dear!" she answered, with a little fluttering sigh.

"Say it, then!" Amelius suggested tenderly.

She took refuge again in her embroidery. "If you would only give me a little time," she suggested, "I might say it."

"Time for what, my own love?"

"Time to wait, dear, till my uncle is not quite so anxious as he is now."

"Don't talk of your uncle, Regina! You know as well as I do what he would say. Good heavens! why can't you decide for yourself? No! I don't want to hear over again about what you owe to Mr. Farnaby—I heard enough of it on that day in the shrubbery. Oh, my dear girl, do have some feeling for me! do for once have a will of your own!"

Those last words were an offence to her self-esteem. "I think it's very rude to tell me I have no will of my own," she said, "and very hard to press in this way when you know I am in trouble." The inevitable handkerchief appeared, adding emphasis to the protest—and the becoming tears showed themselves modestly in Regina's magnificent eyes.

Amelius started out of his chair, and walked away to the window. That last reference to Mr. Farnaby's pecuniary cares was more than he had patience to endure. "She can't even forget her uncle and his bank," he thought, "when I am speaking to her of our marriage!"

He kept his face hidden from her, at the window. By some subtle process of association which he was unable to trace, the image of Simple Sally rose in his mind. An irresistible influence forced him to think of her—not as the poor, starved, degraded, half-witted creature of the streets, but as the grateful girl who had asked for no happier future than to be his servant, who had dropped senseless at his feet at the bare prospect of parting with him. His sense of self-respect, his loyalty to his betrothed wife, resolutely resisted the unworthy conclusion to which his own thoughts were leading him. He turned back again to Regina; he spoke so loudly and so vehemently that the gathering flow of her tears was suspended in surprise. "You're right, you're quite right, my dear! I ought to give you time, of course. I try to control my hasty temper, but I don't always succeed—just at first. Pray forgive me; it shall be exactly as you wish."

Regina forgave him, with a gentle and ladylike astonishment at the excitable manner in which he made his excuses. She even neglected her embroidery, and put her face up to him to be kissed. "You are so nice, dear," she said, "when you are not violent and unreasonable. It is such a pity you were brought up in America. Won't you stay to lunch?"

Happily for Amelius, the footman appeared at this critical moment with a message: "My mistress wishes particularly to see you, sir, before you go."

This was the first occasion, in the experience of the lovers, on which Mrs. Farnaby had expressed her wishes through the medium of a servant, instead of appearing personally. The curiosity of Regina was mildly excited. "What a very odd message!" she said; "what does it mean? My aunt went out earlier than usual this morning, and I have not seen her since. I wonder whether she is going to consult you about my uncle's affairs?"

"I'll go and see," said Amelius.

"And stay to lunch?" Regina reiterated.

"Not to-day, my dear."

"To-morrow, then?"

"Yes, to-morrow." So he escaped. As he opened the door, he looked back, and kissed his hand. Regina raised her head for a moment, and smiled charmingly. She was hard at work again over her embroidery.

CHAPTER 5

The door of Mrs. Farnaby's ground-floor room, at the back of the house, was partially open. She was on the watch for Amelius.

"Come in!" she cried, the moment he appeared in the hall. She pulled him into the room, and shut the door with a bang. Her face was flushed, her eyes were wild. "I have something to tell you, you dear good fellow," she burst out excitedly—— "Something in confidence, between you and me!" She paused, and looked at him with sudden anxiety and alarm. "What's the matter with you?" she asked.

The sight of the room, the reference to a secret, the prospect of another private conference, forced back the mind of Amelius, in one breathless instant, to his first memorable interview with Mrs. Farnaby. The mother's piteously hopeful words, in speaking of her lost daughter, rang in his ears again as if they had just fallen from her lips. "She may be lost in the labyrinth of London. . . . To-morrow, or ten years hence, you *might* meet with her." There were a hundred chances against it—a thousand, ten thousand chances against it. The startling possibility flashed across his brain, nevertheless, like a sudden flow of daylight across the dark. *"Have* I met with her, at the first chance?"

"Wait," he cried; "I have something to say before you speak to me. Don't deceive yourself with vain hopes. Promise me that, before I begin."

She waved her hand derisively. "Hopes?" she repeated; "I have done with hopes, I have done with fears—I have got to certainties, at last!"

He was too eager to heed anything that she said to him; his whole soul was absorbed in the coming disclosure. "Two nights since," he went on, "I was wandering about London, and I met—"

She burst out laughing. "Go on!" she cried, with a wild derisive gaiety.

Amelius stopped, perplexed and startled. "What are you laughing at?" he asked.

"Go on!" she repeated. "I defy you to surprise me. Out with it! Whom did you meet?"

Amelius proceeded doubtfully, by a word at a time. "I met a poor girl in the streets," he said, steadily watching her.

She changed completely at those words; she looked at him with an aspect of stern reproach. "No more of it," she interposed; "I have not waited all these miserable years for such a horrible end as that." Her face suddenly brightened; a radiant effusion of tenderness and triumph flowed over it, and made it young and happy again. "Amelius!" she said, "listen to this. My dream has come true—my girl is found! Thanks to you, though you don't know it."

Amelius looked at her. Was she speaking of something that had really happened? or had she been dreaming again?

Absorbed in her own happiness, she made no remark on his silence. "I have seen the woman," she went on. "This bright blessed morning I have seen the woman who took her away in the first days of her poor little life. The wretch swears she was not to blame. I tried to forgive her. Perhaps I almost did forgive her, in the joy of hearing what she had to tell me. I should never have heard it, Amelius, if you had not given that glorious lecture. The woman was one of your audience. She would never have spoken of those past days; she would never have thought of me—"

At those words, Mrs. Farnaby abruptly stopped, and turned her face away from Amelius. After waiting a little, finding her still silent, still immovable, he ventured on putting a question.

"Are you sure you are not deceived?" he asked. "I remember you told me that rogues had tried to impose on you, in past times when you employed people to find her."

"I have proof that I am not being imposed upon," Mrs. Farnaby answered, still keeping her face hidden from him. "One of them knows of the fault in her foot."

"One of them?" Amelius repeated. "How many of them are there?"

"Two. The old woman, and a young man."

"What are their names?"

"They won't tell me their names yet."

"Isn't that a little suspicious?"

"One of them knows," Mrs. Farnaby reiterated, "of the fault in her foot."

"May I ask which of them knows? The old woman, I suppose?"

"No, the young man."

"That's strange, isn't it? Have you seen the young man?"

"I know nothing of him, except the little that the woman told me. He has written me a letter."

184

"May I look at it?"

"I daren't let you look at it!"

Amelius said no more. If he had felt the smallest suspicion that the disclosure volunteered by Mrs. Farnaby, at their first interview, had been overheard by the unknown person who had opened the swinging window in the kitchen, he might have recalled Phoebe's vindictive language at his lodgings, and the doubts suggested to him by his discovery of the vagabond waiting for her in the street. As it was, he was simply puzzled. The one plain conclusion to his mind was, unhappily, the natural conclusion after what he had heard—that Mrs. Farnaby had no sort of interest in the discovery of Simple Sally, and that he need trouble himself with no further anxiety in that matter. Strange as Mrs. Farnaby's mysterious revelation seemed, her correspondent's knowledge of the fault in the foot was circumstance in his favour, beyond dispute. Amelius still wondered inwardly how it was that the woman who had taken charge of the child had failed to discover what appeared to be known to another person. If he had been aware that Mrs. Sowler's occupation at the time was the occupation of a "baby-farmer," and that she had many other deserted children pining under her charge, he might have easily understood that she was the last person in the world to trouble herself with a minute examination of any one of the unfortunate little creatures abandoned to her drunken and merciless neglect. Jervy had satisfied himself, before he trusted her with his instructions, that she knew no more than the veriest stranger of any peculiarity in one or the other of the child's feet.

Interpreting Mrs. Farnaby's last reply to him as an intimation that their interview was at an end, Amelius took up his hat to go.

"I hope with all my heart," he said, "that what has begun so well will end well. If there is any service that I can do for you—"

She drew nearer to him, and put her hand gently on his shoulder. "Don't think that I distrust you," she said very earnestly; "I am unwilling to shock you—that is all. Even this great joy has a dark side to it; my miserable married life casts its shadow on everything that happens to me. Keep secret from everybody the little that I have told you—you will ruin me if you say one word of it to any living creature. I ought not to have opened my heart to you—but how could I help it, when the happiness that is coming to me has come through you? When you say good-bye to me to-day, Amelius, you say good-bye to me for the last time in this house. I am going away. Don't ask me why—that is one more among the things which I daren't tell you! You shall hear from me, or see me—I promise that. Give me some safe address to write to; some place where there are no inquisitive women who may open my letter in your absence."

She handed him her pocket-book. Amelius wrote down in it the address of his club.

185

She took his hand. "Think of me kindly," she said. "And, once more, don't be afraid of my being deceived. There is a hard part of me still left which keeps me on my guard. The old woman tried, this morning, to make me talk to her about that little fault we know of in my child's foot. But I thought to myself, 'If you had taken a proper interest in my poor baby while she was with you, you must sooner or later have found it out.' Not a word passed my lips. No, no, don't be anxious when you think of me. I am as sharp as they are; I mean to find out how the man who wrote to me discovered what he knows; he shall satisfy me, I promise you, when I see him or hear from him next. All this is between ourselves strictly, sacredly between ourselves. Say nothing—I know I can trust you. Good-bye, and forgive me for having been so often in your way with Regina. I shall never be in your way again. Marry her, if you think she is good enough for you; I have no more interest now in your being a roving bachelor, meeting with girls here, there, and everywhere. You shall know how it goes on. Oh, I am so happy!"

She burst into tears, and signed to Amelius with a wild gesture of treaty to leave her.

He pressed her hand in silence, and went out.

Almost as the door closed on him, the variable woman changed again. For a while she walked rapidly to and fro, talking to herself. The course of her tears ceased. Her lips closed firmly; her eyes assumed an expression of savage resolve. She sat down at the table and opened her desk. "I'll read it once more," she said to herself, "before I seal it up."

She took from her desk a letter of her own writing, and spread it out before her. With her elbows on the table, and her hands clasped fiercely in her hair, she read these lines addressed to her husband:—

JOHN FARNABY,—I have always suspected that you had something to do with the disappearance of our child. I know for certain now that you deliberately cast your infant daughter on the mercy of the world, and condemned your wife to a life of wretchedness.

"Don't suppose that I have been deceived! I have spoken with the woman who waited by the garden-paling at Ramsgate, and who took the child from your hands. She saw you with me at the lecture; and she is absolutely sure that you are the man.

"Thanks to the meeting at the lecture-hall, I am at last on the trace of my lost daughter. This morning I heard the woman's story. She kept the child, on the chance of its being reclaimed, until she could afford to keep it no longer. She met with a person who was willing to adopt it, and who took it away with her to a foreign country, not mentioned to me yet. In that country my daughter is still living, and will be restored to me on conditions which will be communicated in a few days' time.

"Some of this story may be true, and some of it may be false; the woman may be lying to serve her own interests with me. Of one thing I am sure—my girl is identified, by means known to me of which there can be no doubt. And she must be still living, because the interest of the persons treating with me is an interest in her life.

"When you receive this letter, on your return from business to-night, I shall have left you, and left you for ever. The bare thought of even looking at you again fills me with horror. I have my own income, and I mean to take my own way. In your best interests I warn you, make no attempt to trace me. I declare solemnly that, rather than let your deserted daughter be polluted by the sight of you, I would kill you with my own hand, and die for it on the scaffold. If she ever asks for her father, I will do you one service. For the honour of human nature, I will tell her that her father is dead. It will not be all a falsehood. I repudiate you and your name—you are dead to me from this time forth.

"I sign myself by my father's name—

"EMMA RONALD."

She had said herself that she was unwilling to shock Amelius. This was the reason.

After thinking a little, she sealed and directed the letter. This done, she unlocked the wooden press which had once contained the baby's frock and cap, and those other memorials of the past which she called her "dead consolations." After satisfying herself that the press was empty, she wrote on a card, "To be called for by a messenger from my bankers"—and tied the card to a tin box in a corner, secured by a padlock. She lifted the box, and placed it in front of the press, so that it might be easily visible to any one entering the room. The safe keeping of her treasures provided for, she took the sealed letter, and, ascending the stairs, placed it on the table in her husband's dressing-room. She hurried out again, the instant after, as if the sight of the place were intolerable to her.

Passing to the other end of the corridor, she entered her own bedchamber, and put on her bonnet and cloak. A leather handbag was on the bed. She took it up, and looked round the large luxurious room with a shudder of disgust. What she had suffered, within those four walls, no human creature knew but herself. She hurried out, as she had hurried out of her husband's dressing-room.

Her niece was still in the drawing-room. As she reached the door, she hesitated, and stopped. The girl was a good girl, in her own dull placid way—and her sister's daughter, too. A last little act of kindness would perhaps be a welcome act to remember. She opened the door so suddenly that Regina started, with a small cry of alarm. "Oh, aunt, how you frighten one! Are you going out?" "Yes; I'm going out," was the short answer. "Come here. Give me a kiss." Regina looked up in wide-eyed astonishment. Mrs. Farnaby stamped impatiently on the floor. Regina rose, gracefully bewildered. "My dear aunt, how very odd!" she said—and gave the kiss demanded, with a serenely surprised elevation of her finely shaped eyebrows. "Yes," said Mrs. Farnaby; "that's it—one of my oddities. Go back to your work. Good-bye."

She left the room, as abruptly as she had entered it. With her firm heavy step she descended to the hall, passed out at the house door, and closed it behind her—never to return to it again.

CHAPTER 6

Amelius left Mrs. Farnaby, troubled by emotions of confusion and alarm, which he was the last man living to endure patiently. Her extraordinary story of the discovered daughter, the still more startling assertion of her solution to leave the house, the absence of any plain explanation, the burden of secrecy imposed on him—all combined together to irritate his sensitive nerves. "I hate mysteries," he thought; "and ever since I landed in England, I seem fated to be mixed up in them. Does she really mean to leave her husband and her niece? What will Farnaby do? What will become of Regina?"

To think of Regina was to think of the new repulse of which he had been made the subject. Again he had appealed to her love for him, and again she had refused to marry him at his own time.

He was especially perplexed and angry, when he reflected on the unassailably strong influence which her uncle appeared to have over her. All Regina's sympathy was with Mr. Farnaby and his troubles. Amelius might have understood her a little better, if she had told him what had passed between her uncle and herself on the night of Mr. Farnaby's return, in a state of indignation, from the lecture. In terror of the engagement being broken off, she had been forced to confess that she was too fond of Amelius to prevail on herself to part with him. If he attempted a second exposition of his Socialist principles on the platform, she owned that it might be impossible to receive him again as a suitor. But she pleaded hard for the granting of a pardon to the first offence, in the interests of her own tranquillity, if not in mercy to Amelius. Mr. Farnaby, already troubled by his commercial anxieties, had listened more amiably, and also more absently, than usual; and had granted her petition with the ready indulgence of a preoccupied man. It had been decided between them that the offence of the lecture should be passed over in discreet silence. Regina's gratitude for this concession inspired her sympathy with her uncle in his present state of suspense. She had been sorely tempted to tell Amelius what had happened. But the natural reserve of her character—fortified, in this instance, by the defensive pride which makes a woman unwilling, before marriage, to confess her weakness unreservedly to the man who has caused it—had sealed her lips. "When he is a little less violent and a little more humble," she thought, "perhaps I may tell him."

So it fell out that Amelius took his way through the streets, a mystified and an angry man.

Arrived in sight of the hotel, he stopped, and looked about him.

It was impossible to disguise from himself that a lurking sense of regret was making itself felt, in his present frame of mind, when he thought of Simple Sally. In all probability, he would have quarrelled with any man who had accused him of actually lamenting the girl's absence, and wanting her back again. He happened to recollect her artless blue eyes, with their vague patient look, and her quaint childish questions put so openly in so sweet a voice—and that was all. Was there anything reprehensible, if you please, in an act of remembrance? Comforting himself with these considerations, he moved on again a step or two—and stopped once more. In his present humour, he shrank from facing Rufus. The American read him like a book; the American would ask irritating questions. He turned his back on the hotel, and looked at his watch. As he took it out, his finger and thumb touched something else in his waistcoat-pocket. It was the card that Regina had given to him—the card of the cottage to let. He had nothing to do, and nowhere to go. Why not look at the cottage? If it proved to be not worth seeing, the Zoological Gardens were in the neighbourhood—and there are periods in a man's life when he finds the society that walks on four feet a welcome relief from the society that walks on two.

It was a fairly fine day. He turned northward towards the Regent's Park.

The cottage was in a by-road, just outside the park: a cottage in the strictest sense of the word. A sitting-room, a library, and a bedroom—all of small proportions—and, under them a kitchen and two more rooms, represented the whole of the little dwelling from top to bottom. It was simply and prettily furnished; and it was completely surrounded by its own tiny plot of garden-ground. The library especially was a perfect little retreat, looking out on the back garden; peaceful and shady, and adorned with bookcases of old carved oak.

Amelius had hardly looked round the room, before his inflammable brain was on fire with a new idea. Other idle men in trouble had found the solace and the occupation of their lives in books. Why should he not be one of them? Why not plunge into study in this delightful retirement—and perhaps, one day, astonish Regina and Mr. Farnaby by bursting on the world as the writer of a famous book? Exactly as Amelius, two days since, had seen himself in the future, a public lecturer in receipt of glorious fees—so he now saw himself the celebrated scholar and writer of a new era to come. The woman who showed the cottage happened to mention that a gentleman had already looked over it that morning, and had seemed to like it. Amelius instantly gave her a shilling, and said, "I take it on the spot." The wondering woman referred him to the house-agent's address, and kept at a safe distance from the excitable stranger as she let him out. In less than another hour, Amelius had taken the cottage, and had returned to the hotel with a new interest in life and a new surprise for Rufus.

As usual, in cases of emergency, the American wasted no time in talking. He went out at once to see the cottage, and to make his own inquiries of the agent. The result amply proved that Amelius had not been imposed upon. If he repented of his bargain, the gentleman who had first seen the cottage was ready to take it off his hands, at a moment's notice.

Going back to the Hotel, Rufus found Amelius resolute to move into his new abode, and eager for the coming life of study and retirement. Knowing perfectly well before-hand how this latter project would end, the American tried the efficacy of a little worldly temptation. He had arranged, he said, "to have a good time of it in Paris"; and he proposed that Amelius should be his companion. The suggestion produced not the slightest effect; Amelius talked as if he was a confirmed recluse, in the decline of life. "Thank you," he said, with the most amazing gravity; "I prefer the company of my books, and the seclusion of my study." This declaration was followed by more selling-out of money in the Funds, and by a visit to a bookseller, which left a handsome pecuniary result inscribed on the right side of the ledger.

On the next day, Amelius presented himself towards two o'clock at Mr. Farnaby's house. He was not so selfishly absorbed in his own projects as to forget Mrs. Farnaby. On the contrary, he was honestly anxious for news of her.

A certain middle-aged man of business has been briefly referred to, in these pages, as one of Regina's faithful admirers, patiently submitting to the triumph of his favoured young rival. This gentleman, issuing from his carriage with his card-case ready in his hand, met Amelius at the door, with a face which announced plainly that a catastrophe had happened. "You have heard the sad news, no doubt?" he said, in a rich bass voice attuned to sadly courteous tones. The servant opened the door before Amelius could answer. After a contest of politeness, the middle-aged gentleman consented to make his inquiries first. "How is Mr. Farnaby? No better? And Miss Regina? Very poorly, oh? Dear, dear me! Say I called, if you please." He handed in two cards, with a severe enjoyment of the melancholy occasion and the rich bass sounds of his own voice. "Very sad, is it not?" he said, addressing his youthful rival with an air of paternal indulgence. "Good morning." He bowed with melancholy grace, and got into his carriage.

Amelius looked after the prosperous merchant, as the prancing horses drew him away. "After all," he thought bitterly, "she might be happier with that rich prig than she could be with me." He stepped into the hall, and spoke to the servant. The man had his message ready. Miss Regina would see Mr. Goldenheart, if he would be so good as to wait in the dinning-room.

Regina appeared, pale and scared; her eyes inflamed with weeping. "Oh, Amelius, can you tell me what this dreadful misfortune means? Why has she left us? When she sent for you yesterday, what did she say?"

In his position, Amelius could make but one answer. "Your aunt said she thought of going away. But," he added, with perfect truth, "she refused to tell me why, or where she was going. I am quite as much at a loss to understand her as you are. What does your uncle propose to do?"

Mr. Farnaby's conduct, as described by Regina, thickened the mystery—he proposed to do nothing.

He had been found on the hearth-rug in his dressing-room; having apparently been seized with a fit, in the act of burning some paper. The ashes were discovered close by him, just inside the fender. On his recovery, his first anxiety was to know if a letter had been burnt. Satisfied on this point, he had ordered the servants to assemble round his bed, and had peremptorily forbidden them to open the door to their mistress, if she ever returned at any future time to the house. Regina's questions and remonstrances, when she was left alone with him, were answered, once for all, in these pitiless terms:—"If you wish to deserve the fatherly interest that I take in you, do as I do: forget that such a person as your aunt ever existed. We shall quarrel, if you ever mention her name in my hearing again." This said, he had instantly changed the subject; instructing Regina to write an excuse to "Mr. Melton" (otherwise, the middle-aged rival), with whom he had been engaged to dine that evening. Relating this latter event, Regina's ever-ready gratitude overflowed in the direction of Mr. Melton. "He was so kind! he left his guests in the evening, and came and sat with my uncle for nearly an hour." Amelius made no remark on this; he led the conversation back to the subject of Mrs. Farnaby. "She once spoke to me of her lawyers," he said. "Do *they* know nothing about her?"

The answer to this question showed that the sternly final decision of Mr. Farnaby was matched by equal resolution on the part of his wife.

One of the partners in the legal firm had called that morning, to see Regina on a matter of business. Mrs. Farnaby had appeared at the office on the previous day, and had briefly expressed her wish to make a small annual provision for her niece, in case of future need. Declining to enter into any explanation, she had waited until the necessary document had been drawn out; had requested that Regina might be informed of the circumstance; and had then taken her departure in absolute silence. Hearing that she had left her husband, the lawyer, like every one else, was completely at a loss to understand what it meant.

"And what does the doctor say?" Amelius asked next.

"My uncle is to be kept perfectly quiet," Regina answered; "and is not to return to business for some time to come. Mr. Melton, with his usual kindness, has undertaken to look after his affairs for him. Otherwise, my uncle, in his present state of anxiety about the bank, would never have consented to obey the doctor's orders. When he can safely travel, he is recommended to go abroad for the winter, and get well again in some warmer climate. He refuses to leave his business—and the doctor refuses to take the responsibility. There is to be a consultation of physicians tomorrow. Oh, Amelius, I was really fond of my aunt—I am heart-broken at this dreadful change!"

There was a momentary silence. If Mr. Melton had been present, he would have said a few neatly sympathetic words. Amelius knew no more than a savage of the art of conventional consolation. Tadmor had made him familiar with the social and political questions of the time, and had taught him to speak in public. But Tadmor, rich in books and newspapers, was a powerless training institution in the matter of small talk.

"Suppose Mr. Farnaby is obliged to go abroad," he suggested, after waiting a little, "what will you do?"

192

Regina looked at him, with an air of melancholy surprise. "I shall do my duty, of course," she answered gravely. "I shall accompany my dear uncle, if he wishes it." She glanced at the clock on the mantelpiece. "It is time he took his medicine," she resumed; "you will excuse me, I am sure." She shook hands, not very warmly—and hastened out of the room.

Amelius left the house, with a conviction which disheartened him—the conviction that he had never understood Regina, and that he was not likely to understand her in the future. He turned for relief to the consideration of Mr. Farnaby's strange conduct, under the domestic disaster which had befallen him.

Recalling what he had observed for himself, and what he had heard from Mrs. Farnaby when she had first taken him into her confidence, he inferred that the subject of the lost child had not only been a subject of estrangement between the husband and wife, but that the husband was, in some way, the person blamable for it. Assuming this theory to be the right one, there would be serious obstacles to the meeting of the mother and child, in the mother's home. The departure of Mrs. Farnaby was, in that case, no longer unintelligible—and Mr. Farnaby's otherwise inexplicable conduct had the light of a motive thrown on it, which might not unnaturally influence a hard-hearted man weary alike of his wife and his wife's troubles. Arriving at this conclusion by a far shorter process than is here indicated, Amelius pursued the subject no further. At the time when he had first visited the Farnabys, Rufus had advised him to withdraw from closer intercourse with them, while he had the chance. In his present mood, he was almost in danger of acknowledging to himself that Rufus had proved to be right.

He lunched with his American friend at the hotel. Before the meal was over Mrs. Payson called, to say a few cheering words about Sally.

It was not to be denied that the girl remained persistently silent and reserved. In other respects the report was highly favourable. She was obedient to the rules of the house; she was always ready with any little services that she could render to her companions; and she was so eager to improve herself, by means of her reading-lessons and writing-lessons, that it was not easy to induce her to lay aside her book and her slate. When the teacher offered her some small reward for her good conduct, and asked what she would like, the sad little face brightened, and the faithful creature's answer was always the same—"I should like to know what he is doing now." (Alas for Sally!—"he" meant Amelius.)

"You must wait a little longer before you write to her," Mrs. Payson concluded, "and you must not think of seeing her for some time to come. I know you will help us by consenting to this—for Sally's sake."

Amelius bowed in silence. He would not have confessed what he felt, at that moment, to any living soul—it is doubtful if he even confessed it to himself. Mrs. Payson, observing him with a woman's keen sympathy, relented a little. "I might give her a message," the good lady suggested—"just to say you are glad to hear she is behaving so well."

"Will you give her this?" Amelius asked.

He took from his pocket a little photograph of the cottage, which he had noticed on the house-agent's desk, and had taken away with him. "It is *my* cottage now," he explained, in tones that faltered a little; "I am going to live there; Sally might like to see it."

"Sally *shall* see it," Mrs. Payson agreed—"if you will only let me take this away first." She pointed to the address of the cottage, printed under the photograph. Past experience in the Home made her reluctant to trust Sally with the address in London at which Amelius was to be found.

Rufus produced a huge complex knife, out of the depths of which a pair of scissors burst on touching a spring. Mrs. Payson cut off the address, and placed the photograph in her pocket-book. "Now," she said, "Sally will be happy, and no harm can come of it."

"I've known you, ma'am, nigh on twenty years," Rufus remarked. "I do assure you that's the first rash observation I ever heard from your lips."

BOOK THE SEVENTH

THE VANISHING HOPES

CHAPTER 1

Two days later, Amelius moved into his cottage.

He had provided himself with a new servant, as easily as he had provided himself with a new abode. A foreign waiter at the hotel—a gray-haired Frenchman of the old school, reputed to be the most ill-tempered servant in the house—had felt the genial influence of Amelius with the receptive readiness of his race. Here was a young Englishman, who spoke to him as easily and pleasantly as if he was speaking to a friend—who heard him relate his little grievances, and never took advantage of that circumstance to turn him into ridicule—who said kindly, "I hope you don't mind my calling you by your nickname," when he ventured to explain that his Christian name was "Theophile," and that his English fellow servants had facetiously altered and shortened it to "Toff," to suit their insular convenience. "For the first time, sir," he had hastened to add, "I feel it an honour to be Toff, when *you* speak to me." Asking everybody whom he met if they could recommend a servant to him, Amelius had put the question, when Toff came in one morning with the hot water. The old Frenchman made a low bow, expressive of devotion. "I know of but one man, sir, whom I can safely recommend," he answered—"take me." Amelius was delighted; he had only one objection to make. "I don't want to keep two servants," he said, while Toff was helping him on with his dressing-gown. "Why should you keep two servants, sir?" the Frenchman inquired. Amelius answered, "I can't ask you to make the beds." "Why not?" said Toff—and made the bed, then and there, in five minutes. He ran out of the room, and came back with one of the chambermaid's brooms. "Judge for yourself, sir—can I sweep a carpet?" He placed a chair for Amelius. "Permit me to save you the trouble of shaving yourself. Are you satisfied? Very good. I am equally capable of cutting your hair, and attending to your corns (if you suffer, sir, from that inconvenience). Will you allow me to propose something which you have not had yet for your breakfast?" In half an hour more, he brought in the new dish. "Oeufs a la Tripe. An elementary specimen, sir, of what I can do for you as a cook. Be pleased to taste it." Amelius ate it all up on the spot; and Toff applied the moral, with the neatest choice of language. "Thank you, sir, for a gratifying expression of approval. One more specimen of my poor capabilities, and I have done. It is barely possible—God forbid!—that you may fall ill. Honour me by reading that document." He handed a written paper to Amelius, dated some years since in Paris, and signed in an English name. "I testify with gratitude and pleasure that Theophile Leblond has nursed me through a long illness, with an intelligence and devotion which I cannot too highly praise." "May you never employ me, sir, in that capacity," said Toff. "I have only to add that I am not so old as I look, and that my political opinions have changed, in later life, from red-republican to moderate-liberal. I also confess, if necessary, that I still have an ardent admiration for the fair sex." He laid his hand on his heart, and waited to be engaged.

So the household at the cottage was modestly limited to Amelius and Toff.

Rufus remained for another week in London, to watch the new experiment. He had made careful inquiries into the Frenchman's character, and had found that the complaints of his temper really amounted to this—that "he gave himself the airs of a gentleman, and didn't understand a joke." On the question of honesty and sobriety, the testimony of the proprietor of the hotel left Rufus nothing to desire. Greatly to his surprise, Amelius showed no disposition to grow weary of his quiet life, or to take refuge in perilous amusements from the sober society of his books. He was regular in his inquiries at Mr. Farnaby's house; he took long walks by himself; he never mentioned Sally's name; he lost his interest in going to the theatre, and he never appeared in the smoking-room of the club. Some men, observing the remarkable change which had passed over his excitable temperament, would have hailed it as a good sign for the future. The New Englander looked below the surface, and was not so easily deceived. "My bright boy's soul is discouraged and cast down," was the conclusion that he drew. "There's darkness in him where there once was light; and, what's worse than all, he caves in, and keeps it to himself." After vainly trying to induce Amelius to open his heart, Rufus at last went to Paris, with a mind that was ill at ease.

On the day of the American's departure, the march of events was resumed; and the unnaturally quiet life of Amelius began to be disturbed again.

Making his customary inquiries in the forenoon at Mr. Farnaby's door, he found the household in a state of agitation. A second council of physicians had been held, in consequence of the appearance of some alarming symptoms in the case of the patient. On this occasion, the medical men told him plainly that he would sacrifice his life to his obstinacy, if he persisted in remaining in London and returning to his business. By good fortune, the affairs of the bank had greatly benefited, through the powerful interposition of Mr. Melton. With the improved prospects, Mr. Farnaby (at his niece's entreaty) submitted to the doctor's advice. He was to start on the first stage of his journey the next morning; and, at his own earnest desire, Regina was to go with him. "I hate strangers and foreigners; and I don't like being alone. If you don't go with me, I shall stay where I am—and die." So Mr. Farnaby put it to his adopted daughter, in his rasping voice and with his hard frown.

"I am grieved, dear Amelius, to go away from you," Regina said; "but what can I do? It would have been so nice if you could have gone with us. I did hint something of the sort; but—"

Her downcast face finished the sentence. Amelius felt the bare idea of being Mr. Farnaby's travelling companion make his blood run cold. And Mr. Farnaby, on his side, reciprocated the sentiment. "I will write constantly, dear," Regina resumed; "and you will write back, won't you? Say you love me; and promise to come tomorrow morning, before we go."

She kissed him affectionately—and, the instant after, checked the responsive outburst of tenderness in Amelius, by that utter want of tact which (in spite of the popular delusion to the contrary) is so much more common in women than in men, "My uncle is so particular about packing his linen," she said; "nobody can please him but me; I must ask you to let me run upstairs again."

Amelius went out into the street, with his head down and his lips fast closed. He was not far from Mrs. Payson's house. "Why shouldn't I call?" he thought to himself. His conscience added, "And hear some news of Sally."

There was good news. The girl was brightening mentally and physically—she was in a fair way, if she only remained in the Home, to be "Simple" Sally no longer. Amelius asked if she had got the photograph of the cottage. Mrs. Payson laughed. "Sleeps with it under her pillow, poor child," she said, "and looks at it fifty times a day." Thirty years since, with infinitely less experience to guide her, the worthy matron would have followed her instincts, and would have hesitated to tell Amelius quite so much about the photograph. But some of a woman's finer sensibilities do get blunted with the advance of age and the accumulation of wisdom.

Instead of pursuing the subject of Sally's progress, Amelius, to Mrs. Payson's surprise, made a clumsy excuse, and abruptly took his leave.

He felt the need of being alone; he was conscious of a vague distrust of himself, which degraded him in his own estimation. Was he, like characters he had read of in books, the victim of a fatality? The slightest circumstances conspired to heighten his interest in Sally—just at the time when Regina had once more disappointed him. He was as firmly convinced, as if he had been the strictest moralist living, that it was an insult to Regina, and an insult to his own self-respect, to set the lost creature whom he had rescued in any light of comparison with the young lady who was one day to be his wife. And yet, try as he might to drive her out, Sally kept her place in his thoughts. There was, apparently, some innate depravity in him. If a looking-glass had been handed to him at that moment, he would have been ashamed to look himself in the face.

After walking until he was weary, he went to his club.

The porter gave him a letter as he crossed the hall. Mrs. Farnaby had kept her promise, and had written to him. The smoking-room was deserted at that time of day. He opened his letter in solitude, looked at it, crumpled it up impatiently, and put it into his pocket. Not even Mrs. Farnaby could interest him at that critical moment. His own affairs absorbed him. The one idea in his mind, after what he had heard about Sally, was the idea of making a last effort to hasten the date of his marriage before Mr. Farnaby left England. "If I can only feel sure of Regina—"

His thoughts went no further than that. He walked up and down the empty smoking-room, anxious and irritable, dissatisfied with himself, despairing of the future. "I can but try it!" he suddenly decided—and turned at once to the table to write a letter.

Death had been busy with the members of his family in the long interval that had passed since he and his father left England. His nearest surviving relative was his uncle—his father's younger brother—who occupied a post of high importance in the Foreign Office. To this gentleman he now wrote, announcing his arrival in England, and his anxiety to qualify himself for employment in a Government office. "Be so good as to grant me an interview," he concluded; "and I hope to satisfy you that I am not unworthy of your kindness, if you will exert your influence in my favour."

He sent away his letter at once by a private messenger, with instructions to wait for an answer.

It was not without doubt, and even pain, that he had opened communication with a man whose harsh treatment of his father it was impossible for him to forget. What could the son expect? There was but one hope. Time might have inclined the younger brother to make atonement to the memory of the elder, by a favourable reception of his nephew's request.

His father's last words of caution, his own boyish promise not to claim kindred with his relations in England, were vividly present to the mind of Amelius, while he waited for the return of the messenger. His one justification was in the motives that animated him. Circumstances, which his father had never anticipated, rendered it an act of duty towards himself to make the trial at least of what his family interest could do for him. There could be no sort of doubt that a man of Mr. Farnaby's character would yield, if Amelius could announce that he had the promise of an appointment under Government—with the powerful influence of a near relation to accelerate his promotion. He sat, idly drawing lines on the blotting-paper; at one moment regretting that he had sent his letter; at another, comforting himself in the belief that, if his father had been living to advise him, his father would have approved of the course that he had taken.

The messenger returned with these lines of reply:—

"Under any ordinary circumstances, I should have used my influence to help you on in the world. But, when you not only hold the most abominable political opinions, but actually proclaim those opinions in public, I am amazed at your audacity in writing to me. There must be no more communication between us. While you are a Socialist, you are a stranger to me."

Amelius accepted this new rebuff with ominous composure. He sat quietly smoking in the deserted room, with his uncle's letter in his hand.

Among the other disastrous results of the lecture, some of the newspapers had briefly reported it. Preoccupied by his anxieties, Amelius had forgotten this when he wrote to his relative. "Just like me!" he thought, as he threw the letter into the fire. His last hopes floated up the chimney, with the tiny puff of smoke from the burnt paper. There was now no other chance of shortening the marriage engagement left to try. He had already applied to the good friend whom he had mentioned to Regina. The answer, kindly written in this case, had not been very encouraging:—

"I have other claims to consider. All that I can do, I will do. Don't be disheartened—I only ask you to wait."

Amelius rose to go home—and sat down again. His natural energy seemed to have deserted him—it required an effort to leave the club. He took up the newspapers, and threw them aside, one after another. Not one of the unfortunate writers and reporters could please him on that inauspicious day. It was only while he was lighting his second cigar that he remembered Mrs. Farnaby's unread letter to him. By this time, he was more than weary of his own affairs. He read the letter.

"I find the people who have my happiness at their mercy both dilatory and greedy." (Mrs. Farnaby wrote); "but the little that I can persuade them to tell me is very favourable to my hopes. I am still, to my annoyance, only in personal communication with the hateful old woman. The young man either sends messages, or writes to me through the post. By this latter means he has accurately described, not only in which of my child's feet the fault exists, but the exact position which it occupies. Here, you will agree with me, is positive evidence that he is speaking the truth, whoever he is.

"But for this reassuring circumstance, I should feel inclined to be suspicious of some things—of the obstinate manner, for instance, in which the young man keeps himself concealed; also, of his privately warning me not to trust the woman who is his own messenger, and not to tell her on any account of the information which his letters convey to me. I feel that I ought to be cautious with him on the question of money—and yet, in my eagerness to see my darling, I am ready to give him all that he asks for. In this uncertain state of mind, I am restrained, strangely enough, by the old woman herself. She warns me that he is the sort of man, if he once gets the money, to spare himself the trouble of earning it. It is the one hold I have over him (she says)—so I control the burning impatience that consumes me as well as I can.

"No! I must not attempt to describe my own state of mind. When I tell you that I am actually afraid of dying before I can give my sweet love the first kiss, you will understand and pity me. When night comes, I feel sometimes half mad.

"I send you my present address, in the hope that you will write and cheer me a little. I must not ask you to come and see me yet. I am not fit for it—and, besides, I am under a promise, in the present state of the negotiations, to shut the door on my friends. It is easy enough to do that; I have no friend, Amelius, but you.

"Try to feel compassionately towards me, my kind-hearted boy. For so many long years, my heart has had nothing to feed on but the one hope that is now being realized at last. No sympathy between my husband and me (on the contrary, a horrid unacknowledged enmity, which has always kept us apart); my father and mother, in their time both wretched about my marriage, and with good reason; my only sister dying in poverty—what a life for a childless woman! don't let us dwell on it any longer.

"Goodbye for the present, Amelius. I beg you will not think I am always wretched. When I want to be happy, I look to the coming time."

This melancholy letter added to the depression that weighed on the spirits of Amelius. It inspired him with vague fears for Mrs. Farnaby. In her own interests, he would have felt himself tempted to consult Rufus (without mentioning names), if the American had been in London. As things were, he put the letter back in his pocket with a sigh. Even Mrs. Farnaby, in her sad moments, had a consoling prospect to contemplate. "Everybody but me!" Amelius thought.

His reflections were interrupted by the appearance of an idle young member of the club, with whom he was acquainted. The new-comer remarked that he looked out of spirits, and suggested that they should dine together and amuse themselves somewhere in the evening. Amelius accepted the proposal: any man who offered him a refuge from himself was a friend to him on that day. Departing from his temperate habits, he deliberately drank more than usual. The wine excited him for the time, and then left him more depressed than ever; and the amusements of the evening produced the same result. He returned to his cottage so completely disheartened, that he regretted the day when he had left Tadmor.

But he kept his appointment, the next morning, to take leave of Regina.

The carriage was at the door, with a luggage-laden cab waiting behind it. Mr. Farnaby's ill-temper vented itself in predictions that they would be too late to catch the train. His harsh voice, alternating with Regina's meek remonstrances, reached the ears of Amelius from the breakfast-room. "I'm not going to wait for the gentleman-Socialist," Mr. Farnaby announced, with his hardest sarcasm of tone. "Dear uncle, we have a quarter of an hour to spare!" "We have nothing of the sort; we want all that time to register the luggage." The servant's voice was heard next. "Mr. Goldenheart, miss." Mr. Farnaby instantly stepped into the hall. "Goodbye!" he called to Amelius, through the open door of the dining-room—and passed straight on to the carriage. "I shan't wait, Regina!" he shouted, from the doorstep. "Let him go by himself!" said Amelius indignantly, as Regina hurried into the room. "Oh, hush, hush, dear! Suppose he heard you? No week shall pass without my writing to you; promise you will write back, Amelius. One more kiss! Oh, my dear!" The servant interposed, keeping discreetly out of sight. "I beg your pardon, miss, my master wishes to know whether you are going with him or not." Regina waited to hear no more. She gave her lover a farewell look to remember her by, and ran out.

That innate depravity which Amelius had lately discovered in his own nature, let the forbidden thoughts loose in him again as he watched the departing carriage from the door. "If poor little Sally had been in her place—!" He made an effort of virtuous resolution, and stopped there. "What a blackguard a man may be," he penitently reflected, "without suspecting it himself!"

He descended the house-steps. The discreet servant wished him good morning, with a certain cheery respect—the man was delighted to have seen the last of his hard master for some months to come. Amelius stopped and turned round, smiling grimly. He was in such a reckless humour, that he was even ready to divert his mind by astonishing a footman. "Richard," he said, "are you engaged to be married?"

Richard stared in blank surprise at the strange question—and modestly admitted that he was engaged to marry the housemaid next door. "Soon?" asked Amelius, swinging his stick. "As soon as I have saved a little more money, sir." "Damn the money!" cried Amelius—and struck his stick on the pavement, and walked away with a last look at the house as if he hated the sight of it. Richard watched the departing young gentleman, and shook his head ominously as he shut the door.

CHAPTER 2

Amelius went straight back to the cottage, with the one desperate purpose of reverting to the old plan, and burying himself in his books. Surveying his well-filled shelves with an impatience unworthy of a scholar, Hume's "History of England" unhappily caught his eye. He took down the first volume. In less than half an hour he discovered that Hume could do nothing for him. Wisely inspired, he turned to the truer history next, which men call fiction. The writings of the one supreme genius, who soars above all other novelists as Shakespeare soars above all other dramatists—the writings of Walter Scott—had their place of honour in his library. The collection of the Waverley Novels at Tadmor had not been complete. Enviable Amelius had still to read *Rob Roy*. He opened the book. For the rest of the day he was in love with Diana Vernon; and when he looked out once or twice at the garden to rest his eyes, he saw "Andrew Fairservice" busy over the flowerbeds.

He closed the last page of the noble story as Toff came in to lay the cloth for dinner.

The master at table and the servant behind his chair were accustomed to gossip pleasantly during meals. Amelius did his best to carry on the talk as usual. But he was no longer in the delightful world of illusion which Scott had opened to him. The hard realities of his own everyday life had gathered round him again. Observing him with unobtrusive attention, the Frenchman soon perceived the absence of the easy humour and the excellent appetite which distinguished his young master at other times.

"May I venture to make a remark, sir?" Toff inquired, after a long pause in the conversation.

"Certainly."

"And may I take the liberty of expressing my sentiments freely?"

"Of course you may."

"Dear sir, you have a pretty little simple dinner to-day," Toff began. "Forgive me for praising myself, I am influenced by the natural pride of having cooked the dinner. For soup, you have Croute au pot; for meat, you have Tourne-dos a la sauce poivrade; for pudding, you have Pommes au beurre. All so nice—and you hardly eat anything, and your amiable conversation falls into a melancholy silence which fills me with regret. Is it you who are to blame for this? No, sir! it is the life you lead. I call it the life of a monk; I call it the life of a hermit—I say boldly it is the life of all others which is most unsympathetic to a young man like you. Pardon the warmth of my expressions; I am eager to make my language the language of utmost delicacy. May I quote a little song? It is in an old, old, old French piece, long since forgotten, called 'Les Maris Garcons'. There are two lines in that song (I have often heard my good father sing them) which I will venture to apply to your case; 'Amour, delicatesse, et gaite; D'un bon Francais c'est la devise!' Sir, you have naturally delicatesse and gaite—but the last has, for some days, been under a cloud. What is wanted to remove that cloud? L'Amour! Love, as you say in English. Where is the charming woman, who is the only ornament wanting to this sweet cottage? Why is she still invisible? Remedy that unhappy oversight, sir. You are here in a suburban Paradise. I consult my long experience; and I implore you to invite Eve.—Ha! you smile; your lost gaiety returns, and you feel it as I do. Might I propose another glass of claret, and the reappearance on the table of the Tourne-dos a la poivrade?"

It was impossible to be melancholy in this man's company. Amelius sanctioned the return of the Tourne-dos, and tried the other glass of claret. "My good friend," he said, with something like a return of his old easy way, "you talk about charming women, and your long experience. Let's hear what your experience has been."

For the first time Toff began to look a little confused.

"You have honoured me, sir, by calling me your good friend," he said. "After that, I am sure you will not send me away if I own the truth. No! My heart tells me I shall not appeal to your indulgence in vain. Dear sir, in the holidays which you kindly give me, I provide competent persons to take care of the house in my absence, don't I? One person, if you remember, was a most handsome engaging young man. He is, if you please, my son by my first wife—now an angel in heaven. Another person, who took care of the house, on the next occasion, was a little black-eyed boy; a miracle of discretion for his age. He is my son by my second wife—now another angel in heaven. Forgive me, I have not done yet. Some few days since, you thought you heard an infant crying downstairs. Like a miserable wretch, I lied; I declared it was the infant in the next house. Ah, sir, it was my own cherubim baby by my third wife—an angel close by in the Edgeware Road, established in a small milliner shop, which will expand to great things by-and-by. The intervals between my marriages are not worthy of your notice. Fugitive caprices, sir—fugitive caprices! To sum it all up (as you say in England), it is not in me to resist the enchanting sex. If my third angel dies, I shall tear my hair—but I shall none the less take a fourth."

"Take a dozen if you like," said Amelius. "Why should you have kept all this from my knowledge?"

Toff hung his head. "I think it was one of my foreign mistakes," he pleaded. "The servants' advertisements in your English newspapers frighten me. How does the most meritorious manservant announce himself when he wants the best possible place? He says he is 'without encumbrances.' Gracious heaven, what a dreadful word to describe the poor pretty harmless children! I was afraid, sir, you might have some English objection to *my* 'encumbrances.' A young man, a boy, and a cherubim-baby; not to speak of the sacred memories of two women, and the charming occasional society of a third; all inextricably enveloped in the life of one amorous-meritorious French person—surely there was reason for hesitation here? No matter; I bless my stars I know better now, and I withdraw myself from further notice. Permit me to recall your attention to the Roquefort cheese, and a mouthful of potato-salad to correct the richness of him."

The dinner was over at last. Amelius was alone again.

It was a still evening. Not a breath of wind stirred among the trees in the garden; no vehicles passed along the by-road in which the cottage stood. Now and then, Toff was audible downstairs, singing French songs in a high cracked voice, while he washed the plates and dishes, and set everything in order for the night. Amelius looked at his bookshelves—and felt that, after *Rob Roy,* there was no more reading for him that evening. The slow minutes followed one another wearily; the deadly depression of the earlier hours of the day was stealthily fastening its hold on him again. How might he best resist it? His healthy out-of-door habits at Tadmor suggested the only remedy that he could think of. Be his troubles what they might, his one simple method of resisting them, at all other times, was his simple method now. He went out for a walk.

For two hours he rambled about the great north-western suburb of London. Perhaps he felt the heavy oppressive weather, or perhaps his good dinner had not agreed with him. Any way, he was so thoroughly worn out, that he was obliged to return to the cottage in a cab.

Toff opened the door—but not with his customary alacrity. Amelius was too completely fatigued to notice any trifling circumstance. Otherwise, he would certainly have perceived something odd in the old Frenchman's withered face. He looked at his master, as he relieved him of his hat and coat, with the strangest expression of interest and anxiety; modified by a certain sardonic sense of amusement underlying the more serious emotions. "A nasty dull evening," Amelius said wearily. And Toff, always eager to talk at other times, only answered, "Yes, sir"—and retreated at once to the kitchen regions.

The fire was bright; the curtains were drawn; the reading-lamp, with its ample green shade, was on the table—a more comfortable room no man could have found to receive him after a long walk. Reclining at his ease in his chair, Amelius thought of ringing for some restorative brandy-and-water. While he was thinking, he fell asleep; and, while he slept, he dreamed.

Was it a dream?

He certainly saw the library—not fantastically transformed, but just like what the room really was. So far, he might have been wide awake, looking at the familiar objects round him. But, after a while, an event happened which set the laws of reality at defiance. Simple Sally, miles away in the Home, made her appearance in the library, nevertheless. He saw the drawn curtains over the window parted from behind; he saw the girl step out from them, and stop, looking at him timidly. She was clothed in the plain dress that he had bought for her; and she looked more charming in it than ever. The beauty of health claimed kindred now, in her pretty face, with the beauty of youth: the wan cheeks had begun to fill out, and the pale lips were delicately suffused with their natural rosy red. Little by little her first fears seemed to subside. She smiled, and softly crossed the room, and stood at his side. After looking at him with a rapt expression of tenderness and delight, she laid her hands on the arm of the chair, and said, in the quaintly quiet way which he remembered so well, "I want to kiss you." She bent over him, and kissed him with the innocent freedom of a child. Then she raised herself again, and looked backwards and forwards between Amelius and the lamp. "The firelight is the best," she said. Darkness fell over the room as she spoke; he saw her no more; he heard her no more. A blank interval followed; there flowed over him the oblivion of perfect sleep. His next conscious sensation was a feeling of cold—he shivered, and woke.

The impression of the dream was in his mind at the moment of waking. He started as he raised himself in the chair. Was he dreaming still? No; he was certainly awake. And, as certainly, the room was dark!

He looked and looked. It was not to be denied, or explained away. There was the fire burning low, and leaving the room chilly—and there, just visible on the table, in the flicker of the dying flame, was the extinguished lamp!

He mended the fire, and put his hand on the bell to ring for Toff, and thought better of it. What need had he of the lamplight? He was too weary for reading; he preferred going to sleep again, and dreaming again of Sally. Where was the harm in dreaming of the poor little soul, so far away from him? The happiest part of his life now was the part of it that was passed in sleep.

As the fresh coals began to kindle feebly, he looked again at the lamp. It was odd, to say the least of it, that the light should have accidentally gone out, exactly at the right time to realize the fanciful extinction of it in his dream. How was it there was no smell of a burnt-out lamp? He was too lazy, or too tired, to pursue the question. Let the mystery remain a mystery—and let him rest in peace! He settled himself fretfully in his chair. What a fool he was to bother his head about a lamp, instead of closing his eyes and going to sleep again!

The room began to recover its pleasant temperature. He shifted the cushion in the chair, so that it supported his head in perfect comfort, and composed himself to rest. But the capricious influences of sleep had deserted him: he tried one position after another, and all in vain. It was a mere mockery even to shut his eyes. He resigned himself to circumstances, and stretched out his legs, and looked at the companionable fire.

Of late he had thought more frequently than usual of his past days in the Community. His mind went back again now to that bygone time. The clock on the mantelpiece struck nine. They were all at supper, at Tadmor—talking over the events of the day. He saw himself again at the long wooden table, with shy little Mellicent in the chair next to him, and his favourite dog at his feet waiting to be fed. Where was Mellicent now? It was a sad letter that she had written to him, with the strange fixed idea that he was to return to her one day. There was something very winning and lovable about the poor creature who had lived such a hard life at home, and had suffered so keenly. It was a comfort to think that she would go back to the Community. What happier destiny could she hope for? Would she take care of his dog for him when she went back? They had all promised to be kind to his pet animals in his absence; but the dog was fond of Mellicent; he would be happier with Mellicent than with the rest of them. And his little tame fawn, and his birds—how were they doing? He had not even written to inquire after them; he had been cruelly forgetful of those harmless dumb loving friends. In his present solitude, in his dreary doubts of the future, what would he not give to feel the dog nestling in his bosom, and the fawn's little rough tongue licking his hand! His heart ached as he thought of it: a choking hysterical sensation oppressed his breathing. He tried to rise, and ring for lights, and rouse his manhood to endure and resist. It was not to be done. Where was his courage? where was the cheerfulness which had never failed him at other time? He sank back in the chair, and hid his face in his hands for shame at his own weakness, and burst out crying.

The touch of soft persuasive fingers suddenly thrilled through him.

His hands were gently drawn away from his face; a familiar voice, sweet and low, said, "Oh, don't cry!" Dimly through his tears he saw the well-remembered little figure standing between him and the fire. In his unendurable loneliness, he had longed for his dog, he had longed for his fawn. There was the martyred creature from the streets, whom he had rescued from nameless horror, waiting to be his companion, servant, friend! There was the child-victim of cold and hunger, still only feeling her way to womanhood; innocent of all other aspirations, so long as she might fill the place which had once been occupied by the dog and the fawn!

Amelius looked at her with a momentary doubt whether he was waking or sleeping. "Good God!" he cried, "am I dreaming again?"

"No," she said, simply. "You are awake this time. Let me dry your eyes; I know where you put your handkerchief." She perched on his knee, and wiped away the tears, and smoothed his hair over his forehead. "I was frightened to show myself till I heard you crying," she confessed. "Then I thought, 'Come! he can't be angry with me now'—and I crept out from behind the curtains there. The old man let me in. I can't live without seeing you; I've tried till I could try no longer. I owned it to the old man when he opened the door. I said, 'I only want to look at him; won't you let me in?' And he says, 'God bless me, here's Eve come already!' I don't know what he meant—he let me in, that's all I care about. He's a funny old foreigner. Send him away; I'm to be your servant now. Why were you crying? I've cried often enough about You. No; that can't be—I can't expect you to cry about *me;* I can only expect you to scold me. I know I'm a bad girl."

She cast one doubtful look at him, and hung her head—waiting to be scolded. Amelius lost all control over himself. He took her in his arms and kissed her again and again. "You are a dear good grateful little creature!" he burst out—and suddenly stopped, aware too late of the act of imprudence which he had committed. He put her away from him; he tried to ask severe questions, and to administer merited reproof. Even if he had succeeded, Sally was too happy to listen to him. "It's all right now," she cried. "I'm never, never, never to go back to the Home! Oh, I'm so happy! Let's light the lamp again!"

She found the matchbox on the chimneypiece. In a minute more the room was bright. Amelius sat looking at her, perfectly incapable of deciding what he ought to say or do next. To complete his bewilderment, the voice of the attentive old Frenchman made itself heard through the door, in discreetly confidential tones.

"I have prepared an appetising little supper, sir," said Toff. "Be pleased to ring when you and the young lady are ready."

CHAPTER 3

Toff's interference proved to have its use. The announcement of the little supper—- plainly implying Simple Sally's reception at the cottage—reminded Amelius of his responsibilities. He at once stepped out into the passage, and closed the door behind him.

The old Frenchman was waiting to be reprimanded or thanked, as the case might be, with his head down, his shoulders shrugged up to his ears, and the palms of his hands spread out appealingly on either side of him—a model of mute resignation to circumstances.

"Do you know that you have put me in a very awkward position?" Amelius began.

Toff lifted one of his hands to his heart. "You are aware of my weakness, sir. When that charming little creature presented herself at the door, sinking with fatigue, I could no more resist her than I could take a hop-skip-and-jump over the roof of this cottage. If I have done wrong, take no account of the proud fidelity with which I have served you—tell me to pack up and go; but don't ask me to assume a position of severity towards that enchanting Miss. It is not in my heart to do it," said Toff, lifting his eyes with tearful solemnity to an imaginary heaven. "On my sacred word of honour as a Frenchman, I would die rather than do it!"

"Don't talk nonsense," Amelius rejoined a little impatiently. "I don't blame you— but you have got me into a scrape, for all that. If I did my duty, I should send for a cab, and take her back."

Toff opened his twinkling old eyes in a perfect transport of astonishment. "What!" he cried, "take her back? Without rest, without supper? And you call that duty? How inconceivably ugly does duty look when it assumes an inhospitable aspect towards a woman! Pardon me, sir; I must express my sentiments or I shall burst. You will say perhaps that I have no conception of duty? Pardon me again—my conception of duty is *here!"*

He threw open the door of the sitting-room. In spite of his anxiety, Amelius burst out laughing. The Frenchman's inexhaustible contrivances had transformed the sitting-room into a bedroom for Sally. The sofa had become a snug little white bed; a hairbrush and comb, and a bottle of eau-de-cologne, were on the table; a bath stood near the fire, with cans of hot and cold water, and a railway rug placed under them to save the carpet. "I dare not presume to contradict you, sir," said Toff, "but there is *my* conception of duty! In the kitchen, I have another conception, keeping warm; you can smell it up the stairs. Salmi of partridge, with the littlest possible dash of garlic in the sauce. Oh, sir, let that angel rest and refresh herself! Virtuous severity, believe me, is a most horribly unbecoming virtue at your age!" He spoke quite seriously, with the air of a profound moralist, asserting principles that did equal honour to his head and his heart.

Amelius went back to the library.

Sally was resting in the easy-chair; her position showed plainly that she was suffering from fatigue. "I have had a long, long walk," she said; "and I don't know which aches worst, my back or my feet. I don't care—I'm quite happy now I'm here." She nestled herself comfortably in the chair. "Do you mind my looking at you?" she asked. "Oh, it's so long since I saw you!"

There was a new undertone of tenderness in her voice—innocent tenderness that openly avowed itself. The reviving influences of the life at the Home had done much—and had much yet left to do. Her wasted face and figure were filling out, her cheeks and lips were regaining their lovely natural colour, as Amelius had seen in his dream. But her eyes, in repose, still resumed their vacantly patient look; and her manner, with a perceptible increase of composure and confidence, had not lost its quaint childish charm. Her growth from girl to woman was a growth of fine gradations, guided by the unerring deliberation of Nature and Time.

"Do you think they will follow you here, from the Home?" Amelius asked.

She looked at the clock. "I don't think so," she said quietly. "It's hours since I slipped out by the back door. They have very strict rules about runaway girls—even when their friends bring them back. If *you* send me back—" she stopped, and looked thoughtfully into the fire.

"What will you do, if I send you back?"

"What one of our girls did, before they took her in at the Home. She jumped into the river. 'Made a hole in the water'; that's how she calls it. She's a big strong girl; and they got her out, and saved her. She says it wasn't painful, till they brought her to again. I'm little and weak—I don't think they could bring *me* to life, if they tried."

Amelius made a futile attempt to reason with her. He even got so far as to tell her that she had done very wrong to leave the Home. Sally's answer set all further expostulation at defiance. Instead of attempting to defend herself, she sighed wearily, and said, "I had no money; I walked all the way here."

The well-intended remonstrances of Amelius were lost in compassionate surprise. "You poor little soul!" he exclaimed, "it must be seven or eight miles at least!"

"I dare say," said Sally. "It don't matter, now I've found you."

"But how did you find me? Who told you where I lived?"

She smiled, and took from her bosom the photograph of the cottage.

"But Mrs. Payson cut off the address!" cried Amelius, bursting out with the truth in the impulse of the moment.

Sally turned over the photograph, and pointed to the back of the card, on which the photographer's name and address were printed. "Mrs. Payson didn't think of this," she said shyly.

"Did *you* think of it?" Amelius asked.

Sally shook her head. "I'm too stupid," she replied. "The girl who made the hole in the water put me up to it. 'Have you made up your mind to run away?' she says. And I said, 'Yes.' 'You go to the man who did the picture,' she says; 'he knows where the place is, I'll be bound.' I asked my way till I found him. And he did know. And he told me. He was a good sort; he gave me a glass of beer, he said I looked so tired. I said we'd go and have our portraits taken some day—you, and your servant. May I tell the funny old foreigner that he is to go away now I have come to you?" The complete simplicity with which she betrayed her jealousy of Toff made Amelius smile. Sally, watching every change in his face, instantly drew her own conclusion. "Ah!" she said cheerfully, "I'll keep your room cleaner than he keeps it! I smelt dust on the curtains when I was hiding from you."

Amelius thought of his dream. "Did you come out while I was asleep?" he asked.

"Yes; I wasn't frightened of you, when you were asleep. I had a good look at you; and I gave you a kiss." She made that confession without the slightest sign of confusion; her calm blue eyes looked him straight in the face. "You got restless," she went on; "and I got frightened again. I put out the lamp. I says to myself, 'If he does scold me, I can bear it better in the dark.'"

Amelius listened, wondering. Had he seen drowsily what he thought he had dreamed, or was there some mysterious sympathy between Sally and himself? The occult speculations were interrupted by Sally. "May I take off my bonnet, and make myself tidy?" she asked. Some men might have said No. Amelius was not one of them.

The library possessed a door of communication with the sitting-room; the bedchamber occupied by Amelius being on the other side of the cottage. When Sally saw Toff's reconstructed room, she stood at the door, in speechless admiration of the vision of luxury revealed to her. From time to time Amelius, alone in the library, heard her dabbling in her bath, and humming the artless old English song from which she had taken her name. Once she knocked at the closed door, and made a request through it—"There is scent on the table; may I have some?" And once Toff knocked at the other door, opening into the passage, and asked when "pretty young Miss" would be ready for supper. Events went on in the little household as if Sally had become an integral part of it already. "What *am* I to do?" Amelius asked himself. And Toff, entering at the moment to lay the cloth, answered respectfully, "Hurry the young person, sir, or the salmi will be spoilt."

She came out from her room, walking delicately on her sore feet—so fresh and charming, that Toff, absorbed in admiration, made a mistake in folding a napkin for the first time in his life. "Champagne, of course, sir?" he said in confidence to Amelius. The salmi of partridge appeared; the inspiriting wine sparkled in the glasses; Toff surpassed himself in all the qualities which made a servant invaluable at a supper table. Sally forgot the Home, forgot the cruel streets, and laughed and chattered as gaily as the happiest girl living. Amelius, expanding in the joyous atmosphere of youth and good spirits, shook off his sense of responsibility, and became once more the delightful companion who won everybody's love. The effervescent gaiety of the evening was at its climax; the awful forms of duty, propriety, and good sense had been long since laughed out of the room—when Nemesis, goddess of retribution, announced her arrival outside, by a crashing of carriage-wheels and a peremptory ring at the cottage bell.

There was dead silence; Amelius and Sally looked at each other. The experienced Toff at once guessed what had happened. "Is it her father or mother?" he asked of Amelius, a little anxiously. Hearing that she had never even seen her father or mother, he snapped his fingers joyously, and led the way on tiptoe into the hall. "I have my idea," he whispered. "Let us listen."

A woman's voice, high, clear, and resolute, speaking apparently to the coachman, was the next audible sound. "Say I come from Mrs. Payson, and must see Mr. Goldenheart directly." Sally trembled and turned pale. "The matron!" she said faintly. "Oh, don't let her in!" Amelius took the terrified girl back to the library. Toff followed them, respectfully asking to be told what a "matron" was. Receiving the necessary explanation, he expressed his contempt for matrons bent on carrying charming persons into captivity, by opening the library door and spitting into the hall. Having relieved his mind in this way, he returned to his master and laid a lank skinny forefinger cunningly along the side of his nose. "I suppose, sir, you don't want to see this furious woman?" he said. Before it was possible to say anything in reply, another ring at the bell announced that the furious woman wanted to see Amelius. Toff read his master's wishes in his master's face. Not even this emergency could find him unprepared: he was as ready to circumvent a matron as to cook a dinner. "The shutters are up, and the curtains are drawn," he reminded Amelius. "Not a morsel of light is visible outside. Let them ring—we have all gone to bed." He turned to Sally, grinning with impish enjoyment of his own stratagem. "Ha, Miss! what do you think of that?" There was a third pull at the bell as he spoke. "Ring away, Missess Matrone!" he cried. "We are fast asleep—wake us if you can." The fourth ring was the last. A sharp crack revealed the breaking of the bellwire, and was followed by the shrill fall of the iron handle on the pavement before the garden gate. The gate, like the palings, was protected at the top from invading cats. "Compose yourself, Miss," said Toff, "if she tries to get over the gate, she will stick on the spikes." In another moment, the sound of retiring carriage-wheels announced the defeat of the matron, and settled the serious question of receiving Sally for the night.

She sat silent by the window, when Toff had left the room, holding back the curtains and looking out at the murky sky.

"What are you looking for?" Amelius asked.

"I was looking for the stars."

Amelius joined her at the window. "There are no stars to be seen tonight."

She let the curtain fall to again. "I was thinking of night-time at the Home," she said. "You see, I got on pretty well, in the day, with my reading and writing. I wanted so to improve myself. My mind was troubled with the fear of your despising such an ignorant creature as I am; so I kept on at my lessons. I thought I might surprise you by writing you a pretty letter some day. One of the teachers (she's gone away ill) was very good to me. I used to talk to her; and, when I said a wrong word, she took me up, and told me the right one. She said you would think better of me when you heard me speak properly—and I do speak better, don't I? All this was in the day. It was the night that was the hard time to get through—when the other girls were all asleep, and I had nothing to think of but how far away I was from you. I used to get up, and put the counterpane round me, and stand at the window. On fine nights the stars were company to me. There were two stars, near together, that I got to know. Don't laugh at me—I used to think one of them was you, and one of them me. I wondered whether you would die, or I should die, before I saw you again. And, most always, it was my star that went out first. Lord, how I used to cry! It got into my poor stupid head that I should never see you again. I do believe I ran away because of that. You won't tell anybody, will you? It was so foolish, I am ashamed of it now. I wanted to see your star and my star tonight. I don't know why. Oh, I'm so fond of you!" She dropped on her knees, and took his hand, and put it on her head. "It's burning hot," she said, "and your kind hand cools it."

Amelius raised her gently, and led her to the door of her room. "My poor Sally, you are quite worn out. You want rest and sleep. Let us say good night."

"I will do anything you tell me," she answered. "If Mrs. Payson comes tomorrow, you won't let her take me away? Thank you. Goodnight." She put her hands on his shoulders, with innocent familiarity, and lifted herself to him on tiptoe, and kissed him as a sister might have kissed him.

Long after Sally was asleep in her bed, Amelius sat by the library fire, thinking.

The revival of the crushed feeling and fancy in the girl's nature, so artlessly revealed in her sad little story of the stars that were "company to her," not only touched and interested him, but clouded his view of the future with doubts and anxieties which had never troubled him until that moment. The mysterious influences under which the girl's development was advancing were working morally and physically together. Weeks might pass harmlessly, months might pass harmlessly—but the time must come when the innocent relations between them would be beset by peril. Unable, as yet, fully to realize these truths, Amelius nevertheless felt them vaguely. His face was troubled, as he lit the candle at last to go to his bed. "I don't see my way as clearly as I could wish," he reflected. "How will it end?"

How indeed!

CHAPTER 4

At eight o'clock the next morning, Amelius was awakened by Toff. A letter had arrived, marked "Immediate," and the messenger was waiting for an answer.

The letter was from Mrs. Payson. She wrote briefly, and in formal terms. After referring to the matron's fruitless visit to the cottage on the previous night, Mrs. Payson proceeded in these words:—"I request you will immediately let me know whether Sally has taken refuge with you, and has passed the night under your roof. If I am right in believing that she has done so, I have only to inform you that the doors of the Home are henceforth closed to her, in conformity with our rules. If I am wrong, it will be my painful duty to lose no time in placing the matter in the hands of the police."

Amelius began his reply, acting on impulse as usual. He wrote, vehemently remonstrating with Mrs. Payson on the unforgiving and unchristian nature of the rules at the Home. Before he was halfway through his composition, the person who had brought the letter sent a message to say that he was expected back immediately, and that he hoped Mr. Goldenheart would not get a poor man into trouble by keeping him much longer. Checked in the full flow of his eloquence, Amelius angrily tore up the unfinished remonstrance, and matched Mrs. Payson's briefly business-like language by an answer in one line:—"I beg to inform you that you are quite right." On reflection, he felt that the second letter was not only discourteous as a reply to a lady, but also ungrateful as addressed to Mrs. Payson personally. At the third attempt, he wrote becomingly as well as briefly. "Sally has passed the night here, as my guest. She was suffering from severe fatigue; it would have been an act of downright inhumanity to send her away. I regret your decision, but of course I submit to it. You once said, you believed implicitly in the purity of my motives. Do me the justice, however you may blame my conduct, to believe in me still."

Having despatched these lines, the mind of Amelius was at ease again, He went into the library, and listened to hear if Sally was moving. The perfect silence on the other side of the door informed him that the weary girl was still fast asleep. He gave directions that she was on no account to be disturbed, and sat down to breakfast by himself.

While he was still at table, Toff appeared, with profound mystery in his manner, and discreet confidence in the tones of his voice. "Here's another one, sir!" the Frenchman announced, in his master's ear.

"Another one?" Amelius repeated. "What do you mean?"

"She is not like the sweet little sleeping Miss." Toff explained. "This time, sir, it's the beauty of the devil himself, as we say in France. She refuses to confide in me; and she appears to be agitated—both bad signs. Shall I get rid of her before the other Miss wakes?"

"Hasn't she got a name?" Amelius asked.

Toff answered, in his foreign accent, "One name only—Faybay."

"Do you mean Phoebe?"

"Have I not said it, sir?"

"Show her in directly."

Toff glanced at the door of Sally's room, shrugged his shoulders, and obeyed his instructions.

Phoebe appeared, looking pale and anxious. Her customary assurance of manner had completely deserted her: she stopped in the doorway, as if she was afraid to enter the room.

"Come in, and sit down," said Amelius. "What's the matter?"

"I'm troubled in my mind, sir," Phoebe answered. "I know it's taking a liberty to come to you. But I went yesterday to ask Miss Regina's advice, and found she had gone abroad with her uncle. I have something to say about Mrs. Farnaby, sir; and there's no time to be lost in saying it. I know of nobody but you that I can speak to, now Miss Regina is away. The footman told me where you lived."

She stopped, evidently in the greatest embarrassment. Amelius tried to encourage her. "If I can be of any use to Mrs. Farnaby," he said, "tell me at once what to do."

Phoebe's eyes dropped before his straightforward look as he spoke to her.

"I must ask you to please excuse my mentioning names, sir," she resumed confusedly. "There's a person I'm interested in, whom I wouldn't get into trouble for the whole world. He's been misled—I'm sure he's been misled by another person—a wicked drunken old woman, who ought to be in prison if she had her deserts. I'm not free from blame myself—I know I'm not. I listened, sir, to what I oughtn't to have heard; and I told it again (I'm sure in the strictest confidence, and not meaning anything wrong) to the person I've mentioned. Not the old women—I mean the person I'm interested in. I hope you understand me, sir? I wish to speak openly, excepting the names, on account of Mrs. Farnaby."

Amelius thought of Phoebe's vindictive language the last time he had seen her. He looked towards a cabinet in a corner of the room, in which he had placed Mrs. Farnaby's letter. An instinctive distrust of his visitor began to rise in his mind. His manner altered—he turned to his plate, and went on with his breakfast. "Can't you speak to me plainly?" he said. "Is Mrs. Farnaby in any trouble?"

216

"Yes, sir."

"And can I do anything to help her out of it?"

"I am sure you can, sir—if you only know where to find her."

"I do know where to find her. She has written to tell me. The last time I saw you, you expressed yourself very improperly about Mrs. Farnaby; you spoke as if you meant some harm to her."

"I mean nothing but good to her now, sir."

"Very well, then. Can't you go and speak to her yourself, if I give you the address?"

Phoebe's pale face flushed a little. "I couldn't do that, sir," she answered, "after the way Mrs. Farnaby has treated me. Besides, if she knew that I had listened to what passed between her and you—" She stopped again, more painfully embarrassed than ever.

Amelius laid down his knife and fork. "Look here!" he said; "this sort of thing is not in my way. If you can't make a clean breast of it, let's talk of something else. I'm very much afraid," he went on, with his customary absence of all concealment, "you're not the harmless sort of girl I once took you for. What do you mean by 'what passed between Mrs. Farnaby and me'?"

Phoebe put her handkerchief to her eyes. "It's very hard to speak to me so harshly," she said, "when I'm sorry for what I've done, and am only anxious to prevent harm coming of it."

"*What* have you done?" cried honest Amelius, weary of the woman's inveterately indirect way of explaining herself to him.

The flash of his quick temper in his eyes, as he put that straightforward question, roused a responsive temper in Phoebe which stung her into speaking openly at last. She told Amelius what she had heard in the kitchen as plainly as she had told it to Jervy—with this one difference, that she spoke without insolence when she referred to Mrs. Farnaby.

Listening in silence until she had done, Amelius started to his feet, and opening the cabinet, took from it Mrs. Farnaby's letter. He read the letter, keeping his back towards Phoebe—waited a moment thinking—and suddenly turned on the woman with a look that made her shrink in her chair. "You wretch!" he said; "you detestable wretch!"

In the terror of the moment, Phoebe attempted to leave the room. Amelius stopped her instantly. "Sit down again," he said; "I mean to have the whole truth out of you, now."

Phoebe recovered her courage. "You have had the whole truth, sir; I could tell you no more if I was on my deathbed."

Amelius refused to believe her. "There is a vile conspiracy against Mrs. Farnaby," he said. "Do you mean to tell me you are not in it?"

"So help me God, sir, I never even heard of it till yesterday!"

The tone in which she spoke shook the conviction of Amelius; the indescribable ring of truth was in it.

"There are two people who are cruelly deluding and plundering this poor lady," he went on. "Who are they?"

"I told you, if you remember, that I couldn't mention names, sir."

Amelius looked again at the letter. After what he had heard, there was no difficulty in identifying the invisible "young man," alluded to by Mrs. Farnaby, with the unnamed "person" in whom Phoebe was interested. Who was he? As the question passed through his mind, Amelius remembered the vagabond whom he had recognized with Phoebe, in the street. There was no doubt of it now—the man who was directing the conspiracy in the dark was Jervy! Amelius would unquestionably have been rash enough to reveal this discovery, if Phoebe had not stopped him. His renewed reference to Mrs. Farnaby's letter and his sudden silence after looking at it roused the woman's suspicions. "If you're planning to get my friend into trouble," she burst out, "not another word shall pass my lips!"

Even Amelius profited by the warning which that threat unintentionally conveyed to him.

"Keep your own secrets," he said; "I only want to spare Mrs. Farnaby a dreadful disappointment. But I must know what I am talking about when I go to her. Can't you tell me how you found out this abominable swindle?"

Phoebe was perfectly willing to tell him. Interpreting her long involved narrative into plain English, with the names added, these were the facts related:—Mrs. Sowler, bearing in mind some talk which had passed between them on the occasion of a supper, had called at Phoebe's lodgings on the previous day, and had tried to entrap her into communicating what she knew of Mrs. Farnaby's secrets. The trap failing, Mrs. Sowler had tried bribery next; had promised Phoebe a large sum of money, to be equally divided between them, if she would only speak; had declared that Jervy was perfectly capable of breaking his promise of marriage, and "leaving them both in the lurch, if he once got the money into his own pocket" and had thus informed Phoebe, that the conspiracy, which she supposed to have been abandoned, was really in full progress, without her knowledge. She had temporised with Mrs. Sowler, being afraid to set such a person openly at defiance; and had hurried away at once, to have an explanation with Jervy. He was reported to be "not at home." Her fruitless visit to Regina had followed—and there, so far as facts were concerned, was an end of the story.

Amelius asked her no questions, and spoke as briefly as possible when she had done. "I will go to Mrs. Farnaby this morning," was all he said.

"Would you please let me hear how it ends?" Phoebe asked.

Amelius pushed his pocket-book and pencil across the table to her, pointing to a blank leaf on which she could write her address. While she was thus employed the attentive Toff came in, and (with his eye on Phoebe) whispered in his master's ear. He had heard Sally moving about. Would it be more convenient, under the circumstances, if she had her breakfast in her own room? Toff's astonishment was a sight to see when Amelius answered, "Certainly not. Let her breakfast here."

Phoebe rose to go. Her parting words revealed the double-sided nature that was in her; the good and evil in perpetual conflict which should be uppermost.

"Please don't mention me, sir, to Mrs. Farnaby," she said. "I don't forgive her for what she's done to me; I don't say I won't be even with her yet. But not in *that* way! I won't have her death laid at my door. Oh, but I know her temper—and I say it's as likely as not to kill her or drive her mad, if she isn't warned about it in time. Never mind her losing her money. If it's lost, it's lost, and she's got plenty more. She may be robbed a dozen times over for all I care. But don't let her set her heart on seeing her child, and then find it's all a swindle. I hate her; but I can't and won't, let *that* go on. Good-morning, sir."

Amelius was relieved by her departure. For a minute or two, he sat absently stirring his coffee, and considering how he might most safely perform the terrible duty of putting Mrs. Farnaby on her guard. Toff interrupted his meditations by preparing the table for Sally's breakfast; and, almost at the same moment, Sally herself, fresh and rosy, opened her door a little way, and looked in.

"You have had a fine long sleep," said Amelius. "Have you quite got over your walk yesterday?"

"Oh yes," she answered gaily; "I only feel my long walk now in my feet. It hurts me to put my boots on. Can you lend me a pair of slippers?"

"A pair of my slippers? Why, Sally, you would be lost in them! What's the matter with your feet?"

"They're both sore. And I think one of them has got a blister on it."

"Come in, and let's have a look at it?"

She came limping in, with her feet bare. "Don't scold me," she pleaded, "I couldn't put my stockings on again, without washing them; and they're not dry yet."

"I'll get you new stockings and slippers," said Amelius. "Which is the foot with the blister?"

"The left foot," she answered, pointing to it.

CHAPTER 5

"Let me see the blister," said Amelius.

Sally looked longingly at the fire.

"May I warm my feet first?" she asked; "they are so cold."

In those words she innocently deferred the discovery which, if it had been made at the moment, might have altered the whole after-course of events. Amelius only thought now of preventing her from catching cold. He sent Toff for a pair of the warmest socks that he possessed, and asked if he should put them on for her. She smiled, and shook her head, and put them on for herself.

When they had done laughing at the absurd appearance of the little feet in the large socks, they only drifted farther and farther away from the subject of the blistered foot. Sally remembered the terrible matron, and asked if anything had been heard of her that morning. Being told that Mrs. Payson had written, and that the doors of the institution were closed to her, she recovered her spirits, and began to wonder whether the offended authorities would let her have her clothes. Toff offered to go and make the inquiry, later in the day; suggesting the purchase of slippers and stockings, in the mean time, while Sally was having her breakfast. Amelius approved of the suggestion; and Toff set off on his errand, with one of Sally's boots for a pattern.

The morning had, by that time, advanced to ten o'clock.

Amelius stood before the fire talking, while Sally had her breakfast. Having first explained the reasons which made it impossible that she should live at the cottage in the capacity of his servant, he astonished her by announcing that he meant to undertake the superintendence of her education himself. They were to be master and pupil, while the lessons were in progress; and brother and sister at other times—and they were to see how they got on together, on this plan, without indulging in any needless anxiety about the future. Amelius believed with perfect sincerity that he had hit on the only sensible arrangement, under the circumstances; and Sally cried joyously, "Oh, how good you are to me; the happy life has come at last!" At the hour when those words passed the daughter's lips, the discovery of the conspiracy burst upon the mother in all its baseness and in all its horror.

The suspicion of her infamous employer, which had induced Mrs. Sowler to attempt to intrude herself into Phoebe's confidence, led her to make a visit of investigation at Jervy's lodgings later in the day. Informed, as Phoebe had been informed, that he was not at home, she called again some hours afterwards. By that time, the landlord had discovered that Jervy's luggage had been secretly conveyed away, and that his tenant had left him, in debt for rent of the two best rooms in the house.

No longer in any doubt of what had happened, Mrs. Sowler employed the remaining hours of the evening in making inquiries after the missing man. Not a trace of him had been discovered up to eight o'clock on the next morning.

Shortly after nine o'clock—that is to say, towards the hour at which Phoebe paid her visit to Amelius—Mrs. Sowler, resolute to know the worst, made her appearance at the apartments occupied by Mrs. Farnaby.

"I wish to speak to you," she began abruptly, "about that young man we both know of. Have you seen anything of him lately?"

Mrs. Farnaby, steadily on her guard, deferred answering the question. "Why do you want to know?" she said.

The reply was instantly ready. "Because I have reason to believe he has bolted, with your money in his pocket."

"He has done nothing of the sort," Mrs. Farnaby rejoined.

"Has he got your money?" Mrs. Sowler persisted. "Tell me the truth—and I'll do the same by you. He has cheated me. If you're cheated too, it's your own interest to lose no time in finding him. The police may catch him yet. *Has* he got your money?"

The woman was in earnest—in terrible earnest—her eyes and her voice both bore witness to it. She stood there, the living impersonation of those doubts and fears which Mrs. Farnaby had confessed, in writing to Amelius. Her position, at that moment, was essentially a position of command. Mrs. Farnaby felt it in spite of herself. She acknowledged that Jervy had got the money.

"Did you sent it to him, or give it to him?" Mrs. Sowler asked.

"I gave it to him."

"When?"

"Yesterday evening."

Mrs. Sowler clenched her fists, and shook them in impotent rage. "He's the biggest scoundrel living," she exclaimed furiously; "and you're the biggest fool! Put on your bonnet and come to the police. If you get your money back again before he's spent it all, don't forget it was through me."

The audacity of the woman's language roused Mrs. Farnaby. She pointed to the door. "You are an insolent creature," she said; "I have nothing more to do with you."

"You have nothing more to do with me?" Mrs. Sowler repeated. "You and the young man have settled it all between you, I suppose." She laughed scornfully. "I dare say now you expect to see him again?"

Mrs. Farnaby was irritated into answering this. "I expect to see him this morning," she said, "at ten o'clock."

"And the lost young lady with him?"

"Say nothing about my lost daughter! I won't even hear you speak of her."

Mrs. Sowler sat down. "Look at your watch," she said. "It must be nigh on ten o'clock by this time. You'll make a disturbance in the house if you try to turn me out. I mean to wait here till ten o'clock."

On the point of answering angrily, Mrs. Farnaby restrained herself. "You are trying to force a quarrel on me," she said; "you shan't spoil the happiest morning of my life. Wait here by yourself."

She opened the door that led into her bedchamber, and shut herself in. Perfectly impenetrable to any repulse that could be offered to her, Mrs. Sowler looked at the closed door with a sardonic smile, and waited.

The clock in the hall struck ten. Mrs. Farnaby returned again to the sitting-room, walked straight to the window, and looked out.

"Any sign of him?" said Mrs. Sowler.

There were no signs of him. Mrs. Farnaby drew a chair to the window, and sat down. Her hands turned icy cold. She still looked out into the street.

"I'm going to guess what's happened," Mrs. Sowler resumed. "I'm a sociable creature, you know, and I must talk about something. About the money, now? Has the young man had his travelling expenses of you? To go to foreign parts, and bring your girl back with him, eh? I expect that's how it was. You see, I know him so well. And what happened, if you please, yesterday evening? Did he tell you he'd brought her back, and got her at his own place? And did he say he wouldn't let you see her till you paid him his reward as well as his travelling expenses? And did you forget my warning to you not to trust him? I'm a good one at guessing when I try. I see you think so yourself. Any signs of him yet?"

Mrs. Farnaby looked round from the window. Her manner was completely changed; she was nervously civil to the wretch who was torturing her. "I beg your pardon, ma'am, if I have offended you," she said faintly. "I am a little upset—I am so anxious about my poor child. Perhaps you are a mother yourself? You oughtn't to frighten me; you ought to feel for me." She paused, and put her hand to her head. "He told me yesterday evening," she went on slowly and vacantly, "that my poor darling was at his lodgings; he said she was so worn out with the long journey from abroad, that she must have a night's rest before she could come to me. I asked him to tell me where he lived, and let me go to her. He said she was asleep and must not be disturbed. I promised to go in on tiptoe, and only look at her; I offered him more money, double the money to tell me where she was. He was very hard on me. He only said, wait till ten tomorrow morning—and wished me goodnight. I ran out to follow him, and fell on the stairs, and hurt myself. The people of the house were very kind to me." She turned her head back towards the window, and looked out into the street again. "I must be patient," she said; "he's only a little late."

Mrs. Sowler rose, and tapped her smartly on the shoulder. "Lies!" she burst out. "He knows no more where your daughter is than I do—and he's off with your money!"

The woman's hateful touch struck out a spark of the old fire in Mrs. Farnaby. Her natural force of character asserted itself once more. "*You* lie!" she rejoined. "Leave the room!"

The door was opened, while she spoke. A respectable woman-servant came in with a letter. Mrs. Farnaby took it mechanically, and looked at the address. Jervy's feigned handwriting was familiar to her. In the instant when she recognized it, the life seemed to go out of her like an extinguished light. She stood pale and still and silent, with the unopened letter in her hand.

Watching her with malicious curiosity, Mrs. Sowler coolly possessed herself of the letter, looked at it, and recognized the writing in her turn. "Stop!" she cried, as the servant was on the point of going out. "There's no stamp on this letter. Was it brought by hand? Is the messenger waiting?"

The respectable servant showed her opinion of Mrs. Sowler plainly in her face. She replied as briefly and as ungraciously as possible:—"No."

"Man or woman?" was the next question.

"Am I to answer this person, ma'am?" said the servant, looking at Mrs. Farnaby.

"Answer me instantly," Mrs. Sowler interposed—"in Mrs. Farnaby's own interests. Don't you see she can't speak to you herself?"

"Well, then," said the servant, "it was a man."

224

"A man with a squint?"

"Yes."

"Which way did he go?"

"Towards the square."

Mrs. Sowler tossed the letter on the table, and hurried out of the room. The servant approached Mrs. Farnaby. "You haven't opened your letter yet, ma'am," she said.

"No," said Mrs. Farnaby vacantly, "I haven't opened it yet."

"I'm afraid it's bad news, ma'am?"

"Yes. I think it's bad news."

"Is there anything I can do for you?"

"No, thank you. Yes; one thing. Open my letter for me, please."

It was a strange request to make. The servant wondered, and obeyed. She was a kind-hearted woman; she really felt for the poor lady. But the familiar household devil, whose name is Curiosity, and whose opportunities are innumerable, prompted her next words when she had taken the letter out of the envelope:—"Shall I read it to you, ma'am?"

"No. Put it down on the table, please. I'll ring when I want you."

The mother was alone—alone, with her death-warrant waiting for her on the table.

The clock downstairs struck the half hour after ten. She moved, for the first time since she had received the letter. Once more she went to the window, and looked out. It was only for a moment. She turned away again, with a sudden contempt for herself. "What a fool I am!" she said—and took up the open letter.

She looked at it, and put it down again. "Why should I read it," she asked herself, "when I know what is in it, without reading?"

Some framed woodcuts from the illustrated newspapers were hung on the walls. One of them represented a scene of rescue from shipwreck. A mother embracing her daughter, saved by the lifeboat, was among the foreground groups. The print was entitled, "The Mercy of Providence." Mrs. Farnaby looked at it with a moment's steady attention. "Providence has its favourites," she said; "I am not one of them."

225

After thinking a little, she went into her bedroom, and took two papers out of her dressing-case. They were medical prescriptions.

She turned next to the chimneypiece. Two medicine-bottles were placed on it. She took one of them down—a bottle of the ordinary size, known among chemists as a six-ounce bottle. It contained a colourless liquid. The label stated the dose to be "two table-spoonfuls," and bore, as usual, a number corresponding with a number placed on the prescription. She took up the prescription. It was a mixture of bi-carbonate of soda and prussic acid, intended for the relief of indigestion. She looked at the date, and was at once reminded of one of the very rare occasions on which she had required the services of a medical man. There had been a serious accident at a dinner-party, given by some friends. She had eaten sparingly of a certain dish, from which some of the other guests had suffered severely. It was discovered that the food had been cooked in an old copper saucepan. In her case, the trifling result had been a disturbance of digestion, and nothing more. The doctor had prescribed accordingly. She had taken but one dose: with her healthy constitution she despised physic. The remainder of the mixture was still in the bottle.

She considered again with herself—then went back to the chimneypiece, and took down the second bottle.

It contained a colourless liquid also; but it was only half the size of the first bottle, and not a drop had been taken. She waited, observing the difference between the two bottles with extraordinary attention. In this case also, the prescription was in her possession—but it was not the original. A line at the top stated that it was a copy made by the chemist, at the request of a customer. It bore the date of more than three years since. A morsel of paper was pinned to the prescription, containing some lines in a woman's handwriting:—"With your enviable health and strength, my dear, I should have thought you were the last person in the world to want a tonic. However, here is my prescription, if you must have it. Be very careful to take the right dose, because there's poison in it." The prescription contained three ingredients, strychnine, quinine, and nitro-hydrochloric acid; and the dose was fifteen drops in water. Mrs. Farnaby lit a match, and burnt the lines of her friend's writing. "As long ago as that," she reflected, "I thought of killing myself. Why didn't I do it?"

The paper having been destroyed, she put back the prescription for indigestion in her dressing-case; hesitated for a moment; and opened the bedroom window. It looked into a lonely little courtyard. She threw the dangerous contents of the second and smaller bottle out into the yard—and then put it back empty on the chimneypiece. After another moment of hesitation, she returned to the sitting-room, with the bottle of mixture, and the copied prescription for the tonic strychnine drops, in her hand.

She put the bottle on the table, and advanced to the fireplace to ring the bell. Warm as the room was, she began to shiver. Did the eager life in her feel the fatal purpose that she was meditating, and shrink from it? Instead of ringing the bell, she bent over the fire, trying to warm herself.

226

"Other women would get relief in crying," she thought. "I wish I was like other women!"

The whole sad truth about herself was in that melancholy aspiration. No relief in tears, no merciful oblivion in a fainting-fit, for *her*. The terrible strength of the vital organization in this woman knew no yielding to the unutterable misery that wrung her to the soul. It roused its glorious forces to resist: it held her in a stony quiet, with a grip of iron.

She turned away from the fire wondering at herself. "What baseness is there in me that fears death? What have I got to live for *now?*" The open letter on the table caught her eye. "This will do it!" she said—and snatched it up, and read it at last.

"The least I can do for you is to act like a gentleman, and spare you unnecessary suspense. You will not see me this morning at ten, for the simple reason that I really don't know, and never did know, where to find your daughter. I wish I was rich enough to return the money. Not being able to do that, I will give you a word of advice instead. The next time you confide any secrets of yours to Mr. Goldenheart, take better care that no third person hears you."

She read those atrocious lines, without any visible disturbance of the dreadful composure that possessed her. Her mind made no effort to discover the person who had listened and betrayed her. To all ordinary curiosities, to all ordinary emotions, she was morally dead already.

The one thought in her was a thought that might have occurred to a man. "If I only had my hands on his throat, how I could wring the life out of him! As it is—" Instead of pursuing the reflection, she threw the letter into the fire, and rang the bell.

"Take this at once to the nearest chemist's," she said, giving the strychnine prescription to the servant; "and wait, please, and bring it back with you."

She opened her desk, when she was alone, and tore up the letters and papers in it. This done, she took her pen, and wrote a letter. It was addressed to Amelius.

When the servant entered the room again, bringing with her the prescription made up, the clock downstairs struck eleven.

CHAPTER 6

Toff returned to the cottage, with the slippers and the stockings.

"What a time you have been gone!" said Amelius.

"It is not my fault, sir," Toff explained. "The stockings I obtained without difficulty. But the nearest shoe shop in this neighbourhood sold only coarse manufactures, and all too large. I had to go to my wife, and get her to take me to the right place. See!" he exclaimed, producing a pair of quilted silk slippers with blue rosettes, "here is a design, that is really worthy of pretty feet. Try them on, Miss."

Sally's eyes sparkled at the sight of the slippers. She rose at once, and limped away to her room. Amelius, observing that she still walked in pain, called her back. "I had forgotten the blister," he said. "Before you put on the new stockings, Sally, let me see your foot." He turned to Toff. "You're always ready with everything," he went on; "I wonder whether you have got a needle and a bit of worsted thread?"

The old Frenchman answered, with an air of respectful reproach. "Knowing me, sir, as you do," he said, "could you doubt for a moment that I mend my own clothes and darn my own stockings?" He withdrew to his bedroom below, and returned with a leather roll. "When you are ready, sir?" he said, opening the roll at the table, and threading the needle, while Sally removed the sock from her left foot.

She took a chair near the window, at the suggestion of Amelius. He knelt down so as to raise her foot to his knee. "Turn a little more towards the light," he said. He took the foot in his hand, lifted it, looked at it—and suddenly let it drop back on the floor.

A cry of alarm from Sally instantly brought Toff to the window. "Oh, look!" she cried; "he's ill!" Toff lifted Amelius to a chair. "For God's sake, sir," cried the terrified old man, "what's the matter?" Amelius had turned to the strange ashy paleness which is only seen in men of his florid complexion, overwhelmed by sudden emotion. He stammered when he tried to speak. "Fetch the brandy!" said Toff, pointing to the liqueur-case on the sideboard. Sally brought it at once; the strong stimulant steadied Amelius.

"I'm sorry to have frightened you," he said faintly. "Sally!—Dear, dear little Sally, go in, and get your things on directly. You must come out with me; I'll tell you why afterwards. My God! why didn't I find this out before?" He noticed Toff, wondering and trembling. "Good old fellow! don't alarm yourself—you shall know about it, too. Go! run! get the first cab you can find!"

Left alone for a few minutes, he had time to compose himself. He did his best to take advantage of the time; he tried to prepare his mind for the coming interview with Mrs. Farnaby. "I must be careful of what I do," he thought, conscious of the overwhelming effect of the discovery on himself; "She doesn't expect *me* to bring her daughter to her."

Sally returned to him, ready to go out. She seemed to be afraid of him, when he approached her, and took her hand. "Have I done anything wrong?" she asked, in her childish way. "Are you going to take me to some other Home?" The tone and look with which she put the question burst through the restraints which Amelius had imposed on himself for her sake. "My dear child!" he said, "can you bear a great surprise? I'm dying to tell you the truth—and I hardly dare do it." He took her in his arms. She trembled piteously. Instead of answering him, she reiterated her question, "Are you going to take me to some other Home?" He could endure it no longer. "This is the happiest day of your life, Sally!" he cried; "I am going to take you to your mother."

He held her close to him, and looked at her in dread of having spoken too plainly.

She slowly lifted her eyes to him in vacant fear and surprise; she burst into no expression of delight; no overwhelming emotion made her sink fainting in his arms. The sacred associations which gather round the mere name of Mother were associations unknown to her; the man who held her to him so tenderly, the hero who had pitied and saved her, was father and mother both to her simple mind. She dropped her head on his breast; her faltering voice told him that she was crying. "Will my mother take me away from you?" she asked. "Oh, do promise to bring me back with you to the cottage!"

For the moment, and the moment only, Amelius was disappointed in her. The generous sympathies in his nature guided him unerringly to the truer view. He remembered what her life had been. Inexpressible pity for her filled his heart. "Oh, my poor Sally, the time is coming when you will not think as you think now! I will do nothing to distress you. You mustn't cry—you must be happy, and loving and true to your mother." She dried her eyes, "I'll do anything you tell me," she said, "as long as you bring me back with you."

Amelius sighed, and said no more. He took her out with him gravely and silently, when the cab was announced to be ready. "Double your fare," he said, when he gave the driver his instructions, "if you get there in a quarter of an hour." It wanted twenty-five minutes to twelve when the cab left the cottage.

At that moment, the contrast of feeling between the two could hardly have been more strongly marked. In proportion as Amelius became more and more agitated, so Sally recovered the composure and confidence that she had lost. The first question she put to him related, not to her mother, but to his strange behaviour when he had knelt down to look at her foot. He answered, explaining to her briefly and plainly what his conduct meant. The description of what had passed between her mother and Amelius interested and yet perplexed her. "How can she be so fond of me, without knowing anything about me for all those years?" she asked. "Is my mother a lady? Don't tell her where you found me; she might be ashamed of me." She paused, and looked at Amelius anxiously. "Are you vexed about something? May I take hold of your hand?" Amelius gave her his hand; and Sally was satisfied.

As the cab drew up at the house, the door was opened from within. A gentleman, dressed in black, hurriedly came out; looked at Amelius; and spoke to him as he stepped from the cab to the pavement.

"I beg your pardon, sir. May I ask if you are any relative of the lady who lives in this house?"

"No relative," Amelius answered. "Only a friend, who brings good news to her."

The stranger's grave face suddenly became compassionate as well as grave. "I must speak with you before you go upstairs," he said, lowering his voice as he looked at Sally, still seated in the cab. "You will perhaps excuse the liberty I am taking, when I tell you that I am a medical man. Come into the hall for a moment—and don't bring the young lady with you."

Amelius told Sally to wait in the cab. She saw his altered looks, and entreated him not to leave her. He promised to keep the house door open so that she could see him while he was away from her, and hastened into the hall.

"I am sorry to say I have bad, very bad, news for you," the doctor began. "Time is of serious importance—I must speak plainly. You have heard of mistakes made by taking the wrong bottle of medicine? The poor lady upstairs is, I fear, in a dying state, from an accident of that sort. Try to compose yourself. You may really be of use to me, if you are firm enough to take my place while I am away."

Amelius steadied himself instantly. "What I can do, I will do," he answered.

The doctor looked at him. "I believe you," he said. "Now listen. In this case, a dose limited to fifteen drops has been confounded with a dose of two table-spoonful; and the drug taken by mistake is strychnine. One grain of the poison has been known to prove fatal—she has taken three. The convulsion fits have begun. Antidotes are out of the question—the poor creature can swallow nothing. I have heard of opium as a possible means of relief; and I am going to get the instrument for injecting it under the skin. Not that I have much belief in the remedy; but I must try something. Have you courage enough to hold her, if another of the convulsions comes on in my absence?"

"Will it relieve her, if I hold her?" Amelius, asked.

"Certainly."

"Then I promise to do it."

230

"Mind! you must do it thoroughly. There are only two women upstairs; both perfectly useless in this emergency. If she shrieks to you to be held, exert your strength—take her with a firm grasp. If you only touch her (I can't explain it, but it is so), you will make matters worse."

The servant ran downstairs, while he was speaking. "Don't leave us, sir—I'm afraid it's coming on again."

"This gentleman will help you, while I am away," said the doctor. "One word more," he went on, addressing Amelius. "In the intervals between the fits, she is perfectly conscious; able to listen, and even to speak. If she has any last wishes to communicate, make good use of the time. She may die of exhaustion, at any moment. I will be back directly."

He hurried to the door.

"Take my cab," said Amelius, "and save time."

"But the young lady—"

"Leave her to me." He opened the cab door, and gave his hand to Sally. It was done in a moment. The doctor drove off.

Amelius saw the servant waiting for them in the hall. He spoke to Sally, telling her, considerately and gently, what he had heard, before he took her into the house. "I had such good hopes for you," he said; "and it has come to this dreadful end! Have you courage to go through with it, if I take you to her bedside? You will be glad one day, my dear, to remember that you cheered your mother's last moments on earth."

Sally put her hand in his. "I will go anywhere," she said softly, "with You."

Amelius led her into the house. The servant, in pity for her youth, ventured on a word of remonstrance. "Oh, sir, you're not going to let the poor young lady see that dreadful sight upstairs!"

"You mean well," Amelius answered; "and I thank you. If you knew what I know, you would take her upstairs, too. Show the way."

Sally looked at him in silent awe as they followed the servant together. He was not like the same man. His brows were knit; his lips were fast set; he held the girl's hand in a grip that hurt her. The latent strength of will in him—that reserved resolution, so finely and firmly entwined in the natures of sensitively organized men—was rousing itself to meet the coming trial. The doctor would have doubly believed in him, if the doctor had seen him at that moment.

They reached the first-floor landing.

Before the servant could open the drawing-room door, a shriek rang frightfully through the silence of the house. The servant drew back, and crouched trembling on the upper stairs. At the same moment, the door was flung open, and another woman ran out, wild with terror. "I can't bear it!" she cried, and rushed up the stairs, blind to the presence of strangers in the panic that possessed her. Amelius entered the drawing-room, with his arm round Sally, holding her up. As he placed her in a chair, the dreadful cry was renewed. He only waited to rouse and encourage her by a word and a look—and ran into the bedroom.

For an instant, and an instant only, he stood horror-struck in the presence of the poisoned woman.

The fell action of the strychnine wrung every muscle in her with the torture of convulsion. Her hands were fast clenched; her head was bent back: her body, rigid as a bar of iron, was arched upwards from the bed, resting on the two extremities of the head and the heels: the staring eyes, the dusky face, the twisted lips, the clenched teeth, were frightful to see. He faced it. After the one instant of hesitation, he faced it.

Before she could cry out again, his hands were on her. The whole exertion of his strength was barely enough to keep the frenzied throbs of the convulsion, as it reached its climax, from throwing her off the bed. Through the worst of it, he was still equal to the trust that had been placed in him, still faithful to the work of mercy. Little by little, he felt the lessening resistance of the rigid body, as the paroxysm began to subside. He saw the ghastly stare die out of her eyes, and the twisted lips relax from their dreadful grin. The tortured body sank, and rested; the perspiration broke out on her face; her languid hands fell gently over on the bed. For a while, the heavy eyelids closed—then opened again feebly. She looked at him. "Do you know me?" he asked, bending over her. And she answered in a faint whisper, "Amelius!"

He knelt down by her, and kissed her hand. "Can you listen, if I tell you something?"

She breathed heavily; her bosom heaved under the suffocating oppression that weighed upon it. As he took her in his arms to raise her in the bed, Sally's voice reached him, in low imploring tones, from the next room. "Oh, let me come to you! I'm so frightened here by myself."

He waited, before he told her to come in, looking for a moment at the face that was resting on his breast. A gray shadow was stealing over it; a cold and clammy moisture struck a chill through him as he put his hand on her forehead. He turned towards the next room. The girl had ventured as far as the door; he beckoned to her. She came in timidly, and stood by him, and looked at her mother. Amelius signed to her to take his place. "Put your arms round her," he whispered. "Oh, Sally, tell her who you are in a kiss!" The girl's tears fell fast as she pressed her lips on her

232

mother's cheek. The dying woman looked at her, with a glance of helpless inquiry—then looked at Amelius. The doubt in her eyes was too dreadful to be endured. Arranging the pillows so that she could keep her raised position in the bed, he signed to Sally to approach him, and removed the slipper from her left foot. As he took it off, he looked again at the bed—looked and shuddered. In a moment more, it might be too late. With his knife he ripped up the stocking, and, lifting her on the bed, put her bare foot on her mother's lap. "Your child! your child!" he cried; "I've found your own darling! For God's sake, rouse yourself! Look!"

She heard him. She lifted her feebly declining head. She looked. She knew.

For one awful moment, the sinking vital forces rallied, and hurled back the hold of Death. Her eyes shone radiant with the divine light of maternal love; an exulting cry of rapture burst from her. Slowly, very slowly, she bent forward, until her face rested on her daughter's foot. With a faint sigh of ecstasy she kissed it. The moments passed—and the bent head was raised no more. The last beat of the heart was a beat of joy.

BOOK THE EIGHTH

DAME NATURE DECIDES

CHAPTER 1

The day which had united the mother and daughter, only to part them again in this world for ever, had advanced to evening.

Amelius and Sally were together again in the cottage, sitting by the library fire. The silence in the room was uninterrupted. On the open desk, near Amelius, lay the letter which Mrs. Farnaby had written to him on the morning of her death.

He had found the letter—with the envelope unfastened—on the floor of the bedchamber, and had fortunately secured it before the landlady and the servant had ventured back to the room. The doctor, returning a few minutes afterwards, had warned the two women that a coroner's inquest would be held in the house, and had vainly cautioned them to be careful of what they said or did in the interval. Not only the subject of the death, but a discovery which had followed, revealing the name of the ill-fated woman marked on her linen, and showing that she had used an assumed name in taking the lodgings as Mrs. Ronald, became the gossip of the neighbourhood in a few hours. Under these circumstances, the catastrophe was made the subject of a paragraph in the evening journals; the name being added for the information of any surviving relatives who might be ignorant of the sad event. If the landlady had found the letter, that circumstance also would in all probability, have formed part of the statement in the newspapers, and the secret of Mrs. Farnaby's life and death would have been revealed to the public view.

"I can trust you, and you only," she wrote to Amelius, "to fulfil the last wishes of a dying woman. You know me, and you know how I looked forward to the prospect of a happy life in retirement with my child. The one hope that I lived for has proved to be a cruel delusion. I have only this morning discovered, beyond the possibility of doubt, that I have been made the victim of wretches who have deliberately lied to me from first to last. If I had been a happier woman, I might have had other interests to sustain me under this frightful disaster. Such as I am, Death is my one refuge left.

"My suicide will be known to no creature but yourself. Some years since, the idea of self destruction—concealed under the disguise of a common mistake—presented itself to my mind. I kept the means, very simple means, by me, thinking I might end in that way after all. When you read this I shall be at rest for ever. You will do what I have yet to ask of you, in merciful remembrance of me—I am sure of that.

"You have a long life before you, Amelius. My foolish fancy about you and my lost girl still lingers in my mind; I still think it may be just possible that you may meet with her, in the course of years.

"If this does happen, I implore you, by the tenderness and pity that you once felt for me, to tell no human creature that she is my daughter; and, if John Farnaby is living at the time, I forbid you, with the authority of a dying friend, to let her see him, or to let her know even that such a person exists. Are you at a loss to account for my motives? I may make the shameful confession which will enlighten you, now I know that we shall never meet again. My child was born before my marriage; and the man who afterwards became my husband—a man of low origin, I should tell you—was the father. He had calculated on this disgraceful circumstance to force my parents to make his fortune, by making me his wife. I now know, what I only vaguely suspected before, that he deliberately abandoned his child, as a likely cause of hindrance and scandal in the way of his prosperous career in life. Do you now think I am asking too much, when I entreat you never even to speak to my lost darling of this unnatural wretch? As for my own fair fame, I am not thinking of myself. With Death close at my side, I think of my poor mother, and of all that she suffered and sacrificed to save me from the disgrace that I had deserved. For her sake, not for mine, keep silence to friends and enemies alike if they ask you who my girl is—with the one exception of my lawyer. Years since, I left in his care the means of making a small provision for my child, on the chance that she might live to claim it. You can show him this letter as your authority, in case of need.

"Try not to forget me, Amelius—but don't grieve about me. I go to my death as you go to your sleep when you are tired. I leave you my grateful love—you have always been good to me. There is no more to write; I hear the servant returning from the chemist's, bringing with her only release from the hard burden of life without hope. May you be happier than I have been! Goodbye!"

So she parted from him for ever. But the fatal association of the unhappy woman's sorrows with the life and fortune of Amelius was not at an end yet.

He had neither hesitation nor misgiving in resolving to show a natural respect to the wishes of the dead. Now that the miserable story of the past had been unreservedly disclosed to him, he would have felt himself bound in honour, even without instructions to guide him, to keep the discovery of the daughter a secret, for the mother's sake. With that conviction, he had read the distressing letter. With that conviction, he now rose to provide for the safe keeping of it under lock and key.

Just as he had secured the letter in a private drawer of his desk, Toff came in with a card, and announced that a gentleman wished to see him. Amelius, looking at the card, was surprised to find on it the name of "Mr. Melton." Some lines were written on it in pencil: "I have called to speak with you on a matter of serious importance." Wondering what his middle-aged rival could want with him, Amelius instructed Toff to admit the visitor.

Sally started to her feet, with her customary distrust of strangers. "May I run away before he comes in?" she asked. "If you like," Amelius answered quietly. She ran to the door of her room, at the moment when Toff appeared again, announcing the visitor. Mr. Melton entered just before she disappeared: he saw the flutter of her dress as the door closed behind her.

"I fear I am disturbing you?" he said, looking hard at the door.

236

He was perfectly dressed: his hat and gloves were models of what such things ought to be; he was melancholy and courteous; blandly distrustful of the flying skirts which he had seen at the door. When Amelius offered him a chair, he took it with a mysterious sigh; mournfully resigned to the sad necessity of sitting down. "I won't prolong my intrusion on you," he resumed. "You have no doubt seen the melancholy news in the evening papers?"

"I haven't seen the evening papers," Amelius answered; "what news do you mean?"

Mr. Melton leaned back in his chair, and expressed emotions of sorrow and surprise, in a perfect state of training, by gently raising his smooth white hands.

"Oh dear, dear! this is very sad. I had hoped to find you in full possession of the particulars—reconciled, as we must all be, to the inscrutable ways of Providence. Permit me to break it to you as gently as possible. I came here to inquire if you had heard yet from Miss Regina. Understand my motive! there must be no misapprehension between us on that subject. There is a very serious necessity—pray follow me carefully—I say, a very serious necessity for my communicating immediately with Miss Regina's uncle; and I know of nobody who is so likely to hear from the travellers, so soon after their departure, as yourself. You are, in a certain sense, a member of the family—"

"Stop a minute," said Amelius.

"I beg your pardon?" said Mr. Melton politely, at a loss to understand the interruption.

"I didn't at first know what you meant," Amelius explained. "You put it, if you will forgive me for saying so, in rather a roundabout way. If you are alluding, all this time, to Mrs. Farnaby's death, I must honestly tell you that I know of it already."

The bland self-possession of Mr. Melton's face began to show signs of being ruffled. He had been in a manner deluded into exhibiting his conventionally fluent eloquence, in the choicest modulations of his sonorous voice—and it wounded his self esteem to be placed in his present position. "I understood you to say," he remarked stiffly, "that you had not seen the evening newspapers."

"You are quite right," Amelius rejoined; "I have not seen them."

"Then may I inquire," Mr. Melton proceeded, "how you became informed of Mrs. Farnaby's death?"

Amelius replied with his customary frankness. "I went to call on the poor lady this morning," he said, "knowing nothing of what had happened. I met the doctor at the door; and I was present at her death."

Even Mr. Melton's carefully-trained composure was not proof against the revelation that now opened before him. He burst out with an exclamation of astonishment, like an ordinary man.

"Good heavens, what does this mean!"

Amelius took it as a question addressed to himself. "I'm sure I don't know," he said quietly.

Mr. Melton, misunderstanding Amelius on his side, interpreted those innocent words as an outbreak of vulgar interruption. "Pardon me," he said coldly. "I was about to explain myself. You will presently understand my surprise. After seeing the evening paper, I went at once to make inquiries at the address mentioned. In Mr. Farnaby's absence, I felt bound to do this as his old friend. I saw the landlady, and, with her assistance, the doctor also. Both these persons spoke of a gentleman who had called that morning, accompanied by a young lady; and who had insisted on taking the young lady upstairs with him. Until you mentioned just now that you were present at the death, I had no suspicion that you were 'the gentleman'. Surprise on my part was, I think, only natural. I could hardly be expected to know that you were in Mrs. Farnaby's confidence about the place of her retreat. And with regard to the young lady, I am still quite at a loss to understand—"

"If you understand that the people at the house told you the truth, so far as I am concerned," Amelius interposed, "I hope that will be enough. With regard to the young lady, I must beg you to excuse me for speaking plainly. I have nothing to say about her, to you or to anybody."

Mr. Melton rose with the utmost dignity and the fullest possession of his vocal resources.

"Permit me to assure you," he said, with frigidly fluent politeness, "that I have no wish to force myself into your confidence. One remark I will venture to make. It is easy enough, no doubt, to keep your own secrets, when you are speaking to *me*. You will find some difficulty, I fear, in pursuing the same course, when you are called upon to give evidence before the coroner. I presume you know that you will be summoned as a witness at the inquest?"

"I left my name and address with the doctor for that purpose," Amelius rejoined as composedly as ever; "and I am ready to bear witness to what I saw at poor Mrs. Farnaby's bedside. But if all the coroners in England questioned me about anything else, I should say to them just what I have said to you."

Mr. Melton smiled with well bred irony. "We shall see," he said. "In the mean time, I presume I may ask you, in the interests of the family, to send me the address on the letter, as soon as you hear from Miss Regina. I have no other means of communicating with Mr. Farnaby. In respect to the melancholy event, I may add that I have undertaken to provide for the funeral, and to pay any little outstanding debts, and so forth. As Mr. Farnaby's old friend and representative—"

The conclusion of the sentence was interrupted by the entrance of Toff with a note, and an apology for his intrusion. "I beg your pardon, sir; the person is waiting. She says it's only a receipt to sign. The box is in the hall."

Amelius examined the enclosure. It was a formal document, acknowledging the receipt of Sally's clothes, returned to her by the authorities at the Home. As he took a pen to sign the receipt he looked towards the door of Sally's room. Mr. Melton, observing the look, prepared to retire. "I am only interrupting you," he said. "You have my address on my card. Good evening."

On his way out, he passed an elderly woman, waiting in the hall. Toff, hastening before him to open the garden gate, was saluted by the gruff voice of a cabman, outside. "The lady whom he had driven to the cottage had not paid him his right fare; he meant to have the money, or the lady's name and address, and summon her." Quietly crossing the road, Mr. Melton heard the woman's voice next: she had got her receipt, and had followed him out. In the dispute about fares and distances that ensued, the contending parties more than once mentioned the name of the Home and of the locality in which it was situated. Possessing this information, Mr. Melton looked in at his club; consulted a directory, under the heading of "Charitable Institutions;" and solved the mystery of the vanishing petticoats at the door. He had discovered an inmate of an asylum for lost women, in the house of the man to whom Regina was engaged to be married!

The next morning's post brought to Amelius a letter from Regina. It was dated from an hotel in Paris. Her "dear uncle" had over estimated his strength. He had refused to stay and rest for the night at Boulogne; and had suffered so severely from the fatigue of the long journey that he had been confined to his bed since his arrival. The English physician consulted had declined to say when he would be strong enough to travel again; the constitution of the patient must have received some serious shock; he was brought very low. Having carefully reported the new medical opinion, Regina was at liberty to indulge herself, next, in expressions of affection, and to assure Amelius of her anxiety to hear from him as soon as possible. But, in this case again, the "dear uncle's" convenience was still the first consideration. She reverted to Mr. Farnaby, in making her excuses for a hurriedly written letter. The poor invalid suffered from depression of spirits; his great consolation in his illness was to hear his niece read to him: he was calling for her, indeed, at that moment. The inevitable postscript warmed into a mild effusion of fondness, "How I wish you could be with us. But, alas, it cannot be!"

Amelius copied the address on the letter, and sent it to Mr. Melton immediately.

It was then the twenty-fourth day of the month. The tidal train did not leave London early that morning; and the inquest was deferred, to suit other pressing engagements of the coroner, until the twenty-sixth. Mr. Melton decided, after his interview with

Amelius, that the emergency was sufficiently serious to justify him in following his telegram to Paris. It was clearly his duty, as an old friend, to mention to Mr. Farnaby what he had discovered at the cottage, as well as what he had heard from the landlady and the doctor; leaving it to the uncle's discretion to act as he thought right in the interests of the niece. Whether that course of action might not also serve the interests of Mr. Melton himself, in the character of an unsuccessful suitor for Regina's hand, he did not stop to inquire. Beyond his duty it was, for the present at least, not his business to look.

That night, the two gentlemen held a private consultation in Paris; the doctor having previously certified that his patient was incapable of supporting the journey back to London, under any circumstances.

The question of the formal proceedings rendered necessary by Mrs. Farnaby's death having been discussed and disposed of, Mr. Melton next entered on the narrative which the obligations of friendship imperatively demanded from him. To his astonishment and alarm, Mr. Farnaby started up in the bed like a man panic-stricken. "Did you say," he stammered, as soon as he could speak, "you mean to make inquiries about that—that girl?"

"I certainly thought it desirable, bearing in mind Mr. Goldenheart's position in your family."

"Do nothing of the sort! Say nothing to Regina or to any living creature. Wait till I get well again—and leave me to deal with it. I am the proper person to take it in hand. Don't you see that for yourself? And, look here! there may be questions asked at the inquest. Some impudent scoundrel on the jury may want to pry into what doesn't concern him. The moment you're back in London, get a lawyer to represent us—the sharpest fellow that can be had for money. Tell him to stop all prying questions. Who the girl is, and what made that cursed young Socialist Goldenheart take her upstairs with him—all that sort of thing has nothing to do with the manner in which my wife met her death. You understand? I look to you, Melton, to see yourself that this is done. The less said at the infernal inquest, the better. In my position, it's an exposure that my enemies will make the most of, as it is. I'm too ill to go into the thing any further. No: I don't want Regina. Go to her in the sitting room, and tell the courier to get you something to eat and drink. And, I say! For God's sake don't be late for the Boulogne train tomorrow morning."

Left by himself, he gave full vent to his fury; he cursed Amelius with oaths that are not to be written.

He had burnt the letter which Mrs. Farnaby had written to him, on leaving him forever; but he had not burnt out of his memory the words which that letter contained. With his wife's language vividly present to his mind, he could arrive at but one conclusion, after what Mr. Melton had told him. Amelius was concerned in the discovery of his deserted daughter; Amelius had taken the girl to her dying mother's bedside. With his idiotic Socialist notions, he would be perfectly capable

240

of owning the truth, if inquiries were made. The unblemished reputation which John Farnaby had built up by the self-seeking hypocrisy of a lifetime was at the mercy of a visionary young fool, who believed that rich men were created for the benefit of the poor, and who proposed to regenerate society by reviving the obsolete morality of the Primitive Christians. Was it possible for him to come to terms with such a person as this? There was not an inch of common ground on which they could meet. He dropped back on his pillow in despair, and lay for a while frowning and biting his nails. Suddenly he sat up again in the bed, and wiped his moist forehead, and heaved a heavy breath of relief. Had his illness obscured his intelligence? How was it he had not seen at once the perfectly easy way out of the difficulty which was presented by the facts themselves? Here is a man, engaged to marry my niece, who has been discovered keeping a girl at his cottage—who even had the audacity to take her upstairs with him when he made a call on my wife. Charge him with it in plain words; break off the engagement publicly in the face of society; and, if the profligate scoundrel tries to defend himself by telling the truth, who will believe him—when the girl was seen running out of his room? and when he refused, on the question being put to him, to say who she was?

So, in ignorance of his wife's last instructions to Amelius—in equal ignorance of the compassionate silence which an honourable man preserves when a woman's reputation is at his mercy—the wretch needlessly plotted and planned to save his usurped reputation; seeing all things, as such men invariably do, through the foul light of his own inbred baseness and cruelty. He was troubled by no retributive emotions of shame or remorse, in contemplating this second sacrifice to his own interests of the daughter whom he had deserted in her infancy. If he felt any misgivings, they related wholly to himself. His head was throbbing, his tongue was dry; a dread of increasing his illness shook him suddenly. He drank some of the lemonade at his bedside, and lay down to compose himself to sleep.

It was not to be done; there was a burning in his eyeballs, there was a wild irregular beating at his heart, which kept him awake. In some degree, at least, retribution seemed to be on the way to him already.

Mr. Melton, delicately administering sympathy and consolation to Regina—whose affectionate nature felt keenly the calamity of her aunt's death—Mr. Melton, making himself modestly useful, by reading aloud certain devotional poems much prized by Regina, was called out of the room by the courier.

"I have just looked in at Mr. Farnaby, sir," said the man; "and I am afraid he is worse."

The physician was sent for. He thought so seriously of the change in the patient, that he obliged Regina to accept the services of a professed nurse. When Mr. Melton started on his return journey the next morning, he left his friend in a high fever.

CHAPTER 2

The inquiry into the circumstances under which Mrs. Farnaby had died was held in the forenoon of the next day.

Mr. Melton surprised Amelius by calling for him, and taking him to the inquest. The carriage stopped on the way, and a gentleman joined them, who was introduced as Mr. Melton's legal adviser. He spoke to Amelius about the inquest; stating, as his excuse for asking certain discreet questions, that his object was to suppress any painful disclosures. On reaching the house, Mr. Melton and his lawyer said a few words to the coroner downstairs, while the jury were assembling on the floor above.

The first witness examined was the landlady.

After deposing to the date at which the late Mrs. Farnaby had hired her lodgings, and verifying the statements which had appeared in the newspapers, she was questioned about the life and habits of the deceased. She described her late lodger as a respectable lady, punctual in her payments, and quiet and orderly in her way of life: she received letters, but saw no friends. On several occasions, an old woman was admitted to speak with her; and these visits seemed to be anything but agreeable to the deceased. Asked if she knew anything of the old woman, or of what had passed at the interviews described, the witness answered both questions in the negative. When the woman called, she always told the servant to announce her as "the nurse."

Mr. Melton was next examined, to prove the identity of the deceased.

He declared that he was quite unable to explain why she had left her husband's house under an assumed name. Asked if Mr. and Mrs. Farnaby had lived together on affectionate terms, he acknowledged that he had heard, at various times, of a want of harmony between them, but was not acquainted with the cause. Mr. Farnaby's high character and position in the commercial world spoke for themselves: the restraints of a gentleman guided him in his relations with his wife. The medical certificate of his illness in Paris was then put in; and Mr. Melton's examination came to an end.

The chemist who had made up the prescription was the third witness. He knew the woman who brought it to his shop to be in the service of the first witness examined; an old customer of his, and a highly respected resident in the neighbourhood. He made up all prescriptions himself in which poisons were conspicuous ingredients; and he had affixed to the bottle a slip of paper, bearing the word "Poison," printed in large letters. The bottle was produced and identified; and the directions in the prescription were shown to have been accurately copied on the label.

A general sensation of interest was excited by the appearance of the next witness— the woman servant. It was anticipated that her evidence would explain how the fatal mistake about the medicine had occurred. After replying to the formal inquiries, she proceeded as follows:

"When I answered the bell, at the time I have mentioned, I found the deceased standing at the fireplace. There was a bottle of medicine on the table, by her writing desk. It was a much larger bottle than that which the last witness identified, and it was more than three parts full of some colourless medicine. The deceased gave me a prescription to take to the chemist's, with instructions to wait, and bring back the physic. She said, 'I don't feel at all well this morning; I thought of trying some of this medicine,' pointing to the bottle by her desk; 'but I am not sure it is the right thing for me. I think I want a tonic. The prescription I have given you is a tonic.' I went out at once to our chemist and got it. I found her writing a letter when I came back, but she finished it immediately, and pushed it away from her. When I put the bottle I had brought from the chemist on the table, she looked at the other larger bottle which she had by her; and she said, 'You will think me very undecided; I have been doubting, since I sent you to the chemist, whether I had not better begin with this medicine here, before I try the tonic. It's a medicine for the stomach; and I fancy it's only indigestion that's the matter with me, after all.' I said, 'You eat but a poor breakfast, ma'am, this morning. It isn't for me to advise; but, as you seem to be in doubt about yourself, wouldn't it be better to send for a doctor?' She shook her head, and said she didn't want to have a doctor if she could possibly help it. 'I'll try the medicine for indigestion first,' she says; 'and if it doesn't relieve me, we will see what is to be done, later in the day.' While we were talking, the tonic was left in its sealed paper cover, just as I had brought it from the shop. She took up the bottle containing the stomach medicine, and read the directions on it: 'Two tablespoonful by measure-glass twice a day.' I asked if she had a measure-glass; and she said, Yes, and sent me to her bedroom to look for it. I couldn't find it. While I was looking, I heard her cry out, and ran back to the drawing-room to see what was the matter. 'Oh!' she says, 'how clumsy I am! I've broken the bottle.' She held up the bottle of the stomach medicine and showed it to me, broken just below the neck. 'Go back to the bedroom,' she says, 'and see if you can find an empty bottle; I don't want to waste the medicine if I can help it.' There was only one empty bottle in the bedroom, a bottle on the chimney-piece. I took it to her immediately. She gave me the broken bottle; and while I poured the medicine into the bottle which I had found in the bedroom, she opened the paper which covered the tonic I had brought from the chemist. When I had done, and the two bottles were together on the table—the bottle that I had filled, and the bottle that I had brought front the chemist—I noticed that they were both of the same size, and that both had a label pasted on them, marked 'Poison.' I said to her, 'You must take care, ma'am, you don't make any mistake, the two bottles are so exactly alike.' 'I can easily prevent that,' she says, and dipped her pen in the ink, and copied the directions on the broken bottle, on to the label of the bottle that I had just filled. 'There!' she said. 'Now I hope your mind's at ease?' She spoke cheerfully, as if she was joking with me. And then she said, 'But where's the measure-glass?' I went back to the bedroom to look for it, and couldn't find it again. She changed all at once, upon that—she became quite angry; and walked up and down in a fume, abusing me for my stupidity. It was very unlike her. On all other occasions she was a most considerate lady. I made allowances for her. She had been very much upset earlier in the morning, when she had received a letter, which she told me herself contained bad news. Yes; another person was present at the time—the same woman that my mistress told you of. The woman looked at the address on the letter, and seemed to know who it was from. I told her a squint-eyed man had brought it to the house—and then she left directly. I don't know where she went, or the address at which she lives, or who the messenger was who brought the letter. As I have said, I made allowances for the deceased lady. I went downstairs, without answering, and got a tumbler and a tablespoon to serve instead of the measure-glass. When I came back with the things, she was still walking about in a temper. She took no notice of me. I left the room again quietly, seeing she was not in a state to be spoken to. I saw nothing more of her, until we were alarmed by hearing her scream. We found the poor lady on the floor in a kind of fit. I ran out and fetched the nearest doctor. This is the whole truth, on my oath; and this is all I know about it."

The landlady was recalled at the request of the jury, and questioned again about the old woman. She could give no information. Being asked next if any letters or papers belonging to, or written by, the deceased lady had been found, she declared that, after the strictest search, nothing had been discovered but two medical prescriptions. The writing desk was empty.

The doctor was the next witness.

He described the state in which he found the patient, on being called to the house. The symptoms were those of poisoning by strychnine. Examination of the prescriptions and the bottles, aided by the servant's information, convinced him that a fatal mistake had been made by the deceased; the nature of which he explained to the jury as he had already explained it to Amelius. Having mentioned the meeting with Amelius at the house-door, and the events which had followed, he closed his evidence by stating the result of the postmortem examination, proving that the death was caused by the poison called strychnine.

The landlady and the servant were examined again. They were instructed to inform the jury exactly of the time that had elapsed, from the moment when the servant had left the deceased alone in the drawing-room, to the time when the screams were first heard. Having both given the same evidence, on this point, they were next asked whether any person, besides the old woman, had visited the deceased lady—or had on any pretence obtained access to her in the interval. Both swore positively that there had not even been a knock at the house-door in the interval, and that the area-gate was locked, and the key in the possession of the landlady. This evidence placed it beyond the possibility of doubt that the deceased had herself taken the poison. The question whether she had taken it by accident was the only question left to decide, when Amelius was called as the next witness.

The lawyer retained by Mr. Melton, to watch the case on behalf of Mr. Farnaby, had hitherto not interfered. It was observed that he paid the closest attention to the inquiry, at the stage which it had now reached.

Amelius was nervous at the outset. The early training in America, which had hardened him to face an audience and speak with self-possession on social and political subjects had not prepared him for the very difficult ordeal of a first appearance as a witness. Having answered the customary inquiries, he was so painfully agitated in describing Mrs. Farnaby's sufferings, that the coroner suspended the examination for a few minutes, to give him time to control himself. He failed, however, to recover his composure, until the narrative part of his evidence had come to an end. When the critical questions, bearing on his relations with Mrs. Farnaby, began, the audience noticed that he lifted his head, and looked and spoke, for the first time, like a man with a settled resolution in him, sure of himself.

The questions proceeded:

Was he in Mrs. Farnaby's confidence, on the subject of her domestic differences with her husband? Did those differences lead to her withdrawing herself from her husband's roof? Did Mrs. Farnaby inform him of the place of her retreat? To these three questions the witness, speaking quite readily in each case, answered Yes. Asked next, what the nature of the 'domestic differences' had been; whether they were likely to affect Mrs. Farnaby's mind seriously; why she had passed under an assumed name, and why she had confided the troubles of her married life to a young man like himself, only introduced to her a few months since, the witness simply declined to reply to the inquiries addressed to him. "The confidence Mrs. Farnaby placed in me," he said to the coroner, "was a confidence which I gave her my word of honour to respect. When I have said that, I hope the jury will understand that I owe it to the memory of the dead to say no more."

There was a murmur of approval among the audience, instantly checked by the coroner. The foreman of the jury rose, and remarked that scruples of honour were out of place at a serious inquiry of that sort. Hearing this, the lawyer saw his opportunity, and got on his legs. "I represent the husband of the deceased lady," he said. "Mr. Goldenheart has appealed to the law of honour to justify him in keeping silence. I am astonished that there is a man to be found in this assembly who fails to sympathize with him. But as there appears to be such a person present, I ask permission, sir, to put a question to the witness. It may, or may not, satisfy the foreman of the jury; but it will certainly assist the object of the present inquiry."

The coroner, after a glance at Mr. Melton, permitted the lawyer to put his question in these terms:—

"Did your knowledge of Mrs. Farnaby's domestic troubles give you any reason to apprehend that they might urge her to commit suicide?

"Certainly not," Amelius answered. "When I called on her, on the morning of her death, I had no apprehension whatever of her committing suicide. I went to the house as the bearer of good news; and I said so to the doctor, when he first spoke to me."

The doctor confirmed this. The foreman was silenced, if not convinced. One of his brother-jurymen, however, feeling the force of example, interrupted the proceedings, by assailing Amelius with another question:—"We have heard that you were accompanied by a young lady at the time you have mentioned, and that you took her upstairs with you. We want to know what business the young lady had in the house?"

The lawyer interfered again. "I object to that question," he said. "The purpose of the inquest is to ascertain how Mrs. Farnaby met with her death. What has the young lady to do with it? The doctor's evidence has already told us that she was not at the house, until after he had been called in, and the deadly action of the poison had begun. I appeal, sir, to the law of evidence, and to you, as the presiding authority, to enforce it. Mr. Goldenheart, who is acquainted with the circumstances of the deceased lady's life, has declared on his oath that there was nothing in those circumstances to inspire him with any apprehension of her committing suicide. The evidence of the servant at the lodgings points plainly to the conclusion already arrived at by the medical witness, that the death was the result of a lamentable mistake, and of that alone. Is our time to be wasted in irrelevant questions, and are the feelings of the surviving relatives to be cruelly lacerated to no purpose, to satisfy the curiosity of strangers?"

A strong expression of approval from the audience followed this. The lawyer whispered to Mr. Melton, "It's all right!"

Order being restored, the coroner ruled that the juryman's question was not admissible, and that the servant's evidence, taken with the statements of the doctor and the chemist, was the only evidence for the consideration of the jury. Summing up to this effect, he recalled Amelius, at the request of the foreman, to inquire if the witness knew anything of the old woman who had been frequently alluded to in the course of the proceedings. Amelius could answer this question as honestly as he had answered the questions preceding it. He neither knew the woman's name, nor where she was to be found. The coroner inquired, with a touch of irony, if the jury wished the inquest to be adjourned, under existing circumstances.

For the sake of appearances, the jury consulted together. But the luncheon-hour was approaching; the servant's evidence was undeniably clear and conclusive; the coroner, in summing up, had requested them not to forget that the deceased had lost her temper with the servant, and that an angry woman might well make a mistake which would be unlikely in her cooler moments. All these influences led the jury irrepressibly, over the obstacles of obstinacy, on the way to submission. After a needless delay, they returned a verdict of "death by misadventure." The secret of Mrs. Farnaby's suicide remained inviolate; the reputation of her vile husband stood as high as ever; and the future life of Amelius was, from that fatal moment, turned irrevocably into a new course.

CHAPTER 3

On the conclusion of the proceedings, Mr. Melton, having no further need of Amelius or the lawyer, drove away by himself. But he was too inveterately polite to omit making his excuses for leaving them in a hurry; he expected, he said, to find a telegram from Paris waiting at his house. Amelius only delayed his departure to ask the landlady if the day of the funeral was settled. Hearing that it was arranged for the next morning, he thanked her, and returned at once to the cottage.

Sally was waiting his arrival to complete some purchases of mourning for her unhappy mother; Toff's wife being in attendance to take care of her. She was curious to know how the inquest had ended. In answering her question, Amelius was careful to warn her, if her companion made any inquiries, only to say that she had lost her mother under very sad circumstances. The two having left the cottage, he instructed Toff to let in a stranger, who was to call by previous appointment, and to close the door to every one else. In a few minutes, the expected person, a young man, who gave the name of Morcross, made his appearance, and sorely puzzled the old Frenchman. He was well dressed; his manner was quiet and self-possessed—and yet he did not look like a gentleman. In fact, he was a policeman of the higher order, in plain clothes.

Being introduced to the library, he spread out on the table some sheets of manuscript, in the handwriting of Amelius, with notes in red ink on the margin, made by himself.

"I understand, sir," he began, "that you have reasons for not bringing this case to trial in a court of law?"

"I am sorry to say," Amelius answered, "that I dare not consent to the exposure of a public trial, for the sake of persons living and dead. For the same reason, I have written the account of the conspiracy with certain reserves. I hope I have not thrown any needless difficulties in your way?"

"Certainly not, sir. But I should wish to ask, what you propose to do, in case I discover the people concerned in the conspiracy?"

Amelius owned, very reluctantly, that he could do nothing with the old woman who had been the accomplice. "Unless," he added, "I can induce her to assist me in bringing the man to justice for other crimes which I believe him to have committed."

"Meaning the man named Jervy, sir, in this statement?"

"Yes. I have reason to believe that he has been obliged to leave the United States, after committing some serious offence—"

"I beg your pardon for interrupting you, sir. Is it serious enough to charge him with, under the treaty between the two countries?"

"I don't doubt it's serious enough. I have telegraphed to the persons who formerly employed him, for the particulars. Mind this! I will stick at no sacrifice to make that scoundrel suffer for what he has done."

In those plain words Amelius revealed, as frankly as usual, the purpose that was in him. The terrible remembrances associated with Mrs. Farnaby's last moments had kindled, in his just and generous nature, a burning sense of the wrong inflicted on the poor heart-broken creature who had trusted and loved him. The unendurable thought that the wretch who had tortured her, robbed her, and driven her to her death had escaped with impunity, literally haunted him night and day. Eager to provide for Sally's future, he had followed Mrs. Farnaby's instructions, and had seen the lawyer privately, during the period that had elapsed between the death and the inquest. Hearing that there were formalities to be complied with, which would probably cause some delay, he had at once announced his determination to employ the interval in attempting the pursuit of Jervy. The lawyer—after vainly pointing out the serious objections to the course proposed—so far yielded to the irresistible earnestness and good faith of Amelius as to recommend him to a competent man, who could be trusted not to deceive him. The same day the man had received a written statement of the case; and he had now arrived to report the result of his first proceedings to his employer.

"One thing I want to know, before you tell me anything else," Amelius resumed. "Is my written description of Jervy plain enough to help you to find him?"

"It's so plain, sir, that some of the older men in our office have recognized him by it—under another name than the name you give him."

"Does that add to the difficulty of tracing him?"

"He has been a long time away from England, sir; and it's by no means easy to trace him, on that account. I have been to the young woman, named Phoebe in your statement, to find out what she can tell me about him. She's ready enough, in the intervals of crying, to help us to lay our hands on the man who has deserted her. It's the old story of a fellow getting at a girl's secrets and a girl's money, under pretence of marrying her. At one time, she's furious with him, and at another she's ready to cry her eyes out. I got some information from her; it's not much, but it may help us. The name of the old woman, who has been the go-between in the business, is Mrs. Sowler—known to the police as an inveterate drunkard, and worse. I don't think there will be much difficulty in tracing Mrs. Sowler. As to Jervy, if the young woman is to be believed, and I think she is, there's little doubt that he has got the money from the lady mentioned in my instructions here, and that he has bolted with the sum about him. Wait a bit, sir, I haven't done with my discoveries yet. I asked the young woman, of course, if she had his photograph. He's a sharp fellow; she had it, but he got it away from her, on pretence of giving her a better one, before he took himself off. Having missed this chance, I asked next if she knew where he lived last. She directed me to the place; and I have had a talk with the landlord. He tells me of a squint-eyed man, who was a good deal about the house, doing Jervy's dirty work for him. If I am not misled by the description, I think I know the man. I have my own notion of what he's capable of doing, if he gets the chance—and I propose to begin by finding our way to him, and using him as a means of tracing Jervy. It's only right to tell you that it may take some time to do this—for which reason I have to propose, in the mean while, trying a shorter way to the end in view. Do you object, sir, to the expense of sending a copy of your description of Jervy to every police-station in London?"

"I object to nothing which may help to find him. Do you think the police have got him anywhere?"

"You forget, sir, that the police have no orders to take him. What I'm speculating on is the chance that he has got the money about him—say in small banknotes, for convenience of changing them, you know."

"Well?"

"Well, sir, the people he lives among—the squint-eyed man, for instance!—don't stick at trifles. If any of them have found out that Jervy's purse is worth having—"

"You mean they would rob him?"

"And murder him too, sir, if he tried to resist."

Amelius started to his feet. "Send round to the police-stations without losing another minute," he said. "And let me hear what the answer is, the instant you receive it."

"Suppose I get the answer late at night, sir?"

"I don't care when you get it, night or day. Dead or living, I will undertake to identify him. Here's a duplicate key of the garden gate. Come this way, and I'll show you where my bedroom is. If we are all in bed, tap at the window—and I will be ready for you at a moment's notice."

On that understanding Morcross left the cottage.

The day when the mortal remains of Mrs. Farnaby were laid at rest was a day of heavy rain. Mr. Melton, and two or three other old friends, were the attendants at the funeral. When the coffin was borne into the damp and reeking burial ground, a young man and a woman were the only persons, beside the sexton and his assistants, who stood by the open grave. Mr. Melton, recognizing Amelius, was at a loss to understand who his companion could be. It was impossible to suppose that he would profane that solemn ceremony by bringing to it the lost woman at the cottage. The thick black veil of the person with him hid her face from view. No visible expressions of grief escaped her. When the last sublime words of the burial service had been read, those two mourners were left, after the others had all departed, still standing together by the grave. Mr. Melton decided on mentioning the circumstance confidentially when he wrote to his friend in Paris. Telegrams from Regina, in reply to his telegrams from London, had informed him that Mr. Farnaby had felt the benefit of the remedies employed, and was slowly on the way to recovery. It seemed likely that he would, in no long time, take the right course for the protection of his niece. For the enlightenment which might, or might not, come with that time, Mr. Melton was resigned to wait, with the disciplined patience to which he had been mainly indebted for his success in life.

"Always remember your mother tenderly, my child," said Amelius, as they left the burial ground. "She was sorely tried, poor thing, in her life time, and she loved you very dearly."

"Do you know anything of my father?" Sally asked timidly. "Is he still living?"

"My dear, you will never see your father. I must be all that the kindest father and mother could have been to you, now. Oh, my poor little girl!"

She pressed his arm to her as she held it. "Why should you pity me?" she said. "Haven't I got You?"

They passed the day together quietly at the cottage. Amelius took down some of his books, and pleased Sally by giving her his first lessons. Soon after ten o'clock she withdrew, at the usual early hour, to her room. In her absence, he sent for Toff, intending to warn him not to be alarmed if he heard footsteps in the garden, after they had all gone to bed. The old servant had barely entered the library, when he was called away by the bell at the outer gate. Amelius, looking into the hall, discovered Morcross, and signed to him eagerly to come in. The police-officer closed the door cautiously behind him. He had arrived with news that Jervy was found.

CHAPTER 4

"Where has he been found?" Amelius asked, snatching up his hat.

"There's no hurry, sir," Morcross answered quietly. "When I had the honour of seeing you yesterday, you said you meant to make Jervy suffer for what he had done. Somebody else has saved you the trouble. He was found this evening in the river."

"Drowned?"

"Stabbed in three places, sir; and put out of the way in the river—that's the surgeon's report. Robbed of everything he possessed—that's the police report, after searching his pockets."

Amelius was silent. It had not entered into his calculations that crime breeds crime, and that the criminal might escape him under that law. For the moment, he was conscious of a sense of disappointment, revealing plainly that the desire for vengeance had mingled with the higher motives which animated him. He felt uneasy and ashamed, and longed as usual to take refuge in action from his own unwelcome thoughts. "Are you sure it is the man?" he asked. "My description may have misled the police—I should like to see him myself."

"Certainly, sir. While we are about it, if you feel any curiosity to trace Jervy's ill-gotten money, there's a chance (from what I have heard) of finding the man with the squint. The people at our place think it's likely he may have been concerned in the robbery, if he hasn't committed the murder."

In an hour after, under the guidance of Morcross, Amelius passed through the dreary doors of a deadhouse, situated on the southern bank of the Thames, and saw the body of Jervy stretched out on a stone slab. The guardian who held the lantern, inured to such horrible sights, declared that the corpse could not have been in the water more than two days. To any one who had seen the murdered man, the face, undisfigured by injury of any kind, was perfectly recognizable. Amelius knew him again, dead, as certainly as he had known him again, living, when he was waiting for Phoebe in the street.

"If you're satisfied, sir," said Morcross, "the inspector at the police-station is sending a sergeant to look after 'Wall-Eyes'—the name they give hereabouts to the man suspected of the robbery. We can take the sergeant with us in the cab, if you like."

Still keeping on the southern bank of the river, they drove for a quarter of an hour in a westerly direction, and stopped at a public-house. The sergeant of police went in by himself to make the first inquiries.

"We are a day too late, sir," he said to Amelius, on returning to the cab. "Wall-Eyes was here last night, and Mother Sowler with him, judging by the description. Both of them drunk—and the woman the worse of the two. The landlord knew nothing more about it; but there's a man at the bar tells me he heard of them this morning (still drinking) at the Dairy."

"The Dairy?" Amelius repeated.

Morcross interposed with the necessary explanation. "An old house, sir, which once stood by itself in the fields. It was a dairy a hundred years ago; and it has kept the name ever since, though it's nothing but a low lodging house now."

"One of the worst places on this side of the river," the sergeant added, "The landlord's a returned convict. Sly as he is we shall have him again yet, for receiving stolen goods. There's every sort of thief among his lodgers, from a pickpocket to a housebreaker. It's my duty to continue the inquiry, sir; but a gentleman like you will be better, I should say, out of such a place as that."

Still disquieted by the sight that he had seen in the deadhouse, and by the associations which that sight had recalled, Amelius was ready for any adventure which might relieve his mind. Even the prospect of a visit to a thieves' lodging house was more welcome to him than the prospect of going home alone. "If there's no serious objection to it," he said, "I own I should like to see the place."

"You'll be safe enough with us," the sergeant replied. "If you don't mind filthy people and bad language—all right, sir! Cabman, drive to the Dairy."

Their direction was now towards the south, through a perfect labyrinth of mean and dirty streets. Twice the driver was obliged to ask his way. On the second occasion the sergeant, putting his head out of the window to stop the cab, cried, "Hullo! there's something up."

They got out in front of a long low rambling house, a complete contrast to the modern buildings about it. Late as the hour was, a mob had assembled in front of the door. The police were on the spot keeping the people in order.

Morcross and the sergeant pushed their way through the crowd, leading Amelius between them. "Something wrong, sir, in the back kitchen," said one of the policemen answering the sergeant while he opened the street door. A few yards down the passage there was a second door, with a man on the watch by it. "There's a nice to-do downstairs," the man announced, recognizing the sergeant, and unlocking the door with a key which he took from his pocket. "The landlord at the Dairy knows his lodgers, sir," Morcross whispered to Amelius; "the place is kept like a prison." As they passed through the second door, a frantic voice startled them, shouting in fury from below. An old man came hobbling up the kitchen stairs, his eyes wild with fear, his long grey hair all tumbled over his face. "Oh, Lord, have you got the tools for breaking open the door?" he asked, wringing his dirty hands in an agony of supplication. "She'll set the house on fire! she'll kill my wife and daughter!" The sergeant pushed him contemptuously out of the way, and looked round for Amelius. "It's only the landlord, sir; keep near Morcross, and follow me."

They descended the kitchen stairs, the frantic cries below growing louder and louder at every step they took; and made their way through the thieves and vagabonds crowding together in the passage. Passing on their right hand a solid old oaken door fast closed, they reached an open wicket-gate of iron which led into a stone-paved yard. A heavily barred window was now visible in the back wall of the house, raised three or four feet from the pavement of the yard. The room within was illuminated by a blaze of gaslight. More policemen were here, keeping back more inquisitive lodgers. Among the spectators was a man with a hideous outward squint, holding by the window-bars in a state of drunken terror. The sergeant looked at him, and beckoned to one of the policemen. "Take him to the station; I shall have something to say to Wall-Eyes when he's sober. Now then! stand back all of you, and let's see what's going on in the kitchen."

He took Amelius by the arm, and led him to the window. Even the sergeant started when the scene inside met his view. "By God!" he cried, "it's Mother Sowler herself."

It *was* Mother Sowler. The horrible woman was tramping round and round in the middle of the kitchen, like a beast in a cage; raving in the dreadful drink-madness called delirium tremens. In the farthest corner of the room, barricaded behind the table, the landlord's wife and daughter crouched in terror of their lives. The gas, turned full on, blazed high enough to blacken the ceiling, and showed the heavy bolts shot at the top and bottom of the solid door. Nothing less than a battering-ram could have burst that door in from the outer side; an hour's work with the file would have failed to break a passage through the bars over the window. "How did she get there?" the sergeant asked. "Run downstairs, and bolted herself in, while the missus and the young 'un were cooking"—was the answering cry from the people in the yard. As they spoke, another vain attempt was made to break in the door from the passage. The noise of the heavy blows redoubled the frenzy of the terrible creature in the kitchen, still tramping round and round under the blazing gaslight. Suddenly, she made a dart at the window, and confronted the men looking in from the yard. Her staring eyes were bloodshot; a purple-red flush was over her face; her hair waved wildly about her, torn away in places by her own hands. "Cats!" she screamed, glaring out of the window, "millions of cats! all their months wide open spitting at me! Fire! fire to scare away the cats!" She searched furiously in her pocket, and tore out a handful of loose papers. One of them escaped, and fluttered downward to a wooden press under the window. Amelius was nearest, and saw it plainly as it fell, "Good heavens!" he exclaimed, "it's a bank-note!" "Wall-Eyes' money!" shouted the thieves in the yard; "She's going to burn Wall-Eyes' money!" The madwoman turned back to the middle of the kitchen, leapt up at the gas-burner, and set fire to the bank-notes. She scattered them flaming all round her on the kitchen floor. "Away with you!" she shouted, shaking her fists at the visionary multitude of cats. "Away with you, up the chimney! Away with you, out of the window!" She sprang back to the window, with her crooked fingers twisted in her hair! "The snakes!" she shrieked; "the snakes are hissing again in my hair! the beetles are crawling over my face!" She tore at her hair; she scraped her face with long black nails that lacerated the flesh. Amelius turned away, unable to endure the sight of her. Morcross took his place, eyed her steadily for a moment, and saw the way to end it. "A quarter of gin!" he shouted. "Quick! before she leaves the window!" In a minute he had the pewter measure in his hand, and tapped at the window. "Gin, Mother Sowler! Break the window, and have a drop of gin!" For a moment, the drunkard mastered her own dreadful visions at the sight of the liquor. She broke a pane of glass with her clenched fist. "The door!" cried Morcross, to the panic-stricken women, barricaded behind the table. "The door!" he reiterated, as he handed the gin in through the bars. The elder woman was too terrified to understand him; her bolder daughter crawled under the table, rushed across the kitchen, and drew the bolts. As the madwoman turned to attack her, the room was filled with men, headed by the sergeant. Three of them were barely enough to control the frantic wretch, and bind her hand and foot. When Amelius entered the kitchen, after she had been conveyed to the hospital, a five-pound note on the press (secured by one of the police), and a few frail black ashes scattered thinly on the kitchen floor, were the only relics left of the ill-gotten money.

After-inquiry, patiently pursued in more than one direction, failed to throw any light on the mystery of Jervy's death. Morcross's report to Amelius, towards the close of the investigation, was little more than ingenious guess-work.

"It seems pretty clear, sir, in the first place, that Mother Sowler must have overtaken Wall-Eyes, after he had left the letter at Mrs. Farnaby's lodgings. In the second place, we are justified (as I shall show you directly) in assuming that she told him of the money in Jervy's possession, and that the two succeeded in discovering Jervy—— no doubt through Wall-Eyes' superior knowledge of his master's movements. The evidence concerning the bank-notes proves this. We know, by the examination of the people at the Dairy, that Wall-Eyes took from his pocket a handful of notes, when they refused to send for liquor without having the money first. We are also informed, that the breaking-out of the drink-madness in Mother Sowler showed itself in her snatching the notes out of his hand, and trying to strangle him—before she ran down into the kitchen and bolted herself in. Lastly, Mrs. Farnaby's bankers have identified the note saved from the burning, as one of forty five-pound notes paid to her cheque. So much for the tracing of the money.

"I wish I could give an equally satisfactory account of the tracing of the crime. We can make nothing of Wall-Eyes. He declares that he didn't even know Jervy was dead, till we told him; and he swears he found the money dropped in the street. It is needless to say that this last assertion is a lie. Opinions are divided among us as to whether he is answerable for the murder as well as the robbery, or whether there was a third person concerned in it. My own belief is that Jervy was drugged by the old woman (with a young woman very likely used as a decoy), in some house by the riverside, and then murdered by Wall-Eyes in cold blood. We have done our best to clear the matter up, and we have not succeeded. The doctors give us no hope of any assistance from Mother Sowler. If she gets over the attack (which is doubtful), they say she will die to a certainty of liver disease. In short, my own fear is that this will prove to be one more of those murders which are mysteries to the police as well as the public."

The report of the case excited some interest, published in the newspapers in conspicuous type. Meddlesome readers wrote letters, offering complacently stupid suggestions to the police. After a while, another crime attracted general attention; and the murder of Jervy disappeared from the public memory, among other forgotten murders of modern times.

CHAPTER 5

The last dreary days of November came to their end.

No longer darkened by the shadows of crime and torment and death, the life of Amelius glided insensibly into the peaceful byways of seclusion, brightened by the companionship of Sally. The winter days followed one another in a happy uniformity of occupations and amusements. There were lessons to fill up the morning, and walks to occupy the afternoon—and, in the evenings, sometimes reading, sometimes singing, sometimes nothing but the lazy luxury of talk. In the vast world of London, with its monstrous extremes of wealth and poverty, and its all-permeating malady of life at fever-heat, there was one supremely innocent and supremely happy creature. Sally had heard of Heaven, attainable on the hard condition of first paying the debt of death. "I have found a kinder Heaven," she said, one day. "It is here in the cottage; and Amelius has shown me the way to it."

Their social isolation was at this time complete: they were two friendless people, perfectly insensible to all that was perilous and pitiable in their own position. They parted with a kiss at night, and they met again with a kiss in the morning—and they were as happily free from all mistrust of the future as a pair of birds. No visitors came to the house; the few friends and acquaintances of Amelius, forgotten by him, forgot him in return. Now and then, Toff's wife came to the cottage, and exhibited the "cherubim-baby." Now and then, Toff himself (a musician among his other accomplishments) brought his fiddle upstairs; and, saying modestly, "A little music helps to pass the time," played to the young master and mistress the cheerful tinkling tunes of the old vaudevilles of France. They were pleased with these small interruptions when they came; and they were not disappointed when the days passed, and the baby and the vaudevilles were hushed in absence and silence. So the happy winter time went by; and the howling winds brought no rheumatism with them, and even the tax-gatherer himself, looking in at this earthly paradise, departed without a curse when he left his little paper behind him.

Now and then, at long intervals, the outer world intruded itself in the form of a letter.

Regina wrote, always with the same placid affection; always entering into the same minute narrative of the slow progress of "dear uncle's" return to health. He was forbidden to exert himself in any way. His nerves were in a state of lamentable irritability. "I dare not even mention your name to him, dear Amelius; it seems, I cannot think why, to make him—oh, so unreasonably angry. I can only submit, and pray that he may soon be himself again." Amelius wrote back, always in the same considerate and gentle tone; always laying the blame of his dull letters on the studious uniformity of his life. He preserved, with a perfectly easy conscience, the most absolute silence on the subject of Sally. While he was faithful to Regina, what reason had he to reproach himself with the protection that he offered to a poor motherless girl? When he was married, he might mention the circumstances under which he had met with Sally, and leave the rest to his wife's sympathy.

256

One morning, the letters with the Paris post-mark were varied by a few lines from Rufus.

"Every morning, my bright boy, I get up and say to myself, 'Well! I reckon it's about time to take the route for London;' and every morning, if you'll believe me, I put it off till next day. Whether it's in the good feeding (expensive, I admit; but when your cook helps you to digest instead of hindering you, a man of my dyspeptic nation is too grateful to complain)—or whether it's in the air, which reminds me, I do assure you, of our native atmosphere at Coolspring, Mass., is more than I can tell, with a hard steel pen on a leaf of flimsy paper. You have heard the saying, 'When a good American dies, he goes to Paris'. Maybe, sometimes, he's smart enough to discount his own death, and rationally enjoy the future time in the present. This you see is a poetic light. But, mercy be praised, the moral of my residence in Paris is plain:—If I can't go to Amelius, Amelius must come to me. Note the address Grand Hotel; and pack up, like a good boy, on receipt of this. Memorandum: The brown Miss is here. I saw her taking the air in a carriage, and raised my hat. She looked the other way.

"British—eminently British! But, there, I bear no malice; I am her most obedient servant, and yours affectionately, RUFUS.—Postscript: I want you to see some of our girls at this hotel. The genuine American material, sir, perfected by Worth."

Another morning brought with it a few sad lines from Phoebe. "After what had happened, she was quite unable to face her friends; she had no heart to seek employment in her own country—her present life was too dreary and too hopeless to be endured. A benevolent lady had made her an offer to accompany a party of emigrants to New Zealand; and she had accepted the proposal. Perhaps, among the new people, she might recover her self-respect and her spirits, and live to be a better woman. Meanwhile, she bade Mr. Goldenheart farewell; and asked his pardon for taking the liberty of wishing him happy with Miss Regina."

Amelius wrote a few kind lines to Phoebe, and a cordial reply to Rufus, making the pursuit of his studies his excuse for remaining in London. After this, there was no further correspondence. The mornings succeeded each other, and the postman brought no more news from the world outside.

But the lessons went on; and the teacher and pupil were as inconsiderately happy as ever in each other's society. Observing with inexhaustible interest the progress of the mental development of Sally, Amelius was slow to perceive the physical development which was unobtrusively keeping pace with it. He was absolutely ignorant of the part which his own influence was taking in the gradual and delicate process of change. Ere long, the first forewarnings of the coming disturbance in their harmless relations towards each other, began to show themselves. Ere long, there were signs of a troubled mind in Sally, which were mysteries to Amelius, and subjects of wonderment, sometimes even trials of temper, to the girl herself.

One day, she looked in from the door of her room, in her white dressing-gown, and asked to be forgiven if she kept the lessons of the morning waiting for a little while.

"Come in," said Amelius, "and tell me why."

She hesitated. "You won't think me lazy, if you see me in my dressing-gown?"

"Of course not! Your dressing-gown, my dear, is as good as any other gown. A young girl like you looks best in white."

She came in with her work-basket, and her indoor dress over her arm.

Amelius laughed. "Why haven't you put it on?" he asked.

She sat down in a corner, and looked at her work-basket, instead of looking at Amelius. "It doesn't fit me so well as it did," she answered. "I am obliged to alter it."

Amelius looked at her—at the charming youthful figure that had filled out, at the softly-rounded outline of the face with no angles and hollows in it now. "Is it the dressmaker's fault?" he asked slyly.

Her eyes were still on the basket. "It's my fault," she said. "You remember what a poor little skinny creature I was, when you first saw me. I—you won't like me the worse for it, will you?—I am getting fat. I don't know why. They say happy people get fat. Perhaps that's why. I'm never hungry, and never frightened, and never miserable now—" She stopped; her dress slipped from her lap to the floor. "Don't look at me!" she said—and suddenly put her hands over her face.

Amelius saw the tears finding their way through the pretty plump fingers, which he remembered so shapeless and so thin. He crossed the room, and touched her gently on the shoulder. "My dear child! have I said anything to distress you?"

"Nothing."

"Then why are you crying?"

"I don't know." She hesitated; looked at him; and made a desperate effort to tell him what was in her mind. "I'm afraid you'll get tired of me. There's nothing about me to make you pity me now. You seem to be—not quite the same—no! it isn't that—I don't know what's come to me—I'm a greater fool than ever. Give me my lesson, Amelius! please give me my lesson!"

Amelius produced the books, in some little surprise at Sally's extraordinary anxiety to begin her lessons, while the unaltered dress lay neglected on the carpet at her feet.

258

A discreet abstract of the history of England, published for the use of young persons, happened to be at the top of the books. The system of education under Amelius recognized the laws of chance: they began with the history, because it turned up first. Sally read aloud; and Sally's master explained obscure passages, and corrected occasional errors of pronunciation, as she went on. On that particular morning, there was little to explain and nothing to correct. "Am I doing it well today?" Sally inquired, on reaching the end of her task.

"Very well, indeed."

She shut the book, and looked at her teacher. "I wonder how it is," she resumed, "that I get on so much better with my lessons here than I did at the Home? And yet it's foolish of me to wonder. I get on better, because you are teaching me, of course. But I don't feel satisfied with myself. I'm the same helpless creature—I feel your kindness, and can't make any return to you—for all my learning. I should like—" She left the thought in her unexpressed, and opened her copy-book. "I'll do my writing now," she said, in a quiet resigned way. "Perhaps I may improve enough, some day, to keep your accounts for you." She chose her pen a little absently, and began to write. Amelius looked over her shoulder, and laughed; she was writing his name. He pointed to the copper-plate copy on the top line, presenting an undeniable moral maxim, in characters beyond the reach of criticism:—Change Is A Law Of Nature. "There, my dear, you are to copy that till you're tired of it," said the easy master; "and then we'll try overleaf, another copy beginning with letter D."

Sally laid down her pen. "I don't like 'Change is a law of Nature'," she said, knitting her pretty eyebrows into a frown. "I looked at those words yesterday, and they made me miserable at night. I was foolish enough to think that we should always go on together as we go on now, till I saw that copy. I hate the copy! It came to my mind when I was awake in the dark, and it seemed to tell me that *we* were going to change some day. That's the worst of learning—one knows too much, and then there's an end of one's happiness. Thoughts come to you, when you don't want them. I thought of the young lady we saw last week in the park."

She spoke gravely and sadly. The bright contentment which had given a new charm to her eyes since she had been at the cottage, died out of them as Amelius looked at her. What had become of her childish manner and her artless smile? He drew his chair nearer to her. "What young lady do you mean?" he asked.

Sally shook her head, and traced lines with her pen on the blotting paper. "Oh, you can't have forgotten her! A young lady, riding on a grand white horse. All the people were admiring her. I wonder you cared to look at me, after that beautiful creature had gone by. Ah, she knows all sorts of things that I don't—*she* doesn't sound a note at a time on the piano, and as often as not the wrong one; *she* can say her multiplication table, and knows all the cities in the world. I dare say she's almost as learned as you are. If you had her living here with you, wouldn't you like it better than only having me!" She dropped her arms on the table, and laid her head on them wearily. "The dreadful streets!" she murmured, in low tones of despair. "Why did I

259

think of the dreadful streets, and the night I met with you—after I had seen the young lady? Oh, Amelius, are you tired of me? are you ashamed of me?" She lifted her head again, before he could answer, and controlled herself by a sudden effort of resolution. "I don't know what's the matter with me this morning," she said, looking at him with a pleading fear in her eyes. "Never mind my nonsense—I'll do the copy!" She began to write the unendurable assertion that change is a law of Nature, with trembling fingers and fast heaving breath. Amelius took the pen gently out of her hand. His voice faltered as he spoke to her.

"We will give up the lessons for today, Sally. You have had a bad night's rest, my dear, and you are feeling it—that's all. Do you think you are well enough to come out with me, and try if the air will revive you a little?"

She rose, and took his hand, and kissed it. "I believe, if I was dying, I should get well enough to go out with you! May I ask one little favour? Do you mind if we don't go into the park today?"

"What has made you take a dislike to the park, Sally?"

"We might meet the beautiful young lady again," she answered, with her head down. "I don't want to do that."

"We will go wherever you like, my child. You shall decide—not I."

She gathered up her dress from the floor, and hurried away to her room—without looking back at him as usual when she opened the door.

Left by himself, Amelius sat at the table, mechanically turning over the lesson-books. Sally had perplexed and even distressed him. His capacity to preserve the harmless relations between them, depended mainly on the mute appeal which the girl's ignorant innocence unconsciously addressed to him. He felt this vaguely, without absolutely realizing it. By some mysterious process of association which he was unable to follow, a saying of the wise Elder Brother at Tadmor revived in his memory, while he was trying to see his way through the difficulties that beset him. "You will meet with many temptations, Amelius, when you leave our Community," the old man had said at parting; "and most of them will come to you through women. Be especially on your guard, my son, if you meet with a woman who makes you feel truly sorry for her. She is on the high-road to your passions, through the open door of your sympathies—and all the more certainly if she is not aware of it herself." Amelius felt the truth expressed in those words as he had never felt it yet. There had been signs of a changing nature in Sally for some little time past. But they had expressed themselves too delicately to attract the attention of a man unprepared to be on the watch. Only on that morning, they had been marked enough to force themselves on his notice. Only on that morning, she had looked at him, and spoken to him, as she had never looked or spoken before. He began dimly to see the danger for both of them, to which he had shut his eyes thus far. Where was the remedy?

what ought he to do? Those questions came naturally into his mind—and yet, his mind shrank from pursuing them.

He got up impatiently, and busied himself in putting away the lesson-books—a small duty hitherto always left to Toff.

It was useless; his mind dwelt persistently on Sally.

While he moved about the room, he still saw the look in her eyes, he still heard the tone of her voice, when she spoke of the young lady in the park. The words of the good physician whom he had consulted about her recurred to his memory now. "The natural growth of her senses has been stunted, like the natural growth of her body, by starvation, terror, exposure to cold, and other influences inherent in the life that she has led." And then the doctor had spoken of nourishing food, pure air, and careful treatment—of the life, in short, which she had led at the cottage—and had predicted that she would develop into "an intelligent and healthy young woman." Again he asked himself, "What ought I to do?"

He turned aside to the window, and looked out. An idea occurred to him. How would it be, if he summoned courage enough to tell her that he was engaged to be married?

No! Setting aside his natural dread of the shock that he might inflict on the poor grateful girl who had only known happiness under his care, the detestable obstacle of Mr. Farnaby stood immovably in his way. Sally would be sure to ask questions about his engagement, and would never rest until they were answered. It had been necessarily impossible to conceal her mother's name from her. The discovery of her father, if she heard of Regina and Regina's uncle, would be simply a question of time. What might such a man be not capable of doing, what new act of treachery might he not commit, if he found himself claimed by the daughter whom he had deserted? Even if the expression of Mrs. Farnaby's last wishes had not been sacred to Amelius, this consideration alone would have kept him silent, for Sally's sake.

He now doubted for the first time if he had calculated wisely in planning to trust Sally's sad story, after his marriage, to the sympathies of his wife. The jealousy that she might naturally feel of a young girl, who was an object of interest to her husband, did not present the worst difficulty to contend with. She believed in her uncle's integrity as she believed in her religion. What would she say, what would she do, if the innocent witness to Farnaby's infamy was presented to her; if Amelius asked the protection for Sally which her own father had refused to her in her infancy; and if he said, as he must say, "Your uncle is the man"?

And yet, what prospect could he see but the prospect of making the disclosure when he looked to his own interests next, and thought of his wedding day? Again the sinister figure of Farnaby confronted him. How could he receive the wretch whom Regina would innocently welcome to the house? There would be no longer a choice left; it would be his duty to himself to tell his wife the terrible truth. And what would be the result? He recalled the whole course of his courtship, and saw Farnaby always on a level with himself in Regina's estimation. In spite of his natural cheerfulness, in spite of his inbred courage, his heart failed him, when he thought of the time to come.

As he turned away from the window, Sally's door opened: she joined him, ready for the walk. Her spirits had rallied, assisted by the cheering influence of dressing to go out. Her charming smile brightened her face. In sheer desperation, reckless of what he did or said, Amelius held out both hands to welcome her. "That's right, Sally!" he cried. "Look pleased and pretty, my dear; let's be happy while we can—and let the future take care of itself!"

CHAPTER 6

The capricious influences which combine to make us happy are never so certain to be absent influences as when we are foolish enough to talk about them. Amelius had talked about them. When he and Sally left the cottage, the road which led them away from the park was also the road which led them past a church. The influences of happiness left them at the church door.

Rows of carriages were in waiting; hundreds of idle people were assembled about the church steps; the thunderous music of the organ rolled out through the open doors—a grand wedding, with choral service, was in course of celebration. Sally begged Amelius to take her in to see it. They tried the front entrance, and found it impossible to get through the crowd. A side entrance, and a fee to a verger, succeeded better. They obtained space enough to stand on, with a view of the altar.

The bride was a tall buxom girl, splendidly dressed: she performed her part in the ceremony with the most unruffled composure. The bridegroom exhibited an instructive spectacle of aged Nature, sustained by Art. His hair, his complexion, his teeth, his breast, his shoulders, and his legs, showed what the wig-maker, the valet, the dentist, the tailor, and the hosier can do for a rich old man, who wishes to present a juvenile appearance while he is buying a young wife. No less than three clergymen were present, conducting the sale. The demeanour of the rich congregation was worthy of the glorious bygone days of the Golden Calf. So far as could be judged by appearances, one old lady, in a pew close to the place at which Amelius and Sally were standing, seemed to be the only person present who was not favourably impressed by the ceremony.

"I call it disgraceful," the old lady remarked to a charming young person seated next to her.

But the charming young person—being the legitimate product of the present time—had no more sympathy with questions of sentiment than a Hottentot. "How can you talk so, grandmamma!" she rejoined. "He has twenty thousand a year—and that lucky girl will be mistress of the most splendid house in London."

"I don't care," the old lady persisted; "it's not the less a disgrace to everybody concerned in it. There is many a poor friendless creature, driven by hunger to the streets, who has a better claim to our sympathy than that shameless girl, selling herself in the house of God! I'll wait for you in the carriage—I won't see any more of it."

Sally touched Amelius. "Take me out!" she whispered faintly.

He supposed that the heat in the church had been too much for her. "Are you better now?" he asked, when they got into the open air.

She held fast by his arm. "Let's get farther away," she said. "That lady is coming after us—I don't want her to see me again. I am one of the creatures she talked about. Is the mark of the streets on me, after all you have done to rub it out?"

The wild misery in her words presented another development in her character which was entirely new to Amelius. "My dear child," he remonstrated, "you distress me when you talk in that way. God knows the life you are leading now."

But Sally's mind was still full of its own acutely painful sense of what the lady had said. "I saw her," she burst out—"I saw her look at me while she spoke!"

"And she thought you better worth looking at than the bride—and quite right, too!" Amelius rejoined. "Come, come, Sally, be like yourself. You don't want to make me unhappy about you, I am sure?"

He had taken the right way with her: she felt that simple appeal, and asked his pardon with all the old charm in her manner and her voice. For the moment, she was "Simple Sally" again. They walked on in silence. When they had lost sight of the church, Amelius felt her hand beginning to tremble on his arm. A mingled expression of tenderness and anxiety showed itself in her blue eyes as they looked up at him. "I am thinking of something else now," she said; "I am thinking of You. May I ask you something?"

Amelius smiled. The smile was not reflected as usual in Sally's face. "It's nothing particular," she explained in an odd hurried way; "the church put it into my head. You—" She hesitated, and tried it under another form. "Will you be married yourself, Amelius, one of these days?"

He did his best to evade the question. "I am not rich, Sally, like the old gentleman we have just seen."

Her eyes turned away from him; she sighed softly to herself. "You will be married some day," she said. "Will you do one kind thing more for me, Amelius, when I die? You remember my reading in the newspaper of the new invention for burning the dead—and my asking you about it. You said you thought it was better than burying, and you had a good mind to leave directions to be burnt instead of buried, when your time came. When *my* time has come, will you leave other directions about yourself, if I ask you?"

"My dear, you are talking in a very strange way! If you will have it that I am to be married some day, what has that to do with your death?"

"It doesn't matter, Amelius. When I have nothing left to live for, I suppose it's as likely as not I may die. Will you tell them to bury me in some quiet place, away from London, where there are very few graves? And when you leave your directions, don't say you are to be burnt. Say—when you have lived a long, long life, and enjoyed all the happiness you have deserved so well—say you are to be buried, and your grave is to be near mine. I should like to think of the same trees shading us, and the same flowers growing over us. No! don't tell me I'm talking strangely again—I can't bear it; I want you to humour me and be kind to me about this. Do you mind going home? I'm feeling a little tired—and I know I'm poor company for you today."

The talk flagged at dinner-time, though Toff did his best to keep it going.

In the evening, the excellent Frenchman made an effort to cheer the two dull young people. He came in confidentially with his fiddle, and said he had a favour to ask. "I possess some knowledge, sir, of the delightful art of dancing. Might I teach young Miss to dance? You see, if I may venture to say so, the other lessons—oh, most useful, most important, the other lessons! but they are just a little serious. Something to relieve her mind, sir—if you will forgive me for mentioning it. I plead for innocent gaiety—let us dance!"

He played a few notes on the fiddle, and placed his right foot in position, and waited amiably to begin. Sally thanked him, and made the excuse that she was tired. She wished Amelius good night, without waiting until they were alone together—and, for the first time, without giving him the customary kiss.

Toff waited until she had gone, and approached his master on tiptoe, with a low bow.

"May I take the liberty of expressing an opinion, sir. A young girl who rejects the remedy of the fiddle presents a case of extreme gravity. Don't despair, sir! It is my pride and pleasure to be never at a loss, where your interests are concerned. This is, I think, a matter for the ministrations of a woman. If you have confidence in my wife, I venture to suggest a visit from Madame Toff."

He discreetly retired, and left his master to think about it.

The time passed—and Amelius was still thinking, and still as far as ever from arriving at a conclusion, when he heard a door opened behind him. Sally crossed the room before he could rise from his chair: her cheeks were flushed, her eyes were bright, her hair fell loose over her shoulders—she dropped at his feet, and hid her face on his knees. "I'm an ungrateful wretch!" she burst out; "I never kissed you when I said good night."

With the best intentions, Amelius took the worst possible way of composing her—he treated her trouble lightly. "Perhaps you forgot it?" he said.

She lifted her head, and looked at him, with the tears in her eyes. "I'm bad enough," she answered; "but not so bad as that. Oh, don't laugh! there's nothing to laugh at. Have you done with liking me? Are you angry with me for behaving so badly all day, and bidding you good night as if you were Toff? You shan't be angry with me!" She jumped up, and sat on his knee, and put her arms round his neck. "I haven't been to bed," she whispered; "I was too miserable to go to sleep. I don't know what's been the matter with me today. I seem to be losing the little sense I ever had. Oh, if I could only make you understand how fond I am of you! And yet I've had bitter thoughts, as if I was a burden to you, and I had done a wrong thing in coming here—and you would have told me so, only you pitied the poor wretch who had nowhere else to go." She tightened her hold round his neck, and laid her burning cheek against his face. "Oh, Amelius, my heart is sore! Kiss me, and say, 'Good night, Sally!'"

He was young—he was a man—for a moment he lost his self control; he kissed her as he had never kissed her yet.

Then, he remembered; he recovered himself; he put her gently away from him, and led her to the door of her room, and closed it on her in silence. For a little while, he waited alone. The interval over, he rang for Toff.

"Do you think your wife would take Miss Sally as an apprentice?" he asked.

Toff looked astonished. "Whatever you wish, sir, my wife will do. Her knowledge of the art of dressmaking is—" Words failed him to express his wife's immense capacity as a dressmaker. He kissed his hand in mute enthusiasm, and blew the kiss in the direction of Madame Toff's establishment. "However," he proceeded, "I ought to tell you one thing, sir; the business is small, small, very small. But we are all in the hands of Providence—the business will improve, one day." He lifted his shoulders and lifted his eyebrows, and looked perfectly satisfied with his wife's prospects.

"I will go and speak to Madame Toff myself, tomorrow morning," Amelius resumed. "It's quite possible that I may be obliged to leave London for a little while—and I must provide in some way for Miss Sally. Don't say a word about it to her yet, Toff, and don't look miserable. If I go away, I shall take you with me. Good night."

Toff, with his handkerchief halfway to his eyes, recovered his native cheerfulness. "I am invariably sick at sea, sir," he said; "but, no matter, I will attend you to the uttermost ends of the earth."

So honest Amelius planned his way of escape from the critical position in which he found himself. He went to his bed, troubled by anxieties which kept him waking for many weary hours. Where was he to go to, when he left Sally? If he could have known what had happened, on that very day, on the other side of the Channel, he might have decided (in spite of the obstacle of Mr. Farnaby) on surprising Regina by a visit to Paris.

CHAPTER 7

On the morning when Amelius and Sally (in London) entered the church to look at the wedding. Rufus (in Paris) went to the Champs Elysees to take a walk.

He had advanced half-way up the magnificent avenue, when he saw Regina for the second time, taking her daily drive, with an elderly woman in attendance on her. Rufus took off his hat again, perfectly impenetrable to the cold reception which he had already experienced. Greatly to his surprise, Regina not only returned his salute, but stopped the carriage and beckoned to him to speak to her. Looking at her more closely, he perceived signs of suffering in her face which completely altered her expression as he remembered it. Her magnificent eyes were dim and red; she had lost her rich colour; her voice trembled as she spoke to him.

"Have you a few minutes to spare?" she asked.

"The whole day, if you like, Miss," Rufus answered.

She turned to the woman who accompanied her. "Wait here for me, Elizabeth; I have something to say to this gentleman."

With those words, she got out of the carriage. Rufus offered her his arm. She put her hand in it as readily as if they had been old friends. "Let us take one of the side paths," she said; "they are almost deserted at this time of day. I am afraid I surprise you very much. I can only trust to your kindness to forgive me for passing you without notice the last time we met. Perhaps it may be some excuse for me that I am in great trouble. It is just possible you may be able to relieve my mind. I believe you know I am engaged to be married?"

Rufus looked at her with a sudden expression of interest. "Is this about Amelius?" he asked.

She answered him almost inaudibly—"Yes."

Rufus still kept his eyes fixed on her. "I don't wish to say anything, Miss," he explained; "but, if you have any complaint to make of Amelius, I should take it as a favour if you would look me straight in the face, and mention it plainly."

In the embarrassment which troubled Regina at that moment, he had preferred the two requests of all others with which it was most impossible for her to comply. She still looked obstinately on the ground; and, instead of speaking of Amelius, she diverged to the subject of Mr. Farnaby's illness.

"I am staying in Paris with my uncle," she said. "He has had a long illness; but he is strong enough now to speak to me of things that have been on his mind for some

time past. He has so surprised me; he has made me so miserable about Amelius—"
She paused, and put her handkerchief to her eyes. Rufus said nothing to console
her—he waited doggedly until she was ready to go on. "You know Amelius well,"
she resumed; "you are fond of him; you believe in him, don't you? Do you think he
is capable of behaving basely to any person who trusts him? Is it likely, is it
possible, he could be false and cruel to Me?"

The mere question roused the indignation of Rufus. "Whoever said that of him,
Miss, told you a lie! I answer for my boy as I answer for myself."

She looked at him at last, with a sudden expression of relief. "I said so too," she
rejoined; "I said some enemy had slandered him. My uncle won't tell me who it is.
He positively forbids me to write to Amelius; he tells me I must never see Amelius
again—he is going to write and break off the engagement. Oh, it's too cruel! too
cruel!"

Thus far they had been walking on slowly. But now Rufus stopped, determined to
make her speak plainly.

"Take a word of advice from me, Miss," he said. "Never trust anybody by halves.
There's nothing I'm not ready to do, to set this matter right; but I must know what
I'm about first. What's said against Amelius? Out with it, no matter what 'tis! I'm
old enough to be your father; and I feel for you accordingly—I do."

The thorough sincerity of tone and manner which accompanied those words had its
effect. Regina blushed and trembled—but she spoke out.

"My uncle says Amelius has disgraced himself, and insulted me; my uncle says there
is a person—a girl living with him—" She stopped, with a faint cry of alarm. Her
hand, still testing on the arm of Rufus, felt him start as the allusion to the girl passed
her lips. "You have heard of it!" she cried. "Oh, God help me, it's true!"

"True?" Rufus repeated, with stern contempt. "What's come to you? Haven't I told
you already, it's a lie? I'll answer to it, Amelius is true to you. Will that do? No?
You're an obstinate one, Miss—that you are. Well! it's due to the boy that I should
set him right with you, if words will do it. You know how he's been brought up at
Tadmor? Bear that in mind—and now you shall have the truth of it, on the word of
an honest man."

Without further preface, he told her how Amelius had met with Sally, insisting
strongly on the motives of pure humanity by which his friend had been actuated.
Regina listened with an obstinate expression of distrust which would have
discouraged most men. Rufus persisted, nevertheless; and, to some extent at least,
succeeded in producing the right impression. When he reached the close of the
narrative—when he asserted that he had himself seen Amelius confide the girl
unreservedly to the care of a lady who was a dear and valued friend of his own; and

268

when he declared that there had been no after-meeting between them and no written correspondence—then, at last, Regina owned that he had not encouraged her to trust in the honour of Amelius, without reason to justify him. But, even under these circumstances, there was a residue of suspicion still left in her mind. She asked for the name of the lady to whose benevolent assistance Amelius had been indebted. Rufus took out one of his cards, and wrote Mrs. Payson's name and address on it.

"Your nature, my dear, is not quite so confiding as I could have wished to see it," he said, quietly handing her the card. "But we can't change our natures—can we? And you're not bound to believe a man like me, without witnesses to back him. Write to Mrs. Payson, and make your mind easy. And, while we are about it, tell me where I can telegraph to you tomorrow—I'm off to London by the night mail."

"Do you mean, you are going to see Amelius?

"That is so. I'm too fond of Amelius to let this trouble rest where 'tis now. I've been away from him, here in Paris, for some little time—and you may tell me (and quite right, too) I can't answer for what may have been going on in my absence. No! now we are about it, we'll have it out. I mean to see Amelius and see Mrs. Payson, tomorrow morning. Just tell your uncle to hold his hand, before he breaks off your marriage, and wait for a telegram from me. Well? and this is your address, is it? I know the hotel. A nice look-out on the Twillery Gardens—but a bad cellar of wine, as I hear. I'm at the Grand Hotel myself, if there's anything else that troubles you before evening. Now I look at you again, I reckon there's something more to be said, if you'll only let it find its way to your tongue. No; it ain't thanks. We'll take the gratitude for granted, and get to what's behind it. There's your carriage—and the good lady looks tired of waiting. Well, now?"

"It's only one thing," Regina acknowledged, with her eyes on the ground again. "Perhaps, when you go to London, you may see the—"

"The girl?"

"Yes."

"It's not likely. Say I do see her—what then?"

Regina's colour began to show itself again. "If you do see her," she said, "I beg and entreat you won't speak of *me* in her hearing. I should die of the shame of it, if she thought herself asked to give him up out of pity for me. Promise I am not to be brought forward; promise you won't even mention my having spoken to you about it. On your word of honour!"

Rufus gave her his promise, without showing any hesitation, or making any remark. But when she shook hands with him, on returning to the carriage, he held her hand for a moment. "Please to excuse me, Miss, if I ask one question," he said, in tones too low to be heard by any other person. "Are you really fond of Amelius?"

"I am surprised you should doubt it," she answered; "I am more—much more than fond of him!"

Rufus handed her silently into the carriage, "Fond of him, are you?" he thought, as he walked away by himself. "I reckon it's a sort of fondness that don't wear well, and won't stand washing."

CHAPTER 8

Early the next morning, Rufus rang at the cottage gate.

"Well, Mr. Frenchman, and how do *you* git along? And how's Amelius?"

Toff, standing before the gate, answered with the utmost respect, but showed no inclination to let the visitor in.

"Amelius has his intervals of laziness," Rufus proceeded; "I bet he's in bed!"

"My young master was up and dressed an hour ago, sir—he has just gone out."

"That is so, is it? Well, I'll wait till he comes back." He pushed by Toff, and walked into the cottage. "Your foreign ceremonies are clean thrown away on me," he said, as Toff tried to stop him in the hall. "I'm the American savage; and I'm used up with travelling all night. Here's a little order for you: whisky, bitters, lemon, and ice—I'll take a cocktail in the library."

Toff made a last desperate effort to get between the visitor and the door. "I beg your pardon, sir, a thousand times; I must most respectfully entreat you to wait—"

Before he could explain himself, Rufus, with the most perfect good humour, pulled the old man out of his way. "What's troubling this venerable creature's mind—" he inquired of himself, "does he think I don't know my way in?"

He opened the library door—and found himself face to face with Sally. She had risen from her chair, hearing voices outside, and hesitating whether to leave the room or not. They confronted each other, on either side of the table, in silent dismay. For once Rufus was so completely bewildered, that he took refuge in his customary form of greeting before he was aware of it himself.

"How do you find yourself, Miss? I take pleasure in renewing our acquaintance,—Thunder! that's not it; I reckon I'm off my head. Do me the favour, young woman, to forget every word I've said to you. If any mortal creature had told me I should find you here, I should have said 'twas a lie—and I should have been the liar. That makes a man feel bad, I can tell you. No! don't slide off, if you please, into the next room—*that* won't set things right, nohow. Sit you down again. Now I'm here, I have something to say. I'll speak first to Mr. Frenchman. Listen to this, old sir. If I happen to want a witness standing in the doorway, I'll ring the bell; for the present I can do without you. Bong Shewer, as we say in your country." He proceeded to shut the door on Toff and his remonstrances.

"I protest, sir, against acts of violence, unworthy of a gentleman!" cried Toff, struggling to get back again.

"Be as angry as you please in the kitchen," Rufus answered, persisting in closing the door; "I won't have a noise up here. If you know where your master is, go and fetch him—and the sooner the better." He turned back to Sally, and surveyed her for a while in terrible silence. She was afraid to look at him; her eyes were on the book which she had been reading when he came in. "You look to me," Rufus remarked, "as if you had been settled here for a time. Never mind your book now; you can go back to your reading after we've had a word or two together first." He reached out his long arm, and pulled the book to his own side of the table. Sally innocently silenced him for the second time. He opened the book, and discovered—the New Testament.

"It's my lesson, if you please, sir. I'm to learn it where the pencil mark is, before Amelius comes back." She offered her poor little explanation, trembling with terror. In spite of himself, Rufus began to look at her less sternly.

"So you call him 'Amelius', do you?" he said. "I note that, Miss, as an unfavourable sign to begin with. How long, if you please, has Amelius turned schoolmarm, for your young ladyship's benefit? Don't you understand? Well, you're not the only inhabitant of Great Britain who don't understand the English language. I'll put it plainer. When I last saw Amelius, you were learning your lessons at the Home. What ill wind, Miss, blew you in here? Did Amelius fetch you, or did you come of your own accord, without waiting to be whistled for?" He spoke coarsely but not ill-humouredly. Sally's pretty downcast face was pleading with him for mercy, and (as he felt, with supreme contempt for himself) was not altogether pleading in vain. "If I guessed that you ran away from the home," he resumed, "should I guess right?"

She answered with a sudden accession of confidence. "Don't blame Amelius," she said; "I did run away. I couldn't live without him."

"You don't know how you can live, young one, till you've tried the experiment. Well, and what did they do at the Home? Did they send after you, to fetch you back?"

"They wouldn't take me back—they sent my clothes here after me."

"Ah, those were the rules, I reckon. I begin to see my way to the end of it now. Amelius gave you house-room?"

She looked at him proudly. "He gave me a room of my own," she said.

His next question was the exact repetition of the question which he had put to Regina in Paris. The only variety was in the answer that he received.

"Are you fond of Amelius?"

"I would die for him!"

272

Rufus had hitherto spoken, standing. He now took a chair.

"If Amelius had not been brought up at Tadmor," he said, "I should take my hat, and wish you good morning. As things are, a word more may be a word in season. Your lessons here seem to have agreed with you, Miss. You're a different sort of girl to what you were when I last saw you."

She surprised him by receiving that remark in silence. The colour left her face. She sighed bitterly. The sigh puzzled Rufus: he held his opinion of her in suspense, until he had heard more.

"You said just now you would die for Amelius," he went on, eyeing her attentively. "I take that to be a woman's hysterical way of mentioning that she feels interest in Amelius. Are you fond enough of him to leave him, if you could only be persuaded that leaving him was for his good?"

She abruptly left the table, and went to the window. When her back was turned to Rufus, she spoke. "Am I a disgrace to him?" she asked, in tones so faint that he could barely hear them. "I have had my fears of it, before now."

If he had been less fond of Amelius, his natural kindness of heart might have kept him silent. Even as it was, he made no direct reply. "You remember how you were living when Amelius first met with you?" was all he said.

The sad blue eyes looked at him in patient sorrow; the low sweet voice answered—- "Yes." Only a look and a word—only the influence of an instant—and, in that instant, Rufus's last doubts of her vanished!

"Don't think I say it reproachfully, my child! I know it was not your fault; I know you are to be pitied, and not blamed."

She turned her face towards him—pale, quiet, and resigned. "Pitied, and not blamed," she repeated. "Am I to be forgiven?"

He shrank from answering her. There was silence.

"You said just now," she went on, "that I looked like a different girl, since you last saw me. I *am* a different girl. I think of things that I never thought of before—some change, I don't know what, has come over me. Oh, my heart does hunger so to be good! I do so long to deserve what Amelius has done for me! You have got my book there—Amelius gave it to me; we read in it every day. If Christ had been on earth now, is it wrong to think that Christ would have forgiven me?"

"No, my dear; it's right to think so."

"And, while I live, if I do my best to lead a good life, and if my last prayer to God is to take me to heaven, shall I be heard?"

"You will be heard, my child, I don't doubt it. But, you see, you have got the world about you to reckon with—and the world has invented a religion of its own. There's no use looking for it in this book of yours. It's a religion with the pride of property at the bottom of it, and a veneer of benevolent sentiment at the top. It will be very sorry for you, and very charitable towards you: in short, it will do everything for you except taking you back again."

She had her answer to that. "Amelius has taken me back again," she said.

"Amelius has taken you back again," Rufus agreed. "But there's one thing he's forgotten to do; he has forgotten to count the cost. It seems to be left to me to do that. Look here, my girl! I own I doubted you when I first came into this room; and I'm sorry for it, and I beg your pardon. I do believe you're a good girl—I couldn't say why if I was asked, but I do believe it for all that. I wish there was no more to be said—but there is more; and neither you nor I must shirk it. Public opinion won't deal as tenderly with you as I do; public opinion will make the worst of you, and the worst of Amelius. While you're living here with him—there's no disguising it—you're innocently in the way of the boy's prospects in life. I don't know whether you understand me?"

She had turned away from him; she was looking out of the window once more.

"I understand you," she answered. "On the night when Amelius met with me, he did wrong to take me away with him. He ought to have left me where I was."

"Wait a bit! that's as far from my meaning as far can be. There's a look-out for everybody; and, if you'll trust me, I'll find a look-out for *you.*"

She paid no heed to what he said: her next words showed that she was pursuing her own train of thought.

"I am in the way of his prospects in life," she resumed. "You mean that he might be married some day, but for me?"

Rufus admitted it cautiously. "The thing might happen," was all he said.

"And his friends might come and see him," she went on; her face still turned away, and her voice sinking into dull subdued tones. "Nobody comes here now. You see I understand you. When shall I go away? I had better not say good-bye, I suppose?— it would only distress him. I could slip out of the house, couldn't I?"

Rufus began to feel uneasy. He was prepared for tears—but not for such resignation as this. After a little hesitation, he joined her at the window. She never turned towards him; she still looked out straight before her; her bright young face had turned pitiably rigid and pale. He spoke to her very gently; advising her to think of what he had said, and to do nothing in a hurry. She knew the hotel at which he stayed when he was in London; and she could write to him there. If she decided to begin a new life in another country, he was wholly and truly at her service. He would provide a passage for her in the same ship that took him back to America. At his age, and known as he was in his own neighbourhood, there would be no scandal to fear. He could get her reputably and profitably employed, in work which a young girl might undertake. "I'll be as good as a father to you, my poor child," he said, "don't think you're going to be friendless, if you leave Amelius. I'll see to that! You shall have honest people about you—and innocent pleasure in your new life."

She thanked him, still with the same dull tearless resignation. "What will the honest people say," she asked, "when they know who I am?"

"They have no business to know who you are—and they shan't know it."

"Ah! it comes back to the same thing," she said. "You must deceive the honest people, or you can do nothing for me. Amelius had better have left me where I was! I disgraced nobody, I was a burden to nobody, *there*. Cold and hunger and ill-treatment can sometimes be merciful friends, in their way. If I had been left to them, they would have laid me at rest by this time." She turned to Rufus, before he could speak to her. "I'm not ungrateful, sir; I'll think of it, as you say; and I'll do all that a poor foolish creature can do, to be worthy of the interest you take in me." She lifted her hand to her head, with a momentary expression of pain. "I've got a dull kind of aching here," she said; "it reminds me of my old life, when I was sometimes beaten on the head. May I go and lie down a little, by myself?"

Rufus took her hand, and pressed it in silence. She looked back at him as she opened the door of her room. "Don't distress Amelius," she said; "I can bear anything but that."

Left alone in the library, Rufus walked restlessly to and fro, driven by a troubled mind. "I was bound to do it," he thought; "and I ought to be satisfied with myself. I'm not satisfied. The world is hard on women—and the rights of property is a darned bad reason for it!"

The door from the hall was suddenly thrown open. Amelius entered the room. He looked flushed and angry—he refused to take the hand that Rufus offered to him.

"What's this I hear from Toff? It seems that you forced your way in when Sally was here. There are limits to the liberties that a man may take in his friend's house."

"That's true," said Rufus quietly. "But when a man hasn't taken liberties, there don't seem much to be said. Sally was at the Home, when I last saw you—and nobody told me I should find her in this room."

"You might have left the room, when you found her here. You have been talking to her. If you have said anything about Regina—"

"I have said nothing about Miss Regina. You have a hot temper of your own, Amelius. Wait a bit, and let it cool."

"Never mind my temper. I want to know what you have been saying to Sally. Stop! I'll ask Sally herself." He crossed the room to the inner door, and knocked. "Come in here, my dear; I want to speak to you."

The answer reached him faintly through the door. "I have got a bad headache, Amelius. Please let me rest a little." He turned back to Rufus, and lowered his voice. But his eyes flashed; he was more angry than ever.

"You had better go," he said. "I can guess how you have been talking to her—I know what her headache means. Any man who distresses that dear little affectionate creature is a man whom I hold as my enemy. I spit upon all the worldly considerations which pass muster with people like you! No sweeter girl than poor Sally ever breathed the breath of life. Her happiness is more precious to me than words can say. She is sacred to me! And I have just proved it—I have just come from a good woman, who will teach her an honest way of earning her bread. Not a breath of scandal shall blow on her. If you, or any people like you, think I will consent to cast her adrift on the world, or consign her to a prison under the name of a Home, you little know my nature and my principles. Here"—he snatched up the New Testament from the table, and shook it at Rufus—"here are my principles, and I'm not ashamed of them!"

Rufus took up his hat.

"There's one thing you'll be ashamed of, my son, when you're cool enough to think about it," he said; "you'll be ashamed of the words you have spoken to a friend who loves you. I'm not a bit angry myself. You remind me of that time on board the steamer, when the quarter-master was going to shoot the bird. You made it up with him—and you'll come to my hotel and make it up with me. And then we'll shake hands, and talk about Sally. If it's not taking another liberty, I'll trouble you for a light." He helped himself to a match from the box on the chimney-piece, lit his cigar, and left the room.

He had not been gone half an hour, before the better nature of Amelius urged him to follow Rufus and make his apologies. But he was too anxious about Sally to leave the cottage, until he had seen her first. The tone in which she had answered him, when he knocked at her door, suggested, to his sensitive apprehension, that there was something more serious the matter with her than a mere headache. For another hour, he waited patiently, on the chance that he might hear her moving in her room. Nothing happened. No sound reached his ears, except the occasional rolling of carriage-wheels on the road outside.

276

His patience began to fail him, as the second hour moved on. He went to the door, and listened, and still heard nothing. A sudden dread struck him that she might have fainted. He opened the door a few inches, and spoke to her. There was no answer. He looked in. The room was empty.

He ran into the hall, and called to Toff. Was she, by any chance, downstairs? No. Or out in the garden? No. Master and man looked at each other in silence. Sally was gone.

CHAPTER 9

Toff was the first who recovered himself.

"Courage, sir!" he said. "With a little thinking, we shall see the way to find her. That rude American man, who talked with her this morning, may be the person who has brought this misfortune on us."

Amelius waited to hear no more. There was the chance, at least, that something might have been said which had induced her to take refuge with Rufus. He ran back to the library to get his hat.

Toff followed his master, with another suggestion. "One word more, sir, before you go. If the American man cannot help us, we must be ready to try another way. Permit me to accompany you as far as my wife's shop. I propose that she shall come back here with me, and examine poor little Miss's bedroom. We will wait, of course, for your return, before anything is done. In the mean time, I entreat you not to despair. It is at least possible that the means of discovery may be found in the bedroom."

They went out together, taking the first cab that passed them. Amelius proceeded alone to the hotel.

Rufus was in his room. "What's gone wrong?" he asked, the moment Amelius opened the door. "Shake hands, my son, and smother up that little trouble between us in silence. Your face alarms me—it does! What of Sally?"

Amelius started at the question. "Isn't she here?" he asked.

Rufus drew back. The mere action said, No, before he answered in words.

"Have you seen nothing of her? heard nothing of her?"

"Nothing. Steady, now! Meet it like a man; and tell me what has happened."

Amelius told him in two words. "Don't suppose I'm going to break out again as I did this morning," he went on; "I'm too wretched and too anxious to be angry. Only tell me, Rufus, have you said anything to her—?"

Rufus held up his hand. "I see what you're driving at. It will be more to the purpose to tell you what she said to me. From first to last, Amelius, I spoke kindly to her, and I did her justice. Give me a minute to rummage my memory." After brief consideration, he carefully repeated the substance of what had passed between Sally and himself, during the latter part of the interview between them. "Have you looked

278

about in her room?" he inquired, when he had done. "There might be a trifling something to help you, left behind her there."

Amelius told him of Toff's suggestion. They returned together at once to the cottage. Madame Toff was waiting to begin the search.

The first discovery was easily made. Sally had taken off one or two little trinkets—presents from Amelius, which she was in the habit of wearing—and had left them, wrapped up in paper, on the dressing-table. No such thing as a farewell letter was found near them. The examination of the wardrobe came next—and here a startling circumstance revealed itself. Every one of the dresses which Amelius had presented to her was hanging in its place. They were not many; and they had all, on previous occasions, been passed in review by Toff's wife. She was absolutely certain that the complete number of the dresses was there in the bedroom. Sally must have worn something, in place of her new clothes. What had she put on?

Looking round the room, Amelius noticed in a corner the box in which he had placed the first new dress that he had purchased for Sally, on the morning after they had met. He tried to open the box: it was locked—and the key was not to be found. The ever-ready Toff fetched a skewer from the kitchen, and picked the lock in two minutes. On lifting the cover, the box proved to be empty.

The one person present who understood what this meant was Amelius.

He remembered that Sally had taken her old threadbare clothes away with her in the box, when the angry landlady had insisted on his leaving the house. "I want to look at them sometimes," the poor girl had said, "and think how much better off I am now." In those miserable rags she had fled from the cottage, after hearing the cruel truth. "He had better have left me where I was," she had said. "Cold and hunger and ill-treatment would have laid me at rest by this time." Amelius fell on his knees before the empty box, in helpless despair. The conclusion that now forced itself on his mind completely unmanned him. She had gone back, in the old dress, to die under the cold, the hunger, and the horror of the old life.

Rufus took his hand, and spoke to him kindly. He rallied, and dashed the tears from his eyes, and rose to his feet. "I know where to look for her," was all he said; "and I must do it alone." He refused to enter into any explanation, or to be assisted by any companion. "This is my secret and hers," he answered, "Go back to your hotel, Rufus—and pray that I may not bring news which will make a wretched man of you for the rest of your life." With that he left them.

In another hour he stood once more on the spot at which he and Sally had met.

The wild bustle and uproar of the costermongers' night market no longer rioted round him: the street by daylight was in a state of dreary repose. Slowly pacing up and down, from one end to another, he waited with but one hope to sustain him—the hope that she might have taken refuge with the two women who had been her only friends in the dark days of her life. Ignorant of the place in which they lived, he had no choice but to wait for the appearance of one or other of them in the street. He was quiet and resolved. For the rest of the day, and for the whole of the night if need be, his mind was made up to keep steadfastly on the watch.

When he could walk no longer, he obtained rest and refreshment in the cookshop which he remembered so well; sitting on a stool near the window, from which he could still command a view of the street. The gas-lamps were alight, and the long winter's night was beginning to set in, when he resumed his weary march from end to end of the pavement. As the darkness became complete, his patience was rewarded at last. Passing the door of a pawnbroker's shop, he met one of the women face to face, walking rapidly, with a little parcel under her arm.

She recognized him with a cry of joyful surprise.

"Oh, sir, how glad I am to see you, to be sure! You've come to look after Sally, haven't you? Yes, yes; she's safe in our poor place—but in such a dreadful state. Off her head! clean off her head! Talks of nothing but you. 'I'm in the way of his prospects in life.' Over and over and over again, she keeps on saying that. Don't be afraid; Jenny's at home, taking care of her. She wants to go out. Hot and wild, with a kind of fever on her, she wants to go out. She asked if it rained. 'The rain may kill me in these ragged clothes,' she says; 'and then I shan't be in the way of his prospects in life.' We tried to quiet her by telling her it didn't rain—but it was no use; she was as eager as ever to go out. 'I may get another blow on the bosom,' she says; 'and, maybe, it will fall on the right place this time.' No! there's no fear of the brute who used to beat her—he's in prison. Don't ask to see her just yet, sir; please don't! I'm afraid you would only make her worse, if I took you to her now; I wouldn't dare to risk it. You see, we can't get her to sleep; and we thought of buying something to quiet her at the chemist's. Yes, sir, it would be better to get a doctor to her. But I wasn't going to the doctor. If I must tell you, I was obliged to take the sheets off the bed, to raise a little money—I was going to the pawnbroker's." She looked at the parcel under her arm, and smiled. "I may take the sheets back again, now I've met with you; and there's a good doctor lives close by— I can show you the way to him. Oh how pale you do look! Are you very much tired? It's only a little way to the doctor. I've got an arm at your service—but you mightn't like to be seen waiting with such a person as me."

Mentally and physically, Amelius was completely prostrated. The woman's melancholy narrative had overwhelmed him: he could neither speak nor act. He mechanically put his purse in her hand, and went with her to the house of the nearest medical man.

The doctor was at home, mixing drugs in his little surgery. After one sharp look at Amelius, he ran into a back parlour, and returned with a glass of spirits. "Drink this, sir," he said—"unless you want to find yourself on the floor in a fainting fit. And don't presume again on your youth and strength to treat your heart as if it was made

280

of cast-iron." He signed to Amelius to sit down and rest himself, and turned to the woman to hear what was wanted of him. After a few questions, he said she might go; promising to follow her in a few minutes, when the gentleman would be sufficiently recovered to accompany him.

"Well, sir, are you beginning to feel like yourself again?" He was mixing a composing draught, while he addressed Amelius in those terms. "You may trust that poor wretch, who has just left us, to take care of the sick girl," he went on, in the quaintly familiar manner which seemed to be habitual with him. "I don't ask how you got into her company—it's no business of mine. But I am pretty well acquainted with the people in my neighbourhood; and I can tell you one thing, in case you're anxious. The woman who brought you here, barring the one misfortune of her life, is as good a creature as ever breathed; and the other one who lives with her is the same. When I think of what they're exposed to—well! I take to my pipe, and compose my mind in that way. My early days were all passed as a ship's surgeon. I could get them both respectable employment in Australia, if I only had the money to fit them out. They'll die in the hospital, like the rest, if something isn't done for them. In my hopeful moments, I sometimes think of a subscription. What do you say? Will you put down a few shillings to set the example?"

"I will do more than that," Amelius answered. "I have reasons for wishing to befriend both those two poor women; and I will gladly engage to find the outfit."

The familiar old doctor held out his hand over the counter. "You're a good fellow, if ever there was one yet!" he burst out. "I can show references which will satisfy you that I am not a rogue. In the mean time, let's see what is the matter with this little girl; you can tell me about her as we go along." He put his bottle of medicine in his pocket, and his arm in the arm of Amelius—and so led the way out.

When they reached the wretched lodging-house in which the women lived, he suggested that his companion would do well to wait at the door. "I'm used to sad sights: it would only distress you to see the place. I won't keep you long waiting."

He was as good as his word. In little more than ten minutes, he joined Amelius again in the street.

"Don't alarm yourself," he said. "The case is not so serious as it looks. The poor child is suffering under a severe shock to the brain and nervous system, caused by that sudden and violent distress you hinted at. My medicine will give her the one thing she wants to begin with—a good night's sleep."

Amelius asked when she would be well enough to see him.

"Ah, my young friend, it's not so easy to say, just yet! I could answer you to better purpose tomorrow. Won't that do? Must I venture on a rash opinion? She ought to be composed enough to see you in three or four days. And, when that time comes, it's my belief you will do more than I can do to set her right again."

Amelius was relieved, but not quite satisfied yet. He inquired if it was not possible to remove her from that miserable place.

"Quite impossible—without doing her serious injury. They have got money to go on with; and I have told you already, she will be well taken care of. I will look after her myself tomorrow morning. Go home, and get to bed, and eat a bit of supper first, and make your mind easy. Come to my house at twelve o'clock, noon, and you will find me ready with my references, and my report of the patient. Surgeon Pinfold, Blackacre Buildings; there's the address. Good night."

CHAPTER 10

After Amelius had left him, Rufus remembered his promise to communicate with Regina by telegraph.

With his strict regard for truth, it was no easy matter to decide on what message he should send. To inspire Regina, if possible, with his own unshaken belief in the good faith of Amelius, appeared, on reflection, to be all that he could honestly do, under present circumstances. With an anxious and foreboding mind, he despatched his telegram to Paris in these terms:—"Be patient for a while, and do justice to A. He deserves it."

Having completed his business at the telegraph-office, Rufus went next to pay his visit to Mrs. Payson.

The good lady received him with a grave face and a distant manner, in startling contrast to the customary warmth of her welcome. "I used to think you were a man in a thousand," she began abruptly; "and I find you are no better than the rest of them. If you have come to speak to me about that blackguard young Socialist, understand, if you please, that I am not so easily imposed upon as Miss Regina. I have done my duty; I have opened her eyes to the truth, poor thing. Ah, you ought to be ashamed of yourself."

Rufus kept his temper, with his habitual self-command. "It's possible you may be right," he said quietly; "but the biggest rascal living has a claim to an explanation, when a lady puzzles him. Have you any particular objection, old friend, to tell me what you mean?"

The explanation was not of a nature to set his mind at ease.

Regina had written, by the mail which took Rufus to England, repeating to Mrs. Payson what had passed at the interview in the Champs Elysees, and appealing to her sympathy for information and advice. Receiving the letter that morning, Mrs. Payson, acting on her own generous and compassionate impulses, had already answered it, and sent it to the post. Her experience of the unfortunate persons received at the Home was far from inclining her to believe in the innocence of a runaway girl, placed under circumstances of temptation. As an act of justice towards Regina, she enclosed to her the letter in which Amelius had acknowledged that Sally had passed the night under his roof.

"I believe I am only telling you the shameful truth," Mrs. Payson had written, "when I add that the girl has been an inmate of Mr. Goldenheart's cottage ever since. If you can reconcile this disgraceful state of things, with Mr. Rufus Dingwell's assertion of his friend's fidelity to his marriage-engagement, I have no right, and no wish, to make any attempt to alter your opinion. But you have asked for my advice, and I must not shrink from giving it. I am bound as an honest woman, to tell you that your uncle's resolution to break off the engagement represents the course that I should have taken myself, if a daughter of my own had been placed in your painful and humiliating position."

There was still ample time to modify this strong expression of opinion by the day's post. Rufus appealed vainly to Mrs. Payson to reconsider the conclusion at which she had arrived. A more charitable and considerate woman, within the limits of her own daily routine, it would not be possible to find. But the largeness of mind which, having long and trustworthy experience of a rule, can nevertheless understand that other minds may have equal experience of the exception to the rule, was one of the qualities which had not been included in the moral composition of Mrs. Payson. She held firmly to her own narrowly conscientious sense of her duty; stimulated by a natural indignation against Amelius, who had bitterly disappointed her—against Rufus, who had not scrupled to take up his defence. The two old friends parted in coldness, for the first time in their lives.

Rufus returned to his hotel, to wait there for news from Amelius.

The day passed—and the one visitor who enlivened his solitude was an American friend and correspondent, connected with the agency which managed his affairs in England. The errand of this gentleman was to give his client the soundest and speediest advice, relating to the investment of money. Having indicated the safe and solid speculation, the visitor added a warning word, relating to the plausible and dangerous investments of the day. "For instance," he said, "there's that bank started by Farnaby—"

"No need to warn me against Farnaby," Rufus interposed; "I wouldn't take shares in his bank if he made me a present of them."

The American friend looked surprised. "Surely," he exclaimed, "you can't have heard the news already! They don't even know it yet on the Stock Exchange."

Rufus explained that he had only spoken under the influence of personal prejudice against Mr. Farnaby.

"What's in the wind now?" he asked.

He was confidentially informed that a coming storm was in the wind: in other words, that a serious discovery had been made at the bank. Some time since, the directors had advanced a large sum of money to a man in trade, under Mr. Farnaby's own guarantee. The man had just died; and examination of his affairs showed that he had only received a few hundred pounds, on condition of holding his tongue. The bulk of the money had been traced to Mr. Farnaby himself, and had all been swallowed up by his newspaper, his patent medicine, and his other rotten speculations, apart from his own proper business. "You may not know it," the American friend concluded, "but the fact is, Farnaby rose from the dregs. His

284

bankruptcy is only a question of time—he will drop back to the dregs; and, quite possibly, make his appearance to answer a criminal charge in a court of law. I hear that Melton, whose credit has held up the bank lately, is off to see his friend in Paris. They say Farnaby's niece is a handsome girl, and Melton is sweet on her. Awkward for Melton."

Rufus listened attentively. In signing the order for his investments, he privately decided to stir no further, for the present, in the matter of his young friend's marriage-engagement.

For the rest of the day and evening, he still waited for Amelius, and waited in vain. It was drawing near to midnight, when Toff made his appearance with a message from his master. Amelius had discovered Sally, and had returned in such a state of fatigue that he was only fit to take some refreshment, and to go to his bed. He would be away from home again, on the next morning; but he hoped to call at the hotel in the course of the day. Observing Toff's face with grave and steady scrutiny, Rufus tried to extract some further information from him. But the old Frenchman stood on his dignity, in a state of immovable reserve.

"You took me by the shoulder this morning, sir, and spun me round," he said; "I do not desire to be treated a second time like a teetotum. For the rest, it is not my habit to intrude myself into my master's secrets."

"It's not *my* habit," Rufus coolly rejoined, "to bear malice. I beg to apologise sincerely, sir, for treating you like a teetotum; and I offer you my hand."

Toff had got as far as the door. He instantly returned, with the dignity which a Frenchman can always command in the serious emergencies of his life. "You appeal to my heart and my honour, sir," he said. "I bury the events of the morning in oblivion; and I do myself the honour of taking your hand."

As the door closed on him, Rufus smiled grimly. "You're not in the habit of intruding yourself into your master's secrets," he repeated. "If Amelius reads your face as I read it, he'll look over his shoulder when he goes out tomorrow—and, ten to one, he'll see you behind him in the distance!"

Late on the next day, Amelius presented himself at the hotel. In speaking of Sally, he was unusually reserved, merely saying that she was ill, and under medical care, and then changing the subject. Struck by the depressed and anxious expression of his face, Rufus asked if he had heard from Regina. No: a longer time than usual had passed since Regina had written to him. "I don't understand it," he said sadly. "I suppose you didn't see anything of her in Paris?"

Rufus had kept his promise not to mention Regina's name in Sally's presence. But it was impossible for him to look at Amelius, without plainly answering the question put to him, for the sake of the friend whom he loved. "I'm afraid there's trouble coming to you, my son, from that quarter." With those warning words, he described all that had passed between Regina and himself. "Some unknown enemy of yours has spoken against you to her uncle," he concluded. "I suppose you have made enemies, my poor old boy, since you have been in London?"

"I know the man," Amelius answered. "He wanted to marry Regina before I met with her. His name is Melton."

Rufus started. "I heard only yesterday, he was in Paris with Farnaby. And that's not the worst of it, Amelius. There's another of them making mischief—a good friend of mine who has shown a twist in her temper, that has taken me by surprise after twenty years' experience of her. I reckon there's a drop of malice in the composition of the best woman that ever lived—and the men only discover it when another woman steps in, and stirs it up. Wait a bit!" he went on, when he had related the result of his visit to Mrs. Payson. "I have telegraphed to Miss Regina to be patient, and to trust you. Don't you write to defend yourself, till you hear how you stand in her estimation, after my message. Tomorrow's post may tell."

Tomorrow's post did tell.

Two letters reached Amelius from Paris. One from Mr. Farnaby, curt and insolent, breaking off the marriage-engagement. The other, from Regina, expressed with great severity of language. Her weak nature, like all weak natures, ran easily into extremes, and, once roused into asserting itself, took refuge in violence as a shy person takes refuge in audacity. Only a woman of larger and firmer mind would have written of her wrongs in a more just and more moderate tone.

Regina began without any preliminary form of address. She had no heart to upbraid Amelius, and no wish to speak of what she was suffering, to a man who had but too plainly shown that he had no respect for himself, and neither love, nor pity even, for her. In justice to herself, she released him from his promise, and returned his letters and his presents. Her own letters might be sent in a sealed packet, addressed to her at her uncle's place of business in London. She would pray that he might be brought to a sense of the sin that he had committed, and that he might yet live to be a worthy and a happy man. For the rest, her decision was irrevocable. His own letter to Mrs. Payson condemned him—and the testimony of an old and honoured friend of her uncle proved that his wickedness was no mere act of impulse, but a deliberate course of infamy and falsehood, continued over many weeks. From the moment when she made that discovery, he was a stranger to her—and she now bade him farewell.

"Have you written to her?" Rufus asked, when he had seen the letters.

Amelius reddened with indignation. He was not aware of it himself—but his look and manner plainly revealed that Regina had lost her last hold on him. Her letter had inflicted an insult—not a wound: he was outraged and revolted; the deeper and gentler feelings, the emotions of a grieved and humiliated lover, had been killed in him by her stern words of dismissal and farewell.

286

"Do you think I would allow myself to be treated in that way, without a word of protest?" he said to Rufus. "I have written, refusing to take back my promise. 'I declare, on my word of honour, that I have been faithful to you and to my engagement'—that was how I put it—'and I scorn the vile construction which your uncle and his friend have placed upon an act of Christian mercy on my part.' I wrote more tenderly, before I finished my letter; feeling for her distress, and being anxious above all things not to add to it. We shall see if she has love enough left for me to trust my faith and honour, instead of trusting false appearances. I will give her time."

Rufus considerately abstained from expressing any opinion. He waited until the morning when a reply might be expected from Paris; and then he called at the cottage.

Without a word of comment, Amelius put a letter into his friend's hand. It was his own letter to Regina returned to him. On the back of it, there was a line in Mr. Farnaby's handwriting:—"If you send any more letters they will be burnt unopened." In those insolent terms the wretch wrote with bankruptcy and exposure hanging over his head.

Rufus spoke plainly upon this. "There's an end of it now," he said. "That girl would never have made the right wife for you, Amelius: you're well out of it. Forget that you ever knew these people; and let us talk of something else. How is Sally?"

At that ill-timed inquiry, Amelius showed his temper again. He was in a state of nervous irritability which made him apt to take offence, where no offence was intended. "Oh, you needn't be alarmed!" he answered petulantly; "there's no fear of the poor child coming back to live with me. She is still under the doctor's care."

Rufus passed over the angry reply without notice, and patted him on the shoulder. "I spoke of the girl," he said, "because I wanted to help her; and I can help her, if you will let me. Before long, my son, I shall be going back to the United States. I wish you would go with me!"

"And desert Sally!" cried Amelius.

"Nothing of the sort! Before we go, I'll see that Sally is provided for to your satisfaction. Will you think of it, to please me?"

Amelius relented. "Anything, to please you," he said.

Rufus noticed his hat and gloves on the table, and left him without saying more. "The trouble with Amelius," he thought, as he closed the cottage gate, "is not over yet."

CHAPTER 11

The day on which worthy old Surgeon Pinfold had predicted that Sally would be in a fair way of recovery had come and gone; and still the medical report to Amelius was the same:—"You must be patient, sir; she is not well enough to see you yet."

Toff, watching his young master anxiously, was alarmed by the steadily progressive change in him for the worse, which showed itself at this time. Now sad and silent, and now again bitter and irritable, he had deteriorated physically as well as morally, until he really looked like the shadow of his former self. He never exchanged a word with his faithful old servant, except when he said mechanically, "good morning" or "good night." Toff could endure it no longer. At the risk of being roughly misinterpreted, he followed his own kindly impulse, and spoke. "May I own to you, sir," he said, with perfect gentleness and respect, "that I am indeed heartily sorry to see you so ill?"

Amelius looked up at him sharply. "You servants always make a fuss about trifles. I am a little out of sorts; and I want a change—that's all. Perhaps I may go to America. You won't like that; I shan't complain if you look out for another situation."

The tears came into the old man's eyes. "Never!" he answered fervently. "My last service, sir, if you send me away, shall be my dearly loved service here."

All that was most tender in the nature of Amelius was touched to the quick. "Forgive me, Toff," he said; "I am lonely and wretched, and more anxious about Sally than words can tell. There can be no change in my life, until my mind is easy about that poor little girl. But if it does end in my going to America, you shall go with me—I wouldn't lose you, my good friend, for the world."

Toff still remained in the room, as if he had something left to say. Entirely ignorant of the marriage engagement between Amelius and Regina, and of the rupture in which it had ended, he vaguely suspected nevertheless that his master might have fallen into an entanglement with some lady unknown. The opportunity of putting the question was now before him. He risked it in a studiously modest form.

"Are you going to America to be married, sir?"

Amelius eyed him with a momentary suspicion. "What has put that in your head?" he asked.

"I don't know, sir," Toff answered humbly—"unless it was my own vivid imagination. Would there be anything very wonderful in a gentleman of your age and appearance conducting some charming person to the altar?"

288

Amelius was conquered once more; he smiled faintly. "Enough of your nonsense, Toff! I shall never be married—understand that."

Toff's withered old face brightened slyly. He turned away to withdraw; hesitated; and suddenly went back to his master.

"Have you any occasion for my services, sir, for an hour or two?" he asked.

"No. Be back before I go out, myself—be back at three o'clock."

"Thank you, sir. My little boy is below, if you want anything in my absence."

The little boy dutifully attending Toff to the gate, observed with grave surprise that his father snapped his fingers gaily at starting, and hummed the first bars of the Marseillaise. "Something is going to happen," said Toff's boy, on his way back to the house.

From the Regent's Park to Blackacre Buildings is almost a journey from one end of London to the other. Assisted for part of the way by an omnibus, Toff made the journey, and arrived at the residence of Surgeon Pinfold, with the easy confidence of a man who knew thoroughly well where he was going, and what he was about. The sagacity of Rufus had correctly penetrated his intentions; he had privately followed his master, and had introduced himself to the notice of the surgeon—with a mixture of motives, in which pure devotion to the interests of Amelius played the chief part. His experience of the world told him that Sally's departure was only the beginning of more trouble to come. "What is the use of me to my master," he had argued, "except to spare him trouble, in spite of himself?"

Surgeon Pinfold was prescribing for a row of sick people, seated before him on a bench. "You're not ill, are you?" he said sharply to Toff. "Very well, then, go into the parlour and wait."

The patients being dismissed, Toff attempted to explain the object of his visit. But the old naval surgeon insisted on clearing the ground by means of a plain question first. "Has your master sent you here—or is this another private interview, like the last?"

"It is all that is most private," Toff answered; "my poor master is wasting away in unrelieved wretchedness and suspense. Something must be done for him. Oh, dear and good sir, help me in this most miserable state of things! Tell me the truth about Miss Sally!"

Old Pinfold put his hands in his pockets and leaned against the parlour wall, looking at the Frenchman with a complicated expression, in which genuine sympathy mingled oddly with a quaint sense of amusement. "You're a worthy chap," he said; "and you shall have the truth. I have been obliged to deceive your master about this troublesome young Sally; I have stuck to it that she is too ill to see him, or to answer his letters. Both lies. There's nothing the matter with her now, but a disease that I can't cure, the disease of a troubled mind. She's got it into her head that she has everlastingly degraded herself in his estimation by leaving him and coming here. It's no use telling her—what, mind you, is perfectly true—that she was all but out of her senses, and not in the least responsible for what she did at the time when she did it. She holds to her own opinion, nevertheless. 'What can he think of me, but that I have gone back willingly to the disgrace of my old life? I should throw myself out of the window, if he came into the room!' That's how she answers me—and, what makes matters worse still, she's breaking her heart about him all the time. The poor wretch is so eager for any little word of news about his health and his doings, that it's downright pitiable to see her. I don't think her fevered little brain will bear it much longer—and hang me if I can tell what to do next to set things right! The two women, her friends, have no sort of influence over her. When I saw her this morning, she was ungrateful enough to say, 'Why didn't you let me die?' How your master got among these unfortunate people is more than I know, and is no business of mine; I only wish he had been a different sort of man. Before I knew him as well as I know him now, I predicted, like a fool, that he would be just the person to help us in managing the girl. I have altered my opinion. He's such a glorious fellow—so impulsive and so tender-hearted—that he would be certain, in her present excited state, to do her more harm than good. Do you know if he is going to be married?"

Toff, listening thus far in silent distress, suddenly looked up.

"Why do you ask me, sir?"

"It's an idle question, I dare say," old Pinfold remarked. "Sally persists in telling us she's in the way of his prospects in life—and it's got somehow into her perverse little head that his prospects in life mean his marriage, and she's in the way of that.—Hullo! are you going already?"

"I want to go to Miss Sally, sir. I believe I can say something to comfort her. Do you think she will see me?"

"Are you the man who has got the nickname of Toff? She sometimes talks about Toff."

"Yes, sir, yes! I am Theophile Leblond, otherwise Toff. Where can I find her?"

Surgeon Pinfold rang a bell. "My errand-boy is going past the house, to deliver some medicine," he answered. "It's a poor place; but you'll find it neat and nice enough—thanks to your good master. He's helping the two women to begin life again out of this country; and, while they're waiting their turn to get a passage, they've taken an extra room and hired some decent furniture, by your master's own wish. Oh, here's the boy; he'll show you the way. One word before you go. What do you think of saying to Sally?"

"I shall tell her, for one thing, sir, that my master is miserable for want of her."

Surgeon Pinfold shook his head. "That won't take you very far on the way to persuading her. You will make *her* miserable too—and there's about all you will get by it."

Toff lifted his indicative forefinger to the side of his nose. "Suppose I tell her something else, sir? Suppose I tell her my master is not going to be married to anybody?"

"She won't believe you know anything about it."

"She will believe, for this reason," said Toff, gravely; "I put the question to my master before I came here; and I have it from his own lips that there is no young lady in the way, and that he is not—positively not—going to be married. If I tell Miss Sally this, sir, how do you say it will end? Will you bet me a shilling it has no effect on her?"

"I won't bet a farthing! Follow the boy—and tell young Sally I have sent her a better doctor than I am."

While Toff was on his way to Sally, Toff's boy was disturbing Amelius by the announcement of a visitor. The card sent in bore this inscription: "Brother Bawkwell, from Tadmor."

Amelius looked at the card; and ran into the hall to receive the visitor, with both hands held out in hearty welcome. "Oh, I am so glad to see you!" he cried. "Come in, and tell me all about Tadmor!"

Brother Bawkwell acknowledged the enthusiastic reception offered to him by a stare of grim surprise. He was a dry, hard old man, with a scrubby white beard, a narrow wrinkled forehead, and an obstinate lipless mouth; fitted neither by age nor temperament to be the intimate friend of any of his younger brethren among the Community. But, at that saddest time of his life, the heart of Amelius warmed to any one who reminded him of his tranquil and happy days at Tadmor. Even this frozen old Socialist now appeared to him, for the first time, under the borrowed aspect of a welcome friend.

Brother Bawkwell took the chair offered to him, and opened the proceedings, in solemn silence, by looking at his watch. "Twenty-five minutes past two," he said to himself—and put the watch back again.

"Are you pressed for time?" Amelius asked.

"Much may be done in ten minutes," Brother Bawkwell answered, in a Scotch accent which had survived the test of half a lifetime in America. "I would have you know I am in England on a mission from the Community, with a list of twenty-seven persons in all, whom I am appointed to confer with on matters of varying importance. Yours, friend Amelius, is a matter of minor importance. I can give you ten minutes."

He opened a big black pocket-book, stuffed with a mass of letters; and, placing two of them on the table before him, addressed Amelius as if he was making a speech at a public meeting.

"I have to request your attention to certain proceedings of the Council at Tadmor, bearing date the third of December last; and referring to a person under sentence of temporary separation from the Community, along with yourself—"

"Mellicent!" Amelius exclaimed.

"We have no time for interruptions," Brother Bawkwell remarked. "The person *is* Sister Mellicent; and the business before the Council was to consider a letter, under her signature, received December second. Said letter," he proceeded, taking up one of his papers, "is abridged as follows by the Secretary to the Council. In substance, the writer states (first): 'That the married sister under whose protection she has been living at New York is about to settle in England with her husband, appointed to manage the branch of his business established in London. (Second): That she, meaning Sister Mellicent, has serious reasons for not accompanying her relatives to England, and has no other friends to take charge of her welfare, if she remains in New York. (Third): That she appeals to the mercy of the Council, under these circumstances, to accept the expression of her sincere repentance for the offence of violating a Rule, and to permit a friendless and penitent creature to return to the only home left to her, her home at Tadmor.' No, friend Amelius—we have no time for expressions of sympathy; the first half of the ten minutes has nearly expired. I have further to notify you that the question was put to the vote, in this form: 'Is it consistent with the serious responsibility which rests on the Council, to consider the remission of any sentence justly pronounced under the Book of Rules?' The result was very remarkable; the votes for and against being equally divided. In this event, as you know, our laws provide that the decision rests with the Elder Brother—who gave his vote thereupon for considering the remission of the sentence; and moved the next resolution that the sentence be remitted accordingly. Carried by a small majority. Whereupon, Sister Mellicent was received again at Tadmor."

"Ah, the dear old Elder Brother," cried Amelius—"always on the side of mercy!"

Brother Bawkwell held up his hand in protest. "You seem to have no idea," he said, "of the value of time. Do be quiet! As travelling representative of the Council, I am further instructed to say, that the sentence pronounced against yourself stands duly remitted, in consequence of the remission of the sentence against Sister Mellicent. You likewise are free to return to Tadmor, at your own will and pleasure. But— attend to what is coming, friend Amelius!—the Council holds to its resolution that your choice between us and the world shall be absolutely unbiased. In the fear of exercising even an indirect influence, we have purposely abstained from corresponding with you. With the same motive we now say, that if you do return to us, it must be with no interference on our part. We inform you of an event that has happened in your absence—and we do no more."

He paused, and looked again at his watch. Time proverbially works wonders. Time closed his lips.

Amelius replied with a heavy heart. The message from the Council had recalled him from the remembrance of Mellicent to the sense of his own position. "My experience of the world has been a very hard one," he said. "I would gladly go back to Tadmor this very day, but for one consideration—" He hesitated; the image of Sally was before him. The tears rose in his eyes; he said no more.

Brother Bawkwell, driven hard by time, got on his legs, and handed to Amelius the second of the two papers which he had taken out of his pocket-book.

"Here is a purely informal document," he said; "being a few lines from Sister Mellicent, which I was charged to deliver to you. Be pleased to read it as quickly as you can, and tell me if there is any reply."

There was not much to read:—"The good people here, Amelius, have forgiven me and let me return to them. I am living happily now, dear, in my remembrances of you. I take the walks that we once took together—and sometimes I go out in the boat on the lake, and think of the time when I told you my sad story. Your poor little pet creatures are under my care; the dog, and the fawn, and the birds—all well, and waiting for you, with me. My belief that you will come back to me remains the same unshaken belief that it has been from the first. Once more I say it—you will find me the first to welcome you, when your spirits are sinking under the burden of life, and your heart turns again to the friends of your early days. Until that time comes, think of me now and then. Good-bye."

"I am waiting," said Brother Bawkwell, taking his hat in his hand.

Amelius answered with an effort. "Thank her kindly in my name," he said: "that is all." His head drooped while he spoke; he fell into thought as if he had been alone in the room.

But the emissary from Tadmor, warned by the minute-hand on the watch, recalled his attention to passing events. "You would do me a kindness," said Brother Bawkwell, producing a list of names and addresses, "if you could put me in the way of finding the person named, eighth from the top. It's getting on towards twenty minutes to three."

The address thus pointed out was at no great distance, on the northern side of the Regent's Park. Amelius, still silent and thoughtful, acted willingly as a guide.

"Please thank the Council for their kindness to me," he said, when they reached their destination. Brother Bawkwell looked at friend Amelius with a calm inquiring eye. "I think you'll end in coming back to us," he said. "I'll take the opportunity, when I see you at Tadmor, of making a few needful remarks on the value of time."

Amelius went back to the cottage, to see if Toff had returned, in his absence, before he paid his daily visit to Surgeon Pinfold. He called down the kitchen stairs, "Are you there, Toff?" And Toff answered briskly, "At your service, sir."

The sky had become cloudy, and threatened rain. Not finding his umbrella in the hall, Amelius went into the library to look for it. As he closed the door behind him, Toff and his boy appeared on the kitchen stairs; both walking on tiptoe, and both evidently on the watch for something.

Amelius found his umbrella. But it was characteristic of the melancholy change in him that he dropped languidly into the nearest chair, instead of going out at once with the easy activity of happier days. Sally was in his mind again; he was rousing his resolution to set the doctor's commands at defiance, and to insist on seeing her, come what might of it.

He suddenly looked up. A slight sound had startled him.

It was a faint rustling sound; and it came from the sadly silent room which had once been Sally's.

He listened, and heard it again. He sprang to his feet—his heart beat wildly—he opened the door of the room.

She was there.

Her hands were clasped over her fast-heaving breast. She was powerless to look at him, powerless to speak to him—powerless to move towards him, until he opened his arms to her. Then, all the love and all the sorrow in the tender little heart flowed outward to him in a low murmuring cry. She hid her blushing face on his bosom. The rosy colour softly tinged her neck—the unspoken confession of all she feared, and all she hoped.

It was a time beyond words. They were silent in each other's arms.

But under them, on the floor below, the stillness in the cottage was merrily broken by an outburst of dance-music—with a rhythmical thump-thump of feet, keeping time to the cheerful tune. Toff was playing his fiddle; and Toff's boy was dancing to his father's music.

CHAPTER 12

After waiting a day or two for news from Amelius, and hearing nothing, Rufus went to make inquiries at the cottage.

"My master has gone out of town, sir," said Toff, opening the door.

"Where?"

"I don't know, sir."

"Anybody with him?"

"I don't know, sir."

"Any news of Sally?"

"I don't know, sir."

Rufus stepped into the hall. "Look here, Mr. Frenchman, three times is enough. I have already apologized for treating you like a teetotum, on a former occasion. I'm afraid I shall do it again, sir, if I don't get an answer to my next question—my hands are itching to be at you, they are! When is Amelius expected back?"

"Your question is positive, sir," said Toff, with dignity. "I am happy to be able to meet it with a positive reply. My master is expected back in three weeks' time."

Having obtained some information at last, Rufus debated with himself what he should do next. He decided that "the boy was worth waiting for," and that his wisest course (as a good American) would be to go back, and wait in Paris.

Passing through the Garden of the Tuileries, two or three days later, and crossing to the Rue de Rivoli, the name of one of the hotels in that quarter reminded him of Regina. He yielded to the prompting of curiosity, and inquired if Mr. Farnaby and his niece were still in Paris.

The manager of the hotel was in the porter's lodge at the time. So far as he knew, he said, Mr. Farnaby and his niece, and an English gentleman with them, were now on their travels. They had left the hotel with an appearance of mystery. The courier had been discharged; and the coachman of the hired carriage which took them away had been told to drive straight forward until further orders. In short, as the manager put it, the departure resembled a flight. Remembering what his American agent had told him, Rufus received this information without surprise. Even the apparently incomprehensible devotion of Mr. Melton to the interests of such a man as Farnaby, failed to present itself to him as a perplexing circumstance. To his mind, Mr.

Melton's conduct was plainly attributable to a reward in prospect; and the name of that reward was—Miss Regina.

At the end of the three weeks, Rufus returned to London.

Once again, he and Toff confronted each other on the threshold of the door. This time, the genial old man presented an appearance that was little less than dazzling. From head to foot he was arrayed in new clothes; and he exhibited an immense rosette of white ribbon in his button-hole.

"Thunder!" cried Rufus. "Here's Mr. Frenchman going to be married!"

Toff declined to humour the joke. He stood on his dignity as stiffly as ever. "Pardon me, sir, I possess a wife and family already."

"Do you, now? Well—none of your know-nothing answers this time. Has Amelius come back?"

"Yes, sir."

"And what's the news of Sally?"

"Good news, sir. Miss Sally has come back too."

"You call that good news, do you? I'll say a word to Amelius. What are you standing there for? Let me by."

"Pardon me once more, sir. My master and Miss Sally do not receive visitors today."

"Your master and Miss Sally?" Rufus repeated. "Has this old creature been liquoring up a little too freely? What do you mean," he burst out, with a sudden change of tone to stern surprise—"what do you mean by putting your master and Sally together?"

Toff shot his bolt at last. "They will be together, sir, for the rest of their lives. They were married this morning."

Rufus received the blow in dead silence. He turned about, and went back to his hotel.

Reaching his room, he opened the despatch box in which he kept his correspondence, and picked out the long letter containing the description by Amelius of his introduction to the ladies of the Farnaby family. He took up the pen, and wrote the

296

indorsement which has been quoted as an integral part of the letter itself, in the Second Book of this narrative:—

"Ah, poor Amelius! He had better have gone back to Miss Mellicent, and put up with the little drawback of her age. What a bright lovable fellow he was! Goodbye to Goldenheart!"

Were the forebodings of Rufus destined to be fulfilled? This question will be answered, it is hoped, in a Second Series of The Fallen Leaves. The narrative of the married life of Amelius presents a subject too important to be treated within the limits of the present story—and the First Series necessarily finds its end in the culminating event of his life, thus far.

THE END

784833

Printed in Great Britain by
Amazon.co.uk, Ltd.,
Marston Gate.